I Laugh So I Won't Cry

Kenya's Women Tell the Stories of Their Lives

Helena Halp[illegible]

Africa World Press, Inc.

P.O. Box 1892
Trenton, NJ 08607

P.O. Box 48
Asmara, ERITREA

Africa World Press, Inc.

Book Design: Sam Saverance
Cover Design: Roger Dormann
Cover Photo of Margaret Obonyo weeding her shamba by author
Map: Julia Halperin

Library of Congress Cataloging-in-Publication Data

Halperin, Helena.
I laugh so I won't cry : Kenya's women tell the story of their lives / Helena Halperin.
p. cm.
Includes index.
ISBN 1-59221-303-0 (cloth) -- ISBN 1-59221-304-9 (pbk.)
1. Women--Kenya--Social conditions. I. Title: Kenya's women tell the story of their lives. II. Title.

HQ1796.5.H35 2005
305.4'096762'090511--dc22

2005000159

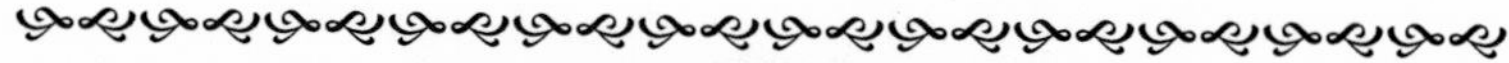

For **Margaret Alosi Obonyo**
and millions of women like her.

Oppressed by international,
national, community and family injustice,
they rise each day to struggle
through courage, work, and laughter.

Sometimes they triumph.

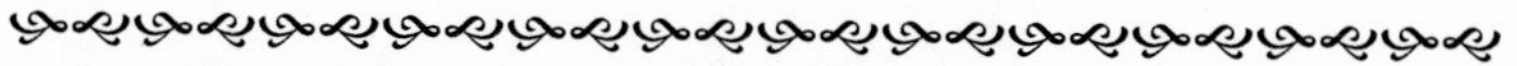

TABLE OF CONTENTS

ACKNOWLEDGMENTS

It has always been obvious that this project could not succeed without help from many different people. Help has been given in measures that exceeded every hopeful expectation. My gratitude for the enthusiastic participation of so many people is boundless.

First, and most obvious, is the willingness of hundreds of women to tell their life stories to a stranger, casual acquaintance, or friend. Those who have done so are not all in the following pages, and some are given only pseudonyms. But, whether or not they are named, all rest in my memory and in my heart. Even if I ultimately had to leave out your own words, what you told me contributed to this book by enlarging my understanding and helping me to think more clearly about the realities of life for Kenya's women.

Many other women who were not interviewed individually came to medium-sized or large gatherings to talk with me about how life is changing in their communities. Those conversations, too, made an important contribution. I hope they were as fascinating to the participants as they were to me. Each one remains a bright memory.

When I began, I asked widely for names of women I should interview, or women who could be liaisons in their home communities. Robert Alison, Prabha Bardwan, Cheryl Bentsen, Ethan Bloomberg, Sandra Boston, Betty Chapple, Karen Cueni and Masambula Igunza, Scot Dingman, Martin Fisher, Heidi Glaessel, Caroline Herberger, Naomi Kipury, Honorine Kiplagat, Jacqueline Klopp, Patricia Kutzner, Deborah and Tony Lustig, Amy McCreath, Mary McVay, Daniel Mindich, Kennedy Momanyi, Margaret Obonyo, Erin Reynolds Peters, Ellen Rosen, Usha Shah, Helen Snook, Sue Standing, Farah Stockman,

Jay Strand, Laura Swinkey, Shawna Tropp, Andrea Useem and David Werner all provided invaluable introductions.

When I was living in Western Province, my friends and the family I lived with did all they possibly could to help me understand my surroundings and saved me from many missteps. The ones who helped me constantly were: Tabitha Nechesa, Margaret Obonyo, John Okumu, and Roselyne Okumu. Many, many others helped me when I needed them, and graciously explained things I could not understand.

To prepare for interviewing people in Kiswahili, I had essential assistance from Oscar Ngaiza and Margaret Sangudi.

In each community, I depended on hosts, translators, and friends to ease my way, assist me with interviews, and help me understand what I was learning. These people did far more than a brief description can convey. They were: In Kakamega and Mumias: Janet Adhiambo, Agnes Mwaro, Margaret Obonyo, Shadrack Okacha, John Okumu, Roselyne Okumu, Bishop Edwin Osera, and Benson Shiundu. At Shamoni: Isaiah Kakai, Jemima Maina and Tabitha Nechesa. In Wajir: Suli Abdi, Nuria Abdullahi, Rukia Abdullahi, Dekha Ibrahim, Ronay Mayow, and the staff of the Pastoralist Rest House. In Kajiado: Irene Katete, Fatuma Osman, the staff of the ACK Guest House, and Emily, the prime mover of Ilbissil Women's Group, whose other names I do not know. In Lusigetti: Njoki Ngige, Michi Vojta, and Rahab Waruguru. In Mombasa and Likoni: Mary Msinga, Damu and Prem Shah, and the YWCA staff in both locations. In Wundanyi: Mary Msinga and the staff of the Hebron Guest House. In Murang'aa and Matuu: Margaret Anyembe and Irene Mahiti. In Malindi: Mariamu Kifeli Ahmed. In Nyansiongo: Wenceslas Momanyi and Beatrice Onduko. In Nakuru: Edward Amani, Denis Kimambo, Muppet, and Stanley Tuvako. In Nairobi: the staffs of the ACK Guest House and the United Kenya Club. In Kisumu: Peter Andajo and Roselyne Okumu.

Denis Kimambo and Stanley Tuvako contributed interviews I could not have gotten on my own. Jacqueline Klopp and Grace Gathone did a much-needed follow-up interview when I could not see Grace Nyawira.

I had competent, prompt, and gracious assistance in transcribing interviews from: Lorraine Bourassa, Rebecca Castleman, Irene Cheng, Megha Doshi, George Fernandes, Samuel Mberere Kabue, Loretta Meshtishdan, Mwashuma Nyatta, Andrea Rackowski, Ravindran, Miranda Richardson, Rafael Sarkisian, Sarah Silbert, Dara Sosulski, Luke Whitmore, Anton Yavkolev, Jo Zasloff and another capable, flexible woman whose name I have lost.

Others who provided valuable information were: Kirra Brandon, Dalya Massachi, Jacqueline Klopp, the Kenya Embassy in Washington, the US State Department, and the extraordinary reference librarians of Robbins Library.

While traveling in Kenya as an outsider, I depended on many people to help me get around, know how to behave, and understand what I was hearing. Some of those who have helped me greatly were: Martin Fisher, Jimmy Kamau, Isaiah Kakai, James Mwangi, Joseph and Joan Nyette, John Okumu, and Judy Shiraku.

I am grateful to the Instituut Lorenz at Leiden University for office space and the use of a computer for the month I spent in Leyden and to Dr. Carlo Beenaker who assisted me when I had computer problems that required more than routine knowledge.

Several friends slogged their way through an early version of the entire manuscript, and gave extensive editorial advice, greatly improving the final product. They were: Prof. Hill Gates, Prof. Bertrand Halperin, Prof. Jacqueline Klopp, John Okumu, Margaret and Genevieve Sangudi, Shawna Tropp and Wachuka Warungu. Jennifer Anderson graciously and expeditiously read a late version and caught many errors and infelicities.

Several others gave me valuable feedback and vital encouragement on specific sections. They were: Sarah Brett-Smith, Pat Harvey, Christopher Junker, Lois Levin, Bernestine Singley, and Helen Snively.

For years, members of my writing group have read sections with close, compassionate, and professional attention. They include: Jeannette Cezanne, Elaine Gottlieb, Irene Gravina, June Gross, Maria Judge, and Carole Vogel. I hope each of you realizes how greatly you have contributed to the readability of the final version.

I am greatly indebted to several people at Africa World Press. Kassahun Checole, the publisher, is always willing to explain their operations and constraints, and has been very helpful in meeting my specific requests when possible. Angela Ajayi, the editor, has given me good advice and answered repeated calls with every appearance of finding my questions as interesting and pressing as I do. They have been a pleasure to work with. I am grateful to Charles Cantalupo, who gave my manuscript very detailed attention, saving me from many blunders; to Roger Dormann, who designed the cover; and to Sam Saverance, who did the typesetting.

My son, Jeffery Halperin, provided a tremendous amount of computer assistance, especially at the beginning, when I was ready to throw my machine, my manuscript, and my vision out the window. When I doubted, he helped me remember why this work seemed worthwhile.

At many stages of this project, my daughter, Julia Halperin, has helped regenerate my enthusiasm through her perceptive and probing questions. At the end, she worked patiently to track down locations too tiny for any map but the one she produced for this book.

My husband, Bertrand Halperin, has assisted with every phase of this project. He contributed airline mileage and supported my work both financially and emotionally. He has spent hundreds of hours over many years discussing Kenya's women, asking wise questions, making invaluable suggestions, and rereading every version. I hope he understands how vital he has been and remains.

Preface

Who exactly is entitled to write about *relationships* between women and men? Hermaphrodites? This is the dilemma upon whose horns I've built my house: I want to know, and to write, about the places where disparate points of view rub together—the spaces between. Not just man and woman but also North and South; white and non-white; communal and individual; spiritual and carnal. I can think of no genetic or cultural credentials that could entitle a writer to do this—only a keen ear, empathy, caution, willingness to be criticized, and a passionate attachment to the subject.

—Barbara Kingsolver, *High Tide in Tucson: Essays from Now or Never*

How This Book Came to be Written

I have always yearned to understand the lives of people whose circumstances are different from my own. In 1989 and 1990, after years of teaching in the United States, I was given an opportunity to teach in a *harambee* [community-supported] secondary school in Kenya. I taught English, Biology, History, and Social Ethics at Shamoni Secondary School in Western Kabras, just north of Kakamega, and about 30 miles from the Uganda border.

For most of my time there, I lived with the family of Margaret and Peter Obonyo. When we grew to trust each other, they took seriously my desire to learn from them, and set out to see how much an outsider could learn in fourteen months.

While there, my favorite activity was sitting with any neighborhood woman in her kitchen and talking about life. I heard numerous tales of resourceful responses to appalling challenges. I talked to many capable and heroic women. From those conversations the idea for this book was born.

This could have been a book about subsistence farmers from Western Province, the segment of Kenya's diverse population that I knew best. Such a book might have been fascinating and inspiring to read, and even more so to research. But it would not have represented the diversity of Kenya's women.

People from afar often believe that almost all Africans are small farmers. Not wishing to add to this misperception, I decided to talk with a comprehensive sample of Kenya's women. Collectively they represent Kenyan women, rather than a small segment of the society.

How can one book hope to represent the diversity of contemporary Africa? Africa is too large and varied to cover both comprehensively and deeply. But all of Africa's major patterns of living are found within Kenya. Kenya has camel herders and cattle herders, commercial farmers and subsistence farmers, international jet-setters and street-corner beggars. This book aims to introduce the continent through the prism of Kenya.

In August 1995, and May to September 1996, I returned to Kenya to do the initial research for this book. I traveled throughout Kenya interviewing women of all ages, many ethnic groups and ways of life. Men asked why I was interviewing only women and ignoring them, but I thought that I could not even begin to talk with men in the intimate way I talked with women. The barriers of distrust and suspicion would be higher with men, as there is much more separation between men and women in Kenya than in my own culture. But, most of all, the women were the ones who inspired me.

In 2001, I returned for three months with a draft of the manuscript. I tried to see my original informants to get updates on their lives, and to show them what I had written about them. Those interviews felt especially intimate. The women were enthusiastic about what I had written, conscientious about correcting any factual errors or any changes of perspective, and seemed to feel that my return showed a genuine, enduring interest in them. Many added a great deal to what they had said earlier about their histories. I stayed until the very end of the period permitted by my ticket, and left feeling sad that I had not been able to see some of the women. Then, in 2002, I had an opportunity to return briefly for some other work, but was able to tie a few last loose ends, and believed I was done.

In the last days of 2002 a new government took over. By the time I was finishing my manuscript in 2003, they had made important changes, invalidating significant parts of my manuscript. I returned for two months in late 2003 with the specific goal of learning how the change of government had affected women in different circumstances, and whether it had changed their expectations. Once again, I failed to see everyone I had hoped to see, but had many inspiring conversations and learned more than I had foreseen.

The Goal

Kenyan women have much to teach about courage and generosity. This book tries to help them tell their stories to the wider world. I have tried to transmit their reflections on their own lives, rather than mine. They speak for themselves. My questions grew out of what women said to me. Many productive questions were added as the research progressed.

At every stage, I tried to be as transparent a lens as possible. My strategy for leaving the basic structure of each interview in the hands of the respondent was to ask very open-ended questions. After explaining my project, I began with a request that the respondent tell me the story of her life "from when you were a little girl until now." As she told her history, I asked questions for clarification and amplification. Afterward, depending on what her experience had been, I asked general questions. I usually asked whether she had ever belonged to a women's group if she had not mentioned one. I asked how her life was different than her mother's had been, or how life in her community was different than it had been ten, fifteen, or twenty years earlier. I often asked mothers what they thought parents could do to help children prepare for the future. Toward the end of the interview, if my informant had not yet discussed the future, I asked what she expected five, ten, or twenty years ahead. Women who expressed grave concerns for the future were asked whether there was anything that could be done in the present to make the future better.

A few women were reluctant at first to talk about themselves. With them, I began with questions about their communities. After we had talked impersonally for a time, they came to recognize that I already knew their world reasonably well, and became more willing to talk about themselves. I attribute this to my long residence with Kenyan subsistence farmers. My questions were usually not those of a visitor from an alien planet.

In writing the book, I have wrestled with how much to insert myself into the text. Many people have advised me to use a first person account of the research process to give a continuing thread. Mostly, I have not done so. I do not wish my experiences and perceptions, however fascinating they are to me, to be at the center of the reader's attention.

Initially, I thought only of a book for American and European audiences. I felt timid offering this work to Kenyan or African readers. I reasoned that as an American, I have nothing to tell Kenyans about Kenya. That was before I began the research. Once I began, my perspective changed. I had extraordinary access to a wider range of women than I had thought possible. Many women I encountered were quite interested in learning about women from other regions, ethnic groups, or ways of life. For some city women, a camel herder seems as exotic as an American, but much more interesting. Therefore, very humbly, I offer this book to readers of every nation who admire valor and resourcefulness.

Many American readers of early drafts said such things as, "By knowing women from another culture, we come to know ourselves better." I think that's true and very valuable, but it misses the point. By knowing people from another culture who live in radically different circumstances, we understand the human condition and the range of human possibilities more broadly. In my view, ultimately the reason for studying people of another culture is that we come to know *them* better.

Is a white American the best person to attempt such a book? Perhaps not. There are many Kenyan women who could have done this project superbly. But no one has. It required a considerable investment of time and love. I felt called to do this after so many women in my village told me their stories. If my book inspires others to extend this work, I will be deeply gratified and will offer any assistance I can.

Until then, this is the only study of Kenya's women with a large sample drawn from many parts of the country and many socioeconomic classes. I hope it will be useful to those who seek to see the whole of a modern African nation and inspiring to those who seek to comprehend and celebrate human strength.

How Respondents Were Selected

When I began, I had many contacts among farmers in Western Province but few others. I combined two approaches to get my sample; haphazard and highly systematic. The systematic part consisted of identifying what segments of the population I would need to interview in order to have a group who truly represented the range of Kenyan women. The haphazard component came from taking advantage of all the contacts I happened to have, and asking them for introductions to the people I needed to meet. Meeting and interviewing women of almost every category I had selected was astonishingly easy. For example, toward the end of my first round of interviews, I still felt that I had not talked to enough young women. I spent a few days in Lusigetti as the guest of Michi Vojta, an American Peace Corps volunteer. I had previously explained my needs to her in a very general way, but now I specifically told her I wanted to interview young women. She found excellent translators for me and introduced me to many women, including a number of quite young women.

Each contact led to quickly widening circles. I could not follow all the promising possibilities I was offered. There was only one group I had trouble meeting: white Kenyans. Until quite near the end of my major round of interviews, none of the people I knew could introduce me to any. Even this ironic problem was eventually solved thanks to the persistence and generosity of many friends, but it took a while.

My goal was to interview a broad enough sample that I could paint a multi-dimensional picture. The obvious variables that concerned me were: race, ethnicity, age, marital status, number of children, education, economic circumstances and means of livelihood. I included at least a few members of each major category, but did not attempt to create a statistically representative sample.

The most significant difference between my sample and a representative sample is that although I interviewed many women who have no schooling, and many who have not completed primary school, well-educated women are heavily over-represented. This occurred for three reasons: 1) My contact in each community was through a woman who spoke English and the local language or languages well, and could translate. To prepare the translator for our work together, I began by interviewing her. 2) In communities where I had not described my needs in detail before arriving, my local contact had often already arranged interviews with whomever she considered the best informants, usually schoolteachers. 3) In addition, I interviewed a number of women whom I met on my own, often through formal-sector employment.

Although all these informants skewed my sample for statistical purposes, my purposes were not statistical. Every woman's comments about changes she has seen, or hopes for the future were informative. Bearing in mind the skewed nature of my sample, generalizations such as "most women worried about the cost of living" are appropriate, but numerical conclusions such as "Taita women average just over 5 years of schooling" are completely inappropriate.

Who They Are

Over two hundred and fifty women were interviewed individually. Over two hundred and twenty five were of African descent; the others were Asian and European Kenyans. The African Kenyans represented the major ethnic groups and some of the smaller groups. They ranged in age from under twenty to over seventy. Most were married for the first time. Some had never married, others were widowed, divorced, or remarried. Over ten percent were childless, but the average number of children was over five. Seventy-three had not been to school, and fifty-three had no more than primary schooling. Seventy-nine were educated beyond primary school, which is extremely out of proportion.

There were many, many farmers, and a substantial number of pastoralists, both camel herders and cattle herders. Most of these supplemented their income with trading of some sort. But there were also many traders who neither farmed nor kept animals. Many women earned money by a variety of trades during their lives, and many had more than one source of income at a time. Many who did not have businesses of their own earned money through a women's group that ran a business or owned some rental property. The microenterprises represented were varied. Some made and sold decorative cloths, batiks or baskets. Others had a kiosk, a henhouse, or rabbit hutch. But there were also many teachers, doctors, and business leaders.

The women for whom I have biographical information are:

Descent:

African 226 Asian 13 European 6

The 226 African-descended women had the following characteristics:

Ethnicity:

Kikuyu	60	
Luhya	40	Kabras, Bukusu, and Wanga
Luo	18	
Kamba	6	
Kalenjin	10	Nandi and Elgeyo
Gusii	3	
Meru	4	
Somali	18	
Maasai	18	
Taita	21	
Teso	1	
Swahili	13	

Other	5
Unknown	7
Immigrants	2

Age:[1]

under 20	12
20-29	43
30-39	39
40-49	44
50-59	19
60-69	5
70 and over	4
Unknown	60[2]

Marital Status:

Never	41
Married(1st time)	118
Divorced/Separated	22
Widowed	33
Married more than once	7
Unknown	5

Number of Children:[3]

0	26
1	14
2	26
3-4	43
5-7	49
8-11	36
12 and over	8
Unknown	24

---

1. At the time the woman was first interviewed.

2. For 42 of these, estimates were made at the time of the interview: 20s – 2, 30s – 7, 40s – 18, 50s – 10, 60s – 4, 70s – 1.

3. These are the numbers of children a woman had borne, not the number living. Many reported losing some of their children. Five women had adopted children. Some of these had borne children, others had not. Since number of children is negatively correlated with years of schooling, and my sample is highly unrepresentative with respect to schooling, this table *must* not be used as a profile of family size for the population as a whole. In addition, this table includes my entire sample, not only those who are past childbearing. Many of the younger women will have more children. In a breakdown of number of children by age, one can see some strong trends, but such a breakdown would be misleading since the overall sample is not representative of the population. This table is included only to demonstrate that the sample includes many childless women, many mothers of large families, and very large numbers of mothers of middle-sized families.

Education:[4]

0[5]	73
0 but can read	3
1-3	12
4-completed primary[6]	46
Some secondary	13
Completed secondary	14
Beyond secondary[7]	58
Unknown	7

Fortutious Additions

In Mumias, a bishop invited many of the women of his church to meet me on a weekday afternoon. I had expected a handful of women ready for individual interviews, but walked into a room filled with over forty women of all ages. I gulped, thanked them for coming, explained my project, and asked, "How is life here changing?" That launched a lively and wide-ranging conversation. My translator and I struggled to keep up, and occasionally asked for clarification, but did very little to guide the conversation. The women had plenty to say about all the subjects I would have asked about, and many others. That set the pattern I followed whenever I was confronted with a group rather than a few individuals.

In Kisii, my host took me to Mass at a huge Catholic Church. Afterward, he invited women to stay and talk with me. Many men wanted to stay too, but my host energetically pushed them out, and left himself. In Nasianda and Mirere, similarly, many women were invited through a network of friends to come on a particular afternoon. Several translators invited groups of her friends to meet me at her home. All of these group interviews were delightful. The level of energy and interest in those conversations exceeded even the individual interviews, but the situation did not permit me to follow all the intriguing conversational threads that developed.

These groups ranged in size from a dozen women to several hundred. They were very helpful in checking my impressions about the prevalence of customs and attitudes, but didn't yield individual life histories.

4. Readers are reminded that this sample greatly over-represents highly educated women. See explanation on p. xi.

5. Adult education is not included.

6. Prior to 1989, primary school was 7 years. Now it is 8 years.

7. Short-term vocational training courses are not included.

Working with Translators

With each translator, I began by explaining my project and interviewing her just as I would later interview the women she introduced me to. There were several parts to the translator's task. First, of course, was to translate my conversations with the informants. The second part was to discuss each interview with me afterward to share her impressions of what the informant might be thinking, and what we could have done differently. Her final task was to go back and listen to the tape and write a full, translated transcription. During the translated interviews, there was much I could not get. Usually, the informant would talk freely, and the translator would translate only the essentials on the spot, just enough that I could have a general sense, and ask the next question. Having the translator transcribe the full conversation afterward gave me the benefit of all that was not translated during the interview. The best translators were active interviewers themselves. They asked appropriate follow-up questions without my prompt. This was wonderful because then the informant could have a genuine conversation with the translator in her own language. Thus, my alien presence was a bit further in the background.

Most translators were very reliable. A few tried too hard to "give me what I wanted." For example, one translator gave the answer "practice family planning" every time I asked, "Is there anything that can be done in the present to make the future better." I do not believe the woman with nine children, whose youngest was sleeping on her lap, gave that answer. So, I was able to use very little from the interviews that translator had helped me with. Another translator added her own comments to those of the respondents. When I realized that, I told her I wanted to know everything she could tell me, but didn't want her to mix her own comments with those in the interviews. After that, she separated her commentary from her translations, and I trusted her translations.

I interviewed a few women in Swahili without a translator, but my Swahili is weak. In those cases, I taped the interview and told the informant that I might not understand everything she was saying, but I would have it translated later so she should say everthing she wanted to say, even if I didn't fully understand her.

A Note on Terminology

Since a major the aim of this book is to help a wide range of Kenyan women tell their own stories, I have attempted to preserve their language. For this reason, I have tried to use the words used in ordinary Kenyan

English, even where they are not accurate from a technical perspective. Although the custom Kenyans call "dowry" would be called "brideprice" by an anthropologist, dowry is the more common term in Kenyan speech, so I have used it. Although "female genital mutilation" is more accurate than "female circumcision," and "excision" or "infibulation" are more precise for specific forms of surgery, they are not the words used in common English-language conversation in Kenya. Kenyans often refer to "the cut," so I have chosen the term "genital cutting."

At first, Kenyan English sounds strange to Americans and Europeans. The vocabulary is different. Some words like "thrice" are rare in the US but common in Kenya. Other words are used differently. "Cheat" is used when I would say "lie." "Conducive" is used as a synonym for benign and has lost connection with the verb "to conduct." So, when an American listens to most English-speaking Kenyans, the impression is one of uneven, unmatched diction. I have tried to leave the language as nearly intact as possible, shortening and rearranging for clarity, but trying to retain the flavor of the informant if the interview was in English, or of the translator if not.

Names, Pseudonyms, and Identification

Pseudonyms are used except where a woman prefers that I use her name. When possible, each woman chose her own pseudonym. When this wasn't practical, I attempted to use ethnically appropriate pseudonyms. In order to be sure that the names I supplied were appropriate to the region, I often traded names. Thus, if I had interviewed Wanjiku Wanjohi, Wambui Gathege, and Njeri Ndungi, I might change Wanjiku Wanjohi's name to Wambui Ndungi.

In the text, I usually identify a woman by her region and means of livelihood. I identify her by ethnic group only when it is clearly relevant. In the first draft, I gave everyone an ethnic label, but Kenyan friends objected. There are commonalities between Kenya's different ethnic groups in many aspects of life. Labeling people by ethnicity perpetuates the idea derived from anthropology that "tribe" determines "custom." Of course there are some differences of custom from one group to another, but there are also great commonalities that can be obscured by thinking about individuals always as members of a particular group. Humans are good at dividing themselves, less good at uniting. In Kenya, ethnic differences have been fiercely exploited to retain political power. As people of good will struggle to build unity, many think it is harmful to use ethnic labels.

I recognize an irony. If I were writing about the USA, I would label us all, to underscore the point that we all love, eat, and think in similar ways, even though we differ in color and circumstance. Those differences are part of our stories because they affect our experiences and shape our perceptions. But in Kenya, imagined differences (as well as real ones) are used to justify politically motivated killing. Perhaps using labels helps build tolerance in the USA, but in the current situation, it is divisive in Kenya. Of course knowledgeable readers may recognize a woman's ethnic background from her region and name, but they can draw their own conclusions about the impact of her heritage.

I don't wish to fuel misunderstandings by repeating resentments people feel against members of other groups. Therefore, I use xxx when a respondent has mentioned another ethnic group negatively. Xxx refers to whatever group the particular respondent happened to talk about, not to one group throughout. Group names are used when the content is neutral, or where the name is essential to understanding the meaning.

I have not been consistent in whether I refer to a woman by her given name or a family name after the first full identification. Often, I made the choice of the less usual name to avoid confusion between women with similar names. Very occasionally, I have used the title Mrs. with a married woman's name. There are a few women who use the title in their own English language activities. For them, I use it as a mark of respect. But it seems an inappropriate import from my culture for most of the women in these pages.

Financial Arrangements

I had help in deciding about gratuities from the African Housing Fund. They provided many of my first interviews by taking me to talk with women in their resettlement project in Kayole, just outside Nairobi. They asked me to give each woman fifty Ksh, which was their standard for a day's wages. For the rest of my interviews in 1995, that was the sum I used. In 1996, I usually gave fifty or seventy-five Ksh but gave 100-500 Ksh. if I was talking with several members of a women's group. Occasionally, I broke my rules and gave individual intervewees 100 Ksh.[8] Later, 100 Ksh became my usual gift.

I had to make some painful judgments. Offering a gratuity to women with significant formal sector employment didn't seem appropriate. I believed the sum I was offering was too small to be significant for her, and offering her more than I offered other women

---

8. I am relying on my memory. I think the lower sum was fifty Ksh, but it might have been seventy-five Ksh.

was certainly not reasonable. This project was self-financed, with the help of my husband's accumulated air miles. I traveled by bus whenever possible and safe, and usually stayed with local people or in low-cost lodgings. Any profits beyond basic expenses will be donated to Kenyan women's groups.

LIST OF PHOTOGRAPHS

MAP OF KENYA SHOWING APPROXIMATE LOCATIONS OF PLACES MENTIONED IN THE TEXT

Portrait A

Zildah Kirwoi

At a sharp bend in the road from Wundanyi to Mbale, a passer-by usually sees a pile of crushed stone. From there, a small farm falls steeply away. Some distance below, there's a substantial mud house with a corrugated iron roof. This is the home of Zildah Kirwoi, a tiny, lively woman who laughs frequently.

I first visited Zildah in 1996 accompanied by her neighbor, Mary Msinga, who served as my community contact and translator.

Zildah was born near where she now lives, and has never travelled far from home. She's a hard-working woman, usually in her fields when I visit.

Since I was born I've never been just sleeping. When I was growing up, I was just looking after cotton, picking firewood, digging, assisting mother with household duties. Father died when we were young. We were three girls and three boys, only one wife.

I don't know the year I was born. When I went to collect my identity card, those people looked at me and guessed 1944.

My mother did piecework to get money. She brought us up nicely, involving us in all the household activites, training us for the future. I would also go and dig somebody's land for cash, but by digging in our own *shamba* [field], we wouldn't often need to buy food.

On special occasions like Christmas, all the villagers would meet together, cook together, celebrate together within their own small villages. That is long gone. Today the only thing which makes people come together is either a wedding ceremony or a funeral. But actual weddings are not common now, only funerals.

When we were growing up, we didn't need to go to the shops for everything. Life was cheap and simple because we got almost everything from the *shamba.*

Now, we have been digging in the same place for a very long time, so the soil has lost its fertility. We are not harvesting enough, so we have to find money to meet our needs.

Those days, girls of my Taita tribe had *Mwari* [a ritual period of instruction for adulthood] when we were starting to mature. Mwari was not circumcision. Taita girls are circumcised when they are about three weeks old, no more than a month. So, that was long healed by the time of Mwari. When I was about 18, the girls of my village were collected together. Our instructors were three aunts. We were taught to abstain from bad practices such as pregnancy before marriage. Those days, if one got pregnant before marriage she would never be married.

During this seclusion we were dressed only in two *shukas* [colorful pieces of cloth]. Special food was given to us, on a special plate which no one else would use. No one was allowed to see us, but we could hear people speaking since we were in a room behind the house. We were not supposed to see anyone. If anyone did speak to us, he would be obliged to pay a fine.

We stayed in seclusion for about a month. If a man who liked one of us wanted to give us a present, we could not even see him. If we liked the man, we would accept the present. We became so clean and brown [light-skinned from lack of exposure to the sun] during this time inside.

A major ceremony with traditional food and plenty of beer was held when we were graduating from Mwari, as we were now mature women. Many people came to that ceremony because no one had seen us for a month.

Mwari is no longer practiced. We were almost the last. Mwari was a very good education. We were taught how to maintain a good relationship with a husband by obeying and respecting him so that the marriage would last. We were taught to co-operate with our husband's family members, and told to persevere through all hardships, beatings, and poverty. The lack of such education has led to the breakup of marriages.

After you come out, you can go to dances and meet men, and find the one of your choice. I stayed for three years after Mwari before I was married. When the two families had agreed, the man's family started to bring some cattle and goats. The numbers of goats and cows varied from family to family, because these animals were given to particular people. For instance, a cow was supposed to go to my mother's sister, and then to a brother to my mother, and then a sister to my father, and then to my mother. Each of them was entitled to a cow and a goat. That was accompanied by some bananas to cook, whatever was available at that time.

When I was married, my husband was working in Mombasa, but it was not right for a man to take his wife to town. She would go to his mother. He would come when he could, maybe every two months. But later, it might even be a year.

Zildah Kirwoi and her husband at home

My relationship with my mother-in-law was not bad, but in any case there is no choice. You must stay with her regardless. No one would employ a housegirl. It was the young wife who helped with whatever needed to be done. I worked in the shamba because I was younger and more active, and she cared for my children. Later, I left to make room for the wife of one of his brothers.

I got my first child as soon as possible. We have four children, three boys and one girl. I am still the only wife.

When we were growing up, we were taught to respect our elders very strictly. But today, children don't have respect for their parents, and not even among themselves. This causes a lot of conflict.

We were not taught to read and write, but only what we needed to know to carry out our daily activites. That was a good way. It was important for a girl to be well trained so she could please her mother-in-law. In fact, when a man saw a girl he was interested in, he would want his friends to go and observe how well she worked.

We were taught to respect our husbands and that we must persevere with him even if we were being beaten. That's why our marriages would last. But today's girls cannot stand that. If her husband cannot give her money and clothes, she might run away.

We parents today find it very hard to train our children. My grand-daughters dismiss whatever I say because I have not been to school. They will say, "That was your time. It is old-fashioned now." Maybe you have never seen a picture of a woman in a book. She's showing you a complicated picture, and you don't understand it, so she thinks you are ignorant.

There are lots of influences reaching the children when they go out and mix with others. Maybe I am teaching the old ways, but another parent is not.

Similarly, when they go to school, teachers teach differently, so they end up not knowing what is right.

The problem is that these children are growing up with two instructors. During my time it was only the parents, but today both parents and teachers are the influential people. So they are growing up under a kind of confusion, but before they were taught to believe whatever their parents said, and that is the right thing.

Despite these problems, I think education is important: It is an eye-opener. Look at Mary,[1] a girl from my own hill here, yet because she did very well in education, she went out into the world, and she was able to meet a foreigner like you and bring you here. She is employed and she has helped her parents. They are old, they can't go looking for money. I am happy when I see Mary because she no longer relies on her parents. Now she helps them.

But children are not all the same. In a family of four like mine, you educate all four, but you find maybe one or two being respectful to their parents. Others aren't. It's not something you can bet on.

In 1996, when I recorded her history, Zildah looked ahead with dread.

I think the future is going to be too terrible. For example, cases of early pregnancies and these STD's. They have been brought about by early relationships and that freedom that young girls are trying to give themselves. During my time we didn't even know about them. We are hearing about them commonly now. Fortunately I have only one daughter. And how will our children afford to live when everything is becoming expensive?

There are many changes I would like to see, but I find it pointless. Perhaps a girl goes to work in town, and the next visit she comes back with a child. I blame this on the problem of two instructors.

In 2001, I visited Zildah again. I found the same lively, hard-working, co-operative person I had interviewed in 1996, but despite the hardships she was suffering during our first interview her life was significantly harder than it had been five years earlier.

Now I have to take care of my grandchildren. Life would be better if we were living only two of us. My husband does not work anymore. I am old and cannot farm the way I used to do.

Tea leaves, match boxes, sugar etc. have gone up by 200%. It is hard for the family like ours to make things work. Paraffin [kerosene, which is the primary source of light after dark] and other essential goods have gone up so we cannot even afford it. We buy five Ksh or twenty at a time. When my

1. Mary Msinga, my translator and host, comes from the same village. She had done well in school, and now has a respected position with the YWCA in Mombasa. Her neighbors are justly proud of her success.

husband was still working, I used to plan our family expenditure so we could get everything we needed.

My daughter left her husband because he is a drunkard. She came back with kids whom I must feed and educate.

One son is living here too, but he does not help. He was a technician at the post office, and he just left the job without consulting anyone. His wife left him and is working as a housegirl because she has to find something. If he were not a drunkard he could help.

HH: Are you able to talk honestly with your son about this?

I can talk to him when he's sober, and we can agree, but when he goes out he always comes back drunk.

When I saw Zildah in 2003, she was deeply discouraged about changes within her family, and clearly unhappy. But she was very enthusiastic about the new government of Mwai Kibaki that had come to power at the end of 2002, replacing the increasingly corrupt government of President Daniel arap Moi that had held power since 1978. The new government's first act was to make primary education free.

Zildah had already benefitted from the change of government. As a result, she was much more optimistic about her own future.

In the future, you'll see some wonderful changes here. I can understand some little Kiswahili so I listen to President Kibaki on the radio and I always appreciate what he says. He gives words of hope, and talks of helping the common person.

I heard the President promise educaton, creation of small industries, microcredit, reduction of prices of commodities like maize and sugar, so we Kenyans will be more equal. These changes will take time. In five or ten years maybe Kenya will be wonderful. If we can all afford life, that will lessen crime, and we will be safer. But, in addition, they should offer free health care. If I could talk to the government that is what I would ask for.

My husband crushes this stone you see. I do all the farming. My eldest grandchild is in secondary school, but we don't pay his fees. My lastborn son is working in Mombasa, so he pays the school fees. Because of free primary education, when I get a little money now I can buy food.

Today, when I go to a shop with a hundred Ksh, I cannot get a packet of maize meal, sugar and salt. If they reduce the cost I will be able to live wonderfully.

HH: Do you think that in your own lifetime you will be able to live as well as you lived long ago.

Yes, I can even grow fat. Today, even if I have a thousand Ksh, I would need to sit for an hour and think carefully to decide what is most needed. If the new government can do what they promised, I could even afford to eat meat once or twice a week, but that is something I never think of now. We eat, not to satisfaction, but just to sustain. I would like to be able to fill my stomach. We don't even get enough for good health. I can't buy tea now because it is not essential, but sometimes I really miss it. Now, I only grow vegetables and maize. A packet of *unga* [maize meal, the staple food in much of Kenya] is fifty Ksh Milk is thirty Ksh a litre. I used to keep a cow, but I don't have one now, so I have to buy milk if we are to have it.

HH: I can't think of anything that would make me happier than to come back and see that you have grown fat because you are able to eat enough.

I wish my husband could help. When I finish in the fields, I go in and cook something for the husband, my son, and the grandchildren. If he could only be loving, if he could only show some appreciation, I would not feel the burden of my work so much. I wish my husband could help me in planting. Some men help, but he never will. This is planting season. He could at least help me now, and crush stones later. His work is not seasonal.

HH: Can a man work in the shamba without other men saying anything?

Some, who are loving to their wives, are even the first ones in the shamba while the wife is finishing the kitchen chores, but he never will. If I ask, he will always give excuses because he wants to concentrate on crushing stones until he gets enough to sell.

My son doesn't help much. He will only take a cup of tea then he leaves. When he's sober, he will agree and maybe even go to the shamba with me, but because of the drinking, his health is very poor and he is weak. When he does go with me, soon one of his friends will come along and he will leave.

HH: Now it is school holidays. Do the children help during holidays?

Some of them are just not willing. The big ones prefer to go walking around with friends. I can't rely on them. I was trying this morning to get the smaller ones to drop the seeds in the ground, but they did not help.

I think with the oldest grandson, it is a matter of peer pressure. I talked about it with him last night, and he just kept quiet. This morning, he left as soon as he had washed himself. He used to help in the shamba very well. He changed very much this year when he got to form three [11th grade]. Sometimes he will just come from school, change his clothes, and go out again, not coming home until after we are sleeping.

This year, when there is a message to bring home from the school, he doesn't bring it. So we never know when there is a meeting. I don't know why he has changed so much, but I am worried about him, and worried about how I can feed them all.

I wish the government would ban illegal liquor. In this, I'm not happy with the new government or the ones before.[2] The worst liquor comes from upcountry. It used to be that people would prepare their own liquor for their families and neighbors. Then it was not so bad, because it had to be safe. With liquor that is brought from far, you can't know whether it is well made or not. Some of it, called ten-ten, has serious side effects, people are going blind, and

---

2. Home production of liquor is illegal, and there are some efforts at enforcement, but illegal liquor is easily available.

it has killed many people. Maybe it is suitable for the people who prepare it somewhere else, but it is not suitable for people here.

HH: Do people here still make their own, or is that over?

They still make it here, but the good local liquor is more expensive. People can buy small pots of ten-ten for twenty or thirty Ksh Although I cannot read, those who can read have told me that in pubs that serve this there is a warning that if you take more than two it can kill you. I don't know how much he takes, but I am so worred because of that. He says he has no money, but when he goes out with his friends, he always comes back drunk.

HH: Does he drink every day?

Every day, and yet he never has money to feed children.

HH: I know that sometimes this problem with alcohol runs in families. How about that grandson who is in secondary school, does he drink?

No, my grandchildren don't drink. They are very upset with their father for his drunkenness, and not happy with his behavior. Maybe it could be a problem in the future, but it is not now.

This last conversation with Zildah took place at the house where I was staying, rather than at hers, so I was able to serve her several cups of tea and buttered bread.

Author's Comment

Oh, Zildah, truly life can be hard! I do not expect you to grow fat, but I hope you will be able to eat to satisfaction.

1

Deliberate Change and Unintended Consequences

When I was young, we used to fetch water from the streams, passing through thick forests. Food was there in abundance. Nowadays when I go home, I really get shocked to see that most of the streams have dried up, the forests are no more, and the food that used to be abundant is not there.

—Maria Kibera, Wundanyi

Long ago people used to live under the coverage of others. They used to care about each other's welfare. Poor people were never seen. My grandmother used to live and eat together with the whole *boma* [village]. We might find a *boma* of fifty homesteads. Steers were slaughtered and eaten by the whole community. But nowadays it is entirely up to you to get something to eat and wear, and many people have no one to help them.

—Irene Katete, Kajiado

As Kenya becomes integrated with the rest of the world, change is disrupting every facet of life. Within memory, there was enough land. When harvests declined because a field had been used too long, people cleared a new field. The more wives a man had, the more land they could work, and the more surplus he could command. Now land available for small-scale farming is scarce, and bitterly contested, while per-acre yields are declining.

Everyone is affected, even those who live far from urban centers and strive to follow tradition. Diets, fertility and mortality, celebrations, the sizes of the cattle or camel herds, social gatherings with friends, even the names people give their children, are influenced by forces outside their control.

Rural elders remember wearing only animal skins and growing everything they ate. Now they depend on cash. Meeting basic needs is becoming harder.

Cascading changes wash away more stability and tradition than anyone could foresee, and create gulfs between generations who have lived in profoundly different worlds.

Economic Changes

These changes are not shrouded in mystery. People understand why their lives are being disrupted. But clear understanding doesn't mean they have ready remedies.

As the global climate warms, the rains have become erratic, devastating farmers. Lucy Lebow married into rural Kajiado. Since she came from a farming background, she raised vegetables amid neighbors who relied on herding rather than agriculture.

> When I came here the rainy season was OK so I used to plant and make the local brew to sell. With the money I bought goats. You used to buy a goat for ten Ksh.
>
> After my husband died, I thought about returning to my home place, but I decided to stay here because of the land. I had five kids to feed. I still try to plant what I did before, but every year it fails because of the short rain. The rains no longer come according to the official seasons.

Sofia Muthoni, a tall, strong former school teacher, lives with her family on a beautiful farm in Murang'aa. They have a well-constructed zero grazing project[1] and a permanent house with concrete floors and glass windows. Everything about their compound suggests a high degree of organization. They are financially comfortable, and provide for a number of local people poorer than themselves. Sofia is deeply worried about neighbors who have less than she does.

> Lands are little and exhausted because we have planted in the same place for long. There is not enough food here and people get terribly hungry. We get enough during the harvest season, but then we finish it all earlier. We starve a few months of the year.
>
> Life was better long time ago because people grew many things they needed, and had enough to eat. Children could go to the shamba, sell some of their produce and get money.

---

1. A pen where confined cattle are brought food rather than being allowed to graze. Their dung, and sometimes urine, can be collected for farm use.

> Nowadays, people are not able to get enough because of the climate. Young people who are not educated are idle. They can't live from their farms and can't find employment; therefore, they engage themselves in bad practices like drugs and stealing.

Herds are also dwindling. Cattle herders like the Maasai and camel herders like the Somali have suffered from dramatic declines in their herds. Even small farmers who cultivate crops and also raise animals now have fewer animals, drink less milk, and eat less meat.

In 1996, we interviewed a group of five *miraa*[2] traders in Wajir. The question "how is life changing here?" elicited lots of animated and overlapping discussion, too much for the translator to sort out. The resulting translation is a composite.

> Life is totally different, even hostile. Our mothers and grandmothers were still pastoralists. They had meat, they had milk. Because of their animals, they were very comfortable. Now, those who have money are going to school and can work in government offices, but we did not go to school so we have no income. Here, we can't do agriculture, can't continue the pastoral life because we don't have animals.[3]

The shift to a money economy began as deliberate British colonial policy. In order to have labor for their projects, the British imposed head taxes and hut taxes that could be paid only in cash, forcing previously self-sufficient farmers and herders to find a source of cash.

Tragically, as harvests and herds decline, the need for money has increased. Rural people need cash not only to share in the opportunities brought by the modern world such as school fees and medical attention, but even to buy the food they used to produce themselves.

For the first forty years of independence, 1963-2002, Kenya became increasingly corrupt, earning a rank of 96th of 102 countries on Transparency International's Corruption Perception Index, tied with Indonesia and leaving only Angola, Madagascar, Paraguay, Nigeria, and Bangladesh as more corrupt.[4] Relentless looting of public funds impoverished the great majority of citizens, leading to widespread hunger.

---

2. Khat [Catha Edulis], a common stimulant.

3. Portraits L and N give background information on Wajir's former herders.

4. Transparency International Corruption Perception Index 2002, http://www.transparency.org/cpi/2002/cpi2002.en.html

From the mid 1980s, poverty increased relentlessly. From the poorest farmers and herders through the ranks of the educated and employed middle class, people felt more squeezed each year. One Nairobi businesswoman, Eileen Waruguru, left a teaching position that didn't pay well to open a hair-dressing salon. With her husband's help, she made a substantial investment in training and equipment. Her salon opened in 1992. At first, it did very well.

> When I started here, we had many clients and made a lot of money. The economy was good. But things changed: there was no money any more, so hair was not of immediate importance. There were so many other needs a woman would want to meet. Somebody who was coming every week in 1992 might come every two weeks in 1993 and maybe only every three weeks later on.
>
> I used to sell clothes in the salon too. Not now. There are so many second hand clothes in the country today that people prefer to buy this cheaper variety, so I can't make any money selling clothes.

When I saw here again in 2001, her salon had failed and she had begun to sell stationery.

As the economy worsened, the value of the Kenya shilling declined, and inflation squeezed government resources as well as individual budgets. Following International Monetary Fund prescriptions, the government of President Daniel arap Moi passed costs for services on to citizens. Under Moi's "cost sharing" system, basic government services such as education and health care, which had been free, were partly paid for by the user. The user's share increased from a small sum to most of the cost, causing the percentage of children enrolled in school to decline and preventing many people from using health services.

Poor people were denied government services in two ways. Cost-sharing from 1985 to 2002 made basic services inaccessible to many through official government policy, but informal corruption had the same effect. Margaret Obonyo's ten-year-old son was injured by a man who threw a rock at him. When she complained to the police, she was told, "Our car is out of petrol, so there is nothing we can do. If you give us money for petrol, we will come to arrest the man." This was routine, unremarkable.

The New Kenya

As I write at the end of 2003, Kenya is struggling to change. In the last days of 2002, a coalition government headed by Mwai Kibaki was elected on promises of zero tolerance for corruption. The National Alliance Rainbow Coalition, NARC, is comprised of many political parties from different regions, representing different ethnic groups. The new government inherited a desperate situation and a population thirsty for changed government policies.

The new government's first big step was to make primary education free with a few days notice. 1.2 million more children enrolled in primary school. As a result, schools became chaotic, and some standard one [first grade] classes had 100 children with one teacher. However, hungry families like Zildah's no longer had to choose between food and school fees.

The first weeks of the new Kibaki government were euphoric. That didn't last, but not because people expected too much too quickly. Everyone from newspaper-reading university graduates to unschooled, radioless villagers seemed to understand that change would take time. Instead, the government squandered the initial euphoria by reneging on some vital promises.

Changing Customs

> We don't have long ears[5] now. We stopped because people go to church.
>
> —Maria Rotich, farmer, Kimaren

Rapid, uncontrollable change creates traditionalists. In any society pounded by too much change, many react by holding tenaciously to their own version of traditional customs. But "tradition" is a problematic concept. Within one community, people will have different interpretations of what "tradition" requires, depending on how they have seen tradition lived and on their individual sense of the meaning of a given custom. For example, a man in Mumias asserted his right to control all his wife's earnings because it is "traditional" for men to keep money.[6] Although money is a comparatively recent introduction, this man generalized "traditional" subordination of women to cover modern contexts.

In any fast-changing society, a gulf opens between generations. The younger generation grows up in a world their parents and grandparents do not know. Formal education in particular creates a gulf. Unschooled parents who respect education may feel profoundly disempowered in

5. Several Kenyan ethnic groups, including the Maasai and the Nandis, used to stretch their earlobes with increasingly large wooden plugs. These stretched earlobes reach to the shoulders but may be twisted into a compact knot around or just below the ear.

6. I am indebted to Dr. Jacqueline Klopp of Columbia University for this example.

conversation with their own children. This is two-sided. The educated generation may undervalue what they can learn from their elders: equally, the elders are often reluctant to guide their children, fearing that what they can teach won't be received with interest and respect.

Christianity is given as the reason for many changes of custom, even those, like earlobe stretching, which are not clearly related to Jesus' teachings. Early missionaries encouraged or coerced converts to abandon customs incompatible with their view of Christian life, calling such customs "heathenish." Yet neither missionaries nor colonial powers intended all the changes that resulted from their interventions.

Christian Kenyans often explain the reason for a particular change by saying, "because we have gone to church." Elders may resent innovations that look like rebellion against tradition, but accept an innovation that is justified as a consequence of Christianity. Even when someone is quite consciously imitating an attractive novelty, it may be more tactful to explain her innovation as accommodation to Christianity.

Joan Kanini, a Catholic Kamba living in Nairobi, sees an irony in the loss of customs that were attacked by missionaries.

> The Kamba were very willing to accept Christianity and make changes. People used to beat the drums, but when they became Christian they stopped that, so they lost the traditional festivals. This is not a good change.
>
> My mother would not want me to dance those dances, but she respected traditions and wanted me to know about them, so it was OK if I watched the dance.
>
> Yet, now the churches are beginning to use drums, and the dances that were abandoned are being replaced by other dances.

Although Christians may explain modernization as a result of Christianity, the same changes have occurred in Muslim regions. The large, arid swath of northeastern Kenya is populated by Muslim camel herders. The only large town of the region is Wajir, a dry, dusty town of 270,000 permanent residents. Bahsan Gedi's home is typical. A large permanent wall surrounds an enclosed courtyard and many rooms. There, I talked with six friends, all in their twenties or thirties. All wore head coverings and voluminous colorful robes over their dresses. The room where we sat was furnished in plush comfort. Dekha Ibrahim and Bahsan explained their mixture of feelings about changing customs.

> Dekha: There are some customs, especially regarding women, that can stop. Traditional ideas like "a woman is a child with a big foot" should go. But there are other customs I'm sorry to see going. Somali culture, as far as poems which

strengthen moral values, is disappearing. We are losing things that strengthen the social fabric. I'm sad about that.

Bahsan: My mother lives here. My daughter is with her right now. It's not like "The only time I see my children is at Christmas" [a reference to her view of family life in the West]. I see my mother every morning and every night.

Dekha: Granddaughters are always with the Granny. When someone is sick, everyone goes there. These things are passed on. I am a modern woman working in an office, but I am still a traditional woman in my dressing, in my talking, in my interactions, and we're not going to let it go.

We are moving. You have to catch up with time, because children are being taken to school to learn to read. Originally the Quran was translated into Somali, and now it is in English, Swahili, and many other languages, so people know much more about it. So religion will get much stronger. But what is going to decline is Somali culture, because that is in the heads of the elders. That I fear. The challenge is to write it out because we are no longer an oral culture.

Bahsan's friend, Hibo Hussein, added, "We are now moving from the culture to the religion," meaning that customs which have no religious sanction are being modified, but with increasing education, people know Islam better and observe its precepts better. The essentials of Islam are being retained, whereas the Somali traditions not required by Islam are changing.

Bahsan supported Hibo's perception, "Our tradition and our religion go together, but the things that are disappearing are just the tradition, not the religion. Now people understand the content of the religion very well."

Names, Ceremonies, and Social Solidarity

Many people can no longer survive by farming or herding as their parents did. Changes in how people support themselves also change their relations with their families and friends; sacred and honored customs disappear. The reasons for some changes are obvious: others are neither obvious nor expected. Why should village gatherings or naming customs, for example, be affected by modernization? Yet they have been, in ways no one predicted or intended. Disruptions created by contact with the outside world spread a sense of powerlessness.

For example, naming traditions have been undermined as an unintended byproduct of other changes. Customarily, Kikuyus, Nandis, and several other groups name the first son for the husband's father, the second son for the wife's father, the first daughter for the husband's mother, and the second daughter for the wife's mother. Only with the birth of a third child of either sex do the parents choose a name. Emily Magut, a Kobujoi farmer born in 1954, explained why the traditional Nandi naming system is disappearing in her village.

> There's no more of naming children after ancestors. During that time of naming, people used to brew traditional beer. Now, since many people have gone to church, things to do with beer have been put aside. That is a bad change because we are losing our traditional ways. We are going to lose our traditional names, and children won't know who their grandparents were.
>
> HH: Could you give the name without the beer?
>
> No, the beer is an offering to the spirits of the ancestors. The ancestor would be angry.
>
> HH: Could you have a celebration with Coca-Cola?
>
> No, it isn't allowed.
>
> HH: But if ancestor spirits would be offended if you didn't give beer, aren't they offended that you don't use the names?
>
> Yes, but we use prayers to control the spirits, and we still give them traditional beer during initiations.

Jane Gathege, a Lusigetti teacher and farmer, expressed a widely shared ambivalence. She worried that traditional observances undermine education. Yet she was concerned about a decline in social life caused by the disappearance of traditional celebrations.

> We have given up some of the traditional rites, like the circumcision rite, singing songs, and so on. It's a good change. If we were circumcising our children, we would start those dances one month early. We would not be doing anything else for that month but enjoying ourselves. Those children would not be going to school. What about that?
>
> But these rites bring the family together, the friends together. By giving up some of these rites we may be losing something good.

The shift to a money economy and increasing poverty have both contributed to a decline of inter-family socializing and increasing isolation. Many rural women have few opportunities to talk with women outside their own families. In Kisii, Selina Onduko, a farmer, lamented the loss of social opportunities and mutual support. For Selina and her family, this is a recent change. They live on land given to her husband by the government in 1965 as a part of a redistribution of white settlers' land. The social life she and her neighbors lament was not the life of the village of her husband's birth, where families had been together for generations. Instead they miss the shared social life of a group of newcomers, which has gone, leaving them feeling isolated.

> When we first came here, we could sit together, we could visit one another. Because of hardships we do not go from one household to another anymore. We used to eat together, especially on Christmas and at circumcisions. Nowadays, children go to hospitals for circumcision and there is no celebration at home.
>
> Long ago, when they had celebrations there was little food and the food was not bought by money, but nowadays food is bought. It is impossible now to bring visitors home because you have to give them sodas, you give them much food. Everybody who comes must get sufficient food. If there are a hundred visitors, you have to kill about two cows, about six goats, and you have to bring a lot of beer, many cases of soda, many hens. Those hundred people don't all eat the same food. This one doesn't eat meat of a cow, that one needs meat of a hen, and where do you get all that? But years ago, it would just be some *busaa* [traditional beer], a cow, and native bread.
>
> Now the cost of living is high. That's what prevents a Christmas celebration with many families. Even weddings are less social. They are done in church. The people eat at the church and then just go home. When we came here, it was done in the homes for many hours, but doing it at church is less expensive.

Loice Mattoi, a Werugha farmer and shopkeeper, was twice sustained by relatives when she met misfortune, but she said that few people can now afford to help others as she was helped.

> After my father died a cousin of my father's was working, so he supported us freely. He sent me and all my brothers to school.
>
> When I had been married for thirteen years my husband went to Tanzania and was gone a long time. He had served the colonial government as an informer. That made him many enemies, so he feared to stay here after Independence. I had three children and never heard anything from him. When he was away, two brothers-in-law helped me very much. Today not many people could do that.

Many other women told such tales of poverty fraying social bonds. It is harder, often impossible, to support relatives who face misfortune, and the social contacts that created solidarity are disappearing. No one meant this to happen — no one planned it — no one even expected it. It is a consequence of hard times.

Position of Women

> During the time of our grandmothers, men would say, "A woman is not supposed to say anything, because if you let her say something, she will shame you." Some still think that way today, but nowadays, many men are making some little changes. The ones who are educated are not like that.
>
> —Wambui Rahab, farmer, Lusigetti

When asked how life in their communities is changing, people of many different circumstances commented first on the changing position of women. "Women of Worth" is a training program for young women who lack the means to support themselves. Each Methodist church in the Meru area sends one girl. For one year, the students are taught cooking, baking, household management, gardening, and business skills. By the end of the year, they are supposed to develop a plan for self-sufficiency. These young women were clearly shy about talking with a stranger. We asked how their lives are different than their mothers' had been.

> Mlero: I can make decisions, but my mother couldn't.
>
> Tina: My mother had no chance to mix with other girls and learn something different.
>
> Karime: The parents of my mother were not free with the girls. The girls were just at home, but now we can read books and are getting information.

Roselyne Choge, a Kobujoi schoolteacher born in 1951, initiated our conversation about women's position.

> Long time ago, women were not regarded as people, but at the moment we are about equal. I sit with my husband at the table and I eat with him. When we go for a walk, we go side by side. A long time ago, the man went ahead and the woman behind, so you can see there are many changes. That comes with civilization.

Nevertheless, when I had dinner with her family, she served her husband, the other male guest, and me at the dining room table, left to feed her children and grandchildren, then returned to eat by herself in the adjoining sitting room. I don't assume a contradiction. Perhaps she eats with her husband when they are alone, but doesn't eat with a male guest.

Among Muslims, seclusion of women is a long tradition. Adey Addeha, a charcoal trader in the Wajir marketplace, grew up strictly secluded, and secludes her daughters. "I was kept at home because my parents feared I might become a prostitute.[7] Now that I am married, I have freedom to go out because all the people I know are married. I keep my daughters at home as strictly as I was kept home."

Although Adey's daughters are secluded, most women are less secluded than a generation ago. Fewer families can afford to forego the women's economic contributions. As women move out to participate in the life of their communities, their economic autonomy is increased. Saumu Hasani, who cooks and sells food on the street in Malindi, appears to be over fifty. Since she has no one to support her, her livelihood depends on freedom of movement.

> It is good for a girl to be going out for the betterness of life. Before, girls were kept indoors and were not allowed to go out, but nowadays, they do. I go out to help with sewing and of course selling, and that supports me, but my daughter also goes out to sell or do any business she can find.

During the conversation at Bahsan's home in Wajir, everyone commented on women's new roles.

> Bahsan: When women want to discuss problems with a man, he doesn't want to listen. You know, the learned women of today realize their problems, and because they are working class[8] they can have security on their own. So they can say, "I want a divorce."
>
> Khadija: Now that women are working, they give their opinions more freely.
>
> Sacdiyo: We all stayed home when we were girls. My mother was very strict about that. In our tradition women are supposed to stay back, but now we are seeing women making decisions. People are seeing that women can do many things. Now women are beginning to talk and even men will listen.
>
> Adey: Maybe now the husband can't get everything the family needs, maybe the man can't get firewood, so the wife now sells miraa to get an income.
>
> Khadija: Our mothers would just stay in. Only the men would do the shopping. In town, our mothers would only go out for weddings or funerals, but when we were in the bush they would go out to care for the animals.
>
> Bahsan: Our daughters can go outside, but you should not just allow them to go just anywhere. There must be limitations. They can go to town if they have something they need to do.
>
> The environment is not the same now. They watch TV. There are people here from outside so we worry about them getting bad habits. A girl from Nairobi lives differently, and some of them are here, so we worry about that influence.

---

7. This is broader than the specific fear that she might exchange sex for money. It is rather that she will become a brazen modern woman who dresses "indecently," speaks to men, and is seen in public.

8. That is, holding formal sector employment, thus well above average in income and financial stability. "Working class" has a social implication almost opposite of what it has in the West. It is often a term of envy.

Changes accepted by urban people are often bitterly contested by rural people. Zuhuru Ali, who was born in 1967, is a nurse in Malindi. Since Zuhuru has an income and no children, several young nieces have been sent to stay with her, but their parents have not always accepted the freedoms that the girls found in the city.

> When my nieces came to me, I gave them freedom to have friends, but with a limit, and let them go to certain safe places without prevention. My sisters and brothers were complaining about it. In fact, one niece was called back home immediately because they thought I gave her too much freedom.

Nuria Yussuf is a Kenyan Somali born in 1973 who lives among Maasai in Kajiado District. She manages a family restaurant, and is the only one who can talk with customers who speak neither Somali nor Maa. Thus, she talks to many people, both friends and strangers. This is something many Muslim families would not welcome for their daughters, but her family is glad to use her sociable nature this way. She told us that although Somalis are Muslim and Maasai are not, their traditions are very similar, and are rapidly changing in both groups.

> Circumcision, rites of baths, are all the same. Like Maasais, Somalis really ignore their wives. A man should not eat where his wife is, and a wife should not attempt to greet men. She should always be behind. All that is the same with Somalis and Maasais.
>
> Those are the old traditions. Even now it is disappearing, It is going to disappear *kabisa* [completely]. Now we can eat in front of people, I can talk to people. I'm very social. My mother and father don't object.

Bahsan and her friends agree that Somali and Maasai customs are very similar, but Bahsan commented, "Of course the religion is different, and that affects everything."

New roles have affected middle-class women the most, but they touch all segments of society. Mariamu Muhammad, a former camel herder now living outside Wajir, has benefited from changing attitudes toward women, but is ambivalent about the goal of equality.

> We got rid of the restrictions on women. In the past, there was no freedom of movement for women. But now they can go anywhere, they can attend meetings. As far as human rights is concerned, it is good to be equal. But as far as the respect and maybe the shyness, women should always be behind men.

Elizabeth Ndunde was born in Nakuru in 1953. Her family was unusual in having an early practice of equality.

My father was a mechanic and a good carpenter. In his free time he would make furniture. I used to like working with his tools. So I did do things in my childhood that were not supposed to be done by a girl. Some of the things I enjoyed as a child were going outside, eating food, planting trees, working with my father.

I do not remember the boys having any different household jobs. I cooked, and they also cooked. They did everything that I did: I never washed their clothes. I washed mine, they washed their own clothes. There was never any discussion of the girls having to forfeit high school. Everybody went to school equally.

When I talk to my husband about things I did as a child, he becomes very shocked. He saw a scar I have on my back, so he asked, "What happened to you?" I told him I got it when my skirt got caught while climbing a tree to eat fruit. He said, "My God! what kind of a girl were you?"

One of our daughters is now in class eight. There was a particular fruit she liked. When she got out of her school she would usually go straight to that tree. My husband does not disapprove, but he finds it very strange. He had not seen that kind of thing when he grew up.

Aoko Odembo, a Nairobi businesswoman born in 1955, is optimistic about the prospects for increasing equity throughout society.

Many women realize that political parties' agendas are not necessarily women's agenda. When we have a meeting we get women from all shades of life. Women are beginning to stand back from political parties and ask, "Why am I part of this fight?" This is really great.

Through the League [of Kenyan Women Voters] we provide information that affects women. We have developed a booklet that we are going to translate into the major languages of the country. That booklet really makes me happy because in many villages, even in my village, the women are exposed to nothing except the Bible.

We tell them how they can collectively fight to have clean water in their villages. We let them know that even if girls become pregnant they can go back to school and continue their education. We are making them aware of how they can use their power to affect Parliament and agitate for better leaders. We are trying to get women to vote for women who will address their concerns.

Husbands will say, "Good wives don't talk about domestic violence." A lot of incest is practiced in this society. Women hesitate to talk about it. I ask them, "If your daughter has been raped by her brother or her uncle, what do you do?" We can now go to a rally and a woman will ask a question like that in public. It's slowly, surely changing.

But opinion isn't as uniform as Aoko Odembo suggests. Sofia Muthoni, the Murang'aa farmer who talked about soil exhaustion, agrees that education and financial independence give women the possibility of striving for equality, but she does not approve. She blames education for spreading a myth that women should be equal, and believes it is undermining tranquil home life.

> Our girls are able to go to school and tend to think that they are now equal. But being a wife, they are supposed to be under their husbands. Now that they have money, they don't want to be under men, so they conflict.

Maria Kibera, the development worker who lamented the disappearance of forests and streams in Wundanyi, searches for opportunities to promote gender equity.

> Everyone in Kenya knows that women need equal rights in development, and any other area, but women are not in great numbers at places of policy making. At the grassroots level, women know their rights. In Kenya women's rights is not rights to fight their men, but rights to be able to realize themselves, rights to able to make their families healthier. Their need is to uplift their status but not to the same as their men, no.
>
> Children should be given freedom to express themselves starting at home. When I was teaching, the girls in the lower level classes used to come to complain that this or that happened. I told them, "You settle your problem with that boy. You don't need any help because you are equal, and that is why you are in the same class."

Although women are beginning to expect more power over their lives, men are changing their expectations more slowly. In rural Kajiado, I visited a kind widow, Sein Milanoi. Sein is well educated and runs a successful shop. She has a good income of her own, and is well respected in the community. Her life is now largely devoted to helping girls stay in school and other issues of empowerment for young women. She is concerned about the attitudes her grown and educated sons have toward women. "I ask my sons, 'Will you help your wives at home?' But they always say, 'No, I can't do that.'"

AIDS: The Dark Void

Anna Wanjiru was an exceptionally beautiful young woman. At seventeen, she was caring for her five younger brothers and sisters. Her mother died in 1999 and her stepfather died three years later of AIDS. When I met Anna, she seemed oppressively sad. What she told me made sadness understandable, but I wasn't told the worst until after she left: shortly before he died, her stepfather raped her. She died about a year after our conversation.

Sammy Kariuki of Nakuru had a healthy young girlfriend before he married someone else. He and his wife had a baby daughter who died at four months old. After an interval, they had another daughter, who also died in infancy.

After the second death, Sammy assumed he had been cursed. Of course, he wanted to know the reason for the curse, and whether it could be lifted. He asked whether his father had completed paying dowry for his mother. Sammy's father found the question insulting and threw him out of the house.

Sammy became terribly sick and was hospitalized, incurring huge medical bills. Being unable to pay his medical bills, his family disowned him. Although Sammy was still too sick to take care of himself, the hospital wanted him to leave because of the unpaid bills. When he left the hospital, Sammy could not go home or to any friend. He was offered shelter in a charcoal shed. Sister Patricia, a nun working in Nakuru, began visiting, bringing food and helping him clean himself. No one else would.

Sammy's friends abandoned him after AIDS was diagnosed. His wife was especially angry, believing that he must have known about the infection when he met her. Sammy was amazed to learn that his former girlfriend was infected, since she looked healthy.

At that point, Sammy planned suicide. He decided to stage a bank robbery, expecting to be shot in the attempt because of the Kenya police's well-deserved reputation for violence. Inside the bank, he ran into an acquaintance who invited him to take a cup of tea. Sammy didn't want to snub the acquaintance, since he had been so lonely, so he went along. Another time, Sammy decided to run into an oncoming vehicle, but was foiled by a traffic jam.

As Sammy grew stronger, Sister Patricia asked him to accompany her on visits to other AIDS sufferers. From this, he developed a new network of friends and founded TAPWAN, The Association of People With AIDS in Nakuru.

Since they have mostly been shunned by families and friends, members of TAPWAN support each other and work to demystify AIDS.

They insist on acknowledging their AIDS publicly though many people advise them to be discrete.

Sammy was not alone in thinking of suicide after his diagnosis. Evelyne Mwanganyi is a teacher in Wundanyi married to a pastor.

> Our first born was born in 1985. In the course of getting her, I was transfused with two pints of blood.
>
> This child began ailing when she was very young. The hospital told us, "This child has a disease which has no cure. This is brought about by unfaithfulness." We told him we cannot believe the results. He said, "Whether you believe the results or not, I would like both of you tested."
>
> We told him, "No, we are not going to be tested for something which we have not done." We told him of the transfusion and he said, "I do not see the way this kid could have been infected because it was you who was transfused."
>
> As we were leaving the clinic, we were told to just go home with the child and wait for her to die, and maybe we would follow. We came home praying that we would get a road accident and just all die.

As she grew, their daughter had intermittent serious health problems. Two other children were born before the first one died in 1998.

> We were asked, "What about the other kids."
>
> We said, "They are all right. We do not want to test them because this is the only one who has problems." When she died was when we learned that a person can get it from a transfusion, so at last we knew that it was true.
>
> That same year, I got very sick and needed an operation. According to our African culture, if a husband dies, and after a few months the wife dies, we say that these people really loved one another. So I prayed to God, "If the same disease is also with us, I ask you to take me when they put me to sleep for my operation."
>
> I asked my husband one time, "Why don't I go for a test because all the signs I am experiencing are the signs our late daughter experienced."
>
> He said, "No, don't go saying things that will make us weak in our faith."
>
> I began to have oral thrush, stopped eating, lost my appetite for anything. I began getting boils. I sort of shied off from going to the doctors because when I went for the first boil, the doctor asked me if I had ever been tested for anything. I knew what he was after. So I told him, "No, never."

After a time, Evelyne told another doctor the whole story. She and her husband were both tested and found positive. "We thought that we were the next to go. We did not share it with any of our family members at first. We thought we would be judged harshly that we got it through immoral ways."

Eventually, she decided to speak openly about her infection.

The year 2002, God told me, "I want you to tell the people that you are HIV positive.

When I heard that voice, I was trying to fight it. Am I imagining? I asked God, "Is that you speaking. Is that your voice? Do you want us to tell everybody?" Even our kids did not know.

From there, we began telling the children. They cried that night thinking that they were going to lose their parents.

In my prayers I said, "I am willing to break the news, but you see I am very weak. In order to know that you are the one sending me and not my emotions, I want strength to help me to talk boldly without crying," because there was not a day I had finished the story without crying.

The next day was a Sunday. Before, I was walking with the aid of a walking stick. That day, I walked on my own, walking fast. I spoke to the congregation without any tear rolling down. We thought that it would have an effect on the Holy Communion; that if I touch anything, people would not want to take it.

Our second born child, now the eldest, said, "Mummy, Daddy, we are also getting questions from the other students in school, 'How about you people? Are you also positive? Do you eat the food your mother cooks? Do you eat from the same plate?'" So the children wanted to go for a test.

We did not want to know their status. I had to take them for a test under their request. They were negative.

One of the problems in Africa is that if people have the virus they do not want to die alone. Immediately one discovers to have the virus, she or he shares it as much as possible. That is what is making the virus spread.

Before we started the anti-retrovirals, I told the doctor that he should give them to my husband instead of me, because he was much stronger. We were using one salary to live on and one to purchase the drugs. We were budgeting 14,000 Ksh every month for the two of us.

Evelyne and her husband were not unusual in their reluctance to be tested. Grace Gathone is a young political activist who recently left Kenya to study abroad.

Most people don't want to be tested, but if they are tested and find they are negative, they may become very determined to stay negative, and will refuse sex completely.

Men resist using condoms. In rural areas, people did not even used to know what they were, but now they are all around, for free. Still, they are not used.

In rural Kisii, you will not find a homestead without at least two graves. There are so many villages with no teenagers. There are orphans everywhere, houses with grass growing over them, and old people struggling to raise the children.

AIDS is surrounded with shame and misunderstanding. Oruko Omina, who has a Masters degree in Public Health, is the person her family consults when they have a medical problem.

> Not long ago I was told to go see my niece. One of her sisters said, "She's finished."
>
> I asked, "What's wrong?"
>
> They couldn't come out and say. They just said, "You go and see her."
>
> When I saw her, I could see she was a typical HIV/AIDS case. So quickly I took her to a hospital. The husband was there and the children. They said, "Don't bother. This one is not a hospital case. She is bewitched."
>
> What is very sad is the husband didn't know. I insisted that the doctor talk to the husband, but he didn't.

Many women over forty have told me, "I am becoming old and tired. I should have grown children to help me. But my son died, then his wife died. Instead I am raising small children."

In every case, I asked, "Do you know why they died?" Many answers were given. The most common was, "I don't know." AIDS was never mentioned: only one woman responded to my direct question about AIDS with, "There is a rumor that it might have been AIDS."

People like Evelyne and Sammy who are willing to speak openly about AIDS are still rare. Silence is one of the problems that contribute to spread. Oruko Omina has an example from her own family.

> My uncle died of AIDS. AIDS was written on the death certificate. It's one of the ways of dealing with the stigma. Even my cousins wouldn't come right out and say. They said, "TB due to immuno-suppressed deficiency."

She thinks a few high-profile people publicly acknowledging that they are infected would help greatly. In September 2003, the Vice President, Michael Wamwalwa, died in London of an unnamed disease.

> The greatest awareness could have come from the VP whom we just lost. My colleague was involved in treating him. It was definitely AIDS.
>
> HH: He didn't look so thin.
>
> Not all of them get that way.
>
> HH: Did people talk to him about going public?
>
> Who would dare? My friend didn't. For one thing, people didn't think he was dying that quickly.

In any community, AIDS is an import. No matter what its origins, each community receives it from the outside. For a long time it is not recognized. People do not speak openly about it, and at first do not know how much it has already affected their community. But, when a community begins to lose all of its young people, they know.

In 1990, my close friend, Tabitha Nechesa, a community health worker, told me there was no AIDS in our community. A few years later, she had stopped other kinds of health work and was caring exclusively for AIDS sufferers. "AIDS came here when West Kenya [the local sugar factory] got big machines and hired outside workers. They came, they had money, and the girls liked them. We do not have many cases now but it is spreading." Social service organizations are struggling to respond. Many provide free condoms, counseling and testing. Health workers like Tabitha are being trained to recognize symptoms. In Kenya, you cannot go far without seeing ads for Trust, a brand of condoms. You don't have to look long to see skeletally thin people, or people with multiple large lesions, and everyone has lost relatives to AIDS.

Reflections on Exposure to the Wider World

The money economy has brought a need for infrastructure, especially roads from rural areas to market centers. Farmers always want good roads to take their crops to market. Roads bring many changes, some welcome, some not.

Roselyne Choge, the Kobujoi schoolteacher who is proud to walk beside her husband, lives in a recently-built permanent house. Although most rural homes are mud, hers is made of concrete building blocks and has a concrete floor. Although her village has no electricity, their house is already wired for electricity, which she hopes will come soon. She and her husband are very modern in their outlook, yet she is not sure she will like all the changes electricity will bring.

> We are always trying to advance. In years to come, people will use electricity for many things, even for milking the cows. But with electricity, you can have TV and videos. These bring outside influences. Instead of studying, children sneak off.
>
> They are talking about tarmacking the road to Serem. If they do, it will bring more change. Nobody is going to remain because the car will always be telling you, "take me somewhere." Even bus fares will be cheaper and you can go anywhere.
>
> Whenever you have growth, you have some problems. It will bring some good things, but normally when a town grows, it grows with thugs and thieves.

We don't have them now. But very soon we shall have them. We will have street children, and all those things that are now in cities.

Rosemary Njeri, a Lusigetti batik artist born in 1963, is enthusiastic about infrastructure development.

Here in Lusigetti we used to spend so much time going for water and sometimes we could not get any. Today it is very easy. As a matter of fact, there's nothing that was good before that has gone wrong.

The old traditions have changed. For example, our grandfathers and fathers used to go out in the fields to graze cattle. It would take the whole day. These days we have switched to zero-grazing where we have one or two good quality cows. We don't struggle much as we used to in the earlier days.

These developments are good. I don't see any problems coming from them.

Roads and electricity are both wanted and regretted. But one form of infrastructure development is universally praised. Wells, water pipes, and anything else that brings water is a clear boon to women who have walked far and carried heavy loads of water.

Rapid change creates conflict between people who are affected differently by the changes, but also produces widespread ambivalence, as the same person sees both good and bad in the changes. Most women like the development of physical infrastructure, even if they have some reservations. But the social effects of exposure to the wider world cause a great deal of concern. Regina Kavindu, an Athi River farmer born in 1945, is very clear in her disapproval of foreign customs.

Modern houses are better because of snakes. Better transportation is good, but cars can also claim lives.

I see white women holding hands with men. This is wearing down our moral standards. They should dress like we dress instead of our young people copying them. AIDS came from there [the home of white people].

Regina's neighbor Anna Mwende does not share her disapproval. "Things used to be very remote, but they are now forging ahead. When I was young, there was no university education, and people didn't travel abroad. Now they do. It is good because it brings progress."

Rural people may fear contact with urban Kenyans as much as they fear contact with foreigners. We have already heard Bahsan's concerns over outsiders living in Wajir. Jane Gathege, the Lusigetti teacher who applauded the demise of circumcision ceremonies, felt ostracized when she moved from Nairobi to her husband's village an hour away.

> Life was strange here for me at first, because I had been born in the city slums and knew nothing about rural life. The way of dressing is different, for example. In the city, we would put on trousers. Here, if we wear such clothes, people take you very differently. It was hard for me to feel accepted until I learned.

On the other hand, Habiba of *Ayuta Women's Group* [Portrait L] believes that cultural contact is very valuable.

> When people see a visitor from outside, they immediately think about getting some money. But one good idea may be just as useful. We got the idea for our group, and the idea of mat making from seminars, so we like to talk with people who have seen other ways of living.

In the rural secondary school where I taught, students feared a new boy from Nairobi. They expected him to be far ahead academically, and contemptuous of rural ways. In his case, the fear dissipated soon because he was neither arrogant about his city background nor a strong student.

Rural and urban, rich and poor, traditionalists and modernizers, all Kenyans carry a mixture of hope and fear heightened by the extremes of change they have already seen. Many have personal experience of both mud huts and microchips and value both, but they can't envision how new trends will be reconciled with traditions they hope to retain.

Portrait B

Irene Katete

Irene Katete is a lively, smiling woman who works for the Department of Social Services. I was given her name as the perfect person to introduce me to Maasai women and translate interviews with them. I met her in Nairobi to discuss my needs. While we sat drinking warm grapefruit soda, she shared her own story with me over the clanging of metal trays in a crowded cafeteria. Despite our surroundings, she talked at length, sharing both intimate details, and her general philosophy.

During the time we worked together in Kajiado District, Katete introduced me to a wide range of people: the district officer and his staff, participants in the rural women's groups she works with, her work mates, and her own friends and neighbors. Thereafter, whenever she came to see me in Nairobi, she was always accompanied by one or several attractive young men.

Her interest in learning showed in many ways. She had taken a course on birds, and could identify everything we saw. I always think of her when I see a bird I cannot identify. Soon after our first collaboration, she enrolled in Daystar University, although she continued to work long hours at her job.

I was born in 1970 to a family of six children. My father has two wives. I wasn't a favorite kid of my father because he thought I was from another father. So I was given to my mother's mother when I was nine months old. She was very systematic about raising children. For example, she made me eat frequently so that I could grow fast.

She never allowed me to mix with other kids, especially boys, saying that I could get spoilt very easily. Whenever I wanted to play, I had to tell her who

I was going to play with and from what time to what time. We played hide and seek, told each other stories and whenever it reached six she would come and say, "Katete, come back home." I would sneak out when I could, but she would find us singing together, sharing stories or a joke. If I was sad to leave, she would pick up the story that I was being told and continue with it. I appreciate that she brought me up like that.

When I was nine, I went to Nyeri, to live with my uncle and started primary school. Later, I went to a boarding school in Kajiado district[1] and did my KCPE[2] and then joined high school.

During a school vacation, my mother came to visit me and said, "Let her come home. She has to know all the family she has never known."

After that, every vacation I had to go home for two weeks, and one week I went to my grandmother's house. Since I had grown up with my grandmother, I could go to her for refuge when there was a problem at home.

There was a time when I was really annoyed. My eldest sister had some new clothes and I also wanted a dress for Christmas. My father refused. The next morning, very early, I sneaked to my grandmother's place because I was not bought a dress. I stayed there for Christmas and the beginning of the next year.

I used to have a long process to get something I needed for school. I could not go to my father. He would just say, "We have no money." If my mother had no way of buying what I wanted, I would go to my grandmother's place and then my uncle's place to get what I wanted. My father favored his other wife and her children over my mother and her children. He was not willing to give things to me, but he gave anything to my eldest sister from my stepmother.

On the other hand, he would sell my mother's cattle, and my mother had no say. My mother went to talk to the chief, who told my father, "Nobody should be selling anybody else's cows. If you sell, you have to give every her every cent because that cow is hers." From then we started having our own money.

Traditionally, it's hard to settle a problem like that. The *wazee* [elders] have to come in and see that you do not favor one side or the other. The chief was there, and the age mates and clanmates of my mother, and the age mates and clanmates of my father as witnesses. After that, my mother sold her own cattle until my brother was initiated, when she handed the responsibility over to him.

I am lucky I did not get married off. There was a rich man, a chief, who had booked me when I was very young to marry his son. When I finished standard eight, I heard him saying, "Now she has finished school, so when?"

My father said, "Let us just wait for the exam results. If she does not pass, you take her. If she passed, she will continue until she is dropped from school." I stayed at home to wait for my results, but the old man came again.

1. A. I. C. Girl's Primary School is described in Portait G.

2. Kenya Certificate of Primary Education, which is achieved by passing a national exam at the end of primary school.

As soon as he came in, I ran to my grandmother's place and stayed until I went to school.

The next time I came home, I heard, "Ah, you are lucky you ran. Your dad accepted some cattle. You would have been married off before your results came."

When she was in form two [tenth grade], the man came again, so she stopped going home during school breaks. Eventually she was brought home.

When he saw me, my father said, "Oh you have come, so today I am going to drink. Now I am going to give you out."

My mother said, "Let her go. You talk with the old man and give the child a chance to go to school." My mother complained to the chiefs, "My husband is intending to give out my daughter who is still in school."

The chief came to visit my father and told him, "The moment I hear that you are going to marry her off, you will go to jail. She will continue with education, even higher education, look for a job and if she pleases, then you can look for someone who will marry her. Let her stay until the time comes."

Since she was a top student, her father decided it would be better to let her continue with school and find a job to help support the family. As he was backing out of an agreement he had made, he offered to let the intended husband's family choose another of his daughters. The girl they chose had already been promised to someone else. The two families fought. Finally, the father returned as many cattle as he had been given and negotiations were dropped. He never again tried to arrange a marriage for Irene.

He never took any more cattle for me. Now I think he will even accept it if I don't get married. I'm not the only one, there are some other Maasai ladies who never married. But they would like to see me married and settled some day.

I say it is always better to be not married. My friends who are married are not happy. The world has changed. Men are hard to trust. Today he will be one person and tomorrow he will be a different person. You have an affair and then you hear that he has another affair somewhere else. I had a relationship when I was in Nairobi. We used to go out, he gave me heaps of promises, but I could not believe him.

I was inspired by my headmistress in elementary school, Mrs. Priscilla Nangurai.[3] She really stands up and protects Maasai girls from being married off. When I was in school, there was a girl who was booked to get married to

3 . Mrs. Nangurai speaks for herself in Portrait G and Chapter 10.

a man who could have been her grandfather. The headmistress intervened so she was able to continue her education. Now she is a nurse and even her father is happy that she was not married off. I used to pray, "Please God let me help others and be remembered like Mrs. Nangurai."

After I finished my O levels, I got a job with an NGO (non-governmental organization) at home from 1991 to 1994 June. I used to go around and teach the women how to plant a kitchen garden.[4] I introduced them to vegetables like pigeon peas, which we gave them free of cost. They learned that they could reuse household water for the plants. My own family started farming then. They were really active; they planted, harvested, ground sorghum flour. But when I left the program, they stopped planting.

While I was working there, my son was born. He's living with my mother because I am working, and I don't really know how to raise a child. She gives him a lot of time, so I think he will not have any problem. I never had the time to think about what should be done. As long as he was fed and clean that was enough for me. But mother is very keen. She has experienced sixteen children herself. Sometimes I feel jealous, but she assures me, "Don't you ever think that I'm taking him away from you. He is still yours." I don't think I'll have any more children unless the right person comes from Heaven.

The experiences Irene recounted with local officials were unusually positive. The chiefs strongly supported her mother's complaint against Katete's father. Likewise, they helped keep young women in school even when their fathers wanted to marry them off. This is typical in Kajiado District, but in some other regions, officials do far less to promote education.

While we were working together, Irene moved to Isinya town, north of Kajiado. When I returned to Kenya five years later, she was not in the same house. Although I didn't know where to find her or any of her friends, I asked around and, since everyone knows her, was quickly told where she lives. Soon after she moved to Isinya, she became friends with one of the most powerful men in town. She has borne him two daughters, but doesn't want to marry.

She has a half acre of land surrounded by a substantial wooden fence, and has built a four room wooden house. The roughly finished boards that form the walls have some spaces between them, so her two tiny kittens could squeeze through at will, but the mother cat had climb in through the eaves.

The first room a visitor enters is a large sitting room with several modern couches, a low table, a rug woven of plastic-like fibre with red and yellow pictures of camels, and a fancy, glass-fronted cabinet. Behind

4. Her Maasai community relies on cattle herding rather than planting.

this room is a kitchen with a portable propane stove. On either side of the sitting room is a bedroom. The larger room on the left is where Irene sleeps with her two daughters. The rest of the room is crowded with baskets of clothes. There is an adjoining small room for bathing. Water is carried in from an outside tap.

The right bedroom is for the housegirl. On my first visit, there was a charming young girl of about fourteen who did most of the housework and took care of the children while Irene worked. On my second visit a few weeks later, everyone was rather depressed because the housegirl had to leave to be married. We all missed her songs, jokes, and the little games she was constantly devising for the girls.

Irene is gradually finishing her house. During my visit, she had cement floors poured in the house and the latrine and bathhouse out back. When she finishes her own house, she wants to build some rental houses in the front to provide additional income. Despite her previous job, she doesn't grow vegetables on the land surrounding her house.

Irene remains the same warm, outgoing person. She continues to work for social services, and seems to know everyone in town. During the three days I stayed with her, there was a near-constant stream of visitors, mostly devoted friends who see her nearly every day.

Portrait C

Margaret Alosi Obonyo

Margaret is a farmer in Kakamega District, Western Province. She lives in a three-room mud house. Her co-wife has a similar house a few feet away. Each wife has a kitchen in a separate building near her house, and a latrine just outside the compound. The remainder of the compound contains houses of several grown sons and a house for distilling *chang'aa*, the local whiskey that supports most families in her neighborhood.

The region is fertile, with ample rainfall. It's green all year, and there is always water from the artesian well less than 1/2 kilometer away. Fields surround the compound on three sides. Margaret farms about five acres of cane and maize. Six of her children ten children are at home, and five of them are still in school.

When I was young, I used to dream of being married to a man who would love me, and whom I would not share with any other woman.

I was born in 1942 on a farm in Mumias. I was the only daughter, so my parents used to love me so much. When I was in standard five, I went to visit my father's brother to seek school fees. Instead of giving me fees, he introduced me to a strange man. A few days later, I was going to the market to buy some groundnuts to cook and sell them to raise school fees. I saw my uncle with that same man again. They grabbed me, forced me into a car, and drove to Kakamega (32 miles away). They locked me up and kept me incommunicado for some days. My father learned of it from someone who had seen them take me, so he came to try to find me. He was told that a dowry had already been paid to my uncle, so I was now a wife.

I was fourteen years old and knew nothing of family way. He kept me locked up there and in the second month I conceived. I wanted to leave

Margaret Obonyo cooking

him and return to school until I saw a girl who had been a friend. I told her I wanted to return and be with my friends. She abused me, saying I should not have run off with that man if I wanted to continue education. I felt so hopeless! After that, I knew I could not return to my old life, so I accepted staying with my husband.

The second year, I got pregnant again. When my second child was barely a month old, and the first one was still little, he gave me 25 Ksh and told me he was going to his farm for Christmas holidays. The money was to meet my needs while he was gone. I thought he should take me with him, but he refused. Immediately after he left, I packed my things and took the children by bus to my home. I thought this was my chance to escape from him.

He felt very furious to be undermined by a woman, contrary to African custom. I stayed with my parents for about a month. After two weeks, he sent two people with two cows for my father, so I would be sent back. At first, my father did not agree, so after another two weeks, he came himself with two more cows. Still, my father did not agree. I was happy to think maybe I could stay with my parents. After another month he came again, this time with six cows. Now my father thought that a fair dowry had been paid, so he sent me back to my husband.

I started again giving birth. I had eleven pregnancies, but one girl died. Now I have three daughters and seven sons.

At first, we lived in town because he was working there. Then later we lived on a farm nearby. But he lost that farm, so he took me to his home place. That was a problem because he had two other wives, so they had to share their little land with me, which they did not want to do.

The second wife had only one child. One day, there was a terrible argument and he beat her so severely that he broke her leg. After that she felt unsafe, so she ran away.

The other wife hated me very much, and has never welcomed me. She does not realize that I only came to her husband by force. I was not trying to take him from her. When her daughter died, she questioned why God would take her child and leave mine living. She plays some bad tricks on me. She poisoned my chickens and a heifer, and she even tried to poison my children. My second daughter has never been really healthy since that time, but she did not die. God loves me and my children, and has protected us.

My co-wife feels jealous of me in many ways. I have more children than she does because she lost many. My children are very good in school. They are often number one in the class. Her children did not complete school, and were never such good students.

My husband leaves the burden of the children on me completely, which is very hard because there is not enough land, so our harvest is small. It is on me to feed them, educate them, provide clothes for them. Even my husband depends on the little I get as he is not capable now. He used to be a driver, but he retired after breaking his arm in an accident. Since that time, he has never worked, nor helped with our farm work. He tells me to dig, while he just sits. He sits all day in front of his house drinking local beer from a very big cooking fat can. He drinks one and a half cans every day.

His other wife has a still, but now sometimes I make whiskey too, or brew local beer when I can't get money any other way. The police know that almost every family here brews, so they sometimes come to see who they can catch. Once I was caught. I tried to run, but they got me and I went to prison. I don't want to go again!

My husband gets a small pension from the work he used to do, but he does not even give me seeds. He has never told me what he gets, but I do not think it is large. He uses all his money to drink, and is always trying to find ways to get more money for drink. He tries to get money from me, or from other people. When I wanted to get new grass for my roof because the rain was coming in, he told me he would find someone to bring grass and repair the roof. He wanted me to give him the little money I had. He was trying to find someone to do it for less, so he could keep the extra, but I did not even have enough to do it. So, you see, he is even willing to steal from me and the children.

In the early years, he pretended to be a good man, but after many children were born, he changed. He tells me I cannot leave, that I am his property, or that if I leave, I will not be able to provide for the children. Sometimes, when he is drunk, he beats me as if I were an animal. Is it fair for a woman to be beaten like an animal? I asked some of my husband's relatives to talk to him about how he behaves. They talked to him, but he didn't change.

In our culture, even a small household misunderstanding can arouse a man to beat his wife. Men differ in temper. Some can start beating any time they are annoyed by the wife. Others take their time until the children are asleep when they start beating the wife. Some give the excuse that the wife is provocative when the children or guests are there, so he will fight when they are alone.

When a family consists of a few members, maybe two children, it will be a happy family as all the needs can be met, especially love, clothes, food, and most important of all, education. My son David is breaking my heart by following his father and drinking every day, but some other children are hard-working and responsible.

I am a member of *Msamaria Mwema* [Good Samaritan], a women's self-help group to assist women who have problems. For example, when somebody dies, the members contribute food and take it to the bereaved family, and they cook for the mourners. I used to belong to another group but it split up after some women struggled for the posts.

Women like me are very desperate and have many problems, especially with bad husbands who do not care about the children or their wives. We live in fear, and do not know what the future will bring, so we just hold our hearts and pray. I cry to God to stay with me and help me.

Not all Africans are like me. Some are rich and others are poor. Some have good land and good tools. Others have a husband who will help. But I don't, so I live like a prisoner in this condition. I pray to God to give my children a good life, not a life like mine.

2

Arranging a Marriage

In most Kenyan communities, traditionally parents arranged their children's marriages. Typically, the family of the husband would approach the family of the intended wife, and negotiations about brideprice began. If the arrangements were satisfactory, the affected young people would meet each other, and perhaps be consulted. In the course of negotiations, elders made promises about expected settlement, but also about good behavior on all sides. A wedding feast was held at the husband's family home. When the guests left, the bride remained, and became a part of her husband's family under the direction of her mother-in-law.

As young Kenyans become more mobile, they often find their own partners, and may move in together without the traditonal rituals. Sometimes, their union is later solemnized with dowry arrangements. Commonly now, it is not. This worries and upsets parents. Parents of daughters resent losing the animals to which they feel entitled. Parents of sons resent finding a woman they have not chosen, and who may feel no obligation to them, in their compound.

Why Marry?

Women anywhere marry hoping for love, companionship, and financial, emotional, or sexual security. Gracilda Mwakio, a Werugha farmer born in 1943, married for reasons common for girls in bad home situations anywhere.

> My father was a harsh man who beat my mother so much. She ran home many times. It gave me a very negative attitude toward marriage. I decided

never to marry. But after my mother died, I thought that since my father was such a cruel man, he might start beating us like he beat her. I resolved to become a nun. I would sneak away from the house for that training, but it was very far, so I did not continue. Instead, I escaped by marrying.

Siyomit, a Kajiado herder who was born sometime before 1946, doesn't regret being single.

> I never got married, but I had six kids. I didn't marry because my parents were too old. I had to look after them. It's not unusual because traditionally, when the parents realize they are old and they need someone to take care of them, no matter whether you are a boy or a girl, you have to stay at home to look after them and then you inherit. I stayed at home and inherited both the father's wealth and the mother's. I was the only child so father gave me everything.
>
> I am happy that I stayed at home because I sweated but I made it with the help of God. I don't know about married life because I've never tasted it.[1]

Mothers hope their daughters will marry, and worry about them if they do not. In Mirere, a group of about 150 women gathered to speak to us. Because of the numbers, we did not attempt to interview them individually, but instead asked questions we hoped would generate lively discussion. We began with "How is life changing here?" as we always did in such circumstances. After someone mentioned a change, we would ask, "Is that a good change or a bad change?" As usual, these questions led women directly into talking about changes in marriage customs. Several women were clearly very worried about their daughters' marriage prospects.

> Woman 1: Since it seems that there are very many girls compared to men, many men will develop the behavior of exchanging women and women will stand a very bad chance of being married.
>
> Woman 2: Many girls will not get married due to frustrations and disappointments they will face from men. Some will engage in actions that may ruin their lives.

Angie Dawa is a physician born in 1961 who married an Air Force Colonel. When she was in college, she joined a Roman Catholic evangelical community, but she felt she was not doing right by her parents since she had not married and given them grandchildren.

1. Siyomit was able to inherit because she was the only child, and perhaps because land in her region is not bitterly contested. Her region is arid, so landholdings are frequently large and not very valuable. If the land had been arable, male relatives of her father's might have claimed it.

> I was not fulfilling my role toward my mother and father. I felt I had cheated them after they had put in so much to bring me to that level. One day I was cleaning the community kitchen. I put in a lot of time, and it was really clean, but I thought, "I wish I could have an opportunity to do it for my own family." Then I realized I wanted to have a family one day, so I left.

In Kenya, patrilocality adds another reason to marry. A family's land is divided among the sons. When a woman marries, she normally goes to live at her husband's home, and works a portion of his family's land. Although the Succession Act of 1981 permits a woman to inherit a portion of her father's land, this rarely happens. Unless a woman's family of origin has excess land, her brothers rarely wish to share the land that feeds their families.

Reasons for Hesitation

Irene Katete doesn't want or expect to marry. She sees most of her friends unhappily married, and doesn't want to follow them. Clarissa Kahala, a tailor born in 1975 who has only one leg, also fears marriage.

> When I look at the condition of the world, I don't think I want to marry. I see people who are whole and they marry, but they have problems and divorce even if they have children.
>
> Maybe the husband will love me when I have a job, but when I get a baby I won't be able to do the work I did before. Then maybe my husband won't love me any more.

Nightingale Wanjiru, a Lusigetti secondary school student, does not have an optimistic view of marriage.

> It's very hard to make the right choice. In our tradition, most men marry a woman so they can stop doing work at home, so they will have someone to take care of them and produce children. I want to marry not really for children, but for companionship. So I want someone who cares for me as much as I will care for him. Even though we are married he may not keep on loving me. And the in-laws will expect a grandson, which I might not be able to give. Will they still love me if I cannot?

Aoko Odembo and her peers approach the question from the perspective of young, educated career women, and face the same issues as career women anywhere.

> Women of my generation have the problem, "Do I get married now, or do I work first? When do I have children?" There is a lot of competition to

get ahead, which pushes family life aside. So people end up not having many children, or having them later in life. Most of us are educated now, and have pressure to use the education, so family life is considered inferior.

THE "IDEAL HUSBAND"

What do women want in a husband? Kenyan women answer this question like women anywhere. Some mention physical appeal. A woman may say she wants a handsome husband, or she may specify what physical type she finds handsome. Margaret Mueni, a teacher in Matuu, knew what she found appealing. "I had many boyfriends, but I had not known my husband long when I decided to marry him. I really admired him. He was very tall, and very black. I didn't want a brown man, I wanted one who was really black."

Other answers concern love and companionship. A woman may say she wants a loving husband, or one who is also a friend, or an understanding man. Some women stress similarity of background. If she is religious, she may want a man of the same religion, and a similar degree of devotion. If she is athletic or musical, she may want him to share those interests. Some women specify that he should be rich, or a good provider. Alice Mwangi, a nurse in Malindi, is quite sure what she wants.

> I'd like to marry a tall, handsome man, very smart-looking,[2] well educated, with a good salary. I want to have two children because it is hard to cater for more. I would refuse a big family because I want my children to have a good education.

Mariamu Khalifa is a Muslim secretary who wears a *bui-bui* [black loose-fitting overgarment] on the streets. Her father is dead. Before she married, she told me, "I will choose for myself and not my mother planning it for me. She will not mind. He should be a Muslim, not a drunkard, not a criminal and a kindhearted one, not one who is fond of beating others unnecessarily, and the one I love."

She later became the second wife of a man who fit those requirements. She told me that what she really apppreciated when marriage was being discussed was that he would permit her to continue to live in her mother's home. When I visited her after marriage, she and several other married sisters were with their mother. Mariamu's husband regularly alternated nights with her and nights with his first wife. Mariamu's mother is pleased with him as a son-in-law.

2. In Kenyan English, this means clean, trim, well-groomed, fashionable. It does not mean intelligent.

We asked women what advice they would give their daughters about choosing a husband. Consolata Mombua, a Nairobi nurse born in 1945, included both culturally specific and universal themes in her advice.

> I think that we should teach our daughters that, if they find men of their choice for marriage, they should learn their backgrounds. They should inquire about their families and should take a keen interest in learning what type of man he is. They should also look for men with whom their hobbies rhyme and make sure that they are not men who will ruin their lives. Once they find their desired choices, they should bring them home to introduce them to their parents. I can also advise my children to have many friends so that they can choose the right one from them. Of course, we should keep our children from marrying night runners.[3]

Agnetta Owire is a Kakamega farmer with inadequate land. Her family is often hungry. She gave her daughter practical advice, "After she became mature, I advised her to look for a person who has a good shamba because her father does not have a shamba, so we have not had an easy life. She has learned hardship, but I wanted her to live better."

Bahsan and her friends gave advice on family and behavior.

> Dekha: I don't know if there's some kind of secret initiation by our fathers, but there's that common aspect of demeaning women. She should find someone who will respect her as a human being and give her the freedom to do what's right for her. That's a basic necessity. If he doesn't give her that respect, if he's the possessive type, it will be difficult.
>
> Bahsan: You should look into the background of the family If so-and-so's grandfather spoiled[4] so many women, you should be careful.

This is very much like women anywhere, except that polygamy adds an extra dimension. Margaret Obonyo dreamed of having a husband she would not have to share. Roselyne Okumu was born in 1970 to a very poor family in Kakamega. When she was still in secondary school, I was talking casually with her about polygamy. I asked why girls are willing to become second wives. Roselyne's family is hungry for some months each year. She replied emphatically, "If he was rich, I wouldn't care."

Selina Onduku thinks polygamy affects the proper choice in a different way.

3. People possessed by evil spirits who run to make mischief at night.

4. Deflowered and abandoned.

> It is better to have the husband older, because women age faster. Then the man sees that his wife is younger, so that will prevent him from marrying other wives. If he marries an age mate, she will age faster and he will want other wives.

Oruko Omina is a public health educator. Her mother worried when she married into a polygamous family.

> We started dating when I was in high school and married immediately after I finished my first training. My mother wasn't happy about it. My father didn't care as long as he got dowry. My mother was more concerned with my welfare. My husband comes from a polygamous family and my mother asked me once, "If this man comes from that kind of background, how are you sure that he's not going to do the same thing to you?" I was too young to be realistic, but now I would advise differently. I have found it very difficult to live in their family.

Love Matches

In some communities, it is traditional for young people to arrange their own marriages. Simanya Machocho is a Wundanyi farmer with beautiful ritual scarifications covering her face. She does not know her age, but was born around 1940. Machocho explains the role parents had in the process when she was young. It began with *Mwari,* a Taita ritual of seclusion and instruction for adulthood that took place at puberty.

> After we came out of Mwari, we were allowed to attend local dances. So the young people met in those places and identified each other. He would inform his parents. She would inform her parents. The man's mother would approach the girl's mother. The parents would arrange everything.

But, as anywhere else, parents sometimes worry about the choices their daughters have made. Olive Majala was born near Wundanyi, a beautiful town between Nairobi and Mombasa. When we first met her at a friend's home in 1996, she was shivering violently although wrapped in a blanket on a warm day. She had a severe case of malaria, but wanted to be interviewed because she needed the small gift I offered. I interviewed her quickly because she was obviously suffering terribly.

Olive's parents were concerned about her suitor's inability to support a family. "My mother was very much against, citing land, food and such things. She disliked that he was born outside marriage. He had no father, so he had no land."

Regina Kavindu, the Athi River teacher who disapproved of hand-holding, had unusually accomodating parents. They allowed her to marry the man she wanted even though they had already made another arrangement and accepted a dowry.

> I married the Headmaster of my school. He told his parents about me, and they went to my parents. My father had already made another arrangement for me, but I refused, because the man was old. My husband had to pay dowry so my father could pay back the other dowry which had already been given for me.

Sophie Mwangemi was a Wundanyi farmer born in 1938, who died in 2001. Her parents objected because her proposed husband had little land, so she and her beloved eloped.

> He came hunting for me, so we agreed together. My father was against it, not against the man himself, but father felt that I would suffer because the man did not have enough land. Where would I dig and get food? But because I loved him, we eloped. I didn't mind about the land since I loved him so much.

Such a romantic beginning may be a prelude to a long, happy marriage, as it was for Fathia Abdi of Wajir who eloped when she was about thirteen and has been married for twenty-four years.

> I met him at the house of some friends. We were of the same age. We were really in love and were together for one year before we eloped. My parents never felt good about it. That's why we eloped. Afterwards, he paid dowry. He had money and he was very good to me. It never changed. Up to now he never married another woman.

Or it may not. Virginia Njeri's happiness did not last.

> There was a young man who wanted me to marry him, but I didn't like him. He told his friend I was "strict and couldn't be won by any man" but he sent his friend to me with a letter. The friend and I fell in love. We had a courtship of one week. I couldn't control my love. I crept out through the window to join him.
>
> I stayed with him for one month, then we sent his parents to tell my parents. Since I thought my parents might come for me, we went to Mombasa so they couldn't get me back. We stayed there for four months. Then he was transferred to Lamu, but I came back to live at his home place. He's not in Lamu any more. He used to come often, but now one or two years can pass without me seeing him. We have two children now. He used to send something for the children, but now he doesn't.

MARRIAGES ARRANGED BY RELATIVES

In some communities, most marriages are still arranged by relatives, usually the girl's father. Some girls are very happy with their father's choice, others are not. Saumu Hasani, a Malindi woman who appears to be in her mid-50s but does not know her age, was happy with her father's decision. "I married according to Islam. Our families knew each other and arranged it for us. We had a big celebration. I was very happy, although the wedding was the first time I saw my husband."

Elmina Okuda, was not happy with her parents' arrangements, but had no choice.

> The mother of the husband made friends with my own mother. They asked my father. When I first saw the man, I refused him. (laughter) But my father had agreed, so I got married. I accepted because once my father had agreed for a man to marry me, I could get beaten, even killed, if I refused. I'd surely get no cows. So I just had to do it.

Where arranged marriages are routine, the bride's reaction often depends on the age of the man selected. If her father selects a young man with no obvious defects, she may be pleased with her luck. If he selects a much older husband, she usually is not.

At Mile 46[5] we talked with a group of twelve herders, members of the *Elangata Wuas Women's Group*. All the married women had husbands chosen by their fathers. Some were pleased, some were not. Soytonado was pleased. "When I was initiated I was married off to a man my age who was the choice of the family. We used to sing together with his family. It was OK. He's a nice husband."

One member of the group, Lucy Lebow, the Kikuyu woman who plants vegetables in pastoral Maasailand, was not so fortunate.

> I was about twenty-five years old. The man who married me was old enough to be my grandfather. Like all men a long time ago, my father wanted property and cattle, so I was forced to marry. My mother never liked it but she had no power to stop it.

Neperon Naironma, another member of the group, who now has many grandchildren, still regrets not being able to marry her childhood sweetheart.

---

5. Mile 46 is an arid spot in a remote part of Kajiado District with a rail line running through. Colonial authorities, perceiving the area as empty, referred to it by the railway mileage, ignoring the local names. Today, although many colonial names have been changed, the name Mile 46 is still used.

Arranging a Marriage

Two Mumias co-wives complained about marrying a much older man.

Mary Obanda: I had not met the man. He approached my grandmother (her custodial parent), and the agreement was made. Then my parents were informed. I did not want to marry when I learned that he had another wife, but I was forced by my parents.

Margaret Obanda: I was fifteen years old when I got married. My marriage was arranged by my parents, so I agreed because I had to obey them. He paid four cattle for my dowry. He had two wives already and was old. This is why I wanted to refuse.

Sacdiyo Ramallah, a Wajir teacher in her thirties, was pleased when her father arranged a marriage with a cousin.

I've been married for five years. We are related. We were brought up in the same compound. Our father decided we should marry. I thought it was a good idea because he was just like a brother. We had been brought up together so I accepted their decision.

In a conversation at Bahsan's home in Wajir with six Somali friends in their thirties, including Sacdiyo, Bahsan, Dekha, and Hibo, we asked, "What customs are changing?" without referring to marriage or any other specific. As often happened, changes in the way marriage is arranged were the first on the womens' minds.

Bahsan: Before there was no discussion between the husband and the wife to be. She could not say I want this and this, but now there should be discussion before they marry and the wife will say her needs.

HH: How will your daughters' husbands be chosen?

Dekha: They will just choose their own.

HH: Do your husbands accept the idea that your daughters will choose their own marriage partners, or will your husbands want to choose someone for them?

Dekha: I don't think so. With the situation now, you can't force a child into marriage.

Hibo: We are moving from the culture to the religion. Islam says that there is to be no forcing of children.

HH: But sometimes women have a different understanding of this than their husbands do.

Several: That's true.

Dekha: One cannot force a boy into marriage either. Here's a case where the teachings of the religion come in very handy. With a traditional husband, it's only the argument of religion that you can use. In Somali culture, you can't marry a daughter if the mother is not for it. For example, if the husband was trying to force the daughter to marry into a family she didn't approve of, she could do everything to prevent that marriage. She can help her daughter to elope with someone else, or sabotage the wedding, or if the wedding takes place she can make life difficult later on, so the husband knows it is better not to do something she opposes.

Hibo Hussein then explained how dowry works among Somalis. "A girl can be given to a man when she is a baby, but he will not take her until she is mature and has been circumcised. When she is circumcised [at about seven or eight years old], her future husband gives a goat. This creates an awareness of him, but she does not go to him until later."

Some men, like Sacdiyo's father, make arrangements that consider the daughter's welfare. Others do not. Roselinda Washika, a Mumias farmer born about 1927, did not think her welfare counted at all when her father arranged her marriage.

I was born after the big hunger called *Keya.* My father was very old. He had twelve wives, 45 daughters and 89 sons.[6] I was one of the youngest ones. My father had a large shamba. There was no conflict over land.

My husband talked to my parents. They agreed on a dowry of nine cattle. My father forced me to marry very young so he could enjoy my dowry before he died.

I was quite holy [a virgin] when I got married. Sacrifices were made for my praise.

Gladys Oluchumba, a younger Mumias farmer, made a disastrous love match. After it failed, she let her parents arrange another marriage, trusting that they would choose well.

I was twenty when I got married without my parents' knowledge. They tried to look for me but did not find me. My husband was a teacher. He used to drink very much, and beat me terribly. It wasn't until I got my first born that life started to be tough, so I went home to be helped. I went back to him and stayed until I had three children. We had been married six years. Then I left him when the frustrations were serious.

I stayed with my parents until an old man approached my parents for me, so I agreed and moved to his home. He had a wife and children already. They

---

6. I wondered whether these numbers had been accurately translated. Two generations ago in Western Province, quite a few men with enough land had twelve or more wives and over a hundred children, so the numbers were not impossibly high.

However, the extreme imbalance between sons and daughters made me doubt the numbers. I wondered whether female infanticide was being practiced. Roselinda confirmed the numbers and said, "Daughters were greatly welcomed because they would eventually bring more cattle."

welcomed me and my children. Since I had tried finding my own choice and failed, I knew my parents would choose a good man.[7]

Kimiri, another member of Elangata Wuas, also had both an arranged marriage and a love match, but in the reverse order.

I was born to a rich family and I was so happy until I was circumcised, initiated, and then from there I was married to the first husband by my father. The husband was very irresponsible and ate[8] all the cattle that we had. I decided to run away and went to another man. I was beaten by my father. At night, while the parents were asleep I went to him. I went once, twice, then the third time the father decided, "Acch!, let her go to that husband."

An unidentified Mirere woman explained the benefits of arrangements assisted by a third party. "Go-betweens know the man and the woman, and they will know best what people to unite. But now, there are no go-betweens. You just get matched up to someone and it isn't because of behavior or character. You might not go well."

Ilbissil is a roadside market town in the midst of an arid cattle region. In a small permanent house just off the main road, we talked with the *Ilbissil Women's Group*. They considered the changes modern life has brought to marriage, and dislike the results. They prefer arranged marriage because they see love matches as lacking commitment when the love is strained.

Tikako Kores: Girls who select husbands for themselves are not restricted to one man. For example, I choose Jimmy,[9] and besides Jimmy, I have somebody else. Maybe one day Jimmy notices I've got another man, so he starts beating me. Girls choose husbands just because they drink together. They don't know each other. They just go drinking and all of a sudden they are married.

Nampasa ene Naanyu: A long time ago, the parents had to survey. They had to know the background of the boy: that he comes from a very good family, not "Is the family rich?" The parents used to talk to both of them and give their concerns, not like today when you meet and you marry without thinking.

In contrast, Soila Tanei, another member of the group, approves of girls choosing their own husbands, "It is better because at least they get along and work together."

7. Years later, she was not so happy with this second husband. A later story about him is told in the Epilogue.

8. This means "used up," possibly sold for drink, not literally "eaten" by the owner.

9. This was the name of the driver who had brought us and was present during part of the interview.

ABDUCTION

Sometimes what appears to be an abduction is actually an elopment to which the woman has consented. When a man and woman decide to marry, if they think her parents might object, they may stage an abduction. But of the 209 indigenous women interviewed in 1995-6, at least three were abducted without their foreknowledge or consent.

Okhukwesa

Among Luos and Luhyas, *okhukwesa* was once a common form of marriage. An outsider might call okhukwesa "abduction," but some Kenyans object that this is too loaded a term, though accurate, for an accepted and common practice. Today, okhukwesa is less accepted than a generation ago and is not common.

An okhukwesa marriage is one in which the groom and his friends capture a girl who has caught his eye. The arrangement may be in fact an elopement between consenting parties, or it may be entirely unsuspected on the girl's part. She may be taken by a man she does not know, as Margaret Obonyo was.

A few days after the abduction, relatives of the husband go to the girl's father to say something like, "We understand that your cow has strayed. We know where she is and will offer you compensation for her." The father is now in a weaker negotiating position than if the daughter were at home.

Having been married by okhukwesa is sometimes a point of pride for a woman. She may feel flattered by her husband's determination. Whether she feels flattered to be irresistible, outraged that her hopes for the future have been stolen from her, or resigned that she must accept whatever men do to her, a woman can do little to resist okhukwesa other than avoiding it by staying close to home, or going everywhere heavily chaperoned.

Other Forms of Abduction

Serah Rahab, who was born outside Nairobi in 1957, is an exceptionally beautiful woman. She has experienced two different abductions. Serah's abductions were not okhukwesa because Kikuyus do not accept okhukwesa, and punish those who try to acquire a bride without either her family's consent or her own. Serah told me this story in a letter which touched me deeply. We had been introduced by a mutual friend, Michi Vojta, an American living in her village. We had a wonderful conversation, and I left. Many weeks later, Michi sent me a letter saying that Serah had forgotten to tell me about the times she was captured, and wanted me to know. She had written out the entire story for me.[10]

> When I was sixteen years old, Wambui, a girl who lived near me, tried to force me to marry her step-brother, Kamau, who was almost thirty. She invited me to visit her aunt's place in Nairobi. While there, I met Kamau. We

---

10. Thank you Serah, and thank you Michi.

Serah Rahab at Michi Vojta's house

stayed one day at Kamau's house, but I was told it was her aunt's house. On the second day, Wambui ran away without saying anything to me. On the third day, since Wambui still had not returned, I began to realize that something was very wrong. I didn't leave because I thought it would be wrong to leave without telling Wambui, and also I did not know the way home. When I asked Kamau where Wambui was, he told me he wanted to marry me. I did not want to marry him because he was very ugly, so I started looking for ways to escape.

I looked for casual work to earn money for the bus fare home. But in the first month, I didn't know anyone and couldn't find work. But all that time we didn't do anything sexual. He was a night watchman. When he would return home in the morning, I would run away and hide.

In the second month, I got the money. I left in the middle of one afternoon. When I got to the road, I met someone I knew and asked directions to Karai (home). Kamau followed me. In the meantime, Wambui had told my mother that I had run away to get married. When I told my mother what had happened, she called the elders and told them the story. They fined Kamau. It is traditional that if a young man takes a woman by force he is fined a number of goats. I was so happy that he had to pay. I mocked him every time we met after that.

The next year, another older man wanted to marry me. He locked me in his room, but I locked the door from the inside so he couldn't get in and he had to sleep outside at a friend's house. Eventually he gave up. I married my husband the next year.

Planning for a Life Together

We asked married women, "When you were deciding to get married, what plans did you and your husband make about your lives together?" There were two reasons for this question. One was to learn more about what went into the woman's choice of husband. What hopes and dreams had the couple spun together?

The other was to learn whether they had agreed before marriage about the number of children they would have, since differing views about this can be a source of significant conflict later. Some made this an important part of planning their future together.

As often happened, the question led in many directions. Some answers concerned numbers of children. Others concerned economic plans, decisions about where to live, and agreements about shared responsibility for care of aging parents. Many others had made no plans together.

Rosemary Njeri, who was married in 1986, made several kinds of plans. Her husband is a batik artist, who has taught her his trade. Now in addition to farming, she helps with batik production.

> At the time we got married, he didn't have his own house, so we decided we would buy a shamba. We decided to have four children so we could feed them nicely, and clothe them well. I didn't want them to face the same problems I had faced. If I had girls only, we would be satisfied with them even if we didn't have any boy.

Doris Mathieu of Meru and her husband are both college educated. Since her husband is more educated than his brothers, he has better economic prospects. He decided to help his brothers by buying his own land rather than taking a share of the family land.

> We decided that when we get married we would have only two children regardless of their sex. And we decided we would not stay with his parents. We would get another portion of land. My in-laws' portion is small and the family is very big. His father has three wives and there are many children.

Nancy Wanjiku, a Lusigetti farmer born in 1960, and her prospective husband made many plans.

> We talked a lot about how we would raise our children and try to be completely independent of our parents, trying to find land somewhere else. We thought we'd raise animals. We didn't have much education, so our plans didn't succeed. Because of inadequate money, problems increased and we couldn't even educate our children.

We interviewed Njoki Ngige while she was very busy with preparations for her wedding, to be held the following week. She told us about many plans.

> About one year ago, I decided to marry my fiance. We are planning to have only one child, and not until we have been married for about five years. He is a preacher, and a singer of Christian music. We are planning to make a cassette together, work together, and live together.
>
> We will live in Kikuyu town in a rented house. I have been called for nursing [admitted to a training program] so I want to study. And I want my child to study. I will keep my kid in school until she or he gets a good post.

Nkatha Murithi is a cheerful young woman from Meru who works in a library, and a devout Christian. She and her husband married against their parents' advice, but followed both the traditional forms and Christian rituals.

> He was not employed, I was not employed, and we were very young. All of the parents thought we should not marry yet. But we decided it was time for us to marry.
>
> We did not know what we would have in future, so we said if we had no job, we would have only one child, but if either of us got a job, we would have another child. Our firstborn was born when we were not employed, but in 1993, I was working and he was working too, so we decided it was time to have another. God blessed us with a boy and a girl. Now we are building a permanent house.
>
> Those are some of the plans we made. But the minimum was we would live together and whether we had or did not have, we would work hand-in-hand.

Angie Dawa, the woman who left her evanglical community to have a family, became a doctor in an important position with an international organization. Since she is a Roman Catholic, she did not plan the number of children she would have. In retrospect, she finds herself surprised at many other things that were not planned before marriage.

> When I was a little girl, I wanted many children. We are very few. I know four is not so few, but it seemed few to me. I thought I should have a large family. And there is my religion.
>
> My husband and I never talked about it. I know he wants a third child. He wants a son. The first was a daughter, the second was a daughter. I think eventually I'll agree to a third but definitely not now. We did not discuss it before marriage.
>
> Our only attempt to discuss our future life was when he proposed. I remember asking just one thing. Would he be intimidated by a wife being a doctor?" He said no. That was a very short session, very romantic.
>
> My main objective in marriage was to get male companionship. I had no problem about money. But we never discussed "Where are we going to live? How are we going to live?"
>
> We never discussed anything serious, not even religion. And all along I was a very religious person, very Catholic. I thought "His people will be my people. His God will be my God." Because he is not a Catholic, I got married in a non-Catholic church, which is taboo for a Catholic.

Aoko Odembo and her husband are both university educated. She thinks they are typical of educated people of their generation in deciding to have only two children.

> My husband agreed to have only two children because economically we could not afford more. All of my generation have two children. It is a true change because when I grew up the average of all the families were five or six. Girls are getting married much later than our parents' generation because of education.

Jane Gathege and her future husband agreed to adopt children.

> We didn't have a hope of having children because I had some problems, so we decided we'd adopt some street children and give them a home. When we got our own children we forgot all about that. We have four children. That is enough. But we still feel that if we came across a homeless child we would take him in.

In the conversation at Bahsan's home in Wajir, Khadija Mayow was the first one I asked about plans she had made with her husband before marriage. She was the only woman there who had no secular schooling. Her husband is a Wajir district official, and a prosperous man. They are happily married, which might have been expected from her answer.

> We decided if we got many children and sometimes didn't have enough, we would be patient with each other. Also, if my parents need help, he will take care of them, and if his parents need help, I will take care of them.

The next two women said they had made no plans. Hibo interjected, "We don't plan for the future. It's not part of our culture." So I asked no more questions about plans that afternoon.

Conflicting Views of Dowry

When I was teaching in Kakamega District, one student, Mary Shitokane, wrote a long, passionate paper arguing that brideprice should be discouraged. She reasoned that if a man pays dowry, he regards his wife as a possession and feels entitled to mistreat her. At that time I knew a family where the man justified beating his wife on the same grounds. I therefore began my research with a clear conviction that dowry tends to lead to abuse.[11]

When I asked rural women over forty, "What customs are changing?" they almost always responded, "Dowry is no longer being paid." I followed this with, "Is that a good change or a bad change?" Because of my initial bias against dowry, I was very much intrigued that they almost always regretted the change.

Oruko Omina, the public health educator who spoke about the lengths people go to in denying that relatives have AIDS, explained how she sees the traditional significance of dowry, and the protection it gives the wife.

> You must not just give your daughter away for free, which means she isn't valuable. The marriage will not be recognized if no dowry is paid. But in this modern age whereby they meet in town and marry, it no longer holds the same importance. Traditionally, it meant recognition, not ownership. It was a gift of appreciation.
>
> Women were protected by dowry. If husband and wife had a quarrel, the elders would sit to discuss it, but they will only sit if they also sat for the dowry. They say, "This is a girl who came in the daylight [not covertly]. She belongs to us. We went to her home, we promised her people that we were going to take care of her, so you are not going to mistreat her." It made it impossible for a man to disclaim his wife.

---

11. "Brideprice," "bridewealth," and "dowry" are three commonly used terms for the same custom. It is not in fact "dowry" but the reverse, a payment from the groom or his family to the family of the bride. I use the term "dowry," although it is inaccurate, because it is the term most commonly used in Kenya. Mary Shitokane used "brideprice."

> The clan was responsible for the wife just as much as the husband was. For example, if the husband went to the city and disappeared for three or four years, it was up to the clan to appoint one member to go and look for him. She would not just be left standing. They would all collectively make sure she had something to eat and was taken care of, and that came about because they recognized her. Recognition came about through dowry. The idea of ownership is modern.

In most communities, dowry should be arranged by negotiation between the two families, as it was for Zildah, but the Maasai do it differently. Sein Milanoi, a Maasai, explained that in her community dowry is uniform, rather than depending on individual circumstances. In her view, this is much better.

> I like the Maasai dowry very much. The Maasai dowry is not for greed. The other tribes will say, "I want ten cows, I want a hundred thousand Ksh., a big drum of water, a hundred goats, what and what" But the Maasai dowry is just to make you feel you've got something left from your daughter. It's only a big ox, and a cow with a calf, those are three, and a he goat, and a ram, five. It was like that for our mothers and grandmothers. It's standard.
>
> This girl has been going to the river, she has been fetching firewood, so that they don't forget about her completely they leave a cow to milk with a calf. The day it arrives they start milking it, they drink the milk, they remember their daughter. The he goat will be slaughtered and eaten between the families. It's nothing much.
>
> But the other tribes will say, "My daughter has been educated, you pay this and this." That one, I don't like it. Because of that, some say it's good if she just goes without dowry.

In Mumias, Nasianda, Mirere, and Kisii, we had conversations with large groups of women, sometimes thirty, sometimes about 200. We always began by asking, "How has life changed here?" The pattern of responses was the same in every community. Economic changes and changes in marriage customs were the major topics. When changes in marriage customs such as dowry were mentioned, we asked, "Does that change the way husband and wife relate to each other? How?"

The answers concerning dowry were contradictory. Almost everyone agreed that the disappearance of dowry was bad. They disagreed about why. Usually, we did not know the names or individual histories of these women, so I report them anonymously. Some agreed with Oruko Omina that dowry protects a woman because parents are involved.

Sein Milanoi (right) with one of her cows and several young relatives

Mumias Woman 1: Now girls do not persevere because dowry is not paid. Parents feel ashamed to approach each other to settle these matters since they do not know each other.

Mumias Woman 2: It has weakened marriage ties. The couple does not respect each other. Parents from both sides do not know each other, and this weakens the relations.

Several women insisted that a man was more likely to beat his wife if he had not paid dowry.

Mirere Woman 2: The husbands desert their wives because there is nothing to hold them. Without dowry, men can abuse the wife at any time.

Mumias Woman 3: Men do not care about their wives because they have not paid dowry. A man can handle his wife in any bad way and does not care whether she leaves because he has not paid dowry. So he can marry another one.

Some thought dowry was valuable because it was part of marriage arrangements that included go-betweens.

Mirere Woman 3:. Someone can see a man before you marry him and watch his behavior.

Mirere Woman 4:. Sometimes a guy and a girl might not know what they are doing. They may not be good at settling their own matters. It was better when parents were deciding.

HH: So now a woman doesn't have as much protection as she used to?

Mirere Woman 5: It used to be a girl and boy would not know each other. Now you can meet before, but the families may not know each other. It's good for the families to know each other because they don't feel like meeting to solve a problem if they haven't met before. So now when a girl leaves her home there's no other help. She can only persevere or leave.

In the time when dowry was paid, people would try to inquire about where their daughter was going. The go-between would try to know. Both sides tried to figure out what man and woman were like. Now it's not practical to do that.

One young Nasianda woman disapproved of dowry.

Nasianda Woman 10: Yes, we brought her up but his parents also brought him up, so there's no need of dowry to compensate the parents.

HH: Are you saying it's the same, and husband and wife are equal?

Nasianda Woman 10: Yes.

HH: : Do husbands and wives treat each other as equals?

(widespread laughter)

Nasianda Woman 10: Somewhere else, away from the husband's home that could be possible, but since she is at her husband's home, she is under him.

Many women said that a woman could more easily go to her own parents for help if dowry had been paid.

Nasianda Woman 1: In the old way, in case the girl experienced any hardship, she could go back to her family. She was not ashamed to go back. But nowadays, since a girl goes without her parents, she feels afraid of going back.

Priscilla Nyette's experience illustrates this point. She is a maid in a Nairobi household in her late twenties who was married after she finished school. After a few years, her husband began to drink, and the marriage fell apart. Her parents refused to help her because they had not arranged the marriage.

Life got worse. My husband started beating me, which he hadn't done before. The *mzee* [his father] asked him why he was treating me like that. Then he beat his own father.

I went to my parents for help, but they said, "We took you to school. You chose your own life. We can't help you now." I started growing thin and thinner from worry.

Some viewed dowry as a payment to the father-in-law to ensure that he will have something to support his daughter's children if she leaves the marriage and returns to her natal home.

Nasianda Woman 3: We like the system where your parents made the decision. Cattle are taken as security in case of problems coming out of marriage. The girl's parents would have something for their daughter's children. In a marriage where no children are involved, the dowry is returned if the marriage breaks up. Today, a woman with many children cannot leave her husband to go back to her parents, because her parents won't be able to raise her many children. She then has to stay with the man even though she may not want to.

Others argued that dowry creates a trap: a woman cannot leave if dowry has been paid unless her parents are wealthy enough to repay it.

Nasianda Woman 5: The husband will have given the wealth to your parents so you cannot leave easily without causing some friction between your husband and your parents. We are trapped in the relationship.

Nasianda Woman 6: Some men can frustrate their wives when dowry is paid, and now that it is not, a woman can leave.

Mumias Woman 5: Since dowry is not paid for our daughters, their lives are very temporary.

Mumias Woman 6: Most girls are able to divorce in case of hardship because there is nothing to hold them back.

Hadija Ali [Portrait J] was able to rescue her daughter from an abusive marriage because no dowry had been paid. "One of my daughters took off with a man who kept harassing her and beating her until I withdrew her because he did not bring me any money and here he is hurting my daughter."

In contrast, Susan Malaso, the assistant headmistress of a rural primary school, believes dowry is beneficial because it makes it difficult for a woman to leave her husband, and thus preserves marriages.

If my son wants to marry, we have to take six cattle, two blankets, two sheets for the mother, beer and tobacco for the old people. These days they can even ask for a sack of sugar. They can ask anything, but those are the most important things.

It is done in every family. During the wedding day, the parents of the boy are supposed to buy food to be eaten by the guests, so it is really expensive. It is hard to get so much money, so the husband should save some money for that.

Dowry should continue because it strengthens the relationship between the husband and the wife. If dowry is paid, the girl is not supposed to go back to her family. She is supposed to stay no matter what, even if he mistreats her, so it cements the relationship between husband and wife. She will not even think of running away if dowry has been paid.

Dowry also brings the two families together. A long time ago it meant that the girl who got married is not supposed to go to her father's place. No matter whether that husband will mistreat her, she has to stick with the husband because the dowry has been paid. If she ran home, old people used to say "I have now sold you, you have been sold."

If they are in good times I don't think a man will abuse his wife just because he has paid dowry. Why he should abuse her?. But long ago men used to say, "I bought you so you should be under me. You should follow whatever I tell you."

Even though dowry gives families a financial stake in their daughters' marriages, some women convince their families to refuse dowry. Irene Katete eventually convinced her father that it was better if she continued in school and sought employment. Sein Milanoi had been betrothed to a man, and part of the dowry had already been paid, when she decided to marry someone else.

I married at age nineteen. I loved him. They had picked another husband, but when I passed the exam, I told them "I don't want him." But even if I hadn't passed, there would have been no problem with the one I chose. I was not marrying another tribe. My father was dead. My elder brother did not want me to continue in school. He wanted me to marry the man who had paid dowry. He said, "I will not return anything."

But my mother paid. She said to him, "You are not my husband. You are my child and I will do what I want."

HH: So the man they chose had already paid part of the dowry?

Yes, when you are circumcised, they bring one ram. But if you refuse, it is returned to them.

Despite the need to return the ram which had already been paid, and her favorable attitude toward the traditional Maasai dowry, Sein did not want her chosen husband to pay any dowry. She believed dowry was a fetter rather than a protection.

For myself I said, "I don't want it." I told my parents, "I may decide to come back and my father is dead, so who will pay that back?" We never took anything as a dowry, but we stayed well.[12] My husband went home to see my mother, and if she had a problem, he would help. So they kept their respect for each other.

Though Hadija Ali [Portrait J] was desperate for money, she rejected her brother's advice that she arrange a marriage for her daughter so she could get dowry. Joan Kanini, a Nairobi woman born in Ukambani in

12. In the next chapter, Sein elaborates on her later relations with her husband.

1945, told me about the quick-thinking of her gutsy younger sister when dowry was paid.

> While I was going to school, somebody started coming to our home to talk to our father. He was a young man who used to come in a car. He wanted to marry either me or my younger sister, but he never talked to us, he only talked to my father. One day my father told us that either of us could marry that man. I said, "not me," and so did my sister. He was a handsome young man, but he did not talk to us.
>
> My father was not happy when we refused. Normally to start an engagement one has to pay three she goats and one he goat. I was away at boarding school, but my sister was still in primary school. One morning, she saw two goats. My father was not around, but she knew where they had come from, so she took them back. She told the man's father, "There is no wife coming from our home to your home, so you can keep the goats."

Often, traditions are abandoned first by the educated urban elite, and later by rural people. That is not the case with dowry. In every rural village, I heard women lament that dowry was no longer being paid, but dowry is still a cherished tradition for some members of the urban elite, who can afford it more easily than poorer farmers. This is true throughout East Africa, not only in Kenya. When my friend Oswald, son of a high Tanzanian official, married Nelida, a Ph.D., his family wanted to "do it right." They agreed on the appropriate sum of money, but wanting to show respect for the bride's family and for tradition, Oswald's family included one token cow, though both families lived in the city. "We had to hire a truck to take the cow to them. It was an awful nuisance! A cow in the city is just not practical."

Nkatha Murithi's husband is a policeman. Thus he is subject to transfer. Currently, he works in Kisumu, 430 kilometers away. They married in 1989 and have two children. Every part of the interview, and other conversations we held with her, suggested a highly successful and very happy marriage, despite the imposed separation. Murithi thinks a cash dowry is more harmful than a traditional dowry paid with animals and other gifts.

> Marriage customs are changing because in past days dowry was cows and goats for the father, millet for the mother, but now most people are paying it in money. Some parents are asking for the education of the daughter. If she has gone to private schools it is more. If she went to university or is employed, it is more.
>
> HH: You went to secondary school. How much dowry did your father ask?

My father didn't ask for cash. They did it customarily. I was the last daughter in the family. For the others they had asked for cattle so they continued in the same way.

In some families, the daughter is not happy with a cash dowry, because it makes the husband regard the wife as one of the things in the house that he has bought. He says, "I bought the sofa set for so much, and my wife for so much." So you see it brings a bad relationship.

When they pay with cows, goats, and millet it shows respect for the parents. And if the parents have a problem, they can ask for help from the son-in-law. But if he has paid money and they ask for help he wonders why he should help since he has already given them so much money.

HH: One woman told me that they agree on an amount at the beginning, but he only pays part of it at the time, and then he pays more from time to time.

It depends on the family. Some won't let their daughters go until it has all been paid.

HH: What will you want to do about dowry when the time comes for your daughter to marry?

I don't know because I don't know what the custom will be at that time. And, we mothers are not the ones to decide. It is the fathers who decide.

HH: But weren't the animals given to the father and the millet given to the mother?

Yes

HH: Won't you have to decide whether or not to ask for millet?

The father will decide.

Mindful of these comments, we asked Oruko Omina whether the form of payment made a difference.

These days, people prefer cash. When cash wasn't there, it had to be cows and goats. Cash has more value now.

In my society, even if you give cash, you still have to pay at least one animal. These days people don't have big land to graze cattle, so they prefer cash which they can use to buy whatever. And these days there is prestige about the amount, whereas before it didn't matter. It's still a source of pride for a woman to know that dowry has been paid.

It didn't mean much to me but it was important to my parents and the parents of the other side, so we let them go ahead and do it.

Consolata Mombua explained how her father reconciled his anti-dowry convictions with accepted practice.

My father does not believe in dowry, but he was given some goats to open a friendship between the families, just as a token. In fact, often the dowry is not paid in full. It is not supposd to be completed, but continuous to keep the relationship going.

Some people would not agree with her. As we have seen, when Sammy Kariuki and his wife had several children die in infancy, they first suspected that perhaps Sammy could not father healthy children because his father had not completed paying dowry.

Whether dowry is being paid or not, many young women want to be sure their ideas about married life and their future husband's are compatible. For better or for worse, with or without family consent and subsequent family protection, more women are choosing whom they will marry. As family involvement and oversight weaken, the question for the future is how women can make marriages in which they will be safe and cared for.

Portrait D

Catherine Obungu

During Kenya's period of one party rule from 1982 to 1991, a legacy of bloody political repression left Kenyans very wary of discussing politics or seeming lukewarm in their support of the ruling party. The school where I taught was an hour and a half walk from the tarmacked road between Kakamega and Eldoret. Once, when President Moi was scheduled to drive by, classes were cancelled for the day so the students could go to the road to cheer the president. The headmaster explained to me that if they didn't go, he would be suspected of supporting the opposition.

Catherine Obungu was one of very few women who hesitated when I requested an interview. She was concerned about whether I would ask political questions. I responded, as I did always before 2003, that although I would ask no political questions, some people had chosen to respond to my questions with political answers.

I was invited to her beautiful home in an elegant section of Nairobi. Clearly, she had been financially comfortable, but had become less comfortable. Her clothing, polyester knit pants, shirt, and hat, had served her a long time.

Throughout the interview, I sensed lingering fear, yet she answered questions fully and intimately. Her eldest daughter, home for a visit, was present during a small part of the interview, and her nephew, a handsome and lively boy of about eight, appeared at the end.

I was born in 1949, the second in a family of nine children, five girls and four boys. In 1957, when I was eight years old, my father went to prison for six years. He used to be a clerk in a government office and some money was lost.

They thought he had taken it. I don't know what my mother thought about it, but certainly we never had any benefit from that money if he did take it. My mother was a very great and brave woman, deeply religious. She suffered quite a lot of abuse from my father.

I was very happy when he was away, even when he went to jail. He used to drink a lot and beat my mother. He was a loving person as I remember, but when he was drunk he became very violent. First he would find fault with my mother and beat her, and then turn towards the children. We would try to hide for protection. Eventually, after my mother was dead, he changed.

When my father went to prison, we could not afford to stay in town. We had to move to the rural area. Mother put up some hasty structure for us to live in. I was in standard three. Mother started brewing local beer to sell so she could keep us in school. I finished fourth in the whole school, but we could not pay the fees so I dropped out. But afterwards I did my school certificate as a private candidate in 1966 at the age of eighteen and I got a second grade.[1] After that, I worked for two years.

Then I met my husband and got married at 1968. We married in church and have a marriage certificate. I was almost twenty, but my husband was eight years older.

From the beginning, anything I said, he did not like much. He did everything without consultation, and any idea I put forward was useless and unnecessary. He was domineering and very secretive.

Everything was in his name, even the car I used to get to work. He decided to sell it without consulting me. I had gone home to see my parents. When I came back, the car had been sold.

People believe that a man has a right to do anything he wants because he is a man. At one point when I complained, "Why are you doing this?" my husband answered, "I am a man."

We have five children. I bore three girls in a row, but we were looking for a boy, so we kept on. The fourth child was a boy. I would have stopped at that but my husband insisted. After the fifth he still wanted to have one more, but I said no. At that point I didn't need to worry about financial problems, but I was worried about my job. So I did not agree.

I did not know the person whom I got married to until something drastic happened. He got involved in a criminal case and had to leave his job. It was something that I should have known. In my case, every time I got some success, I was so proud to tell him; but in his case, he never quite said what was going on. I don't think he realized I ever grew up. He treated me throughout like a child.

When I got married, I was just a telephone operator. I took training as a secretary and was posted to the finance director of a large multi-national corporation, where I stayed for fourteen years. They invited me to set up the secretarial department for a very large new group. The work load in the office

1. At that time, one could take the exams as a private candidate if not enrolled in school. Few private candidates passed highly.

became very heavy and my family life became difficult. On occasion I had to work very long hours and my husband did not appreciate that. It made a bit of tension.

In 1975, he came into quite a substantial amount of money, and then lost his job. He had to start over from scratch. I was completely surprised because he never talked to me about this and at that partiular moment he was courting some woman he wanted to marry. If he hadn't lost that job, I think he would have married then.

By 1990, he decided to discard me. The children were completing their education, his role as a father was coming to an end, he was going to complete his task in life, so he wanted to make himself more happy. We aren't actually divorced, but he is not here now. My life would be happier if my husband was completely gone, but he keeps coming back.

In 1993, he decided to marry another woman. His second wife is the same age as my daughter. He tried to get me out of the house. He wanted to use it for his second wife, but I never moved out. I had to go to court to get restraining orders because he used to come here and harass me. I worried that my children might be hurt psychologically during the long months we were fighting about the house.

We used to economize quite a bit to save for the future. We had quite a few properties that we acquired together. Unfortunately they are all in his name. He was very secretive in his acquisition of properties. Despite all my efforts to try to get my children's names added to them, it has not worked because the system is very, very corrupt. They do not honor restraining orders.

Both the lawyers and the courts are corrupt. It is impossible for a woman to get help. My colleagues and friends of similar age are all alone now and all are experiencing the same situation. The men gang up, they bribe this lawyer, they bribe that lawyer, and various officials, and they tell their wives, "If you try to get help you will never succeed."

My children have all done very well in school and have advanced degrees or are getting them. Four of them are studying abroad. I am tempted to believe that my husband had heard about my success in my studies despite all hardships, and looked me up because of that. Maybe he thought because I was intelligent, I could produce clever children. He wanted to be seen as the father of intelligent children, so he had to look for somebody intelligent to produce his children. After that was accomplished, he had nothing more to do with me. That is just my thought and I have never told it to anybody. Looking down on our long history, it did not seem like a loving relationship. I think I was just used, but it does not bother me. I have beautiful children.

I want to be on my own without any interference. I don't think I'll remarry. When I look back at what I went through, I don't see any purpose in marrying again. It was traumatic, and he was so cruel.

At the same time, I had another problem. A widowed sister died, leaving six children. I took three of them, and my sisters took the others. When they came to me, those children had never seen the inside of a school. I attempted to get them into a government school for orphans, but did not succeed, so I am educating them myself. They are now in primary school. By the time they came, my children were already grown and out of the house.

The way I was cheated for twenty-six years, I never knew what to expect. For example, I never knew what we were earning together or acquiring together. If only I had known when we were getting married that something like this could happen, maybe I would have been able to protect myself. At the moment, I have nothing to fall back to. My daughters see what has happened to me and they are more careful. But it is not easy when there is love. We don't believe that this person we love could do such a thing. I believed it couldn't happen to me. Even my parents were completely surprised. I used to hide it: to cover up: to smile.

All my friends are women who are alone now. When something like this happens to you, the women who are still with their husbands loathe you. These women are in fear of their husbands. They can't even make up their minds to protest, so they keep away from us.

When men used to marry many wives, even if the husband took other wives, he would not interfere with his first wife, and he never took away her rights. But in this case my husband tried everything to take our property away from me. And I see no sign that he really ever cared for me at all. Now, I just work for myself, and of course, my sister's children. That's what keeps me going.

Portrait E

Saadia Abubakar

In the center of Malindi, on an attractive street crowded with narrow house-fronts, is the home of Saadia Abubakar. A mutual friend told her I would be coming to talk with her sometime. I had just arrived in town and found modest lodgings. When I arrived at her family's house, although they had never met me and knew little of me, I was welcomed warmly and told they wanted me to stay with them.

I interviewed Saadia at her home. She declined to be photographed for the book, which I regretted, because I would like to share my enduring image of her. She is a small, laughing woman. I shall always think of her playing vigorously with her infant grandson, lifting him high in the air with a swooshing sound, and lowering him with a chuckle, while continually smoking a cigarette.

While we talked that first afternoon, her youngest daughter, a school secretary, was present. The conversation was interrupted by the call to evening prayers. When the call started, we stopped talking to listen to the muezzin, then Saadia retired to the back of the house for her prayers. When she returned, her daugher left in turn to pray, then returned to talk with me while Saadia gave other daughters instructions about preparing dinner. When it was time for me to leave, the daughter offered to accompany me on the short walk to my lodgings. Saadia insisted that her teenaged son chaperone us.

I returned unexpectedly five years later. She greeted me effusively, and insisted that this time I really must stay with them, although that meant displacing her. To my embarrasment, she slept with one of her daughters so I could have her bed. For two days, I accompanied her as she went to the market, prepared food, entertained friends, answered questions on every topic I could think of, and cooked *maandazi* [doughnuts] to sell. Even though my presence must have been a burden, especially when she was haggling at the market for a good price, she was irresistably hospitable.

I was born in Lamu in 1944. My brother and I were brought up by my mother because my father stayed upcountry. I was six months old when he left. After my father left, my mother thatched houses and wove mats to get money for us.

When I was about six years old my mother remarried. My stepfather had a shamba . I have two younger brothers and a sister from him. My stepfather treated us as well as his own children. None of us went to regular school. We learned to read in Quranic school, though we did not learn to write.

After Quranic school, I helped my mother do household work and look after my young brothers. During my free time I used to go swimming or play with other children. A group of girls would go to the beach with an elderly woman who looked after us. It was only girls, never with boys. We would wear regular clothes, not swimming costumes. Once my breasts started protruding, I stopped swimming and couldn't go roaming around any more. Swimming or going out unnecessarily were not allowed when one had matured.

Instead, we were given duties at home. Since I was happy in helping my mother, that was fine with me. I was a responsible girl. When there was a festival, I could not go unless I went with my grandmother. I used to visit my friends, but under restriction. Some of my friends were similarly restricted and others were not. We were never circumcised.

I got married when I was sixteen years old. My husband came to my parents for marriage arrangements, and they asked me if I was willing to marry him. I had known him before. He was about fourteen years older. He had married three wives and divorced them before he married me. I didn't worry that he would divorce me, because I tried to avoid the mistakes that his other wives made. After marrying me, he did not marry any other woman.

My husband was a good man. He was elderly and I was young; therefore he loved me very much. I was so happy in my life with him. I was much freer after I got married. I was free to invite friends and rejoice with them.

I had a lot of freedom of shopping. I used to buy the groceries, and had a house girl who did some of the shopping. My husband would sometimes buy something he found good, but did not do the shopping usually. He let me go out to do it.

I had seven children with him, four girls and three boys, but unfortunately all the boys died.

We came from Lamu to Malindi in 1975. In 1980, I decided I wanted to divorce him and marry my second husband, an Arab. He is employed by the bank, and is my age-mate. He had a wife before and has had another wife since. I was married to him for eight years. My teenage son is the only child I got with him. I am thankful that this son has survived.

Saadia Abubakar's kitchen where she and her daughters prepare the food they sell

I decided to divorce the second husband because he did not allow me to go anywhere. I was like a prisoner. I could not go to visit my sick child, so I decided to stay alone and try to support myself. It has been hard.

I have a little business of making and selling *maandazi*, *samosas* and *chapatis* [similar to flour tortillas], so I am able to help myself. Something that has really helped my family is this house, which belonged to my first husband. Since my daughters came from him, when he died, this house was given to them, so there is no rent to pay.

All my children went to school. Both fathers helped with school fees, so I did not have to educate the children myself, which I could not have done.

I would like to remarry, someone who will make my life pleasant but who will not frustrate me. I am fed up with poverty and would like a better-off man.

My life is much easier now because my daughters are working so they can help me. I experience almost the standard of life my daughters are living because they are very generous.

It is easier to bring up children now than when I was a girl because people don't have such large families. People then had no knowledge of planning their families and therefore did not have an easy time of caring for their children. But now people try to plan their families and most of them are working class, whereas sometime back, few people had employment.

Nowadays is also better because we are exposed to modern life and educate our children. I am happy about that change.

I compare my life to my mother's. My mother and I both struggled, but I manage better because selling food is easier in a big city like Malindi where there are many busy workers who buy food instead of cooking. But life is safer in a small town than in big towns. In some twenty years to come, that safety will be gone because these towns are developing and the population will be much more.

When I was a child, women had no freedom of doing things independently, so that's why they did not have much knowledge. On the other hand, family life may have been better. Children used to fear and respect their parents but children now are less respectful. For example, your child may ask to go to visit her friend. If you let her go for two hours, she may disregard you and stay as long as she wants.

3

Husbands, Co-Wives, and Mothers-in-Law

In the West, the metaphor of partnership dominates thinking about marriage, and loving companionship is expected. To be sure, western marriages often fall far short of these goals, but the ideal of a loving partnership molds people's assumptions about how they should behave in marriage. Not in Kenya. Instead, many men regard their wives as property, and both men and women commonly believe that a woman should be "under" her husband. Spouses may love each other, but enduring closeness is rare. Physical abuse is common and accepted by many as normal.

Money Arrangements between Husband and Wife

> Some families sit together, husband and wife, and plan how they can use their money. But in other families it is the husband who is the boss and handles all the money and, at times, they conceal. A man wouldn't like the woman to know how much money he has. If a wife asks her husband to buy something that is needed, like soap or tea, he will ask himself, "Now, how did she know that I have money in my pocket?"
>
> —Roselyne Choge, teacher, Kobujoi

> During past days when we didn't need much money, our life wasn't that bad with our husbands. Now so much depends on money. Even if the man has much money, the wives do not know how to get it. Men own the money. Men possess land, so it's the man who does the selling. The woman doesn't know how much money he gets or what he does with the money.
>
> —Unidentified farmer, Nasianda

As anywhere in the world, power is often negotiated between spouses through control of money. More often than not, a woman is expected to provide for the children's needs herself, although she usually has less access to cash than her husband. Men provide land and plow to prepare the fields for planting; when shifting cultivation was possible, men cleared new land. Women grow the food that feeds their families. Men are neither expected to help with the routine farming, nor obligated to provide money to meet their family's cash needs. Some husbands share everything with their wives and children; others may steal from wives who can barely feed their children.

Grace Nyawira [Portrait H] had an extremely selfish husband. She fought her way out of life on the streets through cleverness and tenacity. From what she earned selling fruit, she managed to buy a plot and build a house. Without her knowledge, her husband sold the house for drinking money. One day, she came home to find herself locked out and homeless, so she and the children returned to the Nairobi streets and her husband returned to his mother.

Among herders, ownership of the herds and access to money from selling animals differs greatly from one community to another. Susan Malaso, the teacher who values dowry because it prevents wives from leaving their husbands, describes the common pattern of control of money in Maasai herding families.

> All the buying and selling of animals is done by men. The man is the only one who benefits from that sale because he is the one who is being given that money. He buys some food in a shop, goes home, and sends the wife to fetch it. He won't carry it.
>
> The man decides by himself how money will be spent and whether school fees will be paid. Most of the time a woman relies on the husband. If the cows have milk, sometimes she can sell milk at market. If she has anything, it is only from selling milk.

Despite their husband's ownership of the cattle, some Maasai wives find ways to defend their interests. Kimiri, who is part of a cattle-herding family in Kajiado District, protects her family from economic devastation through joint action with her husband's other wives.

> At first we were very happy. He was always polite with me and also with the children. Then he started drinking. The boys started school but they dropped because we didn't have enough money after he started drinking. He wanted to sell some cows so he could have money to drink, but I said, "These cows are not going to be sold" so he started beating me and abusing me.

His drinking has reduced now because the co-wives and I have been tough protecting the livestock so he can't sell them and the boys are now big enough to stand up for themselves.

Some pastoral communities have very different ownership arrangements than the Maasai. Women may have their own herds and be independent of their husbands. Husbands may be away for long periods, so the women are autonomous.

Among Somali women, this independence may persist even when they have left pastoral life. The Somali women I talked with in Wajir, rich or poor, all had more economic autonomy than women of other communities. Bahsan Gedi explained that financial independence may permit separation on peaceful terms.

Some couples have nothing to do with one another. She works, she pays for the school fees of the children. She's independent and happy because now he has no say over her. He has his own house, she has her own house. She can pay for anything. Now if she wants to buy clothing, she can. She can go where she wants.

In other communities, even when the wife has her own income, it is simply assumed that the man should handle all the money. Since she holds a responsible professional position, Oruko Omina has her own salary. She let her husband manage all the money at first, but later decided to control her own finances. Her husband was not pleased, but had to accept the situation.

Our system is something we worked out after we had climbed our hurdles. It was a battle. I used to give my pay packet to my husband. Then. I'd have to ask. I started feeling very bad, so I said, "I think I'll have my own account.". He thought it was a joke, but then he went to the bank and found he didn't have my pay in his account. I said, "Now we will have to talk to decide what you will pay and what I will pay."

We have one account in common. We decide what it will go for: school fees, repairing the house, whatever. This common fund is for specific expenditures like education, development for the home or a farm to be cultivated. It's for big things. Then we each have our own separate accounts. If I meet you and want to buy you a cup of coffee, I don't want to call him and ask him. We divide small expenses. One pays for electricity, another for school fees, depending on who has the bigger account.

I have a friend who was beaten up because when she went to the bank to collect her salary, she saw a beautiful dress for the daughter and bought it. When she went home she was minus fifty Ksh. The husband demanded to know where it was. He said, "You are not to take a cent. It must all arrive here intact."

In the West, the man knows he is supposed to be a breadwinner. Right from the time they are babies it's ingrained that they are supposed to provide for their families. But here you find men who want to be recognized as the head of the family, and yet they are not providing.

Maria Rotich and her husband are farmers in Kimaren. They split the domestic work: he sells livestock; she sells the farm surplus. She gives her earnings to her husband, and he pays the family's expenses. He is a responsible man, and determined to educate his children well, so in their case, his control of the money is not a problem.

Angie Dawa also has her own salary. Her financial role shifted during the course of her marriage. She believes that she earns more than her husband, and has long taken financial responsibility for the children's school fees and supplies. Eventually, she also took responsibility for household expenses.

Among Muslims, the arrangements are different. Islam has a strong tradition of men being obligated to provide for their wives and children. Today's working Muslim women may contribute to family support, but that does not relieve the husband of providing. Dekha and Bahsan, both educated and employed women in their thirties, described how they share expenses with their husbands.

Dekha: He contributes and I contribute. Whatever I see missing, I add. Whatever he sees missing he adds. Sometimes there might be something where he doesn't contribute, but I don't make a big issue. The religion says he has to pay everything. But truly speaking, if you have a salary...

Bahsan: And with inflation, maybe he can't pay everything.

Dekha: You have to come in. It changes your relationship when you're putting in so much money. He may be criticized by his friends if you have an independent life, but at the back of his heart he knows he can go nowhere without you.

In the group conversation in Mirere, women shifted quickly from describing changes in their communities to a lively discussion of money. There were several men sitting on the sidelines out of curiosity. One added his comments to those of the women.

Woman 1: During the old times, we were relying on our own produce. Now that we depend on money, we have to ask our husbands. That causes a lot of quarreling.

Woman 2: Always talk between men and women is of money.

Woman 3: I find it hard to solve problems because I cannot get money when I need it.

Man: This is the way it should be: women are under the men. Women should have to ask for the money.

Woman 2: Now we are often hungry. Men decide how much maize to sell. We used to plan what we needed for eating and the rest could be sold.

HH: Who makes the decision about selling in other families?

Woman 1: The husband doesn't discuss, he only orders you to prepare the maize to be taken to the market. We grow it and carry it to market, but it's the men who do the selling in the market.

HH: Do most of your husbands take responsibility for meeting the needs of their wives and children, or do they keep the money for their own use?

[Many voices, much heated conversation, most of it not translated.]

Woman 4: Men do not give us enough money. Only a little, so the wives have to come back even the next day and ask again.

Woman 1: Men are different. Some are responsible: they tell their wives when they are leaving and where they are going. On their way back they may buy something that is needed in the house. Others say nothing, and if a wife asks where he is going, she is beaten.

Karen Mahiti is a Nairobi businesswoman whose business activities caused a great deal of friction with her husband.

Usually the responsibilities of the child are left for the woman. For example, after taking a child to school the man can decide to refuse to pay school fees and therefore it is the woman to take the responsibility.

My husband did not behave positively towards the children. I had a business and therefore I tried to pay school fees, but there came a time when I was unable to pay. Since this was a Catholic school, I went to ask the sister in charge to talk to my husband about school fees. The sister told him that he was the father to the children and it was his duty to pay.

He knew this was serious and started paying the fees. That was one advantage with a Catholic school. They offer counseling services to the parents, which is not possible with many other schools.

But, as Roselyne Choge said, there are also men who make financial decisions jointly with their wives. Dorah Zighe, a Wundanyi farmer, is married to a carpenter who shares both money and decision-making fully with his wife.

If I got money, I'd use it to help my husband buy wood and set up a workshop. He and I have a lot of transparency between us. If he gets 100 Ksh he brings it home and we decide together how to use it. Even our children are the same way. If we are trying to think how to buy a packet of salt for ten Ksh, even the children may say, "I have a shilling someone gave me to buy a sweet." Another may have two Ksh.

When control of money doesn't give a man sufficient power over his wife, he may beat her.

Domestic Discord, Beating, and Neglect

Men have wronged their wives repeatedly, but women don't beat them. Beating a wife is just a way of treating her like a little child.

—Mary Obanda, Mumias farmer

In individual interviews, many women told us of suffering frequent beatings. In every large gathering, though women were not telling their own personal stories, they would refer to beating as normal, or widespread. Most believe a woman may seek relief if she is beaten "too much," but some believe a wife should "persevere" under all circumstances.

In Nasianda, we interviewed about fifty members of *Bahengere Women's Group*. A few men sat on the sidelines out of curiosity, and commented when they wished. As usually happened, the subject of beating arose in the course of asking about other things. In this case, I had asked the unmarried women what qualities they'd like to find in a husband.

Woman 1: Well, most girls look for the type we want, but then after staying with them for some time, they behave differently altogether.

HH: Are you saying that men change?

[Widespread laughter]

Woman 2: They don't change at the beginning, but after one or two children when they know the girl is now stable in their homes is when they change. You see one may try to cheat[1] you that he doesn't drink at all, but then he may begin to drink and mistreat you terribly.

HH: : When men mistreat their families, is that mostly because of alcohol, or does that happen even with men who don't drink? Are there men who drink a lot, but are good to their wives?

[lots of muttering!]

Woman 3: All men beat their wives, but those who drink are worse.

HH: They all beat?

[Universal assent and laughter. Answers and translations are inaudible on the tape for nearly a minute, because there are too many voices and laughter from both men and women. Then the conversation resumes.]

1. In Kenyan English, "cheat" is routinely used where others would say "lie to" or "deceive."

> Woman 4: Both those who drink and those who don't drink beat their wives, but mostly those who drink a lot do it more often. We are bitter about alcohol. You see him coming home drunk, and you know you will be beaten.
>
> Man: I do not think they do it when they are not drunk. They only do it when they are drunk, which is not bad at all.
>
> Woman 4: Most of the time when they are not drunk, they just make noise and do not beat.
>
> Woman 3: Some take abuse without any complaint while others fight back.
>
> Woman 2: These men do not hate us. They beat us, yes, but they love us. If we leave them and take on another man, they may even come and fight your new man and kill each other. That shows how much they love us.

While courting, or in the early days of marriage, partners will be on their best behavior. But after many children are born, a wife cannot leave easily, and becomes more dependent on her husband. Economic dependence makes a woman vulnerable. That is when a man is most likely to start beating his wife, or to take another wife. For Margaret Obonyo [Portrait C] beating was not a serious problem until she had many children and could not leave easily. Then, her husband could beat her without fear or constraint. Beatings continued even when she was aging and seriously ill.

When I visited Sein Milanoi, she gave what seemed to be a complete interview while I had the tape recorder on. She had chosen her own husband. He later took two other wives, with whom she had peaceful but distant relations. I believe she was not beaten, but her two uneducated and economically dependent co-wives were.

With the tape recorder on, Sein said of her married life, "We stayed well," which precluded my asking whether she was beaten. Later, after the tape recorder had been put away, she said more. "You know, men don't like laughing with their wives. Other men will say, 'Don't laugh with her. You are showing her that you love her too much. She will shame you. She will make you serve tea.' So they just sit stony-faced."

The next day, Sein took me for a walk around her shamba. When she came to a spot near her husband's grave she said:

> This is where he used to beat his second wife. He would tie her to that tree, beat her, take some beer, and beat her some more.
>
> She got sick and was taken to the hospital. While she was there he would sometimes visit her. Then she died. The hospital called him to bury her. But he said, "She is not my wife. She is my brother's wife and he is not here. I cannot bury her. You bury her."

> What kind of a man would refuse to bury his own wife? You know, he became a very brutal man.[2]

Shaming such as Sein mentions is a common concern. Many men will tell each other not to let their wives do such and such because if they do, their wives will shame them. Men pressure each other to conform to harsh standards in how they rule[3] their wives. A man who does not beat his wife will be badgered with questions like, "Do you mean she has never made a mistake?" and accused of creating problems for other men.

Several women told us that beating is a problem only in large families, only in rural areas, only in economically marginal families, or only in some sector of society to which they do not belong. Susan Malaso believes that beating now occurs only in large families. "Long time ago, men used to think their wives should be under them, and they would beat them very much. That habit is now dying out, but with large families it is still there because a large group is very difficult to control."

In fact, wife-beating occurs in every social sphere. Catherine Obungu [Portrait D] told us about a University lecturer who severely and repeatedly battered his wife. Angie Dawa, the physician who thought she hadn't planned enough before marrying, had quite a few beatings.

> The first time he beat me, I was shocked. The people who were working under me invited me for a fund raising. I asked my husband to accompany me, but he did not want to. Perhaps he did not have the money. I went alone. Just when it was going to end my husband came by with a friend. I said, "Oh fine, he will take me home." He said, "No we are going to a disco." I said, "OK, fine, you go to a disco. I want to go home." The children had been at home all day with the maid, my breasts were engorged with milk, I was tired. He said, "No, you are going to a disco." On the way, he said, "What are you trying to show me? You are trying to show me that you can attend fund-raisers without me, that you can go out without me." And I think I must have answered him badly because he really beat me. Afterwards, he was very apologetic.
>
> The second time it happened, we had gone out again. Now I can't remember why, but I ended up with a black eye. At that time we were living with relatives. My main worry was to make sure no one saw. I made up so many lies, I fell down the stairs, I was bitten by a wasp. The next day I went to a clinic. I asked the nurse to inject me with hydrocortisone. I said I was bitten by a wasp. That's what I remember about that time, that I went to extreme efforts to try to hide it.

---

2. Despite her reluctance to record this, she has seen these paragraphs and given me permission to publish them.

3. This is the word commonly used in Kenyan English. For example, a man might say he would prefer to marry a younger woman, "So I can rule her."

The third time was about money. I had received a quite significant amount of money to do some research. He wanted to control it. I refused and decided to conceal the amount. But I think I was naive. He went with me to the bank and he saw the amount on the bank slip. He said I was trying to cheat him. He said it was a question of trust. That was horrible.

The next time, our daughter was almost three. He refused to eat something that I served him. He poured it on my plate and said, "You eat it." He went into the kitchen, got a jug of water, poured it onto my face, he slapped me a few times. I was so embarrassed. The next day, I made an attempt to let him know that I was really upset, and he appeared to be apologetic.

That was the last time he hit me until recently. But this time I am stronger, and I know about the women's movement. I was tired, but he wanted us to make love. I said no. He hit me. I just refused to have any arguments unless there was a third person there to protect me. I called my sister-in-law, and we discussed it, although it was very embarrassing. But now it is different between us. I have gotten over the idea that for marriage to work, I have to give and give totally.

Gracilda Mwakio, a farmer outside Wundanyi, told us about her mother's experience, "My father beat her a few days after she had given birth to my last brother. He hit her with a big log of firewood across the stomach. She never really recovered. She had internal injuries and pain, but she did not die until later. Beating went on until she passed away."

When we asked Gracilda whether her husband beat her, she explained how she avoided beatings. "Since I came from around here, he knew about my mother. When he was ready to beat me, I would say, I don't want to die like my mother, so he wouldn't beat me. I was always reminding him of my mother's experience."

Just outside Wajir, we interviewed some of the members of *Kulimiya Women's Group*, former nomads who fled to Wajir when drought and clashes killed their animals. They have come together to learn self-employment skills, and are now earning money for the first time. We sat in the shelter they had constructed for group meetings, which is made of sticks lashed upright in parallel between small trees. Because there were many of them and the sun would soon set, I did not get individual names. We had been talking about their economic lives when one woman of about forty brought up the subject of beating.

I am now beaten less because my husband no longer has animals. He is less proud, more appreciative.

HH: Has this been the same for any of the rest of you?

Gracilda Mwakio returning from her shamba. In the background left is a latrine and on the right a neighbor's house

[Much hubbub, many overlapping answers, but this one came out clearly on the tape] As much as there is no beating, we believe that the woman should always be taking the orders from the husband.

HH: Could you say something more. Now that you are businesswomen, and you have accomplished much, would you say something about why you believe that a woman should still take her orders from her husband?

Translator: Because of the Islamic religion. In every house, everywhere, when there are two people, one has to be the head. Through the grace of God a man will be the head. A woman should always respect her husband and will always compromise. That way, nothing will lead him to harm her.

Members of Ilbissil Women's Group were eager to talk personally about domestic violence, even though they had not met me before. One member of the group, Soila ene Silantoi, is greatly afraid of her husband. "If I come home late, I will be beaten up. So I just keep quiet. I fear I may be beaten even to death."

Another member, Tikako Kores, has a much gentler husband. She sees beating as an excusable means of correction, but believes it will become uncommon when more men are educated.

> My husband is a very good man. Since he is a man there is sometimes commotion here and there, but it is not serious.
>
> Among us Maasai, the less-educated people beat their wives most. If he finds you outside, you have done a mistake, he beats you there. Beating of a wife is to make her aware, to think. It's only to rectify her mistake.

Later in the conversation, Tikako described what the bride's parents should say to a young man about to marry their daughter.

> Tell the husband, "This girl we are giving you has no mark on her face. If she makes a mistake, and you have to beat her, don't beat her with your hands. Look for a stick, but not a very big strong stick — something that will just make her feel pain. If she has an affair outside the home, beat her, and perhaps she will come back to the home."
>
> But on the other hand, the parents can also say, "If my daughter comes home several times because you are not taking care of her: you don't clothe her properly, you don't feed her properly, she will become my daughter again, and I will give back what you gave me [the animals or cash paid for bridewealth]."

Her friend Nampaso ene Naanyu has run home to her parents because of beatings.

> My husband is a very harsh man. He has two wives. Originally there were four. Two went away because of the strictness. I am the favorite.
>
> He used to drink and start beating me, so I ran away three times. He came to my parents' place and they talked. He said he made a big mistake and he would never beat me again, but when we reached home, he started beating me again.
>
> He talked so nicely in front of the parents and made it look like he stopped beating me, but when we got home it was the same.
>
> I had to take the beatings because of the children, so even though my parents tried to say, "You don't have to stay with him," I had to come back for the children.
>
> He still drinks, but he is old now, so the beatings are finished.

Traditional mechanisms for solving domestic conflicts by calling on the elders have contemporary equivalents. Chiefs can be asked to protect a wife's rights. Their decisions can be enforced with time in jail. Unfortunately, a woman may not feel safe in using these important sanctions. Monica Mgoye, a farmer in Kakamega District, sought the authorities' help for a different problem, but then couldn't safely expose her husband to their punishment.

> He doesn't help with the shamba or the children. At the beginning he used to buy them clothes. He paid school fees before but now he would not do that. Since he married [again], he does not bring anything to them. For years, he was harsh, even for a small mistake. He could talk evil to the children. Now, he's a bit better with them. He can talk to them without abusing them.
>
> When he married me he had one acre. When he married another wife, he gave that new wife all the shamba, and left me without anything. I only have my house. I went to the sub-chief to be given part of the shamba.
>
> The sub-chief told him to give it to me. He refused. He threatened that if the other woman left, I'd better run. The sub-chief decided to jail him, but another man had died in the jail, so I thought that he might die there. I did not want that because the brothers would say that I killed him. So I decided to leave him alone instead of jailing him. Now, quarreling is not much, but I still do not have the shamba.

Many women think beating is a routine and eternal problem, nearly as much a fact of life as the sunrise. Regina Kavindu is one, "My parents' marriage was ordinary. As usual, men beat their wives. He beat her but was good to the children, so she was happy with him."

Although many women's lives are constricted by fear and embittered by being beaten, surprisingly few complain. To many women, if beating is routine, it is not worth complaining about. A more common complaint is neglect. Flores Mwang'ombe, a Wundanyi farmer, appears to be in her fifties.

> The most problem that married women experience is with drinking husbands, and especially the local beer. Instead of spending time with the family, finding out the problems, they come back home already drunk. The next day maybe he leaves in the morning. So if there's any pressing problem the woman wanted to share with the husband, it is difficult. That really makes life miserable.
>
> I have that problem here. My early days of marriage were OK because we were staying in town. But when we came here, he started to drink too much.

In the group conversation in Nasianda, a woman of about forty whose name was not recorded said, "It would be better if my husband spent some of his free time with me so I can tell him about our problems."

Hearing this, a younger woman said, "If my husband stayed home more, I'd just be beaten more."

Abuse and neglect are common problems for married women, but not universal. Eunice Karoge is a farmer in Lusigetti born in 1963.

> We have a very sweet life together. He's much older than me, seventy years old. We have fourteen children. We sometimes quarrel, but because we have much love, we can solve the problem. We're just like a girlfriend and boyfriend. We even go on picnics.

Advice for Wives Who Are Beaten

We asked many women what a wife should do if she is beaten. The advice differed widely. Many offered ways of keeping husbands happy like making sure dinner is ready when he gets home or giving him good food. Others had suggestions for resolving conflict, like talking with him when he is sober. I asked Charlotte Kogo, a Kobujoi farmer who appears to be in her fifties, what advice she gives her daughter about marriage. She says women should avoid giving their husbands any reason to beat them. "First, before advising her, I want to know if she made some mistake. She can avoid problems by not doing something her husband dislikes."

A group of neighbors of many different ages at Dorah Zighe's home in Wundanyi had varied opinions.

> Lillian Kibuka: If a woman is beaten she should go to someone the husband respects, to see if that person will counsel her husband. Also the wife should find out why he is beating her. If she is at fault, she should change the fault.
>
> A wife can't prevent her husband from beating the children, but if he is beating her daily, she should leave him.
>
> HH: [to the older women] If you had a daughter who was married but didn't yet have any children and she was being beaten, what advice would you give her? Should she persevere, or should she leave?
>
> Olive Majala: You apologize and welcome him home with love, even if he is drunk.
>
> Mary Msinga: I would advise her to pack quickly and leave. No one would support that beating.
>
> HH: And if she has children?
>
> Dorah Zighe: Depending on the number of children, I might advise her to leave. If she has one or two children and I could accommodate them, I might advise her to leave, but if it is many she will have to stay. Also then it will not be easy for the man to agree to release her.

Maria Kibali: I think it is a risk to advise your daughter to stay. She might even be beaten to death, then what would you do? Today life has changed. She can come back home, and even get a job to support her children. So she should come home in that case.

Mary Msinga: Before, a woman was not allowed to leave, but today she can do that if she has money.

I asked what a mother should do if the father beats the children. Conversation became lively and overlapping. Rather than try to translate each comment, the translator, Mary Msinga, said, "Some say the mother should not try to interfere. She should not comment, just keep quiet and observe. Others say the mother should try to withdraw the children. You leave that place, and come home. You should not stay."

Flores Mwang'ombe recalled two wives who responded differently. In one case, despite repeated severe beatings, the wife did not dare leave, although Flores' urged her to. Another wife left after being beaten once. Flores did not entirely approve of her haste.

Susan Malaso advises perseverance because it is better for the children not to be torn between their parents. She does not approve of a wife leaving even when she is well able to support herself and the children.

We are losing some of the good old customs. A woman used to be advised by her parents, if you are abused by the husband you should tolerate. I like that because we women have patience and we should teach to our children to be patient, not just pack and go when you are told something you don't like. Obey your husband, submit yourself to the husband.

HH: Are there any circumstances under which you'd think that a wife should leave her husband?

Maybe if the case is genuine, she can go home to her parents until they can talk over and see who is in the wrong and who is in the right. But she has to go back to her husband. Divorcing is not wise because the person that is going to suffer is the child. The mother will go, and the child will be left in between. He'll have to follow the father or follow the mother. A wife should never do that, never!

The Nasianda women had a lively discussion about what an abused woman should do, reflecting the deep disagreement on this topic.

Woman 5: I used to get beaten, but the best thing to do is to make a lot of noise, so he will be ashamed.

Woman 1: Some leave but end up coming back. Where can one go?

Woman 6: It happens commonly, so if that happens, she just has to persevere.

HH: Would you advise your daughters to persevere?

[many simultaneously] Yes.

HH: Are there any circumstances when you would advise your daughters to leave?

Woman 7: We just can't tell them that, but we don't want them to stay with a man who may kill them. The girls themselves leave when they feel it is enough.

Woman 2: We tell our daughters to try to save the marriage. Problems always exist, so you just let her know it is a part of marriage.

Woman 1: If there are many children, it is very hard to leave and support them yourself.

Woman 2: The husband will have given the bridewealth to your parents so you cannot leave without causing quarrels between your husband and your parents. We are thus trapped.

Woman 4: If the husband does not change after the issue has been raised, the girl's parents may decide to take their daughter back if they can afford. They are reluctant to do this. It is a very severe scenario.

Woman 2: If she leaves, maybe the man rests, and then she can go back and he may improve.

Woman 1: If she goes back when he has made promises, maybe he will be better for a few days, but then he may resume his old ways.

HH: In my country, a woman who is being badly beaten is often afraid to tell anyone because she fears that then the man may become very angry, and might even kill her.

Woman 7: What do you think a woman should do in such a situation?

HH: I think the women here can give better advice than I can, because the situation is different. In my country the advice we give is: the first time he beats you, you leave, and you don't ever go back for any reason whatsoever. But I'm not sure whether that's the right advice for here. What do you think?

[Many simultaneously] NO!

Woman 9: Even if the men beat the children they don't do it cruelly, intending to kill them. So, when a woman goes away, she should only rest at her home, not go away permanently.

Woman 4: When children are involved, we can leave him with or without dowry and he cannot get us back. Our fear, though, is the children. We cannot leave them with him unless they are well grown-up.

Oruko Omina, the public health worker who decided to keep a separate bank account, emphatically disagrees with advice to persevere patiently.

I'm disappointed because women are not doing enough for themselves. Too often, we just take it. Men take their salaries and drink. The woman

> struggles on her small salary, and the children may not be in school. I'd go to his employer and say, "Don't pay him this month for drinking." I'm sure that would shake him, but women aren't willing to do that. They say, "Oh, no! He would kill me."

This divergence of opinion reflects a harsh reality. Many women have no possibility of leaving: nowhere to go, and no means of supporting themselves and their children if they leave. Accommodations must be made, even when there is no satisfactory way of resolving the problem.

Polygamy

Traditionally, all Kenyan ethnic groups practiced polygamy. Muslims were restricted to four wives at a time, but men in non-Muslim areas often had more. When land was plentiful and herds were large, extra wives provided useful labor.

Even when additional wives are an economic liability, polygamy still provides clear emotional benefits: a man can woo any available woman who appeals to him. Then, there is the desire to father many children. Although having many children is now expensive, it is still emotionally satisfying. A man's standing in the community is enhanced. He is regarded as more virile than one who has few.

Another support for polygamy is the myth of surplus women. Although women usually do not want their husbands to marry other wives, they may not be opposed to polygamy in the abstract. Kenyans believe that there are many more women than men. Therefore, some say that without polygamy, many women would never have a chance to marry.[4]

Today, with pressure on land, greatly reduced herds, and exposure to European social norms, polygamy is becoming less common. Even in those areas where most men have several wives, the numbers are smaller. In Western Province three wives is common, but twelve is now almost impossible.

When I visited my friend Shadrack Mbasu at his family home in Malava District, he seemed a bit embarrassed to introduce his two wives. He explained, "It is hard to manage this land since we live in town. I needed someone to manage it, so that's why I married again."

But few men have more land than one wife can manage. Many are hard-pressed to feed one wife and her children on limited land, or land

4. According to the 1999 Kenya census, females outnumber males 1.019 to 1. According to 1996 US CIA estimates, males outnumber females in Kenya 1.002 to 1. In either case, the numbers are very close.

whose fertility has been depleted. Herders do not need to care for land, but there can be other economic advantages to polygamy. Among Somali herders, each wife has her own herd and is economically independent.

This is not true for all pastoral groups. Although the Maasai are also pastoralists, as we have seen, a Maasai husband usually owns and controls all the animals, so his wives are dependent on him, unlike Somali wives.

Catherine Obungu [Portrait D] was one of several women who thought that for her husband, pride was the major motive in taking a second wife. "When these men realize they have something extra, they want to show their ego. They want to show that they are successful so they marry other wives."

As we have seen, many men take little economic responsibility for their children. If fathers do not pay the children's school fees, or don't help to provide food for them, they can believe their own welfare is only enhanced, not diminished, by the arrival of more children.

The traditional saying, "A man with only one wife is like a man with only one eye" is still widely repeated. Polygamous men pressure others to take another wife. Often, this pressure is not subtle at all. A man is made to feel that he is not a real *mzee*[5] while he has only one wife. Angie Dawa's father gave in to that pressure.

> My father was very strong to resist conflict until retirement, when he finally succumbed to pressure from his tribe to have another wife. [His first wife was not of his tribe.] He has taken a little girl who is the age of my last-born sister.
>
> Something very strange, my mother not only gave her permission but she was encouraging. She took part in the negotiations. She actually pushed the process through. But I have heard her complain about wishing that it was different.

Sometimes pressure comes from in-laws who want more grandchildren. Roselyne Okumu, the person who said she wouldn't mind being the second wife of a rich man, worries silently about her mother-in-law's attitude, but does not discuss this with her husband.

> After we got married we decided to control how many kids we were going to have. I talked to my mother-in-law about it and she was against the idea. She said if I don't get enough children then he would need to get another wife, because she wants to have many grandchildren.

Sein Milanoi was sure her husband would not take other wives.

5. Literally "elder." This is an important title of respect for any man of middle age or more. A grown son will refer to his father as "the mzee."

> I was not expecting a co-wife because in the church he was swearing he would not marry somebody else. But the men of my tribe, when they get rich, they take another wife. At first we stayed well, but then he was incited by his friends. The cattle had increased, my shop was doing well, there was a lot of property, so he took more wives.

When he visited me in Kenya, even my European-American husband was repeatedly asked why he had only one wife, and was mildly teased about it.

Pressures for Monogamy

Polygamy still benefits a few men economically and many men in other ways, but there are countervailing pressures for monogamy. The current economic situation, Protestantism, and family problems caused by polygamy are some of the reasons polygamy is becoming less common. Men in cities and towns have fewer wives than rural men. Nuria Abdou, who lives in Wajir, believes living in town has made it impossible for her husband to take another wife. "He has his wife, ten children, his mother, his sister, and his sister's children. Where will he put another wife?"

Since Somali Muslim men take economic responsibility for their wives and children, Dekha Ibrahim's father felt burdened by his two families.

> My father married a younger wife. He has expenses. The first wife's children are grown and she is economically secure, whereas the husband is a slave to the young wife. My mother can take care of her grandchildren, but the husband's going through turmoil.
>
> Most men here have at least two wives, and it gives problems to their elder children because while the young wife is still giving birth he may pass away.

Religion and Polygamy

> I don't think my husband will take other wives because he is a saved Christian.
>
> —Doris Mathieu, social service worker, Meru

When Protestant missionaries arrived in East Africa, they struggled to eradicate polygamy. Catholic missionaries, on the other hand, decided that opposition to polygamy interfered with their larger goal of conversion. Consequently, in Protestant areas, polygamy and Christianity are considered incompatible; however, in heavily Catholic areas, many practicing Christians see no conflict.

Muslim men have always had fewer wives at a time than men in non-Muslim areas, since Islam limits a man to four wives. But a Muslim man can easily divorce a wife. Men on the coast usually have only one wife at a time, but several wives during their lives. This is not true in other Muslim regions. Among Somalis, simultaneous polygamy is still common. Although four wives are permitted, two is more usual.

Polygamy and Family Problems

Aside from their own unhappiness, women's main complaint about polygamy is that it leads to economic strain and lack of harmony at home. Although a man is supposed to treat all his wives equally, many women complain that only the most recent wife is taken care of.

Usually, wives are deeply unhappy when their husbands take a new wife, but they may be reluctant to say all that they feel. Two of my friends let their faces express what they did not wish to put into words. When I was teaching in western Kenya, one of my closest friends was a health worker, Tabitha Nechesa. Tabitha was hospitalized for some months in her thirties. Until then, she had been a sole wife, but while she was away, her husband took another wife.

When Tabitha told me about her co-wife, I said, "That must have been a disappointment." She replied with the saddest face I've ever seen, but said only, "Yes."

A man of the neighborhood later told me that Tabitha's husband had no choice but to take a second wife. There was a real possibility that Tabitha might die. If she died, her husband would have difficulty getting another wife because women would fear that he had somehow caused her death. Therefore, the only wise course was to take a new wife while Tabitha was still alive.

Jane Achieng'o was a sole wife with four young children in Kisumu. When the subject of polygamy came up naturally in a rambling conversation, I asked, "How would you feel if your husband took another wife?"

She looked at me in total horror, and said, "I could not accept that." She has since borne three more children, her husband has taken another wife, and her relations with him have become so difficult that she had to leave, in spite of the hardship this brought her children.

Relations between co-wives are usually difficult. Jealousy is often expressed in tension over financial assistance, or disputes over land.

Giving each wife her own land and her own house is the most important thing a man can do to keep peace among his wives.

Qaudensia Oyiro, who was born in 1957, is a farmer in Western Province. Her husband works in Kisumu, but returns to his land on the weekends. Qaudensia, her co-wife, and their husband worked out an unusual living arrangement that kept the wives separate and kept peace for some years. Eventually, their arrangement ceased to satisfy, and was changed.

> At first, I would stay in Kisumu for a year and she would stay here. Then she would go to Kisumu for a year and I would stay here. For thirteen years, we were exchanging.
>
> At the beginning, things stayed very well. We would eat together. After some three or four years, the changes started. The co-wife started throwing bad words. When I was staying there with him and the co-wife was here, she would come there and quarrel.
>
> Even the husband changed. If I'd ask for something to send the girl to school, oh! So I decided to leave and just come back here. For ten years I have not gone back there. I don't like to be at Kisumu now. The husband ordered me to come back to Kisumu, but I refused because instead of quarreling, I prefer to stay alone.

There is a common assumption that the most recent wife will be loved the most and helped the most. This why many women willingly marry a man who has other wives. In a rural church near Mumias, I met with a group of about forty women whom I didn't know individually. They eagerly discussed the relative merits of being a first wife or a last wife.

> Woman 1: Most men have many wives. Men love their second[6] wives most. So most women prefer to be the second wife, to be loved and cared for.
>
> Woman 2: I'd rather be the second wife. If I were to marry a man with no wife, I might not know what to expect, but if I am the second wife I am sure he can get along with me the same way he gets along with his first wife.
>
> Woman 3: I would like to be the first wife because by the time the second wife is married, my children will be growing up and proceeding with their school. So by the time her children will be big enough to go to school, mine will have finished.
>
> Woman 4: The first wife is respected by people around and in cases of the man's absence, it's the first woman who controls everything.

6. The translator may have translated comments about a "last wife" or a "junior wife" as "second wife" regardless of the actual number.

Woman 5: Some men do not tell the woman they take as a second wife that they already have a first wife. So she does not know until she goes to his home.

Despite their unhappiness, many women accept the arrival of a new wife graciously. We have seen that Angie Dawa's mother took over the negotiations for the second wife, though she was not happy. Although most women would prefer not to share their husband, a few women are really happy to welcome a co-wife. Mateu, who lives in rural Kajiado and walks far to fetch water, was very happy. Her reasons remind us how hard rural women's lives can be. "I was happy because when I was pregnant there was no one to help me but after she came, I really had good help. She could help me bring in firewood and water, and mud the house."

Women may bear children hoping to forestall the arrival of additional wives. This is a topic women discuss often. The Mumias church group had a lively disagreement about this.

Woman 1: Many women reject family planning to have many children, so they may prevent their men from marrying other wives.

Woman 2: I would prefer my husband marrying a second wife rather than having many children. In this way, I will resume my health and my few children will be easy to care for.

Woman 3: Instead of my husband getting another wife, I can give birth to a lot of children because I hate life with co-wives.

Woman 4: The man can convince you in getting lots of children, then after that he still marries the second wife. So he leaves you with the whole burden of caring for the children. I'd better plan the number of children so that I will not be much hurt when he marries.

Life with In-Laws

Since a young bride usually goes to her husband's parents' home, relations with her in-laws are an important part of her married life. She is marrying not only a man but also a family and a home. The tradition of whole families participating in arranging a marriage gave the in-laws and the new bride a chance to learn about each other before they made final decisions. Now, mothers-in-law lament the loss of that opportunity. One of the unnamed women in Mumias said, "The son never asks the mother who she wants him to marry as it used to be. We never know who our daughters-in-law will be and when they will appear. We just get unexpected visitors."

Nuria Abdou's marriage was arranged between her husband and her mother. Her husband's family were far away with their herds, and therefore not involved in the marriage negotiations. Later drought and clan warfare forced them, like so many others, to abandon pastoral life and move to town, living with Nuria and her husband.

The in-laws do not like Nuria, and consider themselves entitled to object to her since they did not consent to the marriage. They are pressuring the husband to divorce Nuria, although she has seven children.

In farming communities, the new bride works under her mother-in-law's direction until her husband sets up his own homestead, which takes several years. Among the Luo, for example, a man may build a family home outside his parents' compound when his oldest child can walk. Until then, he and his wife live in his bachelor cottage within the family compound. His wife will not have her own kitchen until they have their own compound, though she may cook separately in the cottage.

Even if she cooks separately, a wife's farm work and chores will be carried out according to the matriarch's wishes. Even after her husband has his own compound, she may still farm under her mother-in-law's supervision until her father-in-law formally divides his land late in life. The entire harvest may go to the mother-in-law, so the wife will have to ask her mother-in-law for each basket of maize.

The matriarch is powerful within her domain. Roselyne Choge, a middle-aged school teacher with eight children and a substantial permanent house of her own, does not think it strange that whenever she buys something for herself, her mother-in-law will ask, "Where's mine?" So, Roselyne never buys anything for herself without buying the same for her mother-in-law. She also washes her mother-in-law's clothes.

The mother-in-law has the right to insist that the children be named as she wishes. Wambui Rahab, an educated Kikuyu woman who was born in 1963, disagreed with her mother-in-law over naming her eldest son, but had to yield. Since Kikuyus name the first son for the husband's father, and married sons continue to live on the family land, in one compound there may be many grandsons who have the grandfather's name.

> There were five Joseph Maina Ngangas in our compound. I wanted to make a small change in my first son's name; to change it to Maina Joseph Nganga. My mother-in-law was outraged, and would not allow it.
>
> Because of the names, you must have at least four children so all the grandparents have a namesake.

A mother-in-law has ample room for tyranny if she chooses to use her power that way. On the other hand, she can be a great ally in times of marital troubles. When we asked the Nasianda women whether married women generally have trouble with their mothers-in-law, one young woman responded immediately, " The mother-in-law will help her when the husband is quarreling or beating her."

Taboos regarding in-laws are broader than incest taboos in the West. There are high barriers of "respect" that must be observed between a woman and her father-in-law, or between a man and his mother-in-law. A bride will relate very differently to her father-in-law than to her mother-in-law. My friend Zipporah Masai ran out of her mother-in-law's kitchen with her face covered when her father-in-law entered, though she had been living at her in-laws' homestead for seven years. When I asked her about this she explained that she respects him very much. Although others describe this as fear, neither word exactly describes the feelings accompanying this ritual avoidance.

Although respect/avoidance is an important aspect of proper behavior, the precise form that it will take differs from family to family. Generally, a man who chances to meet his mother-in-law on the road will go to great lengths to avoid her, will hide from her, or will at least cover his face while she passes. Despite the obligation to avoid his mother-in-law as a matter of respect, Sein Milanoi's husband would visit and help Sein's mother, which made Sein proud and happy.

> You don't go to a son-in-law's house often and he likes staying away from you. But my mother is far away, so whenever my husband went to Letoktok he would visit them. A son-in-law can go, but a mother-in-law cannot just be coming here often. Maybe once in two years.
>
> Likewise, a father doesn't go to a daughter-in-law. If they go, they might even sit outside and not eat the food prepared by her.

Roselyne Okumu was born in Kakamega District, but married a man in Kisumu, about seventeen miles away. She has five younger brothers. When her family wants to communicate with her quickly, they send Juma, who is about twelve years old, although there are two brothers considerably older than that, and one of them is neither working nor attending school. Roselyne's mother told me that a husband would not like a mature brother to visit, but would not mind a small boy.

In those Muslim families that practice seclusion, a wife might have no social contacts other than her in-laws. One of the women I was most drawn to was Fathia Osman, barely eighteen years old, mother of two small children, at home in a city on the coast. When the interview began, her husband was at home, and showed no objection to the interview. When she wasn't sure how to answer one of my questions, she consulted him. But soon he had to leave. She continued talking with us until her much younger brothers-in-law came in, angrily questioned why she was talking to strangers, and made her stop. It was an incomplete interview, but one part of it underscored her isolation. She rarely talks to her mother now; each of them is secluded in her own home.

Oruko Omina's husband would like to retire and live "at home" but she is strongly opposed because she finds his family difficult.

> I get along well with my mother-in-law, though she is very petty. It's my step-mother-in-law with whom I don't get along. She looks at me as a rival. She has all daughters, six in a row. My husband being the youngest of his mother's sons, she was looking to inherit him as a son. So she thought my being close to the mother was going to draw my husband from her, and prevent her from adopting him.
>
> Now, we fight about the cow that I keep there. When I am in Nairobi, she can use all the milk, but when I visit, she resents that I take some of the milk.

Virginia Njeri, the woman who went through a window to elope, came to her in-laws without their foreknowledge. Her husband has now abandoned her, but she cannot return to her natal home because there is no land for her there. "My in-laws mistreat me because my husband has left. Once, my mother-in-law told me to leave, and she beat my children thoroughly. Sometimes I think they might even poison the children. I only stay with them because I don't have anywhere else to go."

Agnetta Wanjiku grew up living on the street in Nairobi with her older brother. She remained homeless after her brother had established himself.

> Eventually, my brother married and had somewhere to live, but my sister-in-law didn't want me to come around. She thought my son would grow up to be rough, and would harm her children. So whenever I went there she sent me away. Once, she really attacked me. I reported the incident to the chief, but she bribed him and he made no report.

Occasionally a married couple may live at the wife's family home, as Agnetta's brother did. But their tenure may be insecure because a woman has no traditional right to inherit land, although Kenyan law now allows her to. Despite the new law, brothers rarely want to concede part of their father's land to her heirs in perpetuity. When I made a return visit to Maggie Mwasi of Mwatate, she had moved.

> Where we were staying was my family land. It was offered to me by my father. He said, "I have given this land to all my children, to live here." My father passed away in 1999 and problems started.
>
> According to our culture, those who are not enlightened feel that the woman cannot inherit, so I felt I should move to avoid clashes with my brothers. When the children grew up, it wouldn't be their land. We needed to have a place we called our own, so the children could be saying, "This is our home, from our parents," so they could be confident, and not clash with their cousins over land.
>
> Once my father died, my brother wanted me out. Now he's bedridden from a stroke, and his wife is in control of everything. My sister-in-law told me, "Your brother says you have to leave by July."
>
> I was given that ultimatum, so I couldn't even discuss the question with my brother. He's not in his proper state of mind. None of my relatives assisted me, but they pushed me to move.

Barrenness

Life without children is unthinkable for many families. One reason is practical: children can be a great help for fetching water and firewood or doing other the work. But it is not only a practical matter: life without children is regarded as unbearably dreary.

Kenyans consider barrenness the greatest tragedy that can befall a woman. It creates problems between husband and wife, and with the in-laws. Grace Namanda, the childless first wife of a teacher, is sure that's why her husband took a second wife. She gamely refers to her co-wife's children as "our children." Shortly after our conversation, Grace was banished. Her husband bought land elsewhere. Despite her employment as a primary teacher, she was sent to develop the new land, while the younger wife stayed with their husband on his family's land.

A wife who doesn't conceive risks being sent away. Why should she be given permanent use of family land if she can't contribute children? Elizabeth Anton, a Mwatate farmer who was born sometime around 1940, was fortunate.

> I was married twice. I stayed for about twenty years without getting a child so that husband divorced me. Then I married again. This husband had six children with his first wife but they were not getting along well so he set out in search of another woman without worrying about getting more children. But just the following year I got a child.

Sophie Amolo is an extraordinarily charismatic woman. Few people would want to risk being compared with her. Her personal magnetism ultimately doomed her childless marriage.

> Our time together was very good. There was nothing bad except not having children. We loved each other. He respected me and I respected him. But his family were funny.[7] There was a time when they wanted him to divorce me, but I shook it off because my husband loved me, and I relied on that.
>
> We did not adopt because if I adopted children and didn't know their background I might one day be disappointed. They might not respect me. Also, if God wanted me to have children, he would send them.
>
> He didn't divorce me, but after eight years he asked me to leave because I couldn't have children. Of course, he could have taken another wife with me still there, but my in-laws knew me well and knew the other woman would just get scared, because those around me respected me. They thought that I would be a threat to the new wife.
>
> I couldn't believe it when he gave in to his family's pressure. I said, "Now, is it you, or somebody else?"
>
> He said "I cannot do otherwise because my parents want this and that. But one day if you want to come back, you may."
>
> The one he married after me also did not have children. I didn't want to remarry. I had already tried it, and see what happened.

Some families will adopt instead of sending a barren wife away. Informal adoption is common and done for a variety of reasons: to get more children, to get sons if one has only daughters, to help a family that cannot care for its children, to establish closer ties with another family, or to care for relatives orphaned by AIDS. Constance Tanui [Portrait F] adopted several children in addition to her own, even though she was not married.

Childless women commonly adopt in any number of informal arrangements. For example, a child with many siblings may be adopted permanently or temporarily by a childless neighbor. One of Margaret Obonyo's sons lived with a childless neighbor for several years, both to give the other woman a child to care for, and to relieve the economic burden on Margaret's family. Irene Katete was brought up by her grandmother, as many children are. In her case, the decision was made because her father didn't want her, but it also enriched her grandmother's life. After Irene grew and left, the grandmother adopted other children. "I was the only child staying with her, because my mother was the last-born.

7. "Funny" is a term of disapproval in Kenyan English.

So when I left she was abandoned. There was nobody else, nobody to talk to, no one to share her food with, so she took another grandchild."

Separation and Divorce

Separation and divorce are becoming more common. Most women over fifty are alarmed by this, but many younger women consider it a healthy change. Regina Kavindu sees the increase as the result of greater autonomy for women. She does not approve.

> When I was young, there were no divorces, now it is frequent. There were no pregnancies outside marriage. Now it is common. There's a lot of prostitution because of freedom given to girls. Women should stay with their husbands and find a way to solve problems, not go off with other men.

Many women stay in unhappy marriages: marriages where they submit to frequent abuse, marriages that give them little love or respect, and inadequate sustenance. Why do they stay? For rural women, land is often the reason. If they leave their husbands, they may have no way to feed themselves and their children.

Tabitha Nechesa lives on a small plot of land with her young son, Zachariah Mutanyi, her widowed daughter, and three grandchildren. She came from a family with a huge shamba. All her brothers have large plots. If she left her husband she could easily feed herself and her dependents on part of her parents' land. She is unhappy with her husband, and her part of his land is inadequate even to feed herself and Zachariah. Still, Tabitha cannot leave. Although her brothers will give her land for her own use, they are not willing to give Zachariah his own permanent land to raise another family. Zachariah's only right to land comes from his father, and he will lose even that if she leaves. In this case, the problem is the father's individual stubborn pride. Many other women in this region leave their husbands, and their sons still inherit, but Tabitha's husband has made it clear that Zachariah will not inherit if she leaves. Tabitha takes this threat seriously because Zachariah is not the only male heir. Her husband has sons by his other wife.

Even educated and employed urban women may be forced to stay with their husbands for economic reasons. Eileen Waruguru, a Nairobi woman who left a position as head teacher to become a hairdresser, stayed with her husband for economic security, but insisted that her daughters get as much education as possible so they would be spared dependence on abusive marriages.

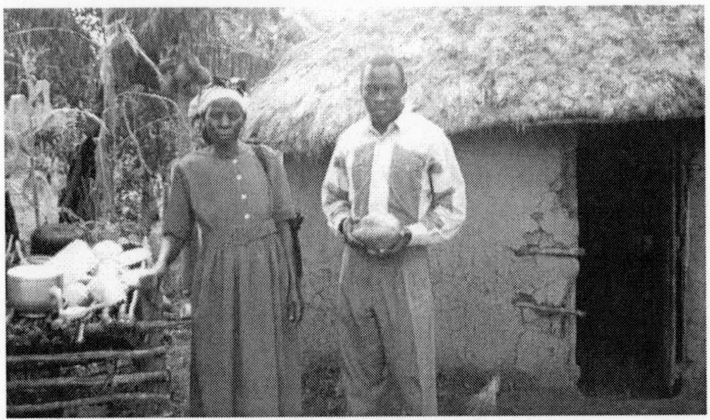

Tabitha Nechesa at home with her nephew. On the left is a drying rack made of sticks and chicken wire to keep clean dishes off the grass and away from animal droppings

All of my life I lived under my husband in fear because I knew that if I came out on my own, I would not have enough money to run a family. We clung to our husbands because of the upbringing we had.

Now, today's young women have numerous choices. They go to the universities, they earn their own money. My girls are earning enough. So why should a man come and give orders? Maybe she is in a position to get a loan and buy a house of her own. So what does she want from a man? Nothing. When my daughters used to listen to our fighting, the oldest one would say, "if this is the kind of life that I am expected to live, I would rather not marry." I think life will be easier for them because of what they have seen. They will not stand nonsense.

Tikako Kores of the Ilbissil Women's Group agreed that an educated woman is in a better position to leave.

Those who are educated can say, "He's not the only man. Let him go. I've got my education. I've got my certificates, I'll get a job and look for another husband." But for us, if we are beaten, we must still come back here because of the children.

When Jane Gathege's mother left her father, the whole family suffered materially.

My father married a second wife when I was ten. My mother and the other wife lived together for a short time. Then she left. We went with my mother. She didn't have the hotel[8] any longer, or a shamba. We had been rich, now we

8. Small food kiosk or cafe.

> were poor. I was out of school until someone from the church sponsored us for school. My father would come to see us, but didn't give us money.

As anywhere in the world, considerations of the children's welfare weigh heavily in decisions about separation. In many communities, children stay with the father unless they are very small. A man can say to his wife, "You came without children. You go without children." In truly desperate situations, a woman may leave without her children, even though that may rupture her relationship with them, but many other women stay with abusive husbands despite daily beatings and constant abuse, so they can care for their children.

Often a woman is tied not only by her desire to remain with her children, but also because her husband does not make sacrifices for the children's welfare. She knows that if she leaves, they may be severely neglected. That was Margaret Obonyo's reason for staying despite beatings and insults. "Many women leave their husbands because of his evil doings. Some leave their children, and some take their children. I often think about wanting to leave, but how can I? My children would die or starve. Therefore I have no alternative but to persevere."

Karen Mahiti is an urban businesswoman who separated from her husband. She left at his urging, but reconciled when he came to appreciate her in her absence. After their reconciliation, her husband tried to help her obtain contracts for her new milk supply business, even though his resentment of her business activities had caused the split.

> Sometimes this issue of working brings misunderstanding because you have to contribute in the house and you also have to employ a house girl, buy food and pay for the house rent. This caused our separation. My husband used to mistreat me. He would not even buy me what I needed. He abused me and would tell me that he did not want me. He told me to pack up and go. So I left for one and a half years. I told him that I came with no child and therefore I was not going to leave with any child,[9] and then I went.
>
> He found caring for the children hard. He changed greatly and understood that it was his responsibility to take those duties. I alerted him that he was an office worker therefore he was bound to get his salary under whatever circumstances, whereas I could sometimes work at a loss or not get customers. My earning was not certain.
>
> So I can say that it's sometimes good to pack up and go because this gives husbands time to change. Since I came back, he is the one who is supporting me. He asks me about anything that is missing, he can purchase anything we need in our house.

9. I was surprised to hear this phrase used by a woman who wanted to leave without her children. It is more often used by a man as a threat to keep the children if his wife leaves.

Mahiti preferred to leave her children with their father. Halan Ahmed also left her older son. It has not created problems for her. She sees him frequently, and they have remained close. We talked at the home of her friend Bahsan, who contributed her own comments.

> My younger son is in kindergarten. He is with my mother. The older one, who is seven, went with his father when we separated, but he comes to see me often. I see as much of him as I can, so he will have a mother's love. On Friday when there are no classes, he comes. He stays with me the whole day and then I return him in the evening.
>
> What happens to a woman when she leaves her husband depends on her parents. If they are not poor, they can take care of her.
>
> Bahsan: But every man will always say, "Why was she divorced?" So it will always have an implication on the woman's side, not on the man's side.

Even women assume that a divorce is probably the result of some fault of the wife. Among Muslims, divorce is asymmetrical. A Muslim man can divorce his wife by saying "I divorce you" three times. No reason need be given. But a woman cannot easily divorce her husband. In addition, since the wife is often financially dependent on her husband, and may live secluded in his house, she is less likely to be secure after divorce, and is therefore less likely to seek one, however great her grievances. Thus, among Muslims divorces are almost always initiated by the husband. Saadia Abubakar [Portrait E] didn't worry at all about marrying a man who had three times divorced a wife.

Attitudes toward separation and divorce are quite different among younger women. The friends assembled at Bahsan's home were all Muslim women in their twenties or thirties. They explained the chasm that separates their views from their parents.

> Bahsan: There's a Somali saying, "It's better to marry thirty men than stay with difficulties." You know, the learned women of today realize their problems, and because they are working class they can have security on their own. So they can say, "I want a divorce." When we want to discuss problems with a man, he doesn't want to listen.
>
> Halan: You know, we educated women do not agree with our parents. When there were harassments they would tell us not to leave the husbands. They say, "In this generation it is not the women who are married [*kuolewa*] it is the men who are married.[10] If you tell them why you cannot stay with your husband,

10. In Bantu languages, men "marry" but women "are married." The active form for the man and passive form for the woman implies that it is the men who decide and initiate. Here, Halan uses the semantic difference to express her mother's generation's strong disapproval of growing symmetry in marriage.

you get no co-operation from them. Your mother will say, "I had the same problems, but I stayed."

Hibo: If a woman leaves, people will say, "She's a curse," or they may even curse her. That's very serious in Somali culture.

HH: What's your advice to women? When should they leave, when should they stay?

Bahsan: They should not stay under any pressures! Because even now most of the households are being taken care of by women. Whatever little the husband gets, some goes to his parents, some goes to enjoyment like chewing *miraa* or whatever, and whatever comes to the home is minimal, so the women have to struggle really hard. Under these conditions, why should you stay if he puts pressure? If you don't feel comfortable, you should just go and stay comfortably on your own.

Hibo: But husbands say "If you leave, I'm going to bring brothers, cousins, everyone, to bring you back."

Sacdiyo: She can't stay where she's being beaten, and not being taken care of.

Halan: It's better for the woman, but not for the children.

Adey: You know, she can't stay where she's being beaten and not being taken care of.

HH: Are there marriages that remain close throughout life?

Dekha: I think the percentage of marriages that remain close all through is very small. Also with the nomadic life, you know separation is not divorce or anything. Pastoral families have to be separated often anyway.

Eileen Waruguru, the teacher-turned-hairdresser, regards the possibility of divorce as a great blessing.

I am a good reader of novels, so I know how it is done in other places. What I like in American life is, when they are fed up, they just walk out. There is no fight about it. If it is the man who thinks that he is fed up with the wife, he is the one who walks out of the home. He would even leave you the home because he is not happy with you. Whereas my husband bought the home for us. If I am the one who wants to go, he cannot part with his property. If he throws me out, I will have to go out and start afresh. When I think that I have to start all on my own, I am not going to go. That way we suffer so much.

For a woman who is formally and legally married, a legal divorce may not be easy. In addition to social stigma and poverty, she may face legal hurdles like those Catherine Obungu [Portrait D] faced. Esther Wangui, a Nairobi lawyer, has had the same kinds of legal problems that Catherine had.

I'm getting divorced. The reason people don't get divorced more in Kenya is that it's such a problem getting it through the courts, even for a lawyer. You find the file has disappeared, for example. The men are very acrimonious. They want to make sure you don't get anything. In my marriage, I walked out after two years and two months, so we don't have a fortune together. But there's still this whole African thing about the woman. He may mistreat you like crazy, but he'll ask, "What do you mean, 'She's going?' She can't go!"

I didn't think very well. Here I am with education and a good job, but there's this whole mentality that's so traditional. He's living with someone else, and he has other children but still he's arranging for the file to disappear from court and things like that.

WIDOWHOOD

Despite the hardships that often plague marriage, widows talked most about the mistreatment they suffer as widows. In many communities, the traditional way to protect widows was "widow inheritance." A brother or other married male relative of the deceased husband would marry the widow and take responsibility for her. Some interpret this as giving the widow the right to choose which male relative she will marry. Now, feminists are urging widows to refuse to be inherited. But rural women may have no other form of protection.

Widow inheritance contributes greatly to the spread of AIDS. When a married man dies of AIDS and his widow is inherited by a male relative, that relative and his other wives will be infected. If he dies first, those widows will also be inherited. Oruko Omina knew one woman who protected herself in that situation.

My uncle from my mother's side died of AIDS. My cousin asked me what he died of because he inherited the wife and they got a baby. The baby died. His first wife came crying to me that she would be infected, but in fact she had already decided to stay away from him for three years unless he brings an AIDS-free certificate. But if she stays away, he'll go out and infect other women.

Widows often have trouble protecting their claims to their husband's land. Because of today's shortage of available land, many, many widows are chased away from their husband's land by his surviving relatives, and have to return to their parent's home or join the thousands of landless, jobless women living in every city. Georgetta Njoki, who was born in Kikuyu after World War II, fled to Nairobi to live in the streets with her children and work as a prostitute because that was safer than remaining on her husband's land after he died.

My childhood was very stable. I had loving parents. At that time, we didn't use to go to school. I got married in the same neighborhood. I was not yet twenty, maybe seventeen, but since we did not go to school it was a good age.

My husband's father had three acres of land It was not enough for the whole family my father-in-law, and his two sons.

I was my husband's only wife. He died. His brother harassed me and beat me up. He wanted me as his wife so he could have all the land for himself. I didn't want to be his wife. He kept beating me. I resisted.

He wouldn't care about what we ate. We were hungry. So I was forced to go to other people's farms to pick coffee. My children were still not big, but they were big enough to help me pick.

One son was badly beaten by the brother-in-law. He was struck in the head and became mentally sick. He was taken to a hospital, but he never stayed two days. He just died in the halls. When this child died, I realized we were not safe. So I just ran away.

Sofa Nanzala married an age-mate and lived with him on his family's land in Malava. It was beautiful, rich land, energetically cared for, with a zero grazing project. When I first knew Sofa, her husband was taking a business training course and starting his own business. A few years later, in the middle of the night, thieves came to their compound. He went out to confront the thieves, and was killed. After that, his family chased Sofa and her son, their grandson. They went to live with her mother, one of the poorest women I knew in Kenya.

In Kabras, I interviewed a series of women at the home of my host. One woman, Salome Onyango, sat in the doorway. I assumed she was there to enjoy the breeze until I learned that as a widow she could not enter anyone else's house. She brews and digs. In the past, she was a trader, but could earn more money brewing. She had wanted to limit her family but her husband wanted many children because he had been an only child. So now she is a widow with nine children. The two oldest are married daughters. She supports the remaining seven with her hoe and her brewing. She cannot be inherited because she has no brothers-in-law to inherit her. But there is also no one to chase her from her land.

Benadette Nechesa, a recent widow in Malava, urged me to include a section about widowhood. Her husband had a highly paid position and was able to improve his land. She is sure he was murdered by jealous relatives.

When a husband dies, it should be the duty of the relatives to be sure that the children are maintained, which is very different than what happens. Once the husband dies, the children remain entirely on the wife. Secondly, something

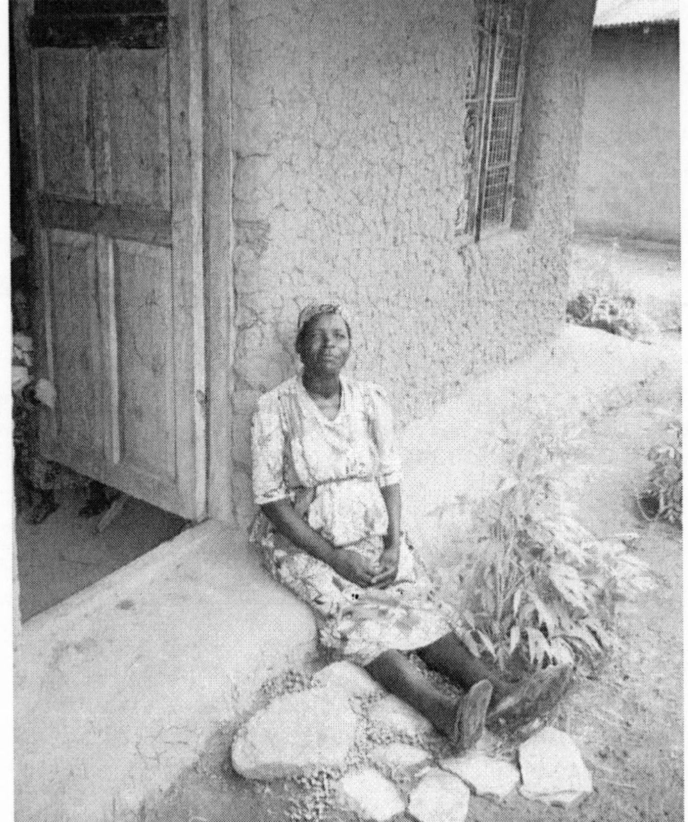

Salome Onyango sitting in Margaret Obonyo's doorway. As a recent widow, she cannot enter.

should be done to ensure that widows inherit the husband's property instead of the relatives claiming it.

These days when you get someone to inherit you, he has only come to inherit the property that the brother left. Widows have a very lonely life. If someone visits a widow, it is assumed that he is going for that property. This makes people avoid visiting widows. Women become very jealous if they see their husbands visiting a widow, so there are no close associations. I've lost many friends. My only company is now widows.

She has said it better than I could say it for her.

Women Marrying Women

In some communities, a widow who has no sons and is too old to bear more children may protect her land by marrying another, younger woman who can give her sons. This is not a universal custom. When we told Kenyans whose communities did not have this practice about it, they were amazed and fascinated. In Matuu, Filomena Syokau, a farmer born in 1956, explained that this was the only way to protect land without sons, because her community has no tradition of adoption.

> I have five children. I was married to a man, but he died after just one year. Now I'm married to an old woman who has only daughters. I married her three years after my first husband died. Actually, before he died, her husband picked me for her to marry. I had three children by then, so I agreed to marry her to take care of my children. She encouraged me to have more children but it's not necessary because I already have sons and daughters.
>
> A woman marries a younger woman if she has land and no sons. We do not have a tradition of adoption, so marrying me was the best way for her too.
>
> She doesn't have other wives, and won't take any more because she is too old. When she dies, I will stay as a widow so my children will have title to her land.

When I returned, Filomena introduced me to a friend who was also married to another woman, very happily, but her own marriage had deteriorated.

> The woman I am married to is too old and sick now. We do not get on well. She refused to educate my kids. Our life together was hard because we had money problems and interference from her daughter. When she heard we had married, the daughter came back and made problems. She wanted the land because she has sons.
>
> The woman I am married to has moved to her daughter's house. After her daughter came back she ignored me.
>
> When my daughter was ready to get married, I advised her to marry a man because of the problems I am experiencing. You are not really loved when you are married to a woman. When you are married to a man you are loved. In fact, two of my daughters are married to men. Their husbands are working too. They are good and helpful husbands. They depend very much on their husbands.

Filomena's arrangement is an unusual form of marrying to insure inheritance. But only the form is unusual. The goal is fundamental to marriage.

* * *

Neither men nor women can count on finding marriage emotionally satisfying. Men look to other men for companionship and esteem. Likewise, women rely on other women for many of their needs. Marriage does not exist primarily to provide emotional support. That is neither the object, nor usually a collateral benefit. Marriage exists to protect property and ensure the orderly inheritance of land, herds, or other assets.

Portrait F

Constance Tanui

Kobujoi is a beautiful community overlooking the Rift Valley. From Kakamega or Kisumu, a traveler reaches Kobujoi by taking three *matatus* [vans which are the basic local transportation] or by driving, unless rain has swamped the roads. On one of my visits, there had been rain. Twice my car slipped off the road, but I was immediately helped by hordes of young men who ran to lift the vehicle back onto the road. When I arrived, I asked for Constance, and was quickly taken to her, since everyone knows her. She greeted me enthusiastically, but was in the middle of work, so she asked a young relative to take me to her home to meet her mother and await her there.

Her farm is wide and treeless with a large permanent house and several outbuildings. A water pump stands near the verandah. From the verandah, there is a broad view of the neighboring hills through which I had come with such difficulty. Cows and dogs mingle in front of the house.

After the young woman left, Constance's mother and I felt a bit shy with each other since I don't speak Kinandi. Soon Constance came and talked about herself and her community at length. Constance is a strong, straight woman with a squared face and an easy laugh. Talking with her is a pleasure because she enjoys explaining. Even a new acquaintance can see that she is a talented teacher.

> I was born near Kitale, around 1942. Our parents did not know how to write or read, so they could not record our ages. My father was working for a white settler, and we lived on his farm. We came to Nandi when I was ten years old. My father had three wives then, and later married two more. My mother is the first. She had only daughters.

When I was fourteen and had been in school for five years, my sister and I were circumcised. After the surgery, we stayed in the house because no one is allowed to see you during that time. We stayed for nearly a year and a half. During the day, we stayed strictly inside, but at night we would walk around outside. You can see people through the window, but you cannot be seen by anybody.

We got fat. We could only exercise in the evenings, walking outside around the house. There were some things we could do. We could mud the house, smear the floors, wash the eating calabashes, any work we could do without being seen.

Normally, each girl is at her own home for that time unless a girl's family has nothing to feed her. If they have nothing, they'll ask another family, "Can my daughter stay with your daughter?"

At the end of it, we were taught how you will have to stay with your husband, the respect you have to give your husband, what you can tell your husband and what you cannot tell. You know men can try to seduce any woman, even a married woman, so if another man tells you some things, you say, "No, I don't like that" but you don't tell your husband. They did not really teach us how to do sex.

Some of the things we were taught I don't think are applicable now. We don't circumcise our daughters anymore. My sons were circumcised but not my daughters. The church has come and told us not to do that, so it has stopped.

When I came out, I continued with school up through form two. Then I went for training in social work. After my training, I came here and taught social work. We taught young girls how to promote health, personal care, housewifery, gardening, nutrition. Now there are boys doing this social work too.

I really liked that teaching, but eventually I had to change from teaching to doing direct work with the farmers. You see, there are now many girls here who have finished form four. I couldn't teach girls who had finished form four when I have only finished form two because they would not respect me. In my work with the farmers, I encouraged building cattle dips, schools, and all kinds of community work.

I didn't marry because my mother had only daughters but a son is essential, so I had to take responsibility for her. I'm the first. Usually it's the last one who does that, but my sister didn't want to, so I did. When I started teaching, I looked for land, and brought my mother here. At first, I built a small hut, and she stayed there. I brought a child of my sister to stay with us. You know its not easy in an African home to stay without children. We are two, my mother and I, and we have my community, my church. So, if you compare mine with another family with a husband and wife, it is the same.

We like children, so I brought a child of my sister first, then my cousin came here, and we had also a friend who came and stayed here.

After I got the land and bought some cows, I had my firstborn boy. I have five children of my own. The three oldest are boys, the last two are girls. When my son was born, my cousin stayed on, but the rest left. I educated that cousin

Constance Tanui at home

up to form six.[1] My own children have had a lot of schooling too. The first one went to University and graduated in 1990. The second-born also went up to University and he graduated last year. The third boy one is now in form four. He didn't do well last year, so he repeated. I have a daughter who is now in second year in a private university in Nairobi, Daystar. That school is very expensive. The last is away at school. She's in form three. So now, they are all gone. I am left with only my mother. I would like to have some more children come to live here with me, girls or boys, it doesn't matter.

We want more children. We always ask my eldest, "What's happening? Why don't you have any children yet?"

My youngest son, my third born. says "You people leave us alone," He has read a lot about Europe, so he says, "European families don't force their children to give many grandchildren. As long as you finish schooling, you are left alone. But you still pressure us. Why can't you leave us alone?" We are waiting for a grandson.

Life here in Kobujoi is changing very much. Our children don't hear us, and we wonder, 'How, why, did that happen?' because children should listen to their elders, but they don't.

Most of my generation didn't go to school, but the children went to school. Now they know English, they know Swahili, they have gone to Eldoret. The parents have not reached Eldoret, have not reached Nairobi. The children know things we, the parents, don't know. The children look at us as ignorant. They don't listen to us because they think we don't have anything to tell, but

1. The educational system was reorganized in 1989. Until then, form six was the end of secondary school, but form two and form four were also logical stopping points with terminal exams. After the reorganization, secondary school ended with form four, which means twelve years in principle, but many students repeat one or more years.

they should. Before schools came, there were elders teaching the young ones. Now the young don't listen.

In Kobujoi, we have better roads, not really good, but better than how it was when I came here. Development has brought a lot of things, good and bad. Now we have diseases we have never had. We have visitors from outside who dress differently from the way we do and in the end, the young people grab that very quickly.

There are good things too, of course. We have telephones now, we have light, and we can reach the district headquarters easily. School supervisors can reach us very easily. We can export: we take our things from the garden, from the *shambas*, like milk from the cows, we can take to the factory. We can get our produce to the nearest shop to sell. I think those are the good things.

In the future, we shall have more robbers. We shall have maybe more diseases because people will be moving. Maybe in twenty years we can have tarmacked road and movements will be very easy. People here will be able to move even to Nairobi. We can have an easier life because we have more things to transport to towns, and maybe we will have factories here in Kobujoi itself for tea, for milk, for vegetables. But life will be more difficult. We shall have more robbers and thugs.

Many of our young people go outside. Now as I talk, four of my children are in Nairobi. And I know many children from other homes who have gone to Nairobi, Eldoret, or Kisumu.

I worry that my sons may want to settle in town, not come home. We tell them, "Bring money, we'll build you a house." They laugh, "Oh, how do you know we'll like to come there and settle?" But they know they'll have a share of my land. Everyone knows that I have to get some people on the land, so I'm sure one of them will come to build a house here.

As for the daughters, we don't know where they will go, because they have to get married somewhere. When they are married, they have to go to their husband's place, so they are not thinking of settling anywhere for themselves.

4

Raising Children for an Inscrutable World

Children are born for many reasons: because adults love them, and each other; or because women may be unable, reluctant, or forbidden to use contraception. Adey Addeha lives in Wajir on what she can earn selling miraa. On that small income, she struggles to feed her nine children. Yet she hopes eventually to have fifteen.

But the realities of meagre land and high school fees lead many women to want smaller families. Many who already have numerous children, and love them, regret not having used contraceptives earlier. Filomena Jeptanui is a schoolteacher and farmer near Kobujoi who was born in 1959.

> You know, in any family, the first thing is to have children. When we were getting our first children, we had not even heard of family planning, but later we decided that's enough. We could see that life is becoming very hard. We have six, but if we had known earlier, we could have had fewer.

Ironically, in the course of accomodating themselves to new customs from the outside, many people have abandoned traditional practices that effectively spaced births. Roselyne Choge tells of a widespread traditional means of spacing births.

> When a woman gives birth, she was considered unclean for some time, and the man would sleep outside with the cows, up to the time when the child could communicate. So when a child could be sent to bring something, the father would know it was time for another child, and he could come home. But now, after delivery you can finish one month and you are pregnant. We

> stayed apart for about three months, but that was too long. Now, I don't think people would stay that long.

Although Choge is speaking of Nandis, many other groups have essentially the same custom. Among Luos, the husband's return is initiated by the wife. When the child is old enough, the mother gives the child a calabash of liquid to carry to the father. This is the signal for him to return.

From the earliest times, in every community, some women used abortifacient herbs to conceal the results of incestuous or otherwise shameful liaisons. But herbs were not used to limit family size. Until recently, there was no reason to do so.

Most young women now think about limiting their families. Whether or not they are able to depends on their husband's attitude. Elizabeth Ndunde knows several men who encourage their wives to stop.

> You'll hear men saying. "If you get another child, you'll have to take care of it yourself."
>
> I met a young man of twenty-seven who was going to have a vasectomy. In his tribe, if a man has children outside, he is expected to bring them home. So even if his wife had her tubes tied, he'd have too many children to care for.

Priscilla Nyette, a Nairobi housemaid born in 1969, and her husband set a limit of three children before they married. After their third child was born, she had her tubes tied, with her husband's complete agreement.

Before she was married or betrothed, Mariamu Khalifa, said she would like to have as many as she could afford. She thought the number of children she would have should depend on her economic circumstances. "I don't want a very large family, maybe with only four children, but not beyond six. This will depend on the way of life we have. Maybe I will be still working and if my husband has work, we can maybe afford five children." When we talked again after her marriage and the birth of her first child, her views had not changed.

Attitudes about desirable family size have changed quickly as poverty has deepened. In 1990, when I was teaching in a village secondary school in Kakamega District, I often asked girls, and sometimes asked boys, how many children they hoped to have. Almost all answered quite emphatically that they would certainly not have a large family. When pressed for numbers, most girls said not more than six, or five. The lowest number mentioned was four, by a girl who came from extreme

Rosemary Shinachi at Shihome Clinic

poverty. In dramatic contrast, the five girls I interviewed in 1996 from the same school gave much lower numbers. Three said they wanted two children, and two said they wanted only one so they could afford school fees. I asked whether they would consider having no children, but all five emphatically rejected that suggestion.

Rosemary Shinachi, who oversees the work of a rural clinic in Western Province told us that contraception has begun to be widely used by rural women. When she started it was uncommon, but now half the women in her region use some form. Injections are the most common, both because women fear forgetting to take a pill and because many want to conceal contraceptive use from their husbands.

> Competition between co-wives used to be a major reason for having many children, but no longer. Sex preference is now the major reason. People here would like to have boys. They feel a boy will stay with his mother but a girl will marry away and leave the parents alone.
>
> When family planning started here, it used to be restricted to proven bearers. The clinics would say, "You must first prove that this woman can deliver." Now we even serve schoolgirls if they come. Most parents would not like their children to come, but once a client comes, they should not go away without some method.
>
> These days, you don't need to push people to come. Even women who haven't been to school come when we have a mobile clinic.
>
> Now prestige is not through having large families. You know when we talk to a woman who has a very large family, she will say, "We were stupid. We didn't know in time. But we can tell our children."
>
> Some men come. Some are sent to collect pills for their wives. When a man comes, we discuss everything. Maybe in my clinic I just have one method, but I discuss others. I tell them, "A vasectomy will not disturb anything. You will be happy with your wife, but the sperms will not pass."

> We also tell them of safe days, but most men don't accept that one. Maybe they work elsewhere, so if they come home on a non-safe day, they wouldn't like to go away before they share. It is a bit hard for men, but there's one here who uses calendar methods for religious reasons.

Flores Mwang'ombe, the farmer who complained that her husband ignored his family after he began drinking, wanted to stop bearing children for medical reasons as well as economic ones. But, she had to accede to her husband's wishes.

> We never practiced any family planning. We just left it to God. I gave birth to all the ten children at hospital. So every time I went to give birth the nurses and helpers attending me reminded me of family planning. I was interested. I didn't want more children because when I was giving birth I had problems.
>
> But the husband was against it because his mother died when he was young so he didn't have brothers and sisters. Having many children was making up for what he didn't have in childhood, a kind of revenge for loneliness.

Although some husbands now agree to limit family size, many more do not. A wife has three options if her husband objects. She can accede to his wishes and give him as many children as he wants, she can use birth control secretly, or she can openly refuse to bear more children than she wants. Only the first two are common. Women often accede despite economic hardship.

Some women use methods which do not require their husband's co-operation and which he cannot detect. But we have seen that many women fear their husbands will marry other wives if she doesn't give him (or his mother) enough children. Many of the women in the groups in Mumias, Nasianda and Mirere used secret methods with trepidation.

> Nasianda 1: We are afraid to plan families because our husbands may use it as an excuse to marry. If he asks us to do it, it may be a sign that he wants a second wife.
>
> Nasianda 2: What are you talking about? He does not just get married to a second wife. He beats you up for planning the family.
>
> Mirere 1: When they do these family planning efforts, some people are finding it unhealthy because women here have to work very hard. Those who take injections become unhealthy. If you're taking pills, sometimes you'll still get pregnant. And the coil sometimes disappears. So there are problems.
>
> Mirere 2: Most of the men in the area do not support this. Most women just hide [contraceptive use]. So when they get these problems, they don't want their husbands to know.

HH: Do most women here have to use something secret from their husbands?

(Many voices chorus "Yes!")

Mirere 3: Some men may agree to family planning before marriage, but then after the marriage, he will change his mind. Then he doesn't allow his wife to use contraception because he wants to show that he is a real man.

Although their husbands' objections prevent many women from using contraceptives, sometimes it works the other way. Mitau Silantoi, who was born in 1959 in a cattle-herding family, is limiting her family only because her husband insists.

Oruko Omina and her husband agreed before marriage to have a small family. They stopped after having three girls. He did not object, but his relatives kept pressuring her to have more children. Now they are pressuring him to take another wife and provide sons.

> I've told him he can go ahead for all I care because I have done my bit. It is just so difficult economically and socially to bring up children in this era. Who wants to send herself to her grave before her age because of children? Whether I have ten, or two, or one, I'm still a mother. If that is what is the most important thing to a woman, I've got it.

Omina has helped other women to get their husband's agreement.

> One time at home[1] a neighbor who had eight said, "You know this uncle [her husband] won't even let me take those pills. Do you think there's something I can take so that he won't know?" I said, "You can get an injection, or there are other things you can do, but would you like me to go and talk to him?" She thought she would be murdered, but I went to my uncle and we got to talking.
>
> He talked about the problem of school fees. I asked, "How about if you had another one?"
>
> He said, "Oh, my God, I don't know what we would do."
>
> I said, "But Auntie is in the child-bearing years. What are you doing about it?"
>
> "Oh, she should go to a women's clinic," he said. "If she gets another one, she'll have to take care of it."
>
> It's so sad when I go home and see fourteen year olds who are mothers. Your mother is angry with you because she has ten already and you are adding an eleventh. I don't think this thing about women's empowerment is addressing the real issue until the rural woman gets to be educated about her own body.

1. Although she and her husband live in Nairobi, she refers to her husband's family land as "home." Many city people continue to think of their rural base as home, spend weekends and holidays there, and eventually retire to the farm.

Oruko Omina at home

Right now our girls have absolutely no idea of how their bodies work. I think about myself. The first time I had my menstrual period I was shocked. I had no idea what it was. My mother had not talked to me about it.

HH: Were you among the first of your girlfriends to get it?

I don't know. Before I got to high school, we didn't talk about it and when I started, I had no idea what this was.

HH: Did you ask your mother about it?

I couldn't! I didn't know what had caused it. I thought all sorts of crazy things. I thought it was something to do with a boy, so if I told my mother she would kill me. That was not talked about at all, at all!

HH: How long was it before you said something to somebody?

When I was just starting high school. There were bigger girls and they stared talking about sanitary pads and things like that, so I got to know, "Oh, this thing is normal!" It could have been even about two years. When I was much younger, I saw the elder girls washing their clothes. I used to wonder where that blood was coming from, was it coming from the anus. And then when we started talking, I heard stories from older girls like, "If you don't want to get pregnant, take a sanitary pad you have used and put it under the roof thatch, and even if you sleep with a man you won't get pregnant," and all sots of crazy things. That was not a good way to learn.

FATHERS AND CHILDREN

> Most African men leave the controlling of children to women. When a child behaves well, he says he is his child and when a child misbehaves he is the mother's child. The man can refuse to pay school fees and therefore it is the woman who takes the responsibility.
>
> —Karen Mahiti, milk trader, Nairobi

> I can't advise my sons. It is only fathers who advise sons. So if you find the father drunk it is very hard.
>
> —Joan Kanini, textiles trader, Nairobi

These contrasting comments reveal more than differing viewpoints. They indicate a complexity in expectations for fathers. Responsibility for small children often belongs exclusively to mothers. Growing the food to feed them and raising money for their school fees[2] may rest entirely on the mother. Usually, small children eat their meals in the kitchen with their mother, while the father is served separately in another room.

Fathers have an important role in raising sons after they leave early childhood. As they grow up, eventually boys are invited to take their meals with their father, and sitting in the kitchen with their mothers becomes inappropriate. Growing boys are encouraged to regard the tenderness they shared with their mother as babyish, and those bonds loosen. In the past, groups of adolescent boys would sleep in the home of a male elder, but that no longer happens. Through formal initiation and informal men's conversation, boys are taught to treat women with little respect, which diminishes the mothers' influence. Since mothers are gradually removed from guiding sons, and elders no longer have the large role they once played, there is a void to be filled by fathers and other adult males.

With daughters, however, the father's role diminishes as they mature. A father can play with a small daughter, but when she reaches puberty, she is taught to be more reticent with her father, and he is expected to respect a growing distance between them. Nevertheless, one woman in the Mirere group said that "since the father is the most important person in the family," fathers should help guide daughters as well as sons.

Many, many women said that mothers cannot advise sons. Mariamu Khalifa believes fathers are better guides for sons than mothers, but thinks her mother guided her brother well.

---

2. Although primary school became free again in 2003, parents must still pay for secondary school and preschool. Chapters 5 and 6 discuss schooling before and after the abolition of school fees.

> For boys, it is better if they have conversations with their father. But for my brother's case, his father is far away. My mother has to teach the son. Maybe she may see that some of the things my father used to do to her were not good, so she has to advise the son, "Do not do this to your wife."

Some women we talked with in Nasianda were wrestling with raising a son without a good role model.

> Woman 2: Even if the father is abusive, we try to tell our sons and daughters to respect them. This is their father and they must respect him no matter what he does. The father is supposed to take care of the home. A drunkard father may make noise, but if he takes care of the family well, it is okay. However, we do tell our boys the importance of being decent and responsible, no matter how the father may behave.
>
> Woman 1: If the father is not responsible, the mother will have to talk to her son and ask him, "Suppose you behave that way, how will your home be?"

Several college graduates with professional positions credit their success to their father. Dekha Ibrahim was one.

> Traditionally, girls fear their dad and don't go out with them, but my father told us stories. He was with us in the evenings. I grew up being very close to my father. I travelled with him and I remember many times his friends telling him, "You are spoiling your daughter. Why are you treating her like a boy?"

When there was a crisis in Elizabeth Anton's childhood, her father put his children's welfare ahead of both his marriage and his employment. "After my mother passed away, the father married a second wife who was mistreating us. He was working in Nairobi, but when he learned what was going on, he chased the wife away and stayed home with us himself for quite some time."

Except for Elizabeth Anton and a few professional women, none of the women we talked with recalled their fathers as gentle, loving, or interested in their welfare. Many women of all levels of education and economic circumstances spoke of their fathers as very harsh. This was not always a criticism. Many expressed their approval of a very strict upbringing and were grateful that their parents had been harsh.

Irene Katete's father sent her to live with her grandmother when she was nine months old, and showed his dislike when she visited home in childhood. Catherine Obungu was very much afraid of her father, and glad when he was away in prison, because it spared the family many fights and beatings.

But a generation later, fathers may be beginning to change. A few women praised their husbands' fathering skills. Jane Gathege speaks of the contrast between her husband, a schoolteacher, and fathers of the previous generation.

> My children can play and joke with their father, but we would never have done that. Our parents believed in total discipline. Whatever mistake we made, it was a beating. My dad's harshness used to frustrate my mother so much that she would take it out on us.
>
> My husband's dad was much harsher than my Dad was, so he feels he should not do the same.

Informal Education

> The future will be very difficult. The best thing we can do is to have few children and to educate them. Also, we should teach them respect.
>
> —Agnetta Owire, farmer whose father refused to educate his daughters

Many women are deeply dissatisfied with the way their lives have turned out. The reasons are beyond their control: years of corrupt governance and an international economy that impoverished the vast majority of Kenyans; and a culture which permits men to mistreat their wives and neglect their children. Most women have limited power to protect their children from these injustices. They can only prepare them.

The obligations of parents have increased in recent times. Before urbanization, there often was a village to raise each child. Grandmothers had responsibility for small children while mothers were at work in the fields. The elders, not the parents, provided sex education and chaperonage when children became youths.

But now, urbanization has increased mobility. Many young people grow up with neither a network of elders nor a community with shared values. This has greatly increased the parents' role, while the issues facing young people and their caretakers have become more complex.

Many Muslim women were secluded as girls and young women. As the roles available to women expand, they are ambivalent about the degree of seclusion or protection they want to give their daughters. Saadia Abubakar [Portrait E] represents this ambivalence.

> For the sake of freedom of movement, our daughters should not be restricted when they go out with a reason, but they should not go out to waste time. Roaming around aimlessly should not be allowed. If one of my

daughters is going to visit someone, I must know who she is going to visit and the dress she is putting on.

Dekha Ibrahim's advice is formed by her interpretation of Islam and her reflections on a rash of killings in Wajir, her home.

In the Islamic community, you are supposed to raise your children equally. So they both have to learn to do all the work. My maternal uncle is a very good practitioner of Islam. He helps his wife literally with everything. When you visit him, we will be shocked. He will be fetching water and taking it to the bathroom; he will help you with your tea; prepare a bed for you and all that. And how could he do that if he didn't learn when he was a little boy?

HH: What do you think about protecting daughters more than sons keeping them at home or providing escorts when they go out?

It depends on where you live. Right now, in Wajir, though we have gone through all that violence, we don't fear somebody raping a daughter when she just steps outside the compound. I think overprotectiveness is not necessary. When she goes out in the afternoon, she doesn't need a special escort. But at night, anybody requires an escort. That is OK. But even a boy, if he has a business to do, he does. But if there is no business outside the home, why loiter? Loitering is not acceptable in Islam whether it is a daughter or son. They should have a reason for being outside the home. He shouldn't loiter outside because he is a boy. If he loiters as a boy today, then he will loiter as a husband tomorrow.

Consolata Mombua, who has one daughter and four sons, surprised me with her ideas about raising boys. "It should be left to their fathers to teach boys during their adolescence and to prepare them to be good men in future. They should be told that they should choose a decent girl, a girl that is respectful. They should choose girls who can bear with them under all circumstances." I was struck that she emphasized choosing a wife who can "bear with them under all circumstances" rather than treating the wife well in all circumstances.

Angelina Mganga had a very hard life working as a bar girl. After she became a Christian, new friends were able to help her find other work and her life improved. Her advice to her nine children grows from the troubles of her past life.

I teach my girls about Christian life and to read the Bible and to avoid men. I tell them to learn from my example of getting into a difficilt life. I also teach them to be selective in choosing their marriage partners so that they may not end up divorcing. I have told my sons to avoid concentrating on any leisure things or any bad ways but to concentrate on school and try to get jobs they

> can rely on. That's when they can think about marrying. They should avoid moving with girls at their early ages and think about their futures first. I also tell them to choose good wives in future and to respect them.

The question that most divides women with different attitudes toward changing social norms is the question of women's independence. Oruko Omina has a very modern perspective on teaching her daughters how to relate to men. "My daughters are assertive, and I'm very happy about it. Their father always tells them, 'You will not get men.'

"They say, 'Look at mother. She got a man.'

"I say, 'If being strong means not getting a man, that's fine.'"

Sofia Muthoni, the Murang'aa teacher with a zero grazing project, does not value independence. She stresses the importance of submission. "When a girl is small, she must learn to understand that the husband is the head of the house and therefore she should respect him whether she has got money or not.

Even very traditonal women may have broad aspirations for their daughters. Dekha Ibrahim's mother defied Somali tradition in order to raise an intelligent and capable daughter.

> A woman is supposed to stay indoors for forty days after childbirth. Sometime after the fortieth day the child is taken outside the house for the first time. Traditionally, girls are supposed to be taken out in the dark of the night when there is no moonlight. If they are taken out during the full moon, they will be very bright and they will challenge men. My mother reversed this saying, "Who wants a stupid child taken out in the dark? I want my daughter to be bright so I will take her out on a full moon day."

Dekha works in an office and has a modern perspective, yet community, extended family, respect for tradition, and a firm grounding in religion are her core values. She believes it is vital for girls to be economically self-sufficient, as well as grounded in their culture and religion. Her explanation for the decline of respect is quite different from that of many older, less educated women.

> My daughter and son spend more of their time with my mother than with me. My mother lives close by so we are always together. This is very important because the children then can grow up not as individuals, but as part of a community right from when they are young.
>
> One thing that our modern society now does not have, and which we should develop, is dialogue with the children. If you lock yourself in your job and the children lock themselves up in their schools, if they don't see their

> grandfather and grandmother, don't see their uncles and aunts, then the social fabric becomes loose. They will not respect elders.

Generational Conflicts

In any society that is changing rapidly, splits between generations are exaggerated. When asked about changes, nearly all rural women older than forty answer that young people no longer respect their elders. There is more to this than the complaints by the older generation that are a part of any culture. It is exacerbated by rapid social change, by the spread of formal education, by recently increasing poverty, by migration, and by new contact with other cultures. The young grow up in a new world, and believe that their parents cannot give them answers to the dilemmas of their generation. It is easy for children whose parents have not been schooled to believe them ignorant and out of touch with modern realities. Tragically, if the parents respect education, they may share these views.

Any change that an elder disapproves of may be perceived as lack of respect. Zuhura Ali, the nurse who brought several nieces to live with her, gives changes in dress as an example.

> Customs are really changing, some for the better and others not. Traditionally, women had special way of dressing, but nowadays, our children have adopted the western ways and styles of dressing, which does not please the elders. That is seen as lack of respect.

Jerusha Wawuda, a middle-aged Wundanyi farmer, feels defeated in her attempts to guide her children.

> Things have changed a great deal since I was growing up. When your mother says no to something we were taught not to question.
>
> Now, the moment you try to show a girl that you want to sit with her, they have no time to listen. If I want to say something, I have to be very tactical. I have to go to my son or daughter, but before the children used to come to you. So I think generally things have changed from high to low.

Elders are not the only people who hold these opinions. Although Njoki Ngige is only twenty-four years old, she agrees.

> Earlier, children had a lot of discipline, but now children are undisciplined. Some have turned to be prostitutes, others have turned to be devil-worshippers. The cause of these changes is lack of money. Because of lack of employment

> and lack of money, people are turning to be thieves. Even some who have degrees are just loitering with no work.

Margaret Njoroge, a Lusigetti farmer born in 1948, had a different explanation for why young people no longer respect their elders. "Life between husband and wife has changed greatly. Many times, the husband comes home drunk. If the woman asks for some money, the man rises up saying many things and quarrels start. This happens in front of children and this is where the low rate of dignity begins."

When unschooled parents educate their children, they are especially conscious of the gulf between the world in which they were raised and the world in which their children will live. They are distressed that the younger, educated generation has less respect for elders than they themselves had when young. They often feel powerless to guide their children. This sense of helplessness, a surprise to me, was an often repeated theme. Tikako Kores, one of the Ilbissil group, who never attended school, expressed the disempowerment that disturbs so many parents.

> Once they are going to school, it is hard to try to bring them that life that used to be at home. They are hard to talk to, not the same sort of children they used to be.
>
> With daughters, we mothers must do it all. Fathers usually tell the daughters, "talk to the mothers." Whatever we try to tell them, most children say in their heart, "Oh, she just couldn't be talking to me."
>
> Children used to learn about their culture naturally as they grew and experienced the world. But into that way of life has now come the teachings of another way. Putting the two together, the child can have a mixture of two different ways and not really know what is right.

In response, her neighbor, Soila Tanei, who finished primary school, described how she has taught her children to live in two disparate realms of contemporary African life.

> It's not a problem in my family, because I manage the two cultures. I still teach them about the traditional way of life, but they are not supposed to be that way. Since they have education, they can follow another way of life. Mixing two cultures seems to be working, although they are still young. During the week, I have books. I read them to bed. And I later elaborate to them what the book says. On Fridays I take them home to my parents so that they can know what they must do there. They can help raise the animals.

Joyce Mitau, who attended primary school for five years until her marriage, echoed Soila.

> I have also to make sure that the girl knows how to milk, how to bring the cows in, how to respect the elders, how to serve them, and how to interact with those other, more traditional girls. Every weekend we go home and stay there so they can have time to see what other girls see. I don't want them to know just educated city and town life.

Town Life versus Country Life

> One thing I remember about my childhood with a lot of nostalgia is the freedom. If you are told to collect firewood, it is not a bad thing. When you go to the forest there are so many things you want to do. There is wild fruit you can pick. You have a rope to tie firewood. Before you collect firewood, you make a swing with the rope and swing for a long time, eat wild fruits and have a lot of fun.
>
> —Elizabeth Ndunde, Nairobi office worker
> who grew up in rural Nakuru

Many women throughout the socio-economic spectrum have lived in both town and country and expressed definite preferences for themselves or, more commonly, for their children. Those who preferred to raise their children in town cited the advantage of having better schools.

Karen Mahiti's father was one of the many who left his rural home for employment in the city. He was unusual in bringing his daughter to stay with him so she could have a city education. Karen is grateful for this advantage. "When I was young, I stayed in Nairobi comfortably with my father so I was able to go school. My mother stayed home and worked on the farm. My first sister was already married. I was the only girl now, so my father had love for me and determination to educate me."

People who are employed in town may be much more prosperous than their rural relatives. Yet jobs in cities are scarce, and many who go to cities do not find what they had hoped for. Diane Kimunda was one of those. "I decided to come back home and educate my children here. In Mombasa, we depended on our little income only. We had no shamba, so we were not able to afford education."

Many others prefer to raise their children "at home" because they consider rural life more wholesome. Susan Omulindi, a Mumias farmer born in 1963, came home from Nairobi so her five children could grow up in the country. "I didn't want the children to get used to the city type of life. Children learn bad habits in the city. Children raised in the country are more respectful and easier to guide."

Concern over the erosion of respect leads many to prefer raising their children at their rural homes. Although Flores Mwang'ombe was more prosperous in town, she preferred raising her children at home for cultural reasons. "I prefer home life as compared to town life, because at home the children are involved in daily household activities like digging, which prepares them for their future. But in town, they are exposed to funny things."

Cecilia Kimundo of *Kitivo Women's Group* prefers to raise her children in her village near Wundanyi because she dislikes the mixed ethnicities and different customs in cities. "I think life at home is better. In town there is a lot of outside influence from other tribes and other kinds of life. Here they grow up in a specified community with one religion, and it helps them."

Sex Education

Giving guidance about sexual matters is one area where parents have dramatically less community support and more responsibility than formerly. During adolescence, young people used to sleep in same-sex groups under the supervision of an elder. These elders were responsible for sex education and for the guidance appropriate to that stage of life. Oruko Omina was too young to have experienced the collective instruction by village grannies, but had been told about it.

> One of my grandmothers in the village told me what used to happen in the past was that when girls and boys reached the point where they were beginning to be sexually active, all the girls of the village slept in one grandmother's house, and all the boys slept in one grandfather's house. the role of the grandmother was to teach them how to behave when they get married, how to behave with men, and so on. My grandmother said that it's not very easy for men to abstain, so they allowed the men to get together with a woman, and fondle, and release their sperm on her thighs, but not penetrate.
>
> When I was dating my husband, we used to do that. If you are feeling very sexual, you fondle and the man is relieved. The woman, if she's never had sex, doesn't know whether she's relieved or not, but she is left feeling nice. There are no pregnancies, and girls still marry as virgins.
>
> But that no longer goes on because of contact with westerners. That kind of teaching, if it was brought back, would be very useful.

Simanya Machocho told us about the traditional Taita sex education.

Where we were kept there were elders to teach us. They would come up with hidden things for your eyes only. They show you something and you never say what it is. Among yourselves you don't even tell. For the rest of your life you are threatened. It's kind of a bad omen to tell: you might never be married because what kind of a man would want to marry a woman who is not going to keep secrets?

Everything was explained about sexual matters, and that's why the pretest was how to keep a secret. So whatever they tell you about how to live with a man you are not supposed to share with anybody.

After that we were to keep away from younger girls because we could be tempted to tell juniors what happened. And they were curious to know because they are going to be the next lot. Everyone is supposed to learn for themselves and experience for themselves.

Traditonally, parents were supposed to leave their children's sex education entirely to grandparents and other elders. They were never supposed to discuss sexual matters with their children. Since parents now have new responsibilities in this area, we asked, "What should daughters be told about boys?" and "What should sons be told about girls?"

A group of farm women gathered at the home of Dorah Zighe in Wundanyi had a passionate discussion about how to handle sex education. They were diverse in age, education, and degree of economic security.

Dorah Zighe [mid forties]: It is difficult for a mother and daughter to talk frankly. Especially if the daughter is more educated than the mother, there is a gap. The mothers fear the daughters because they feel inferior. When my mother tried, I would not listen, but she did try.

With my aunt or another older relative, it was easier. Whatever knowledge I had was from my aunts and others outside, not directly from my mother, although my mother was very willing to talk to me.

Lillian Kibuka [recent high school graduate]: You must do it before they are mature, before they get their menstrual cycle. They should be prepared early and be informed about what will happen if they involve themselves with boys, so they will not get early pregnancy.

Olive Majala [probably in her forties]: I did not discuss anything about men with my mother. Nothing at all.

Roda [early twenties]: I just learned from friends. Even if I had something to ask my mother, I felt shy and did not ask.

Sophie Mwangemi [mid fifties, five years of school]: When my mother would come up with that topic, I would look for a reason to leave the house. I think what the teacher taught me in class was enough.

HH: What will you try to tell your daughters and when will you do it?

A young woman: I feel shy about it. It will be better if they go to another woman to learn.

Mary Msinga [the translator]: That is according to our custom. We were brought up with mothers not saying anything to daughters about this. We[3] would like to have a forum where we gather together, maybe two or three mothers and daughters. Then we can try to talk to them as a group. It will be easier. Maybe that will succeed, but approaching your own mother is difficult.

Karen Mahiti used to have a generally secretive approach to issues concerning sexuality, but has recently decided that she needs to discuss birth control openly with her daughter.

I conceived when I was still in form four. Once I noticed that I was pregnant, I was ready to marry. I did not tell my parents because I felt shy.

When I got married, family life was just a secret. Since I was a staunch Catholic, I was not allowed to use contraceptives. My husband he has never used a condom but I protected myself secretly.

Today's generation is in a better position because things are talked about freely. The use of birth control is common. Since there are a lot of diseases, there is no way children are going to be safe unless they are talked to about these ways.

My oldest daughter got pregnant while she was still in school. She decided not to marry the boyfriend because she wanted to finish education first. Her father also supported that decision. I am glad because most African men would not take the responsibility of such a girl. Many men would chase her and her mother away because the mother is the one who did not teach her daughter how to behave.

I am sure it would have been better if I talked to her about this, but I didn't want to say anything contrary to the church. After what happened to her, I wanted to be sure to protect my younger daughter. I talked to her about family planning but told her that this should not encourage her to have boyfriends.

3. She is the YWCA liaison to women's groups in the area. Here she is talking about a YWCA project.

Portrait G

A. I. C. Girls' Primary Boarding School

The A. I. C. (African Inland Church) Girls' School in Kajiado has enabled many Maasai girls to stay in school when their fathers wanted to marry them off.

Entering Kajiado by road, you cannot fail to notice the school. The gate is right on the main road, and well marked, welcoming visitors. A visitor is greeted by the nearest person, and taken to whomever is on duty. Some of my visits to the school have been unannounced, yet each time someone would talk with me and answer a long, wide-ranging list of questions. The headmistress, Mrs. Priscilla Nangurai, dresses in fashionable western clothes, but honors the beauty of local culture. As you enter her home, there is a long wall covered with a bright display of Maasai beaded jewelry. Mrs. Nangurai is a dynamic, noticeable woman with a true vocation as a teacher. From the time she started secondary school, she wanted to be a teacher. She spent the early part of her career teaching at Kajiado High School. During that time, she was also very active in the affairs of the A. I. C. church, so when the former headmistress of the primary school resigned, the Board of Governors appointed her. Through her creative efforts to keep girls in school, she has become well known in Kajiado, and abroad, as a crusader for girls' education.

> When I arrived here, I looked at the reports of how many girls had gone to secondary school, how many had dropped out, why they dropped. The numbers of pregnancies and forced marriages were alarming. So we started very quietly allowing girls to come back after giving birth. Now the Ministry of Education has allowed it officially, but before that we had to keep it a top

Susan Malaso teaching a class at A. I. C. primary school. Irene Katete is on the left

secret. When I'd admit young mothers from other schools, I'd say she couldn't tell the other girls, and I wouldn't tell the teachers. This year I have ten young mothers.

Later, I allowed girls to stay on until they were about to give birth, but the education officer saw a pregnant girl, so he chastised me because it was not allowed. What was I to do? Sometimes when I asked a girl, she would deny it.

Many girls used to drop out when their fathers found a husband. After they are threatened with marriage, I keep them here during school holidays. Before we fenced off the school, sometimes the bridegrooms would come to persuade them to leave. For the last three years I have not encountered any. I think the men now know that we are serious.

If a girl has been threatened with marriage, we don't let her go home again unless we're very sure because there are parents who'll pretend everything is okay but once we let the girls go they'll start everything all over again. And sometimes they try and get her pregnant because they think when they got her pregnant that is the end, she can't come back.

We also have some former students who still cannot go home, so they come here for holidays throughout high school. There is even one girl in university who still comes here because she doesn't want to be forced into marriage.[1]

Marriage is common at thirteen. There are cases of eleven, even nine or ten, but that's not tradition. I've talked to some of the parents who give away girls when they are young. They send her away early because she's not yet able able to make decisions. They think, "Daddy says I should do this," but when they are about fifteen, they know they should go to school.

Now, my policies are becoming known, so if a girl is at another school and marriage has been discussed and the mother is not happy about it, she will

1. In 2003, there were forty-five primary students who had to stay at school for this reason. In addition, twenty-eight secondary students and one university student returned to A. I. C. during their holidays.

try to bring the girl here. The last two years, I have received three cases from other schools. But I insist she makes arrangements, gets uniforms, gets the fees, exercise books.[2]

Some of the fathers around here say, "I am not going to take my daughter to A.I.C. I will not be able to get her when I want."

There have been many cases of girls who started here and then when they are about standard five or six, marriageable age, the father would come and say, "I am not able to pay school fees."

We will tell him, "I want school fees. If you do not pay school fees, I will report you." They are scared of the police, so they pay. If it's not a case of marriage arrangements, but real hardship, I say, "You continue paying what you can. The rest of the money I am going to forget."

Traditionally I am not supposed to face a man and make all these rules. Of course I was scared to threaten, and I do not know who to report and who not to report. But now I just face them, even though I am scared and ashamed.

Most of the teachers support me on this. There are some who feel, "If he wants to give her away, let him. Anyway she is not good in school.".

But I say, "Give the girl a chance. Whether she is bright or not, let us just try."

Mrs. Nangurai has also defied parents, and local tradition, in other ways.

One of the problems we have is circumcision. When the girls reach class five or six, they are circumcised. And circumcision brings them to another stage where they are treated as adults, ready for marriage. After circumcision you are free to have sexual relationships.

From the age of twelve or thirteen, when these girls go for holidays they might be circumcised. So, at that stage. we counsel them to think about their future. It has made some changes; pregnancies are less.

About sex education, we are being very careful because it is not accepted. When the medical staff comes here, we get them to mix with the girls because girls are freer with them. We tell them if any girl asks questions, answer them fully. But we as teachers, at the moment, cannot discuss this openly. In a private situation, I have told the teachers, if a girl asks, give her the correct information.

Most are of our girls are Maasai, but we have Kamba, we have Kalenjins, Taita, and some Indian girls. We tell them, "When you come through that gate, you belong to one family." Sometimes I wish some cleansing rain would come and wash out all these clashes, but here in school we don't have tensions between different tribes.

Money is very hard for us. We are continually looking for sponsors because we must try to keep these girls. That may be the last time the girl sees school. We are in debt. Sometimes, money promised by sponsors does not arrive.

---

2. This conversation took place before the Kibaki government reinstituted free primary education.

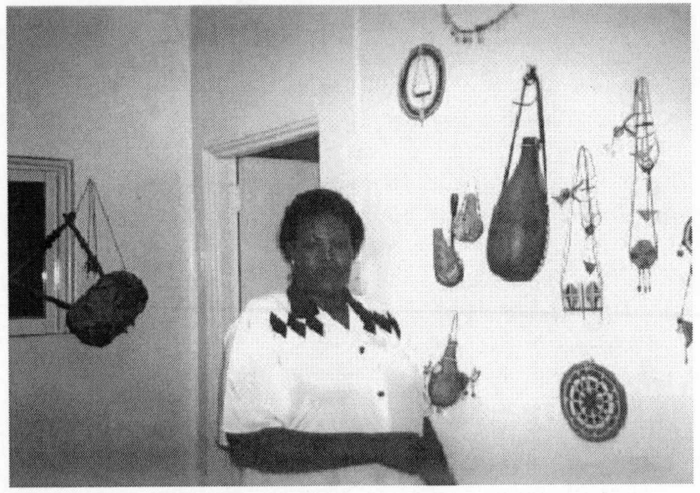

Mrs. Nangurai at home with her local crafts display

Although we have enough dormitories we do not have toilets in the dormitories. We lock them in at night for safety, so between nine and six if they have a short call [need to urinate] they cannot go. That has disturbed my mind but I have not been able to do anything because every time we get a little money, there is always another pressing issue.

There are still lots of girls around here who have not been to school, so I would like to continue going to the villages to persuade the parents to bring their girls to school.

The government is not providing anything. It started as cost sharing, "We shall provide this, you provide that." Then it changed gradually until everything is on the parents. Problems are going to be worse unless the government comes in and resumes their responsibilities.[3]

Parents are running the schools now and things are getting worse every year. Prices are going up, food especially. I see a lot of families where the parents are not able to cope.

At the end of last year, I saw every girl's parents, even the ones whose kids have been living here during holidays. The fathers came to me to say, "Thank you. My daughter left home under very difficult circumstances but I've come to say I'm sorry for what happened. I was just being a Maasai. I can't do what you are doing for my daughter. When I see other girls finishing their education, I understand why you want to keep my daughter at school." When the old men from different areas came to say, "Sorry," I knew we were getting somewhere.

Some girls here start school very late. I've a girl who started at fifteen. They find it childish being in lower classes, the activities are childish, so if they are

3. Of course, this changed in 2003.

not determined, they have a lot of confrontation with the teachers and the administration. When they're determined, they can succeed.

We had a training on self expression. It's called "Speak Out Program." We had training for the teachers to help these girls to be able to express themselves, not to keep problems to themselves. If the can't say directly what's worrying them, write a story about themselves, write a poem. After the training session, we had an open day where we invited parents and friends to see what the girls were doing. Through drama, they came out with the problems they are facing and had not been able to talk about.

As a result of the introduction of free primary education in 2003, enrollment went up dramatically at many day schools. That didn't happen at A.I.C. The deputy headmistress, Mrs. Katherine Karamboi, explained why.

In January and February, we had a drop in enrollment. With these new policies, the parents expected everything to be free. A boarding school is different from a day school. Even though the government is providing certain things like maize and beans, there are other things that need to be bought like tomatoes and onions. When the parents were told to produce something little, many were not willing. So we had to withdraw their children from school. Now, the parents are beginning to understand that we are doing more than just educating their daughters, we are also feeding and housing them, so we need a watchman, and many other things. Now, finally, most are willing to bring a little something.

When the school committee talks to the parents, they come to a consensus on the parents' contribution. But sometimes after they agree that they are going to pay a certain amount of money, when they meet again, they say, "We never agreed to that." In our Parent Teacher Association (PTA), we have so many people who are not educated. Even though we have the minutes, they still do not believe. They sometimes accuse us of having made it up because it is written.

The PTA meets in the middle of the term when we have a parents' day. And because of this parents visiting day, if they want to see their children, they have to come to these meetings, but it is mostly the mothers who come.

It is the man who has the money. When it comes to real paying, the women will be told, "You are the one who said you are going to pay, so can you go and pay."

There is a big advantage to being in a boarding school. Distances here are very great. Many children have to walk far to reach school. That is especially a problem for big girls. They may meet any boy on the way. In these times the parents are beginning to understand that even if she has been circumcised, she is at risk of disease if she befriends boys.

Rescue cases are sometimes brought through the district commissioner's [DC's], or chief's offices, or the girls come on their own. When they come alone, we have to send them to bring their chiefs so that we can be able to have the true picture of what happened, i.e., whether it is true that the girl is being forced into early marriage hence her running away, or it is a story that has been made up.

HH: Are most of the chiefs here quite sympathetic to your work or do they see you as interfering in family concerns?

At first they used to see us as interfering with the family life. But we have offered workshops for the chiefs on the importance of girl child education. They have come to understand and they are helping us in the rescue process.

In September we will have another workshop. They will be bringing their reports on their *barazas* [public meetings] in every district with parents about educating girls.

5

1985-2002: We Go Hungry to Educate Our Children

Unequivocally, most mothers believe that the most important thing parents can do for children is to send them to school. Even those who fear that their educated children will not respect them, strongly advocate educating children, although many could not afford to send their children to school before the reintroduction of free primary education.

Most of the children in school now are the first generation to attend. The average amount of schooling has risen dramatically.

Who Goes to School?

When formal education was new in Kenya, there were many fewer girls than boys in school. Parents were often reluctant to send children to school, but more reluctant to send girls than boys. There were two reasons: fear that the girls would "become prostitutes," and a conviction that money invested in educating a daughter would not return benefits to her family of origin. The concern that daughters would "become prostitutes" exceeded the specific fear that a girl would exchange sex for money; it was that she would abandon valued traditions and the respectful behavior toward her elders on which her culture rested.

Most women in rural areas are much less educated than their brothers. But now, even in rural areas, a girl is as likely to start school as a boy, although she is less likely to finish primary school. Pregnancy or early marriage prevent many girls from completing school.

In the early years, parents could choose whether to educate their children or not. To encourage parents to send children to school, primary education was made free and legally compulsory at the time of independence. Even though it was free, enrollment was never close to universal. Enforcement was uneven. In many Nandi, Maasai and Turkana communities, taking children to school by force was common. In other areas, parents were encouraged, but there was no enforcement. Fees were reintroduced in the 1980's under a "cost-sharing" program. The percentage of children in school fell as fees rose.

Schools in rural areas are often built by the community rather than the government. These harambee schools rely on donations for building and expansion, and, before 2003, sometimes for operating expenses. Contributions to the harambee fund were officially voluntary, but abuse was common. Children might be chased [sent home] for fees when all that was due was the "voluntary" contribution to the harambee fund.

Government Enforcement

Many of the people who were taken to school by force, or their parents, are very glad it happened. Njoki Maina is a former Nairobi sex worker and paper collector who appears to be about 40 years old. "My daughter had gone to see in town a three-legged cow out of curiosity. That's where she was caught by policemen, arrested, and taken to school in Kiambu. She was happy because she liked school so much."

Sein Milanoi is very grateful that she was taken to school by force.

> My parents were not educated, so they did not value education. I was a small herdsgirl. The chief came around looking for parents who did not take their children to school. Fortunately, the good Lord had seen Sein somewhere without going to school, and my parents were forced to take me to school. My mother wanted me to go, but my father did not. In 1958, I was taken for five years.
>
> My mother took one brother to Nairobi. She did not tell my father he was going to school. She said he was going to Nairobi to stay with an uncle. That's how my brother got a chance to go to school. My mother had seven children. Only one brother never attempted going to school.

Sayioyio, who lives in rural Kajiado, regrets that her grandmother's pleading spared her from being taken to school.

> I never went to school. The chiefs used to go around and my name was written down to go to school, but when they came, my grandmother started crying, crying. "People are coming to take her away from me. Why? why? why? I don't have a child, I'm old."
>
> So I was left with her, not sent to school. I stayed with her for three months after that, and then went to marry.

Money Constraints

Deepening poverty made it hard for families who used to educate their children to keep them in school when fees were reintroduced. In a beautiful village in Kisii, Selina and Wenceslas Onduko live on a large, fertile *shamba* in Nyansiongo with a stunning view across a valley. They have substantial land, good rainfall, and two sons employed in Nairobi. In 1996, they also had a number of smaller children in elementary school. They lived frugally, scrimped and struggled like anyone else. "We don't have enough money to educate the children. Some of the children are going to stay at home. Although we have two children who are working, they need their money for their own house rent where they work. Their money doesn't reach us. We are going to be poor."

They are deeply devoted to education, have made sacrifices to send their children to school, and have benefitted from that investment because two sons have modest employment. They would do everything possible to send their younger children to school. A third child, Beatrice, did well in her KCPE[1] in 1996, but could not attend secondary school because they could not pay her school fees. She is now supporting herself by selling second-hand clothing.

Agnetta Owire, a Kabras farmer born in 1958, could not educate her daughter. She minded terribly because she thought her own lack of education had made her life very difficult.

> My father had many wives, and didn't believe in educating girls. I went to standard one and was first in my class, but then I had to stop. Life has been difficult because of not having schooling.
>
> My eleven year-old daughter does not go to school either. My husband is now in Nairobi. He stopped sending money for her to go. He comes here about once a year, and stays for one day. I want her to go back to school, but I cannot manage on my own.
>
> My son is in a special school in Nairobi because his bones don't grow. He matures, but he is wasted and thin. Because of his illness, he is sponsored by the government. I can't afford to go to visit him.

Many students worked to raise part of their fees. In 1989 and 1990, students at Shamoni Secondary School, where I was teaching, made building blocks from mud, wove and sold sissal ropes, raised chickens and sold eggs, took surplus maize from the family harvest to market at times

1. This is the national exam administered to students finishing primary school, which determines whether the student will be admitted to secondary school.

when local prices were high, raised sheep or goats, raised cane, plowed for other families, tended others' cattle, brewed, distilled, or (I was told obliquely) prostituted themselves. Judith Kakai's father is a mason. She and her siblings made bricks from the clayey soil in her family's shamba. She commented, "If we just do laziness, it is we who will suffer."

But often, even if the student earns part of the fees, the nuclear family may not be able to pay everything. Relatives often help. It used to be perfectly acceptable to ask any relatives, but this too has become harder as people become more desperate.

There are government funds intended to assist children of poor families with their schooling, but these funds often did not reach needy students during the Moi years. Doris Mathieu, an educated social worker in Meru, a rich cattle-raising area, recalled the children who went to school with her.

> Of the forty who finished primary school with me, only two boys and three girls went on to secondary school. The rest just finished standard eight. A number of them were quite clever but they could not go on. Bursaries [scholarships] didn't reach the people who needed them. Now there are fewer students going to secondary school because the fees are very high and only those who are employed can manage.
>
> In standard one there were double classes. By standard four, many had already dropped. It went to single classes. By standard eight, there were very few students. Many girls had dropped.

Even when a family could raise the necessary fees, they may not have been able to get their children into desirable schools unless they were willing to pay a bribe. On the other hand, if they were willing and able to bribe, their children might get into schools they were not otherwise qualified for. Nightingale Wanjiru was disappointed that she was only called to a secondary day school, and tried to find a place at a boarding school.

> In joining form one, the marks I had were not enough to take me to a good boarding school. I was called to a day school, but I felt I couldn't concentrate there. I asked my Dad to see if there was any boarding school which would take me. He went to one of the schools, but he was told that he would have to pay an extra 5,000 Ksh. So he told me I'd have to accept the situation because he was not ready to pay a bribe. So I just went to the school that called me. I didn't do well there.

Government bursaries often disappeared, but there were and are NGOs that sponsor some children. Just outside Nairobi, in Kayole, we talked with a number of former street women. Several have been able to find sponsors for their children. Margaret Wagatwe's children were sent to school through private sponsorship while she was still living in the streets.

> By the time I came here, my children were already in Mathare. They stay together. The older ones care for the younger ones and they are doing well. I did not bring my children here [to Kayole] because I don't have the money to send them to school, so they must stay near the school where they are sponsored.

Poverty can prevent children from going to school even if there are no fees to pay. Hunger; not having a uniform; embarrasment over dirty, torn clothing; or needing to work or beg also keep children out of school. Some of Sarah Mwalime's children were sponsored, but poverty prevented others from going to school even though it was before "cost sharing" required parents to pay for their children's schooling. "The ones who did not get aid often could not go to school because of lack of food. My children went to school if they'd eaten. If they had not eaten, they did not go."

Boys versus Girls

We talked to many women who had not been sent to school because their fathers objected to educating girls. Philiciah Munyovi, a Mumias farmer born in 1933, was one.

> My parents would only take the boys to school but not the girls, because girls could not do any job. But by good luck, I know how to write because of the Bible. For my baptism I was supposed to know how to write and read, so I was taught by the missionaries.

Flores Mwang'ombe's father changed his mind.

> My father decided to educate the boys only. The mother was so much interested in having the daughters go to school. But only the father was earning, so mother had no way to educate us. I wanted to go to school but I was not allowed.
>
> The girls were just to get married. The boys were to be educated, go to work, support a family.
>
> My two followers were brothers. When the brothers grew up and started working, they disliked the idea of the father not educating girls, so the younger girls were educated. But I was among the first two, who were not educated.

Flores Mwangombe at home

> Later on, the *mzee* [her father, referred to respectfully as "elder"] felt guilty and asked for forgiveness from us two who never went to school.

Although many women said their fathers educated boys in preference to girls, yet none, not one, of the over 250 women we interviewed said they or their husbands educated boys rather than girls, and only one of the young women said her father was reluctant to educate her.[2]

We talked to many who were not schooling their children, and many more who were, but none of the parents whose children are not in school said they would spend scarce money for fees on boys rather than girls. In fact, some believe that parents reap more financial benefit from educating their daughters because daughters are more dutiful, and therefore more likely to help their parents, even though they will leave home when they marry.

Khadija Mayow of Wajir, the unschooled wife of a driver, has come to care deeply about educating her daughters.

> You should educate all your children the same, even if you can't send them all the way through. You know, two or three years ago, parents would say, "Never send your girls to school, because they will become prostitutes." But ideas are

2. This change is real but not universal. Highly educated women are greatly over-represented among my informants.

changing. Now parents are beginning to realize that girls are much more likely to help their parents than boys. It's more important to educate girls.

Nuria Yussuf was born in 1973 in a village in Kajiado district. Her parents, who are ethnic Somalis and devout Muslims, moved into town so the children could go far with their education.

Mother went to school a bit, just a bit, but my father is not educated at all. That's why my Mom is thinking of education, she's thinking of no circumcision, she's thinking of her daughter to study so hard, so we can get by. My Mom is very strict and strong.

My Dad doesn't have a say. He always has in mind, "if ladies go for education they are going to be spoiled," but my Mom, she's the best. She has really fought for our future.

All my elder bothers are finished education. All of them went to universities, They have degrees.

Although my parents are rich, they believe we should know problems also.

Nuria's father is the only one we heard of who was reluctant to educate girls now, but his wife's determination overcame his reluctance.

Cultural Resistance

In the early days, many children were kept out of school because of fear caused by cultural unfamiliarity. Now, there are educated people in nearly every village, and everyone has seen the material advantages education can bring, so this fear no longer prevents parents from sending their children to school. Roselinda Washika, the Mumias farmer from a huge family, learned to read and write in church, like Philiciah Munyovi.

People came to take us to school but some of us refused. We did not know the importance of school. We thought school would cause us some harm.

We were taught by the church, but not school. We were given some chalk and a board on which we learned to read and write. Although we refused school, we accepted going to church because church was meant for all people. We felt safe there because we could go with our parents, who went to listen to the Word of God.

I forgot how to read and write after I got married.

Some were not sent to school because of fear of religious conversion. Mariamu Khalifa is the first generation in her family to attend school because her grandparents feared for their children's Muslim identity.

Our grandparents did not send their children to school. The schools were set by [Christian] missionaries, and they had a fear that if their children went to school, they would become converts. Now that some people have gone to school, and still remain Muslims, there is no fear. My mother did not go to school but she insists that her children must go.

PROBLEMS CREATED BY EDUCATION

At Shamoni Secondary School, the Headmaster asked five of the most articulate form four girls to talk with me. All were ambitious and eager for more education. Four hoped to study medicine and the fifth hoped to become a lawyer. We had a lively and passionate conversation. Comments were often overlapping, so the written account has non-sequiturs. Although the girls want as much education as they can get for themselves, they blame education for Kenya's, and the world's, central problems.

Bettye Khayati: Me, I just blame people who brought education. Due to this education, there are some big problems. For example, these bombs, which are very dangerous. And due to this education we have discrimination. Those who are educated look at those who are uneducated as if they are not human beings, which is not good. Also, the equipment which they have come up with because of education, vehicles and so on, they are destroying the atmosphere, destroying the ozone layer. If I think of the coming years, we will die because ultraviolet radiation will reach us, so education is destroying us.

HH: What do the rest of you think about what Bettye said?

Knight Opaka: I think that education is now becoming useless. For example, suppose my friend gets an A and I get an A, but she has money and I don't, she'll go ahead. I won't. Now what is the benefit of going to school?

HH: Would Kenya be better off if there weren't an educational system? What can be done?

Carolyne Ashiko: Before colonization, our African countries lived in peace. If natural problems arose, they would just be solved. But now if there is a certain tribe fighting the tribe of our President, it will involve weapons from outside, so his tribe or community will win. But if they just used arrows, it would not be so bad.

Since education has come, everyone is struggling to have the best. If there are two people fighting for one position, we will not have peace. One will die. And also, we have people who are not educated fearing those people who are educated. We don't have understanding.

Carolyne Molenje: We need to work with equal levels of education, equal development of resources.

Although we talked with a number of women whose children are not in school, concern about respect was never given as a reason or even a contributing factor in keeping their children out of school. Their children are kept at home only because of inability to pay school fees. Of

Caroline Ashiko, Knight Opaka, Caroline Molenje, Bilha Chiluyhi, Bettye Khayati outside Shamoni Secondary School

course, families differ greatly in how seriously they will struggle to raise money for school fees. For many, it is the highest priority. For others, it is more easily displaced by other needs.

Simanya Machocho lives in the hills overlooking Wundanyi. For her, the central problem of modern life is that outside influences undermine traditional culture [two instructors, in her words]. We interviewed Simanya at home. Her daughter and granddaughter were nearby and occasionally joined the conversation. Simanya's granddaughter, Lucinda, joined this part of the conversation.

> Simanya: I blame lack of respect on two instructors. I think education has contributed to problems. Whatever knowledge I have, I try to impart to my daughter or my granddaughter. When she goes to school, teachers give other instructions altogether. Other people are also outside influences, and I feel this has created a big gap between my generation and this generation.
>
> HH: Could you comment on what your grandmother has said?
>
> Lucinda: OK it's true, because the education parents used to give is quite different from the education we get at school. For example, our parents used to hide the secrets about our growth, especially about matters between boys and girls, but at school you see you are taught everything about the changes from childhood to adolescence, so we knew everything.[3]

3. I believe Lucinda's agreement with her grandmother's opinion can be taken as genuine rather than deferential. Simanya had not been to school and did not speak or understand English. Since Lucinda spoke English well, she spoke directly to me in English, instead of in Kitaita through the translator. If she had wanted to express a differing opinion, she could have done so without her grandmother suspecting the difference.

HH: Do you agree with your grandmother that this harmed relations between your generation and hers?

Lucinda: Yeah, I agree with her because you find that now we don't give respect. Ladies of about eighteen years to twenty years used to give much respect to parents. But you find that these days a girl of about fifteen years shows no respect, though she is still young.

HH: From both of you I'd like to hear if you think that is a good change or a bad one.

Lucinda: It's quite a bad change.

Simanya: It is a bad change. It is creating a barrier between the parents and the children. But we don't only look at the bad side. We look at the whole thing. When you educate a child she becomes self-responsible. If she gets employment, that lessens the burden of the family and one way or another maybe she supports the family. But knowing the children have some valuable skills we lack, we fear our children are wiser than us. We may be ridiculed or despised if we try to guide the children.

Education is Even Better than Cows: The Benefits of Education

When they have to pay to educate their children, many parents struggle. Most families live on such a slim margin that money spent for fees has concrete and immediate consequences: a longer period of hunger each year, foregone medical care, inability to sustain or expand a small enterprise. The cost is high. Yet for most mothers, education is a very high priority.

Why are mothers willing to make these sacrifices to school their children? Some who have not been to school see concrete benefits for themselves in having educated children. Siyiomit, a member of Elangata Wuas women's group, is one. "Once they are educated they can help me. When I want something to be written I won't have to go look for someone else. The children will write for me."

Mothers gave many reasons education will help their children. Olive Majala, the unschooled mother of nine whose parents worried when she married a landless man, has often wished she could read, and is happy her children can.

> I have never seen a classroom. I was really interested, but the mother refused. She wanted me to assist with the household duties.
>
> I want to educate my children so that they don't fall victims to the kind of life I have led. We people from small homes have to find money to educate our children so they will succeed in future. Since my husband had no land, I decided to educate the children so that maybe they would get employment

and be able to buy their own land somewhere. My land is not enough to share amongst the children.

I don't want them to be illiterate like me. Whenever my children send me a letter I have to get someone else to read for me and I'm never sure whether I have been given the right information.

I cannot write a letter. If I have an important message to pass to the children, even if it is a family secret, I have to use somebody, and that means exposing the secret.

Lucy Lebow of Elangata Wuas sees other benefits to literacy.

When I go to Nairobi, I see signposts and I can't read so I have to ask people about the signs. When they are educated, the children know how to take themselves. My daughter was only shown the way to school once. The rest of the time she went alone and came back alone.

Education is very important because one becomes aware of so many things. Also, education helps people because they can get employed after their studies. I have no education so the only job I can do is just to sit and sell vegetables.

Robina Mukera is an unschooled woman living in rural Kisii who educated her five children. She had several reasons. Some were the same reasons other women gave. One was unique and interesting.

When children have been to school, they can use a different language. They become more respectful toward their parents, because they can understand a good example. They start to dress differently, and tell the parents what to do. They advise the mother about how to change, how to dress, what to buy. This is not disrespectful; it is very helpful.

Joan Kanini explained that education is important not only for individual advancement, but for the whole community.

Women lag behind. It affects the whole community if they are uneducated. Where we have our small farm, there are many who are not educated. The mothers do not even know to boil or sterilize baby bottles. They just give the baby any water.

Diane Kimunda, who did not attend school, believes that educated people are more likely to lead useful, constructive lives than less educated people.

I am very worried about my children who are not schooling now. They might not become useful citizens in the future, whereas those I managed to take to school have become responsible. Only one son got to form four level. He has managed to build the house we are sitting in. (It was a large, well-built, permanent house.) The ones who are less educated are involved in bad activities, so I am worried about them.

When we raised the subject of education with Fatma Omar, the young woman in Malindi whose interview was curtailed because her younger brothers-in-law objected, she immediately started telling us about her desire for education for herself. "If I can go to school myself I will go too. My husband doesn't refuse, but at the moment I don't have an assistant to take care of the baby, so I can't go. I've wanted to go for a long time." I hope someday to learn that her wish has been fulfilled.

In contrast to the many people who believe that education undermines respect for elders, I was surprised to hear that several women in Nasianda think that learning respect is one of the benefits of formal education. Some in that group hope their children will be able to find employment. Others who think that may not be realistic still believe education will help them economically.

Woman 3: Education helps in that there are some people who don't respect their parents, but if they go to school, they will be disciplined.

HH: Do you mean that people learn to be more respectful from going to school?

Yes.

HH: Do most of you agree with that?

Many murmurs of assent.

HH: I've heard some people say that if the parents don't have much schooling, and the children get more, that may make them disrespect their parents. What do you think about that?

Woman 4: I disagree. In school, children are given regulations and taught how to behave.

HH: Do you mean that in general you think schooling makes people more respectful?

More murmurs of assent

Woman 1: In years coming, everything will depend on schooling. Even a houseboy or a housegirl will need to read and write. So getting even the simplest employment will be a problem for our children if they haven't gone to school.

HH: In ten years, do you think people will have better luck getting employment than now, or will it be even harder than now?

Woman 5: It will not be easy to get employment, but education is still very important because many people will have some business of their own, and that may need reading and writing.

Monica Mgoye is a farmer in Western Province who has eleven living children. Although she has not been to school, she expressed a broad understanding of the value of education.

> Some of my children were taken to school for a few years. In those days, there were no school fees, so they could go.
>
> If the children could have learned to form four, there would be something more they could do. I even took one boy to Kakamega for a driving course. But I didn't have enough money for him to complete the course, so he just came back home.
>
> HH: Do you mean that if they go all the way through school, then that's worthwhile, but if they have to stop early, a few years of schooling won't really help them?
>
> No, there are other reasons. I sent my children to school so that they might learn how to socialize with others, get knowledge, know much about the world and how to handle things, and also to get jobs. The benefit they can get is that they learn more than me. I didn't go to school so I don't know what is going on all over the world. When I take the children to school, I learn more and know how to stay in the future.

Susan Omulindi, a Mumias farmer who has finished primary school, sees benefits that extend far beyond the specific skills learned in school.

> Women who have been educated are respected. Their fellow women respect them very much. Their husbands treat them better. A husband knows that she is also an independent person and can do things on her own. The man is scared. He thinks maybe that if he hits her she is free to leave, but an uneducated lady is just forced to stay even if she gets problems in her marriage.

Nancy Karamana believes education was quite unnecessary until recently, but is important now. "Before, if there were many girls, the father was very rich, because cows will come. But now there is no marriage even, so you have to educate your daughters the same as your sons. I think they forgot about polygamy because of that. Education is even better than cows."

Portrait H

Grace Nyawira

I met Grace Nyawira in 1995 through the African Housing Fund (AHF). She was one of many former street women who had been given housing in their project in Kayole. Several of these women, including Grace Nyawira and Habiba Ali [Portait K] had been given loans of 3,000 Ksh to start a business. For reasons that are apparent in this interview, I was greatly impressed with Grace's resourcefulness, determination, and pluck. Several times, she had lost everything and begun again, each time finding a way to create shelter and a source of income. Her mother's fate illustrates the frequent consequences of rural people's migration to cities.

My mother came to Nairobi with a friend when she was young. I don't know why they came, but I never visited her home place. I was born in 1963. My mother, my older brother and I lived outside the wholesale market with many other street dwellers. When I was small, our houses were demolished by the police. Immediately our mothers built again so we could cook and sleep there.

I was able to go to school until standard four. My mother took me to school as much as my brother. You cannot separate your children. But of course the girls have more duties to take care of than the boys and so the boys did better than the girls in schoolwork.

My brother died. Then my mother also died and was buried at Langata because I did not know her home place. I was left in the care of her friend, Sarah, who is now here at Kayole with me. I stopped schooling. We lived in the open, with no real shelter. We built some structures using plastic sheets, and lived in them. They were demolished by the police, so we returned to Nairobi.

I married and lived in a house for three years. It was a real house with a roof, but a slum house, not sanitary or strong. I didn't get children. I started hawking fruits on the streets. My husband never used to help me. The little money I got he would take, and we would fight. He could be very harsh to me because I was an orphan and didn't have relatives to protect me.

He never had a job. He used to sell papers, then drink all the money he'd made. He beat me and left me to do all the work on top of that. I was always supposed to find enough money to feed us with no help from him. He would beat me up for asking for help.

When he left, I stayed six years without a husband. Then I married another man, and got two children. My second husband was also rough, although he never beat me. He worked at the post office. His name was Kinyua, which means a person who likes drinking. The name rhymed with the person.

Kinyua was not very clever. He could not reason properly. He was born in 1948, and stayed for long without a wife because of his mental problems. Despite his shortcomings I loved him because we rhymed. When I suggested something that we could do together, he would agree.

At first we stayed with his mother. Later, from my earnings, I bought a plot at Kaserani where we constructed a two-room house. After we moved away from her, my mother-in-law started saying I was taking her son away.

At every end of the month when he received his pay, he had a routine. He went to his mother's house and they would spend all the money together. When he missed coming home and I went looking for him, I would find him in his mother's house. Then I had to beg for bus fare for the month.

One day I went to his place of work and complained about his behavior. His boss said that from then on we were going to get the pay together. After that, every month Kinyua would give the whole amount to me, and I would give him some for drinking.

One day, when I came home I found that Kinyua had sold the plot I bought. The children were locked out and we were homeless. They stopped going to school. So I lived in the streets again, this time with two children to care for. We found another place to live and opened a Post Office account in his name. The house and the piece of land was in his name too because traditionally everything has to belong to the man, even if the woman bought it.

We saved for a year until he took the account book without my knowledge and withdrew all the money. He drank so much that he was arrested. I looked for him for two weeks and finally found him in a police station. He had been charged with robbery. They said that he was trying to steal a car. I don't believe that because of how his brain works. Probably he got drunk and fell near the car and they arrested him.

He stayed in remand for too long and was suspended from his work. His mother felt so angry because of the son losing his job. She said that I am a prostitute who only stayed with her son because his mind was not very good. When he got out, Kinyua decided that he wanted to stay with his mother. My

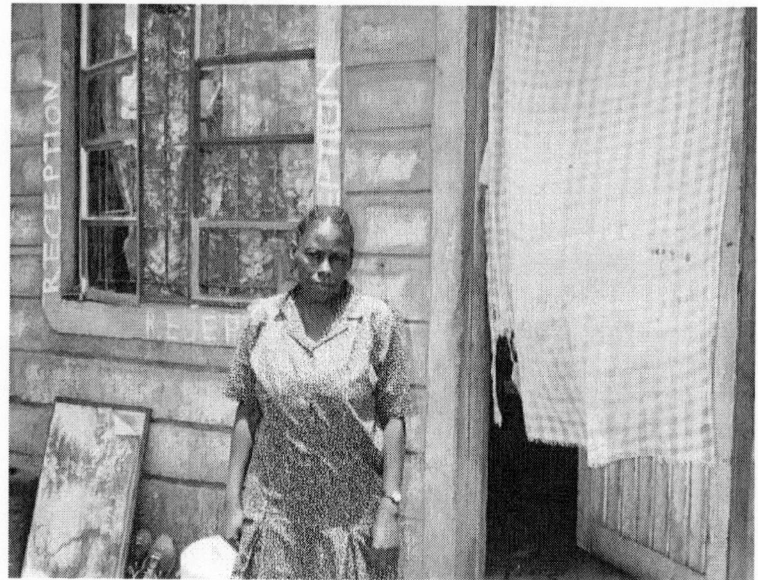

Grace Nyawira in her rented house, 2003

children and I were locked out of the house where we had been living, so I went to live into the streets once more with my kids.

I continued my business while I was living on a verandah in town. The children and I stayed in the streets for three years: 1992, '93, '94. It was tough. I was often arrested for hawking without a license. When I was arrested, my children went with me to prison because they were still small and were not in school.

My business didn't do well because of my arrests. One time, I was away for a whole month. But people living on the streets used to cooperate and help one another. Usually whenever one of the women I knew was arrested, other women would help to raise the money to pay her fines, so she could get out. I survived by borrowing[1] money.

The last time I got out of jail, I learned that other beggars had been brought to Kayole by African Housing Fund, so I came here on my own. My children were with me in the streets up to when Ingrid [the director of AHF] rented the houses at Kayole for us. She has helped us a lot as she's paying for our rent even today.[2]

When I first came here, I was part of a *kiondo* [basket] making project. I also got money from doing odd jobs, like fetching water for people. It's a good life for me here. Finally I have shelter over my head.

1. To spare humiliation, all kinds of asking others for money is referred to as borrowing, even when neither party can foresee repayment.

2. This is no longer true. AHF was taken over by the government, ran into financial difficulties, and went out of existence. Meanwhile, Ingrid Munro, founder of AHF, started Jamii Bora, a revolving loan fund. At first, it served primarily the people AHF had brought to Kayole, but has grown rapidly and now works in several parts of Kenya serving any group that wants to join.

To start again, I went to the wholesale market to collect potatoes and other foods that had fallen on the ground to sell them. A woman I met there understood my problems and had a better idea. She gave me fresh vegetables to sell. I did not have to pay her until I had sold them, and I kept all the profit.

My children were out of school from the time I lost my house in 1991 until I came here in 1994. They began attending an informal school here, but there were a lot of immoral practices at the school, like children pressuring them for sex, so it was better for them to stay home. Since last May, they have been going to a school at Upendo. One is in standard five and the other one is in standard two. The younger one caught up quickly and is doing well.

Soon after I moved to Kayole, we were given a loan of three thousand each by the *mzungu*[3] to start some business. I started hawking. Also, with other women here, I was in a merry-go-round[4] with fifteen women Mostly we paid for bail when one of us was arrested. In fact what inspired us to start that group was the arrests of most of us for hawking.

In 1998, my friend Jacqueline Klopp talked to Grace to get an update. Grace had been suffering severe ulcers. She was unable to drink tea, and had been driven by pain and fear to seek medical help, but had gotten no relief. She had borne a third child, a son. Her children were no longer in school, which distressed her terribly.

Now I am not working and I don't have money. I live in faith and look for vibarua [casual labor]. But it is hard for me to do even that because of the pain.

My older daughter had a serious accident. I sent her to take 100 Ksh to the grandmother, Sarah, who was sick. On the way, my daughter was hit by a car. The driver stopped and took her to Nazareth Private Hospital.

I continued selling my goods for two months after the accident, but it was too much because I had no time to care for her in the hospital, so I stopped hawking. Also, my third child, a boy, was born about that time.

The hospital refused to release my daughter unless the bill was paid. I tried every possible way to get a lawyer. I found a lawyer who helps poor people. The lawyer gave me 7,000 Ksh and wrote a letter to take to the hospital so they would release the child. The child wrote a statement about the accident, and I called for a *harambee* [fund raising event]. We raised 13,000 Ksh only. I paid this and they released my child from the hospital. I still have a hospital bill of 40,000 Ksh. They threatened to arrest me if I don't pay it. I had been told to take her back to the hospital with ten thousand for the plaster to be removed.

3. Ingrid Munro. The word "mzungu" means "white person."

4. A system of pooling their money and giving it all to one member, which gives each member an opportunity to have a larger sum than she could accumulate by herself. Such arrangements are described in detail in ch. 9.

I didn't have the 10,000, so I removed the plaster myself. She will need X rays in October.

The father to my small boy helped me a lot. We separated because I didn't want to get married again. I love my children and want to care for them the best I can, so I don't want more.

My biggest problem is that my children cannot afford to go to school. I want them to have an education so they won't have the problems I have. And, I won't bring my boy up in 'man' style. He will be taught to help.

If my children go to school they can come up very well. The girls are obedient and hard-working. Ever since I fell sick with this ulcer, I haven't done any work. They do all the cooking. They push me to take them to school because they like education very much, but I am not able now.

I have not been back to the streets to hawk because I don't have any capital. There is woman who promised to show me where avocados are bought if I can find only 1,000 Ksh. We buy them unripe, we wait for them to ripen, and we sell them along the road. I will start this when I can get the money.

In 2001, when I returned to Kenya I tried several times to find Grace, but missed her each time. A mutual friend took me to the stone house where she was living, but she was out working. Grace was reportedly doing well, supporting herself and educating her children.

In 2003, I was able to see her. Her life had taken a dramatic turn for the worse. She had sent her oldest daughter through a hairdressing course, but the girl had not found regular employment. She was no longer living with Grace and her siblings. Grace had been sick again, but continued trying to hawk, despite harrassment. She was five months behind on her rent, had no stock for sale, and had been desperate for several months. We were able to arrange a small business grant for her and she is back in business.

6

Chaos and High Hopes: The Reintroduction of Free Primary Education

There are high prospects for the new government: not only free schooling, but the children are also given textbooks and exercise books. The common person here cannot even afford a pencil, so being given those things is very important.

I have five grandchildren with me now. Before they were often chased from school. Any money we got went to the school and we would go to bed hungry many nights, even the children. So we can eat better now.

—Zildah Kirwoi, farmer, Wundanyi

A few days before the school year began on January 6, 2003, the new government announced that primary education would be free. The reaction was nearly universal delight.

At a minimum, free primary education has meant that poor parents who struggled to find money for fees had more money for food or other necessities. And it has meant that most of the children who had not been in school were enrolled.[1] For some, it also made life easier in other ways. Simanya Machocho's grandchildren are in a school that can provide lunch from government-donated maize and beans.

We are very happy about free education and the lunch program. It means that we don't have to rush in from the shamba to make the children lunch. We can work the whole day, and our children are learning.

The first year was difficult for schools. They were prohibited from charging parents, but the first disbursement of government funds didn't arrive until March, and was only 28,000 Ksh[2] regardless of the size of

1. According to official figures, 1.5 million school age children were on the streets in 2002. In 2003, school enrollment increased about 1.2 million, but 300,000 were still not in school.

2. The exchange rate was about 76 Ksh=$1 US.

the school. Later disbursements, though larger, left most schools unable to provide for students as they had in the past.

St. Mary's Mixed [coed] School in Machakos placed first in the district music competition in 2003, but there were no funds to pay for travel to Meru to compete at the next level. It was a severe disappointment to the students who had worked hard and done well, and a blow to the school's pride.

Many St. Mary's students have a long walk to get to school. For them, it is not practical to go home for lunch. Until 2003, the school had a cook, a watchman, and an accountant. In 2003, the school could only pay a night watchman. Even though the government gave the school sacks of maize and beans, they could not provide lunch. Not only could they not pay a cook, they couldn't afford the firewood to cook lunch or salt to season it. Paradoxically, the poorest of the students who were able to attend before were worse off because of the loss of lunch. For some, it was the one full meal they could rely on each day.

Shamoni Primary School in Kakamega District approached the lunch problem another way. One of the standard eight parents was a very active supporter of the school. Since the school could not provide lunch, standard eight parents organized their own lunch program. They do not give money to the school, but run and pay for the lunch program themselves. They also provide snacks for pre-primary children.

Throughout the country, there are huge unfilled needs for additional teachers. At almost every school, a shortage of teachers was and still is the biggest problem.[3] The worst situation I encountered was at Pandpieri Primary School in Kisumu. There were 298 students in standard one, some as old as ten. There were only three teachers, so there were ninety-nine or a hundred student in each class, with one teacher. The children sat three to a desk. The headmaster, James Opwapa, used his limited discretion to control the numbers. For example, he would not admit students who didn't have complete uniforms.

Other schools were more lax about the question of uniforms. Hibo Hussein's school in Wajir didn't insist.

> Uniforms are not required, so every child can go to school. Now, if you can, you buy your child a uniform. If not, it's not a big problem.
>
> We have short supplies of extra books, pencils, textbooks, manila papers. Every term there is some money for expenses. It is not enough, but it is better than nothing. And we cannot blame the government because the little money

3. The increase in enrollment is only part of the reason. Another reason is that since young teachers are often posted far from their families, they are disproportionately affected by AIDS.

> they have is divided for all. Schools have less, but they are supposed to just use what they have to the maximum. The headmaster will have to use his own initiative to get more but he cannot ask the parents.
>
> The situation is new, and people are not used to, not the teachers and not the students, but they have coped up with it.

Pandpieri was not alone in having problems of severely overcrowded classrooms. One teacher in Ninguni, who previously taught standards four through eight was transferred to standard one to help meet extreme needs. In her class, there were fifty-nine students. She admitted, "It's impossible to teach them all well. We do what we can, but if some are having difficulty learning, we just have to leave them."

In contrast to the headmaster of Pandpieri, Filomena Too, headmistress of Kimaren Primary School, worked actively to keep every child in school. At Kimaren, many parents had been to school themselves, and valued education greatly. As a result, there had been very high enrollment even during the cost-sharing era. Since almost all Kimaren children were already enrolled, Kimaren was far less pressed by increased enrollment than most primary schools. Their enrollment in 2003 was 537 compared to 494 in 2002. And they had another advantage: their very active parent's committee had held a major drive for building funds in 2002. So they were able to accommodate the newly enrolled children. Filomena Too tried to ensure that lack of uniforms would not keep any child away.

> Last term, we had a girl who didn't have a uniform. She feared to come to school. I told her, not to worry and talked to the class. Her friends all said, "She should still come to school."
>
> HH: Some schools worry that if they start relaxing the rules about uniforms, some parents will get lazy about uniforms. Have you had any problem with parents saying, "They are not really requiring the uniforms. This one does not have a uniform. Why should I buy that new shirt?"
>
> There are seasons when there is a lot of hunger. Then, nobody's talking about any other thing but what they are going to eat. But this is the time [October, after the harvest] when we encourage parents to buy parts of the uniform that may be lacking.

The reforms of 2003 posed other problems for Kimaren. Like most other schools in Kenya, they need more teachers. But the change that worries Filomena most is the new record keeping and accounting systems. To control corruption, the Kibaki government has put systems of accountability in place throughout the government. Schools have a questionnaire of about thirty pages they are expected to fill out with details of enrollment and expenditures. For Filomena Too, this is both a real burden and a significant worry.

> There are a lot of records to be made. I don't have a school secretary or an accounts person. Before, we didn't have a lot of records, so we didn't need and accounts person. We have not been trained so much in how to make those records. I do the accounts work, but I worry if I don't do it right, since this government is trying very hard to make sure money is properly accounted. What if I make some mistake? And the District Education Office comes to monitor.
>
> I teach as many classes as other teachers in addition to office work, the supervision of the teachers, the supervision of discipline. Sometimes when I come back home, I am so tired I cannot talk. My husband is away often because he's in the army. So, when I come home, I have to do everything for the family, and even for the cows.
>
> Free education has really helped the schools relate to parents. Previously when we held meetings, we talked about money, which kept some parents away. Now they come because they know they are going to get news of how the government has funded education. They're happy to come and see the textbooks and see their children have been given exercise books. Before we'd send the children home to bring their parents to a meeting. But these days, the parents just come on their own.
>
> We have a very active Board of Governors. They built the latrines for the children. We had latrines before, but not enough. With money collected last year, we repaired the leaking roof.
>
> When we collected money we'd come and we'd tell them, "We have used it on this and this," so they see where the money has gone. We were always very transparent.
>
> If I want to talk to the education officers, it is easy to talk to them now. Before, there was some laxity in the office, but now everyone is working, so we can at least go and talk with them.

Even parents have mixed reactions to free primary education. Overcrowding is so severe that some very poor parents send their children to private schools. Grace Nyawira [Portrait H], who spent most of 2003 hungry and perpetually fearing she would lose her house for nonpayment of rent, is sending her children to a small private school that costs only 100 Ksh.

> They like school very much. The boy is eight. Before this year, he had been repeating preschool because I didn't have enough money to take him to standard one.

The government schools are not teaching well. When my children went to private schools for their pre-education they started to read. The main problem in the government school is, with very many students in the class, and only one teacher, it's too hard for that teacher to give students homework because he can't look at it all, and is not even able to look at every child and to know their problems.

Patrick Wanjohi was educated at some of Kenya's best primary and secondary schools. He and his daughter live with his mother, Rose, at Umoja Estates in Nairobi. He was out of work for some time. His daughter is out of school until he can afford to send her to a private school.

Patrick: My daughter was going to a high cost school. When I stopped working in May, I had to move to where my mother is staying.

There are a lot of kids crowding the City Council schools and there's not much learning going on. A child who has been to a good privately run school is well ahead.

Because of the kind of education she knew, taking her to a City Council school would only make her very confused. If I can afford, I would like to send my daughter to a good school so that she can go further than I have. She can go to college, you know, become a professional, and that takes a good foundation. If she becomes confused at this stage, her education will be disrupted for the rest of her life. In City Council schools, even to talk is a problem. You find, you have about 100 kids in a room like this, and one teacher. The kids are just playing in the corners, without listening to what is being taught. She will not see the importance of education if she goes to school to play.

HH: What were the City Council schools like when you went?

Rose: They were good. But now, in the Council schools, children go to school, study for two hours, and come back.

Patrick: The implementation for free primary education was very poor. This was a populist kind of act. You know, to try and show the public that we promised this and immediately it has come.

What I hope is the Ministry of Education has people working round the clock to put a proper structure in place. There is so much money from the donors for this free education project, so now they can channel the money to the schools and make sure quality education is provided.

But there is also the issue of the school buildings. You are asking two million more kids[4] to go to school without building any more structures. I was expecting that the government would build new classrooms in every district. We are only hearing of purchasing of books, purchasing the writing material etc.

4. In fact, this is an overestimate.

They had suggested that they would even put up tents as temporary classrooms. I am not seeing any tents. They are just piling up kids in tiny rooms and the teacher stands there, makes them sing for an hour or two, and then they go out and play. In Umoja, I see no change at all.

Kenya has a parallel system of adult education, but in some schools, adults are attending classes along with the children. In Kobujoi, there is one standard four student who is twenty-four years old, and several mothers going to school with their children.

In September 2003, the Ministry of Education decided that if parents wished to raise money for school needs, as in the past, that would be permitted. This may be a backdoor step toward charging parents again, but it may be the only reasonable accommodation in the short run. Perhaps future years will be easier.

Although secondary school is not free, the NARC government has impoved on administration of bursaries [scholarships]. Now, they are reaching poor students. Gracilda Mwakio of Werugha received some support, and described the process used to select recipients.

In spite of the fact that secondary education is not free, local leaders have said, "Those who are widows, come out, go and see the chief, fill out some forms, say, 'I am a widow, I have so many children in school,'" and they look at paying the school fees for those children.

This was a big benefit for me. They paid 3,000 Ksh for my daughter, and I paid the rest. Those children who perform well and come from poor families are called in front of the chief. They may say, "I'm going to support three children," so it is upon the community to identify three bright children from families who cannot meet this education cost. For us, it is such a relief, because some bright children cannot go to secondary school. But the leaders are committed now.

Some get government funds, and in addition to that, the chiefs give personal support. When we go to the leaders for help, the chief may say we'll find ways to support three children, and I personally will support one, which means that the government is influencing the local leaders to help.

Portrait I

Wanjiru Mwangi

I never intended to interview Wanjiru. She is a friend of a friend. In 1999, she immigrated to the US, hoping to find work. She had relatives in Boston, so she went there. Since I live near Boston, I asked her to visit. Over a cup of tea, she told me her story. Engrossed, we talked for hours, and shared a simple supper. After she left, I continued to think about her story, so I wrote it as I recalled it. The next time she visited, I showed her what I had written, asked for corrections, and requested permission to use it. She filled in details of her experience at Brooke Bond. What follows is the corrected and expanded version.

I was born in 1956 to a landless family. My father was detained[1] so after independence, we were given land in Molo. At first everyone was given two and a half acres. We were to farm cooperatively to repay the government for acquisition cost. Later we were given five acres with title deed.

I'm the second born of ten. We were very poor, but we ate well until I went to school. After that, we never had a good meal.

When I was little, I had only one dress and two pairs of panties. My dress was torn. I slept in a bed with three sisters, two up and two down. We had one blanket. I went to school barefoot and had no school uniform.

I adored my father, who was very attentive and would joke with me. He had little education, but could read and write. He had a contract to supply chickens to a nearby army base. When he went to deliver them, my brother and I would accompany him. We worked together to pluck and eviscerate the chickens. My father would explain the functions of the various parts of the chicken. He also told me about the stars and the galaxies.

1. Imprisoned by the British for participating in the struggle for independence.

One day there was a rooster. We skinned it for family consumption. I found the testicles, which looked to me like small white kidney beans. I asked him what they were, but he told me "Just throw them away." He would not explain, but sent me to my mother for an explanation. My mother also refused to explain, and beat me. I continued to hold onto them. At dinner time, all the family was eating, but I refused to eat. I was still holding the testicles. Finally, my father asked "Why are we all eating, when my mother is not eating?"[2] When he found out I was still upset he told me, "Those are the testicles," but did not explain. Satisfied for the moment, I ate.

I noticed through observation that women who have large bellies no longer do after they get a new baby. I didn't know how the baby got out, but I figured out that the babies come from the belly. When I was in standard two, my baby sister was born. My mother had been very thin, so I had even been able to see the baby moving. My littler sister asked where the baby came from. Mother answered, "I got her from the market." When she left the house for some chore, I explained to the sister that the baby really came from mother's stomach. As she was asking about this, Mother returned, and was very angry. She asked me who had told me, and I said no one had.

Before I got my period, I had a very heavy white discharge, which worried me very much but I had no one to ask about it. My grandmother was not near, and my mother was not very approachable. I was the first to wake in the morning to make the tea. I would wash out my panties and hide them under the mattress. One day I couldn't find my panties in the dark, so I had to go to school without washing them. My mother happened to do a general cleaning that day, and found them under the bed. She saw the white discharge and became very angry. When I returned from school, my mother asked me what it was and beat me very severely.

Father paid my brothers' fees, but he said he couldn't pay mine because he had no job. He was a mason, and only had work irregularly. I loved school and was an excellent student. When I was in standard three, I went to the principal to beg for fees remission, and it was granted. I didn't have to pay the twenty-three Ksh tuition. In principle, all students paid a six Ksh games fee, but I didn't pay that either. I only had to pay the ten Ksh CPE fee in standard seven.[3]

I went on to secondary school. My brother finished form six, but I didn't get that far. When I was in form four, I became pregnant. My mother agreed to raise my son. I went to secretarial training, and then was employed in Nairobi as secretary to the administrator for the high court.

My father always came to me on payday to insist I give him my money. I refused. He finally said it was useless that I was working because he got nothing from it. He didn't drink, but much later I realized that he gambled. He'd give his money to my mother, and would ask her for it bit by bit. She was

2. Wanjiru is the oldest girl, and therefore was named for her father's mother. He jokingly refers to her as "my mother."

3. The Certificate of Primary Education, the national exam that everyone takes at the end of primary school. At that time, primary school ended at standard seven.

very submissive and always gave it to him without arguing about using some for family needs. I remember seeing my mother sitting with her head in her hands, crying, after giving my father money.

While I was working, I paid school fees for all my younger siblings, but this didn't satisfy my father. He thought he should get the money, and was very abusive when I refused. I pleaded that I was paying school fees for the children, but he dismissed that as boasting.

He made an appointment with my boss and asked to have me dismissed, saying there was no point in my working because I wasn't doing anything for him. We had a co-operative [credit union] at my workplace. When money was borrowed for school fees, a letter from the school stating the fees was required, and the check was made out to the school. My boss was head of the co-operative, so he knew that my loans went for school fees. When my father went to talk with him, the boss asked, "Doesn't she have a son?"

"Yes"

"Isn't she educating him?"

"Yes"

"Well, then, isn't she doing what she should be doing?" My father left unsatisfied.

After I refused, he would go to my mother and berate her for her daughter's bad behavior. The mother would plead with me to give in to my father, but I would reply, "He is not my husband. Your marital problems are not my problems."

Another time, my father came to me, again on payday, and asked me for money to rent an acre of land from a neighbor who wasn't using it. That time, I gave him the money. The next payday, he came to me with exactly the same story and no covering explanation about the earlier money. He became extremely abusive when I refused. He had always threatened to curse me and disown me. The day after that he wrote me a long letter cursing me.

I was terribly upset. If my son had been with me, I would have killed him and myself that day, but since he was with my mother, I couldn't do that. The thought of him prevented me from killing myself. After that, I didn't speak to my father for eight years even though we were often together at home.

My favorite aunt begged me to take the first step to reconcile. She begged my father to welcome me back. To please her, I visited my father and was warmly and tearfully received. A few years later he became ill. By this time, he had separated from my mother. Many of the younger siblings were now living and working in Nairobi. They pleaded with our mother to come and take care of my father, which she did, but he died anyway. Mother still lives in Nairobi.

After seven and a half years, I left the job I loved at the high court for more money at Brooke Bond Company. I worked in Kibwezi, then in the Nairobi office, and later in Mombasa on a sisal plantation they had bought. I was working in Mombasa at the time my father cursed me and at the time I reconciled with him.

In government service, there can be some sexual harassment, but they can't fire you. In private companies it's much easier to lose a job. When I worked at Brooke Bond, harassment was not just one person, it included so many senior people. The women who are so exploited seem to think it is the only way they can climb the ladder. I was first sent to a sisal plantation in Kibwezi. The whole staff was twenty-one people: I was the only woman.

Part of my compensation package was that I would be provided with transportation to the market center once a week because it was seven miles away. Instead of giving me a driver as he was supposed to, the Personnel Manager would take me himself. That created an attitude among the other people that I was his woman. He would be so "generous." At the market, he wouldn't let me buy my own stuff, so that even to the shopkeepers, he was creating a picture that we were a couple. The whole town got the idea that I belonged him. I didn't care much about that, but I wanted to be clear with him. I would tell him, "I don't want you buying these things for me. When I go shopping, I want to buy my own stuff with my own money."

He would brush it off with, "It's OK. It's nothing, I just like buying for you."

There was a staff club, which was meant to be a recreation center for us with videos, ping-pong, darts, beer. He would come in the evening with a vehicle to pick me up to take me to the club, so I wondered how I could get rid of him. I would not answer when he knocked, and let him think I was out. Or I would go to the club by another road and let him find me already there. He would be angry with me. He said, "It is dangerous. I was coming for you with the vehicle, and you are already here."

I asked, "When did you become my husband or whatever it is you imagine you are, that you have the authority to get angry with me. It's my life, and if I want to walk to the club, I will do it. Who are you to get angry?"

So, the people in the club realized that the picture he was trying to create was not so. When the others realized that I wasn't sleeping with him, they thought I was up for grabs for anyone. I discovered later that they used to sit and place bets on who would be the first to sleep with me. It was not that anyone was looking for a special relationship with you. They were just arguing, "I'll be the first." They didn't even want to be the only one, just to be first, to brag to the others.

Some of the staff had vehicles, so they would go to town in the evening. I would sometimes ask one of them to buy me something. But when I did that, they would come to me very late at night. Then I'd have to open to get my stuff. One man who seemed respectable demanded to sleep at my house. This was his way of seducing me: no romancing me, but he was there and demanding to sleep in my house. I literally fought with that guy, pushing him out, and I even threw all the things I had sent him to buy out after him.

After that, I decided I had to have a means of transport. Since it is a semi-arid area, you find old women, even as old as my Mum, riding bicycles for miles and miles. So I went to town, and settled on a bicycle that I was going to buy. There was a company bicycle for the office manager, who taught me how to ride.

When you take your vacation, the company gives you a vacation allowance. At that time it used to be 1,400 Ksh. The bicycle was going to cost me 2,200 Ksh. I had saved some money, then I started to take two days vacation here and there so I could get the vacation allowance to pay for my bicycle.

I became the freest woman in town. I would ride my bicycle to work, then go home. You know, back home, a woman wearing pants is unheard of. But I sewed myself some shorts, not even long pants, but shorts. I'd go home, put on my shorts, and ride my bicycle. I'd go to town and buy my stuff. I loved my bicycle. Those guys started seeing me differently. After that, they'd be happy to do things for me with no strings attached.

But then Brooke Bond decided I was too good a secretary to remain in Kibwezi, so I was sent to the head office. I expected that at head office there would be more sophisticated minds, but it was much worse because these were the real bosses who can make or break you, and they used that power over the women to the maximum. Even if there is a policy about sexual harassment, it's not real, and you don't have anywhere to turn. Either you use it to your advantage, or put up with it and accept the frustrations of the job, or lose that job. The personnel manager had gone through every woman in that office, married, single, short, fat, tall, whatever. They had all given in to him, looking for promotion, for good reviews, whatever.

It seemed he looked around and said, "There is one woman I haven't had." I used to work in another office, but I was shipped to his office. Everyone then knows what is going to happen. Nobody says anything directly to you, but if you go into another office, you hear derogatory remarks that you know are meant for you.

We'd leave the office at five. He'd wait until five minutes to five, and then buzz me and tell me that he had an urgent letter that must go today, which is a lot of crap. The post office closes at five, so it cannot go out today anyway. So, I'd prepare my notebook. Meanwhile he'd pretend to be on the phone long distance. He's waiting for everyone to go home, for the office to clear, then he'll call me for dictation. It's getting dark outside. This is when he'd start saying, "What a beautiful girl you are!"

Then I was supposed to smile and giggle say humbly, "Thank you." Even when I was a teenager, I never behaved like that, and I don't admire girls who do. So, when I'd go in to take dictation, he'd start giving me all these compliments, talking about personal things, asking me personal questions. Everybody in the office knew that I wasn't married and was a single mother. So he'd ask me about my son, I'd answer his questions, but with a wall of formality. He'd say I'm beautiful and I'd say, "Thank you sir." The "sir" was essential, because what he wanted was for me to become familiar.

He'd ask, "Don't you consider me a friend?"

I'd say, "I suppose you're not an enemy, so I could say you are a friend."

He'd say, "Why do you insist on calling me 'sir?' You can call me Frank. Everybody calls me Frank."

I'd say, "Even if we are friends, I don't think I'd feel comfortable calling you that because you and I know that in our community, you are more like a father to me. I can only call an elder formally. It doesn't mean I don't know their given name, but I don't use it. I keep that person in a place of respect."

I think I looked stupid because I seemed not to be getting his message. So he would get angry and say, "I've changed my mind about that dictation." He would grab his coat and walk out, or he'd give meaningless dictation and say he wanted that letter ready on his desk tomorrow morning.

It might be late at night when I leave, and have to walk in the dark streets and catch a late bus home. I used to live in a place that was very scary by nine o'clock. When I came to the office the next morning, I'd act as though nothing happened. He'd be upset with me, but I'd pretend not to see it.

He would watch me for a few days, and then start again with a different dictation, and again asking personal questions. "What time will you be done? Can I come back at eight?" I was supposed to feel flattered, taken care of. In the car he would try to make the conversation as personal as possible. I'd be so formal, playing the picture of innocence. The first time, when we got home and I just alighted and went in. He stayed there for at least fifteen minutes. The next morning he was so mad.

After two or three days, he asked, "Why is it I gave you a ride and you didn't even have the courtesy to say, 'Thank you.' You're an enlightened girl and usually very polite." Of course I apologized very much for my oversight.

"But I don't believe you forgot. You know, you're a very conservative girl, but at the same time, there are certain aspects of our society that you seem to miss."

"What is that?"

"In our African culture, if someone takes you home, its not normal for you to just say 'Bye' and let them go. It is normal to invite someone in."

"I'm sorry it didn't occur to me to invite you in because it was very late and I assumed you were tired. I knew I was."

Now, he has told me that is what he expected. Now, he imagines that next time it will be different. So next week he makes another opportunity. I said, "I could invite you in, sir, but I have this headache." Luckily enough, that day I really was sick. I had a horrible cold.

Now, he wants to be the one to take care of me, come in and make sure I am safe. For God's sake!! Could there be a monster in my house? "I'll just make you a cup of tea and tuck you into bed." That is the closest he ever came to telling me he wants to sleep with me.

After about six months, people stopped making those catcalls, those derogatory remarks. Everybody else was starting to treat me differently. How they knew he didn't get me, I don't know. I never discussed it.

I was working two steps higher than my grade and my pay. I wasn't getting any acting allowance. I was supposed to understand that he could give it or not give it. I never asked for anything. Everyone, including the most senior managers were impressed by the quality of work coming out of our office. So I got a promotion with the least benefits that he could give me, and I was moved down to the office where I was before. The last time he ever said anything personal, he said, "You know, I have never met a woman like you."

I smiled. I really smiled. I said, "And you know, you won't!" I think I walked two inches taller.

I was laid off in 1996 and haven't been able to find work since then.

7

Women's Work

At the equator, the sun rises quickly, leaving less than half an hour between first light and full light. Margaret Obonyo rose before dawn, dressed, and started a fire for tea and porridge. It was February 1990, and Margaret had agreed to let me follow her through an ordinary day. By the time it was light and I was up, breakfast was ready, and the nine children were awake. The older girls were helping the younger children wash and dress.

Margaret does not need to fetch water at first light because she lives near a well. Families who fetch water from a river must go very early to get their water before cattle come to drink and stir up the mud.

Margaret gathered the dung left overnight by the cattle and sheep tied in the compound and put it on the dung pile. Later, it would be used in the fields or for repairs to the walls of the mud houses or resurfacing the floors. One of the older boys milked the cows and brought the milk into the kitchen.

While the younger children were finishing their porridge, Margaret and her daughters washed the dishes that had been piled up after dinner last night. Daylight is precious, so the evening meal is eaten after dark, and the dishes are saved until morning when they can be washed in good light. Margaret's second daughter swept the house with a straw broom. The small animals that had spent the night in the house — the hens, rabbits, and cat — were chased out. There were no chicks or ducks and ducklings just then, although there often are.

One of Margaret's older boys went off with the cattle. Once a week, the cattle are taken to the local cattle dip, where they walk down a cement slope through a trough of disinfectant, and up the slope on the other side. This provides protection against insect-borne disease.

It was time for Margaret and the children to go to the fields. She refused my help. It was an old battle between us. I had lived with her family for four months and gradually concluded that insisting on holding to my own sense of equity was childish and resented. They weeded until midday, then went home to prepare lunch for the children. There is usually something for lunch when food is in reasonable supply, but for the last three months before the maize harvest, when there is little food, the adults and older children will not eat at midday. When the children had finished, Margaret returned to the fields for two hours. Shall I admit that I felt sick and took a nap?

After fieldwork, Margaret often goes to the market or the mill to grind her maize, but on this particular day, she gathered firewood. Carrying her *panga* [machete] on her head, she walked about half a mile to a wooded area where she gathered a huge bundle of sticks, slashed a leaf off a sisal plant, and peeled some fibers to tie her bundle together. I gathered some sticks too, but was pitifully slow compared to her. By the time she had finished, another woman had come to gather wood, and was able to help her lift her bundle to her head. She firmly refused to allow me to carry any wood. In an hour and a half, she was able to gather enough wood for three days.

When Margaret got home, she went to the tiny river behind her house for her weekly bath, since this was Saturday. Then, she began preparations for the evening meal. She chopped a large bunch of *sukuma wiki* [kale] very finely, using the dull blade of her only knife, which had lost its handle. The small children were playing nearby and the older children were studying before dark fell. When it became too dark to read, Margaret and her daughters began making supper for the family.

Cooking is done over a fire on the floor of a separate mud-walled kitchen. Pots are balanced on three stones, and Margaret sits on a low stool while stirring the pot. Every night, and at noon on the days when lunch is served, there is *ugali* [a stiff, white corn meal paste] and sukuma wiki cooked in fat with an onion and a tomato. Margaret grows the maize, sukuma wiki, tomatoes and onions, but buys the cooking fat. Often, there is something else too. This time it was tiny Nile perch caught 17 miles away in Lake Victoria, smoked on the banks of the lake, and sold in Kakamega market.

The older boys took the food they share with their father to his sitting room. The daughters and younger sons ate with Margaret in the kitchen, saving some ugali for the cats and rabbits.

Margaret's circumstances and work are much like those of Kenya's millions of farm women. Of Kenya's total population of 29 million, only 1.6 million are wage or salary earners. eighty two percent of Kenya's women and seventy three percent of the men rely prmarily on agriculture.[1] Of these, many more are planters than herders, although there do not seem to be any reliable statistics. Like Margaret's family, most planters also keep some animals.

FARMING

In highly industrialized countries, people make a distinction between domestic and economic tasks [work], since most people rely on their employment for sustenance. For most Kenyans, these are not separate realms. Even the difference between subsistence crops and cash crops may not be clear. A family that keeps a few chickens will sometimes eat the eggs produced, and other times sell them. Families who rely primarily on maize for food, and grow other crops for cash, may also grow some vegetables for subsistence, and sell what they don't eat. A family that has cows will drink some milk, and sell some, but leave enough for a calf. Whether they sell or eat depends on the balance between hunger and need for cash. Thus, describing small-scale farmers as subsistence farmers or cash croppers is an approximation.

Cattle, sheep, or goats used to be slaughtered for a feast to which many neighbors, friends and relatives would be invited. That is now rare. Even killing a sheep or a goat for consumption is uncommon. Increased population density means that there are more close neighbors, so the number of people who would know of the slaughter and expect to share in it has become too large. The sheep or goat would have to be split among so many people that there would be little left. If the neighbors were not invited they would resent the slight.

When farm families eat red meat now, it is usually purchased from a butcher, even though the family raises goats, sheep, or cattle. Animals that are not being used for milk, breeding, or fieldwork will be sold to a butcher. Meat is now bought and sold, and interfamily socializing has declined.

Cooking fuel and even water are becoming commodities. Gathering firewood and fetching water have always consumed many hours of a woman's week. If water is far away, some women walk a long time to fetch it, but others may buy what they need at a water stand run by the owner of a donkey. The donkey carries large barrels of water, which will then be sold by the jerrican.

1. US Government Statistics 2001.

Kenya is rapidly becoming deforested. Many rural women can no longer gather firewood. They cook with purchased charcoal, which is an economic hardship, and — being a less efficient use of trees — hastens deforestation. A few years later, the copse where Margaret had gathered wood was gone, and she had to buy charcoal for cooking.

Plowing is men's work. Planting, cultivating, weeding, and harvesting are generally done by women alone or, less commonly, by women and men together. Most families grow both food and cash crops.

Many farmers concentrate on cash crops and have reduced the acres devoted to their own food. This means more hunger, especially for women, who commonly starve themselves before cutting into the food they serve their husbands or children. Rose Barmasai, [Portrait M], who co-ordinated a church funded social welfare program, described the effect of cash cropping on the smallholders she worked with.

> The benefit of our farming has been robbed away. We plant coffee—we don't decide how much that coffee can cost. We plant tea. The tea will go abroad, and who decided the price? The women who plant pineapples get little. Those pineapples are canned, and the cans are sent abroad to earn foreign exchange for Kenya. The canning factory employs almost 4,000 women who would be sacked if they were found tasting the pineapple. They can't afford to eat it, though they work hungry. When it goes to the market, it is too expensive for them. And that price is decided by others.

In 1996, Mary Wambui, a Murang'aa farmer, didn't see any way farmers could earn enough to eat well under existing political conditions.

> Sometime back, someone with milk would go to the market and exchange it for potatoes, but now, we just must use money and the value of the money is very low.
>
> We farmers rely on money from our coffee and sometimes we end up not being paid. If we don't get paid for our produce, we find it hard to feed our cattle and therefore they are not able to produce milk for sale. Most of these problems come from the top-most people of this country.
>
> We are not able to solve it. If things can be solved at the top, then our local market can help us also.

Jean Wanjugu, who grew up in Central Province but has spent her career as a very high-level business executive in Nairobi, explains why cash cropping provides women so little benefit. "In Central Province, our economic activity is tea, coffee etc. The payment is made to the registered owner of the land, who is a man because women are not supposed to own land.[2] Women get about ten percent of the cash even though they are responsible for ninety percent of farm work."

Ideally, it would not matter whether the money went to the husand or the wife, if both were committed to using the cash to meet family needs. But that cannot be assumed.

Farmers prefer to work together. It's more enjoyable and more efficient. If a matriarch has several daughters-in-law, she may put all to work in the same field so they can help each other. If a woman has no relatives to share work, she may form a group with neighbors to work each other's fields in rotation, planting, weeding, and harvesting. The woman whose field is being worked will feed the others. Usually no money will change hands, unless the labor needs of various families are grossly unequal. Then money may be used as a way of compensating the women who give more.

Increasing population and decreasing soil fertility have left many women without enough land to feed their large families adequately. As a woman ages, her ability to cultivate her land declines. Ideally, by this time, her children are growing so there will be plenty of people to work the land, though there may not be enough land to feed all of them. Tragically, during the last decade of the Moi regime, powerful figures in the government often "grabbed" land to give to supporters. This became one of the most important sources of patronage, greatly increasing pressure on the remaining land.[3]

While increasing population has meant that the parcels held by individual farmers are being divided into smaller pieces, the increased cash value of land has led people with surplus money to accumulate more land. If there are not enough family members to work the land, a prosperous family may leave some fallow, hire assistance, or rent out parts of the land.

Most farmers keep livestock as well. Often, there are several cattle, a few goats or sheep, and some chickens running loose in the compound. Land pressure is changing the way livestock are raised. As grazing lands become scarce, many families install zero grazing facilities. Rosemary Njeri, a Lusigetti farmer and batik artist, sees this as an easier way to raise cattle, though she did not construct the facilities. "In the old days our grandfathers and fathers used to go out in the fields to graze cattle. It would take them almost the whole day. These days we have switched

2. About 5% of the land is owned by women.

3. I am indebted to Dr. Jacqueline Klopp for her useful analyses of "land grabbing."

to zero-grazing, where we have one or two good quality cows. We don't struggle as much as we used to."

HERDING

When pastoral life yields enough for survival, it is deeply loved. The communities that have been least beguiled by the possibilities of modern life (and that have had the least opportunity to abandon their traditions for modern comforts) are pastoral communities: the Maasai, Samburu, Boran, Pokot, Turkana and Somali are all pastoral.

Herding is becoming much more difficult. In the South, the Maasai are cattle herders. Their diet used to be milk, sometimes blood, and occasionally meat. But it is changing. During the colonial era, great tracts of traditionally Maasai land were taken over by white settlers. More recently, individual Maasai have sold part of their grazing land to farmers. Unfortunately, the land that has been sold or taken for farming, the land with water, is also the best grazing land. Now animals are grazing more intensively on drier land, endangering vegetation. The great herds have become memory through disease, land alienation, and climatic disruption creating repeated droughts. Families that used to prosper now have only a few head of cattle and no other resources.

Poor women use enormous resourcefulness as they contrive to get money and food. Other necessities may not be plentiful either. Water and firewood are increasingly scarce. Getting them takes a great deal of a woman's time, and she may never have enough for comfort. Even in the rainy season, women who live at Mile 46 in Kajiado District walk a long way to fetch water. In the dry season, there is not enough. Some families have dug wells, but even they may not have enough water for their cattle. They certainly don't want to endanger their herds by sharing the insufficient water in their wells with many neighboring families. Beatrice Wanjiru, a Kikuyu living among Maasai, has no well, and is sometimes desperate for water. She rises very early to take water from a neighbor's well before the neighbor gets up. Her attitude toward this is pragmatic. She feels neither indignation at the owners who will beat her to keep her away from their wells nor shame about her need to steal the water.

> During drought people have to come and steal water from the wells. When their owners come they'll beat you if they find you. It's not only me. It's all the people. Sometimes the water in the well is not even enough for the cattle. So it's not that they don't want us to drink the water. It's only that it's so hard to share with everybody.

Nomadism, the herder's traditional safety net, has been greatly restricted by encroaching settlements. A generation ago, migration during a dry season was easy and common. Now, there are few places that can sustain incoming herds.

To compensate, some Maasai are beginning to grow grain and vegetables. Development projects encourage agriculture as a way of diversifying a family's resources, and giving women their own source of income. Acceptance of new foods is slow. Men may be especially reluctant to eat vegetables, regarding them as women's food.

Intermarriage between pastoral Maasais and agricultural Kikuyus is fairly common. Several of the women we met in rural Kajiado were Kikuyus married to and living among Maasai. They grow vegetables, serve them to their neighbors, and sometimes inspire imitation. Lucy Lebow is one. She came to live in what is now quite an arid part of Kajiado District. She told us about her early years there, when the rain was more regular.

> At that time this place had good rains, so I used to plant and brew. With the money I got, I bought goats. During that time you used to buy a goat for ten Ksh.. Life was so cheap and everything was good. We used to plant maize, beans, pigeon peas, cow peas. I was not the only one who knew how to plant. There were some other women from away[4] who would also plant. My neighbors would eat when I'd cooked but if I went to their homes they didn't have vegetables and they didn't want to buy vegetables from me. The only thing I could sell was the local brew.

As Susan Malaso mentioned, among the Maasai, proceeds from the sale of animals go entirely to men. Among Somalis it is different. According to Bahsan Gedi, Somali women have greater autonomy and more voice in family decisions.

> A woman's herd comes from the animals her father gave her. Often it is goats. These she can sell as she wishes. But even if the camels are the husband's, he can't sell without the consent of the wife, because it's a big asset, like selling the house. Little things like goats, he can sell or she can sell.

In the arid Northeast of Kenya, people rely on camels and goats. War in Somalia has spilled into Kenya, disrupting their nomadic lives [Portrait N]. The fighting raging among the different clans made life dangerous for people in towns, and even for dispersed herders. Drought from 1991 to 1994, and clashes from 1993 on, made herding dangerous

4. That is, not Maasais.

and drove many people from their pastoral lives into town, severely straining the available social services.

In the village of Barwako, just outside Wajir, the houses are made of heavy thatch over a wooden frame. They are under two meters high and four or five meters apart. A short adult stoops to enter. Although, there is limited light in the houses, the members of Ayuta Women's Group [Portrait L] have a common shelter with walls covered in plastic sheeting. This provides a well-lighted place for weaving mats or other shared tasks. Most members of the group moved to town when their animals died in the drought, or after relatives and friends were killed in clashes. Some would gladly return to herding. Others want to stay where they can educate their children.

> Maryam: I was a pastoralist and so were my parents. Our animals died in the drought, so we came to the village to receive relief handouts. If I had animals now, I would go back to pastoral life. From when I was a child up to now, everything that I have known is animals.
>
> Halima: I am in between. I am a pastoralist and also a villager. I was brought up in the village part of the time and part of the time with the animals. The animals are fewer now and my brothers and sisters wanted to stay as pastoralists, so I decided to leave the animals for them and stay here, but I still love pastoral life. You will never be without in pastoral life because you get the meat and the milk from the animals. Even in town we need this food and it would not be there if there were no herders.
>
> Saadia: When I was young I was a pastoralist. When I got married to a villager, I settled in town. If you have animals and there is peace, pastoral life is very comfortable when there is enough rain.
>
> Habiba: Personally, I would not go back to pastoral life even if I got enough animals and there was peace. I was not able to go to school when we were with the animals. I want to stay in town to send my children to school, so that they have a bright future.
>
> Muslima: I came to this village because animals died. If I had animals now and there was peace, I would still not go back to pastoral life. When we were staying in the bush, our children were brought to school, and used to stay with relatives in town. I want to stay near the school so I can be with my children.

Formal Sector Employment

Kenya shares the unemployment problem common throughout the third world: There are not enough jobs for people at any level of education. The general perception is that one must have connections or pay a bribe to get a job. Yet many of the employed women we talked to said that they got their jobs just by applying. If some had paid a bribe, they did not say so. During the later Moi years getting a government or parastatal[5] job almost always required a bribe and connections. This form of corruption was common in the private sector too.

At the beginning, the new government made great efforts to reduce this and other forms of corruption.

The practice of hiring friends has its positive side as well. Esther Muthoro tells how her family was helped in time of great need because her father's former employer had a sense of responsibility for his family.

> My dad was a driver for a tourist company in Nairobi. He died in a car accident when my mother was pregnant with my brother. I was six and my sister was eight. To help my family out, my mother was hired where my father used to work. She is a messenger and also cooks for the staff.

Esther's story illustrates something else about the practice of hiring relatives of employees and former employees. Relatives of an employee will be given a job when possible, but they will usually be offered a much less remunerative job. Only proteges of the top people will get good jobs.

When Jean Wanjugu finished high school in the 1970s, a British company sent her to secretarial college. She worked for that company for four years, and rose quickly to the point where being an African blocked further promotion. She switched to a locally owned company, but it became part of a British conglomerate. There, she believes that gender discrimination kept her off the board of directors. Jean found ways to use being a woman to great advantage in solving company problems.

> When I was a young woman, administration of the office fell under me. There was a person who was supposed to be cleaning toilets. When I told him that the toilets were not clean, he went to the head of the Human Resources Department and said, "I have got a knife here and I am going to knife that girl. I don't like the way she talked to me yesterday. I am a fully-grown man, recognized, I have gone through the rituals [been circumcised]. She should know that and she can't talk to me like that."
>
> The Head asked me about the incident. I said, "Have the rituals got anything to do with his job? All I want is that the toilet is clean." Later he came and apologized.
>
> After work, all the factory workers have showers. The Kikuyus wanted their places separated from the Luos[6] because of circumcision. The issue came to

5. A parastatal is a government-owned business.

6. Unlike Kikuyus and other Kenyan ethnic groups, Luos do not circumcise either boys or girls.

> me. I said, "I'll go and talk to them. I want them to tell me exactly what the problem is and if they can't, then there isn't a problem." That stopped their complaints.
>
> Another time, we were losing a lot because parts were being stolen. We put in metal detectors. The workers feared that metal detectors make men impotent. I said, "How can the people working in the airport have so many children if they become impotent? The people who work there pass through it five or ten times a day." Nobody came back to me after that.
>
> Once, when we needed to employ a personnel manager, the best candidate was a lady. The managing director said "the job has got a higher profile than the men. Do you think she can manage?'
>
> I said, "I have been managing very well."
>
> He said, "Jean, just get me somebody who is half of you."

Frustration at not being put on the board of directors caused her to leave and set up her own company. She has found the uncertainties of independence distressing, and has a different set of disadvantages as an independent businesswoman.

> There aren't many woman-headed companies here. Consequently, many other women look up to me to see how I am doing, before they set up on their own. There are just some places I can't go. I can't walk into a club and talk to the chap next to me, even though he may be a prospective client.

Doris Masinde is the Kenya publicity manager for internationally marketed personal care products sold in practically every *duka* [small shop] in Kenya. She is far more suited to that work than to government or NGO work because she loves the glamour of her job and likes "working with people, but not people in tragedy." Despite the lure of the business world, she does not plan to remain permanently. She wants to study public or environmental health in the United States. She hopes to get a scholarship as a result of being on the board of an NGO serving women. Although she has enjoyed her high-powered job, it has had a high personal cost. It ruined an intimate relationship because her beloved was jealous of her professional success.

Nuria Yussuf, the young woman whose family had many years earlier moved from an outlying village into Kajiado town so she and her siblings could go to good schools, works many hours a day running a restaurant. It is in the center of town, so there is a constant flow of customers. She is almost always in front to greet people, find out their needs, and make sure they are accommodated. Nuria is an energetic hard-working young woman who wants to be independent, whereas her family wants to offer her some degree of protection and shelter. When we first interviewed her, she was hoping to leave soon for study in India. She would have preferred to be working in something other than her family's business, but that was not permissible. She believed that after her return, her family would not object to her seeking outside employment. When we saw her again five years later, she had not gone to India but had taken over management of the restaurant. Her father had been reluctant to give her such a public responsibility, and to free her from family oversight. But she has always been very close to him. He told her frankly what his worries were for her, and she was able to satisfy him that she could handle any situation. She made a solemn promise that she would not "get spoilt" (lose her virginity), and he consented to give her ownership and full responsibility for the restaurant. Since she has taken over, she finds it very difficult to leave even for a few hours during the week. On the weekends, one of her brothers manages the restaurant so she can leave. When we took her for a Sunday outing, she felt unsure until the last minute that she would be able to accompany us. She had not been away for more than an hour for months.

Because of the desperation people feel about employment opportunities, young people struggle to get training and qualifications. NGOs sponsor various kinds of training programs. When these aim at preparing people to run their own businesses, they often succeed. When they aim at fitting people for employment in either the private or public sector, they increase the number of overqualified, underemployed people. Eventually, the subsidy that offers companies an incentive to take on trainees ends. Often the trainee is neither kept on nor hired elsewhere. Permanent jobs may go only to those with influence, connections, or ready cash for a bribe.

When Jared Shiundu finished secondary school, he enrolled in a sponsored training program at Trans-Nzoia Sugar Refinery. He was trained in all phases of welding and electrical work, then sent to a school in Mombasa for five months of further training. Despite making excellent progress and having good references he was not kept on at the end of the training program. He later worked for another refinery at a salary below what he was earning as a trainee. That factory was closed for many months, so Jared went to Nairobi as a casual laborer. He found little work, and went back home with no realistic prospect of a job.

Hellen Wambui, a former sex worker living in the streets of Nairobi got a break when a Catholic nun found her a place in a job program at a food packaging industry, but lost it because of corruption. "The Catholic Sister took me to True Foods as a casual laborer. By end of the first year, the Sister had left. The supervisor expected a bribe, and since I couldn't pay, I was not rehired."

Of the 1.6 million people with paid employment, forty three percent work for the government. All of them, even the local chiefs, work for the national government. Local, district and provincial posts are all filled by the national government.

Public service attracts people for the best of reasons, and the worst. When the government is known to be as thoroughly corrupt as it has been in Kenya, some are attracted to public employment primarily by the opportunity for looting. But the positions that offer substantial payoffs are rarely held by women. Despite the frustrations inherent in working in a corrupt public sector, government employment in Kenya, as anywhere else in the world, still attracts people who genuinely want to serve their community. Like most of us, Maggie Mwangi, a nurse in Malindi, had many reasons for choosing her eventual career.

> When I was in secondary school, I was very sick. Most of the time, there was no one to care for me. Lying in bed day after day, I thought a lot and decided to be a nurse. I love the work because sick people appreciate us very much. Also we are very smart.[7] But we work long hours. Generally, the hospital lacks many things that we should have, so we improvise. We just do the best we can for patients with what we have here.

For Mariamu Khalifa, the security of government employment gave her more flexibility than she might have had in the corporate world. When she became dissatisfied with teaching, she was able to retrain and change without leaving.

> I came home to Malindi after form four and started teaching from 1987 to 1992. Teaching was giving me a very hard time because you have to talk a lot. In an office, there is not as much talking as in the classroom. I was able to train in the evening and then given employment as a secretary in the same institution. I think I will stay with that for so long.

She has stayed. She has since married and borne a child, but is still working at the same job, and still satisfied with it.

The "glass ceiling" that keeps women from rising as far as similarly qualified men, operates a bit differently for government workers. Oruko Omina, a public health specialist, believes that being a married woman

7. In Kenyan English, this means well-groomed. It does not refer to intelligence.

interfered with her career mobility in some ways that could happen anywhere in the world, and in some ways that might not occur in other places.

> The authorities have it in their minds that women can't do certain things, yet we sit in the same class and score the same grade. But when it comes to positions, the man gets the higher position.
>
> If you're married, you can be denied a promotion or a transfer. If I wanted to be transferred to Busia district and my husband was in Nairobi, they'd say, "Oh, no, we can't transfer you because your husband is here." My husband can only work in Nairobi, so I was only placed here, as much as I wanted to go elsewhere and explore. Unless you have a kind of husband who is very understanding and will tell them "You may take my wife anywhere" you'll never be posted away.

These public sector jobs rarely pay enough to live on. Many excellent public employees cannot afford to remain. That's why Eileen Waruguru, who had been a head teacher for years, and relished the respect it earned her, left to take up hair dressing. Others leave out of overwhelming frustration with inadequate funding, theft of public property, protection of favored incompetents, and harassment by higher-ups.

Desire to serve also leads people to employment in the non-profit or NGO sector. Josephine Mwaura is a college graduate who worked as a writer for the African Housing Fund [AHF].

> I came to work here because I so disliked the negative reporting of the news media. I wanted to work with an NGO which was doing something positive. AHF truly works with the poorest of the poor, and the work is interesting.
>
> Before I came here, I didn't realize that there is money in the streets. I didn't know that people who live in the streets don't necessarily go hungry. Now, when I'm approached by a street person, I'm much more comfortable than I used to be. I feel I know these people, though their stories are different than mine. They ask me for money, but I ask questions. Now, I'm more likely to give food than money.

Dekha Ibrahim left government employment for an NGO. She had taught in a school for nomadic children, and later became Headmistress of a girls' school. The District Education Officer in Wajir was worried about the low enrollment of girls, so he encouraged her to expand the school. After 1991, the problem of education for girls was superseded by a more pressing need. Drought killed thousands of animals in Northwest Province, and sent many nomadic families into town for relief food.

> We started a feeding program for the students. Soon hungry neighborhood children were coming. We could not turn them back. My free afternoons and weekends, I spent mobilizing women in my neighborhood, collecting food, clothes, water containers, anything that could be used by people destituted by the drought. I started income generating projects for women. One way of alleviating our community is through the school, but there is more to be done outside the school. The drought was a turning point for me to work on wider issues.

As the civil war in Somalia spread into Northeast Kenya, waves of killings sent more families into town, and brought the fighting to town as well. Dekha and a few friends began a successful effort to end the clashes and restore peace to Wajir [Portrait N]. She left her school and joined an organization doing health care work with nomadic families. Several times, she has been asked to stand for election to Parliament, but has refused because she does not feel ready. Eventually she probably will enter politics, joining the many people who conclude that the work of NGOs can't solve Kenya's problems until there is committed and effective government support for their efforts.

Self-Employment

Although there are women in visible positions with prominent corporations, the great majority of Kenyan women who work in the private sector are not office workers but self-employed, *jua kali*[8] micro-entrepreneurs.

For millions of women who have no job, self-employment is the only way to earn cash. Yet, many women who have regular employment and feel fortunate to have it yearn to leave and go into business for themselves. Some, like Wanjiru Mwangi [Portrait J], want to escape sexual harrassment; some crave more autonomy; some believe they'll make more money as independent entrepreneurs. A person with education but no specialized skills can often earn far more in her own business than as an employee.

At all economic levels, there are women yearning to leave safe jobs to start a business. Jean Wanjugu started her own business as a woman at the top. Nancy Karamana is a woman in the middle. She was born in Meru but works in Nairobi, at the airport information booth, answering

8. Literally "fierce sun." This refers to the many small-scale enterprises carried out outdoors. These may be micro-enterprises or larger businesses such as metalworking with several non-family employees.

traveler's questions. She plans to leave this secure employment when she has saved enough.

> I hope to retire in four years to run a big shop, so I get some money every day, not wait for the end of the month.
>
> I'd like to have a self-service shop that sells everything — in Nairobi, not Meru. In Meru they are just farmers. When they sell their produce they have money, not other times. In Nairobi, there is money all the time.

Even at the lower end of the economic scale there are pockets of opportunity for women to earn a bit of money buying and reselling. Mary Kiungu left a job in the Nairobi sales office of an electronics company to begin trading on her own. Although she has lost the security of a regular wage, she is very happy about the change.

> I don't want office work anymore. They pay very little. Buying and selling is better. I am selling perfumes and earrings to shops, just going door-to-door.
>
> My daughter learned hairdressing. She would like to have her own salon, but it is hard to find a place. She earns 2-3,000/- a month,[9] but she'd get that much from only two or three customers if she had her own salon.

Women with a bit of capital may stock and run a *duka* [small shop] from home. Roselyne Okumu runs a duka in Kisumu like thousands of other duka*s* in every corner of any city or any rural neighborhood. She lives with her husband and four children in a four-room apartment. It is the sort of housing that abounds in any African city: one story, iron roofed, made of concrete, attached to other identical apartments. Usually, four adjacent apartments constitute a building, but Roselyne's has six. Each has a separate door off a common verandah. The apartments of one building share a latrine, another small room for bathing, and perhaps a clothesline. Roselyne's building has a many-branched tree for hanging laundry, too. Just across from Roselyne's door is a spigot for the neighborhood. Although this is a city, goats wander among the buildings. Without rubbish collection, there is no reason to have trash barrels. Rubbish accumulates near the spigot and in the alleys between buildings. The small window of Roselyne's kitchen and the large window of her shop flank the door. One enters her apartment through a tiny hall crowded with pots and pans, and a large clay jar of drinking water. The small kitchen on the left contains two kerosene stoves, plastic buckets and washbasins, more pots, utensils, open bags of maize and sugar, today's

9. This was 1995.

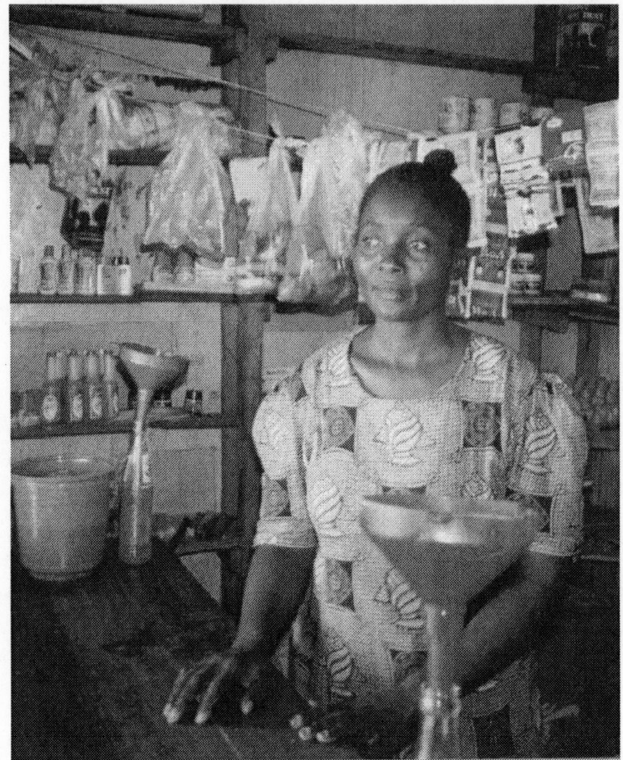

Roselyne Okumu in her shop

vegetables, tea, porridge, and some very pretty ceramic dishes with blue birds, that were a present from her husband when they married.

At the end of the hall is a sitting room with a back window. The room is crowded with furniture for six and piled sacks of maize, sugar, and other bulk commodities for the shop, but Roselyne has made it attractive with the standard decorative items of Kenyan homes: pictures on the walls and crocheted covers on the chairs and low table. To the right of the sitting room is a bedroom and in front of the bedroom is the shop. The windows are covered with a strong metal grate, and can be closed by shutters. Beneath her shop window, Roselyne has a large wooden counter, where she sits most of the day.

On her left is a large jar of cooking oil. On the right is a jerrican of paraffin [kerosene]. Although paraffin is often sold separately because it can endanger other goods, Roselyne sells it from her shop, and the air is permeated with the odor. On the other three walls of the shop are shelves with merchandise: condoms, soap, plastic slippers, salt and seasonings, clothespins, washing powder, solid cooking fat, combs, toilet paper, sanitary napkins, tea, eggs, maize, sugar, toothpaste and toothbrushes, razor blades, and bread. The smallest merchandise — candy, tiny packages of tea, and individually packaged aspirin and malaria tablets — hang from strings overhead. Against the back wall there is another chair, so a family member or trusted friend can join Roselyne in the shop. Cigarettes are one of the most frequently sold commodities. Many customers come every morning and every evening for a single cigarette, or two or three.

The shop opens soon after seven, when most neighbors are rising and making tea, and stays open long after dark. Most of the time, Roselyne sits behind the counter. When she leaves to buy supplies, one of her children takes over temporarily, or she closes the shop for an hour. Her husband works eleven hours a day at a local supermarket. When he comes home, he tends the shop while Roselyne works with the house girl to prepare dinner. Often, he eats at the shop counter while she feeds the children.

Roselyne struggles to keep her shop stocked. Although she earns a small profit on each item she sells, relatives' requests for merchandise are very hard to refuse, and consume much of her profit.

Rural women with some surplus, but not enough to stock a duka, may buy a large quantity of maize or other agricultural products and spend their afternoons sitting with other women at a market to sell their goods. Tabitha Nechesa, a desperately poor farmer in Kakamega District who serves as a volunteer health worker, spends her afternoons selling aspirin and malaria tablets in single doses in the marketplace.

Lucinda Mattoi is a young Taita farmer with a thriving business selling maize in a village outside Wundanyi. She goes beyond simply selling her own surplus.

> I transport maize from Taveta and sell it from my house. My container is a little less than a kilo, so if they are selling at fifteen Ksh per kilo mine will be at fourteen.
>
> My business is seasonal. From July to November demand for maize is very high, but when people are harvesting, they don't buy maize.

In rural areas, reselling of legal goods can be done with no license, but in Nairobi a hawker's license is required. Women who lack the license are arrested repeatedly. People who have a license commonly try to protect its value by complaining to the police when someone sells without a license. This was quite profitable for the police during the Moi years because those arrested often paid a bribe to be released.

For Margaret Wagatwe, hawking was always a struggle. The problem of being continually arrested became so severe that it drove her from selling beer into prostitution.

> I was arrested so many times. I would be released the next day, and maybe rearrested the day after that. All the money went to the police, so I decided it would be better to go to town.[10] That way, when I was arrested, nothing would be taken from me. Later, when I got two or three hundred Ksh., I would get some vegetables to sell. But I did not have a hawker's license, so I was often chased away from selling.

Even when they grow the family's food (and fetch its water and firewood), women's lives increasingly depend on selling. Millions of Kenyan women support themselves by selling products they can make or buy with minimal expenditure. In cities, women like Saadia Abubakar cook *sambusas* [samosas] or *mandazi* [doughnuts] for sale in the market, on the streets, or in small eating establishments called hotels. Others sit on the street with a brazier, roasting maize cobs. These occupations depend on a base of customers who have a cash income but limited time or cooking facilities. They are therefore profitable in cities, but not usually in rural areas.

Many women support themselves by tailoring or sewing, but to succeed they need training and a substantial expenditure for a sewing machine and cloth. Clarissa Kahala, who lost a leg in childhood, was trained in sewing and tailoring at a workshop for disabled girls near Mombasa run by the Girl Guides with financial assistance from the Lions Club. She had just told us in detail how she lost her leg.

> I thought I would have to stay at home doing nothing. There was one project that helps orphans. I went to that college for two months, but it was too difficult for me because it was very far.
>
> Now that I have finished my training, I will stay around here, and not try to go home because there is no market near. I do not need to be in a city, but it is good to be near a school where there are school uniforms to be made.

School uniforms may be custom made by local tailors, but only prosperous people have other clothing made to order. Eileen Waruguru used to supplement the income from her hairdressing salon by keeping a few ready-made dresses for sale. That part of her business collapsed even before she closed the salon. In the 1990's, a flood of second-hand [*mitumbo*] clothes poured in from US manufacturers. This trade was

10. To become a prostitute.

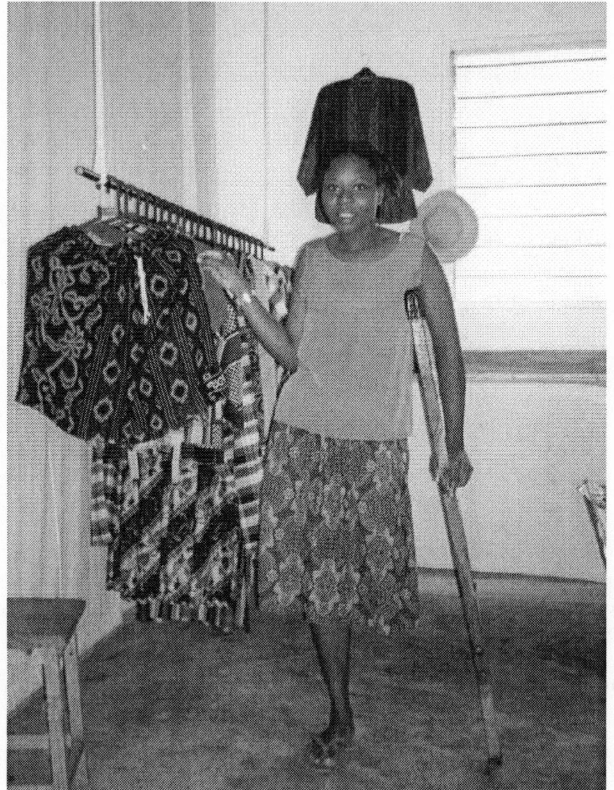

Clarissa Kahala with some of her creations

controlled by people with good political connections, and undermined the livelihood of small sellers like Eileen and tailors like Clarissa. Now, women with training as tailors often find jobs stitching in the Export Processing Zone at Athi River instead of working for themselves.

Although self-employed tailors are only likely to succeed at market centers near schools, there are a number of trades that rural women pursue close to home. Brewing and distilling grain supports many rural families. The trade is illegal, and therefore risky, but profitable. Most brewers sell part of their beer or whiskey to neighbors, but transport jugs of it by matatu to large towns or cities, where brewing is more dangerous. It is risky. Brewers can be arrested at home, and often are, or can be intercepted when transporting their goods. During the Moi years, on the road, as at home, a bribe often bought freedom, but this was not automatic. The police generally knew who brewed, and came around regularly for a bribe or a drink, but when under pressure, would make arrests. Young people who could run fast might escape, but older people were arrested. This was and still is one of the drawbacks to brewing. Another is that alcohol is visibly harming many families. When your neighbor's husband is drinking and her children are hungry, pity may weigh more than Ksh.. Rosemary Setei was one of many who gave up brewing for reasons of conscience.

> I'm a Born-Again Christian, saved about four years ago. The Lord has been with me through all the difficult times.
>
> I used to brew but I saw that it was not good because many people got ruined. They eat[11] even the money that was meant to feed their children. So I started praying, praying so hard that I decided to forget about brewing. I started praying, "I've decided to leave this business. Please show me the right way."

For millions of women, selling sexual favors is a dreaded last resort. Mary Mukuhi was born in 1966 and married young. She began life in a household with two parents, but when she was five, they separated. Both died when she was twelve. After she had borne four children, her husband began beating her frequently and seriously. Her face bears conspicuous scars as a result of being slashed with a panga. For the sake of the children, she stayed with her husband for three years after the beatings started. Eventually, she left in fear of her life.

> When I left him, I never imagined I would go with other men for money, but I had to. I couldn't find work, couldn't feed the children. I could sometimes get money by digging in other people's fields, but most of the year, that was hard. So I went with any man who would give me money. Some were brutal, but I was desperate, so I persevered as long as he was giving me money.
>
> Some men wanted sex on credit. In that case, I considered how well he provided for his family. If they were fed and clothed, I considered him a good risk and would go with him. Sometimes men would agree to use condoms, but then when I was with them, they wouldn't.
>
> Now I am getting old for that. It is hard for me to attract men, so I collect firewood to sell. I prefer selling firewood because no one bothers me, but I have less money.

The oldest profession takes many forms. Sex workers may be young or middle aged, fun-loving and outgoing, or reticent but available. The patterns are different in rural and urban settings. Most enter the profession from desperation, but some have other reasons.

No topic is harder for an outsider, and a woman, to study. I have interviewed many former sex workers, but not in circumstances that

11. Misuse, in this case by buying her liquor.

Mary Mukuhi with two of her children

led them to talk about that work. After I was frustrated in many attempts to interview currently active sex workers, a group of young men volunteered to help me. They are members of Anford Self-Help Group in Nakuru. All are deeply involved in the fight against AIDS, have taken a lively interest in my research, and tried to follow my interview instructions carefully

Stanley Tuvako contributed an interview with Patricia Nanzala, whom he believed to be about forty in 2004. He began with his account of her background.

Patricia was just a primary school girl when she bore Janet. The community protected the father, who was a teacher, since teachers were highly prized in rural areas. Her parents believed she had flirted with boys and got pregnant. She was sent packing, and went to stay with one of her aunts. At her aunt's place she was fed, clothed and cared for. After she gave birth, the situation changed because her uncle started making advances. She told her aunt, thinking that way she would save herself. Instead, her aunt became furious with her.

When Janet was three years old, Patricia married and had another child called Felicia. Her marriage did not last long because her mother-in-law mistreated her, and once her husband's cousin raped her.

In western Kenya back then, women could not speak about such things. Moreover, her experience with her aunt scared her from speaking. She had no job and nowhere to go. She was told that if she left, she could take Janet, but not Felicia. Luhya traditions do not allow wives to take the children. Janet was not considered a daughter of the husband, though Felicia was. So, Patricia kidnapped Felicia and fled to Nakuru.

She tried serving as a housegirl, but clashed with all the families because of sexual harrasment by the men and boys. In one household, she was defiled again and contracted gonorrhea. For months she ignored the infection due to fear; she stank awfully and was sent packing again. The pain was so severe that she was hospitalized for a week with her children. Fortunately, drugs were still free then.

She felt that since she had been defiled, she had no worth anymore; and she had nothing to be proud of. With no other prospects, she moved to the bars. At approximately nineteen, she was forced into prostitution.

Through hard work, she has been able to send her daughters to good schools. "I struggled to ensure that they never beg from anybody, and Felicia has really made me proud."

Stanley quotes the rest of his conversation with Patricia:

ST: If you feel that you cannot answer any of these questions I ask, please feel free not to answer. What are the difficulties you encounter during your work?

Sometimes arrest from the police, sometimes attacks from thugs, but I think the worst is when men refuse to pay. Some of the things we do are not easy to talk about. Especially the very young boys who, despite my age, come for me, then lock me in a hotel room and run off. I blame the hotels for this; but to most of you, we are not people, we are just pits to be used.

I don't like boys one single bit, in fact I don't even like operating with African men, but most of the year the *mzungu* [white, usually a foreigner] is not around, and we are forced to go off with these African men. I have had relationships with some very high-profile individuals. They always start by paying very well, then start evading, and then disappear completely. The young ones, on the other hand, are terrible. All they do is get drunk and try crazy experiments on us; I have many times had to leave, or fight them, or embarrass them by screaming.

ST: Doesn't it also make you look bad?

My friend, where I have come from nothing can make you ashamed. I have been done things by men that have left me looking down at myself, but I learnt something: give them what they want for a higher fee.

ST: Is it you who approaches the men, or is it the men who come to you?

[giggles] I know you are wondering why anybody would think of approaching an old person like me, but men are so stupid, especially when

drunk. At my age, I have learnt to identify the men who will definitely pay. I have to compete against very young, sweet-looking girls. To get people, I have to approach them and ask if they wish to go with me. Nowadays, I have to lure them.

ST: There is much danger? Do you have a way to protect yourself from HIV/AIDS?

I used to be so careless before. Those days the worst that could get to you was syphilis, which was very curable. It reached a point that I was common to my doctor about these infections. Now, I insist on the use of the condom without a twitch of hesitation, because I have seen people die of AIDS. My young colleagues ask for a higher charge without, and some of the amateurs don't even ask, but I insist on a condom. I do not want to die.

ST: How do you know so much about AIDS?

I do not know how to read that well, and in any case most of the materials we receive are not in my language, but I came across groups and listened to their messages, especially when I was in Mombasa. The radio has also helped, but mostly I became cautious from tragedy that befell my friends of trade.

ST: Do men ever insist on putting on a condom?

Do you? Most of them who come to me are drunk, so they are in a hurry.

ST: Do you think you'll ever stop doing this?

I don't know what else I can do. Although I have saved something in bank, I see myself locked in this world. There is part of me that is addicted. I have raised my girls through this trade. I hate men though I use them to make ends meet.

Janet's life has started taking a bad turn and I know soon she too will begin this kind of life. I have no bad feeling towards her, but she is a fool; she got pregnant from a jobless drunkard and now she is pregnant from another drunk man.

ST: What do your daughters think of you?

Janet talks bad of me, saying I wasted her life though I schooled her. Felicia I pray doesn't change. She looks as beautiful as I was when I was young, but she is more pure. We have had our quarrels but she made me a proud mother.

Eunice Wanjiru and Anna Wambui, two stunningly beautiful teenage orphans, live outside Nakuru in an area that some nearby residents believe is uninhabited. Their house and kitchen/distillery are made of split sticks nailed to cross rails, and topped with rusted corrugated iron. There is enough space between the sticks to let in a comfortable amount of light, but the walls offer only a little protection from weather. From their mother, they learned how to brew *chang'aa* [maize whiskey]. Their mother sold chang'aa and her favors. She became sick and moved to Eldoret, leaving her children in the care of her best friend. The friend died of tuberculosis[12] two months after the children came to live with

12. Many people with AIDS die of tuberculosis. I have no way of knowing whether this woman had AIDS.

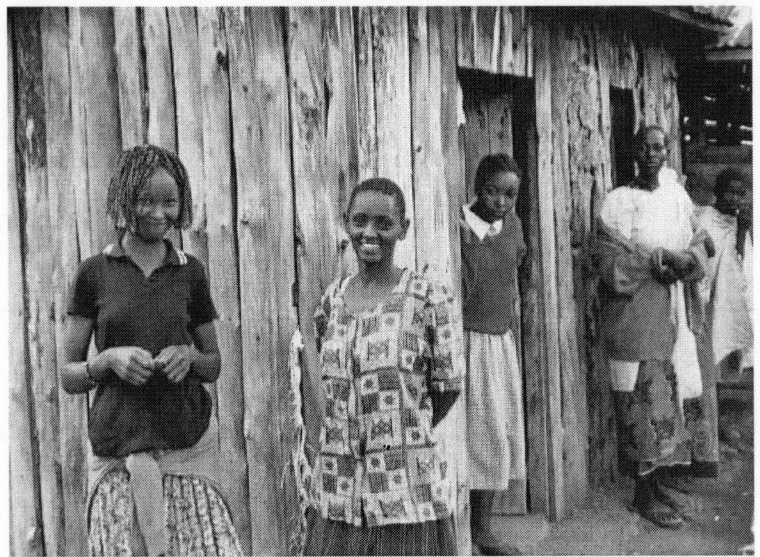

Anne Wambui and Eunice Wanjiru at home with friends

her, so they returned to their original home, supporting themselves in the way they had learned. Neither girl asks customers to use condoms. The elder, Eunice Wanjiru, is fifteen and has a son seventeen months old.

> We do not sell chang'aa because we like it. If we get a different source of income we would welcome it. Customers come one by one. Some get abusive and rape you when they are drunk. There might be a customer who wants to be friendly, helpful and generous. He might say he has fallen in love with you. Then you become friends for some time. But life is full of disappointments. Such a one goes away after a while.
>
> Some men have asked me to marry them. I would like to get married, but I don't want to marry any of them. One smokes *bhang* [marijuana]. When he is high, he says he wants to marry me, but he is not a good man. One man assaulted me because I refused to accompany him to his home. Only my screams saved me that time.
>
> If I get married, I would like to do business like selling clothes in the market or opening a small shop. This would have to come after marriage because I would need protection of a husband.

Eunice went to school until her mother left home. She was in standard four, and an average student. Her sister, Anna, a year younger, has no child yet. In 2003, the two girls were given a home by Josephine Kiarie, a big-hearted local teacher. Josephine was trying to help them leave their old life. But they found life with her too restrictive, and not fun. They left Josephine's care to return to their former home and livelihood. While they lived with Josephine, Anna went to school. Because of her age, she was placed in standard four, but she wasn't well prepared. Soon, the school wanted to move her to standard three, but she felt insulted and refused to join a class where everyone else was younger. Her frustrations with school contributed to her decision to leave Josephine's protection.

The circumstances of the interview made it difficult to ask the girls more about their work. Josephine was translating. She was still feeling hurt and angry that the girls had left her. Her disapproval of their decision was clear.

With her permission, Denis Kimambo of Anford Self-Help Group sent me an account of a conversation he had with his childhood friend Martha Mbugua, who was born in Nakuru but now works in Mombasa.

> Denis, I left school 'cause I did not belong there. I decided to stay home and get married to a rich guy, but my Mum could not allow me to stay home without going to school, so I would put on school uniform and go to town, spend the day there, come back home with a packet of cigarettes for Dad. There are many men in town and with little favors for them a girl can get a lot of things.
>
> What kept me going back was the challenge, and sense of power. As a young girl, I could play with adults' minds and get what I wanted. There were a few times when men hurt me, but you get used to that.
>
> These days I am queen in Mombasa. That's why you are seeing this house here [which she built for her family]. I have manipulated a few rich guys who keep me as their mistress, but I still go back to the clubs to sample and keep my skills on constant trial.
>
> In this business you have to be the best and always getting new customers to make more money. What I do is not evil. Look at you. You went to school but you have done nothing yet. My Mum used to dislike what I do but when I bought this land and built this house she accepted me.
>
> I went to Europe with one of my clients. In Germany the *kuros* [prostitutes] are blacks from here and they welcomed me, but the competition is high. During my one stint in the field there, a guy agreed he would use a condom but when we got into the room he became violent. Though he paid me lots of money, I don't want such men again.
>
> DK: .So how violent does it get with guys here?
>
> It's not fun, this job, especially when dealing with foreigners. The things that they do to you I should not tell you.
>
> DK: Kagoni [her brother who died] is gone and you have heard how he died. Have you gone for the tests?

AIDS, (pauses) no I haven't, despite being told to. If I become sick that's the end. I take precautions, but when you are in a room with a guy and you insist, most of them try to persuade you not to use condoms and they pay you more money. I have been paid up to 30,000 Ksh by a Kenyan so that we don't use condoms.

DK: If you are tested and found positive, what would you do?

Can we talk of something else, Denis? You are boring me now.

For girls who work in upscale clubs, sex work allows them to dress well, earn enough money, and enjoy the self respect that comes from being at the top of a trade. Stanley, Denis, and their friends know several sex workers who come from very wealthy families. They think they know what draws these wealthy girls to commercial sex: because of Kenya's desperate poverty and poor public security, many wealthy families chauffeur their daughters from home to school, and limit their contact with the wider world. Some girls growing up in that cocoon are intoxicated by the taste of danger when they achieve independence, and crave the wildness of life as a high-class sex worker.

Getting by in Desperate Circumstances

If a woman has land, she farms. If she has animals, she herds. If she has a job, she relies on her income. If she has capital, she can start a business. But a woman who has no land, no animals, no job, and no capital depends solely on her own resourcefulness and the generosity of others. Casual labor such as digging for others in rural areas, or scavenging in town, begging, or prostitution are almost the only ways women in those circumstances can survive.

Sayioyioi was born in Kajiado district. She married a man who had two other wives. He drank and eventually lost all his cattle. When there was nothing left, all three wives went back to their natal families. Sayioyioi now lives with her seven children where she grew up. She lives primarily by begging from her neighbors. In better times, two of her children went to school, but have no jobs. One other boy has some work tending other people's cattle. When that's not enough, Sayioioi begs from her neighbors.

Many women who used to live on the streets of Nairobi were brought to Kayole by the African Housing Fund,[13] which was building permanent homes for homeless families. They had come to live on

13. The African Housing Fund has since gone out of existence, but many of these women have stayed in Kayole. Along with thousands of other people, they are now helped by Jamii Bora, a microlending organization founded by the former head of the AHF.

the streets for many different reasons. Each had a dramatic story of surviving in a city despite homelessness and hunger. Alice Ndege was born in 1958 in Murang'aa. "My husband drank a lot, so there was no money for food. I used to sell beer, but the money was not enough, so I left him and brought the children to town. We stayed at the Mosque with a lot of fear of being arrested by the City Council."

Like Alice Ndege, many of the women we talked to in Kayole were forced to live in the streets after some piece of bad luck or injustice had caused them to lose their homes or livelihoods. Barbara Kamau, who was born in Machakos in 1952, has lost her home three times. The first time, her mother was chased after being widowed.[14] Later, Barbara's husband's family lost their land to private land grabbers. The third time, the Nairobi City Council took over the land where her family and many others were living. Now, Barbara lives in Kayole. After telling the misfortunes of her early life, she told us of her life in Nairobi. The loan she mentions is a small business loan given by the African Housing Fund.

> I came to Nairobi in 1970 with my mother-in-law. She had some small money as compensation for the land she was chased from, and got a kiosk. But that failed so I went to town to take care of myself [as a prostitute]. I had two children one and two years old. I met a lot of bad people, including police. I was arrested many nights. Sometimes, I could only collect food.
>
> Later, I sold vegetables and plastic bags at the Kikomba market. I was lucky to get a house in Korogosha. At that time we had more to eat, but I had no hawker's license. I was arrested four or five times a month. When I was arrested, I would always bribe the police to release me because my inventory was worth more than the cost of the bribe. I would sometimes pay up to 500 Ksh bribe. The licensed hawkers would report us unlicensed ones to the police.
>
> More children were born. Now I have eleven. Twelve years ago, the City Council took over all the housing in Korogosha, so I had to leave. One important thing happened when I was living in Korogosha. I was hit by a stone and hospitalized. My children were taken in by friends, who came to me and brought food and money. That was really something special because before that we hadn't helped each other. Of course, I lost my business, but neighbors really helped me.
>
> I went to town and was living on the streets for two years until I met Ingrid.[15] It was worse than before because there were more arrests. Also, my children were older. I had nine children then. The oldest three were grown, but I had to care for the others. I was very glad when I was brought here because it meant my children could go to school.

14. Widow chasing is discussed in Chapter 3.

15. Ingrid Munro, founder of the African Housing Fund and, later, Jamii Bora.

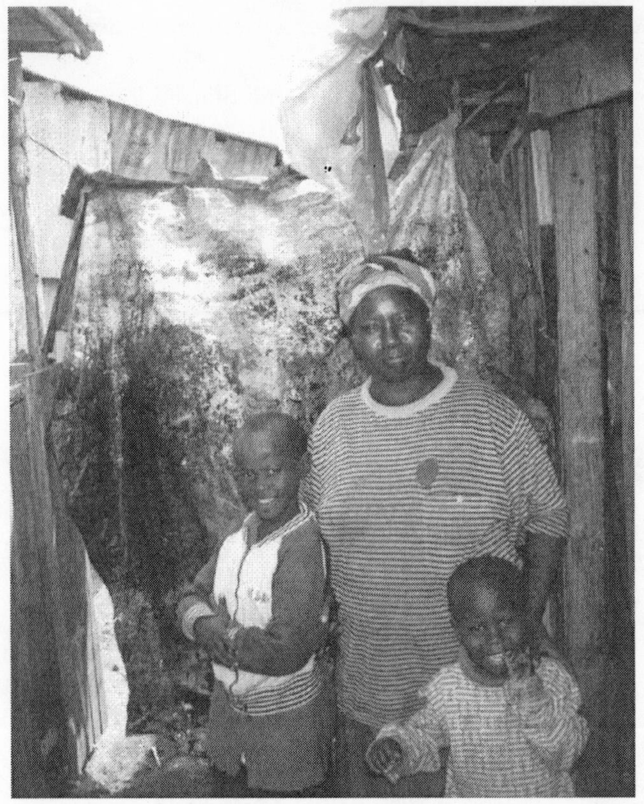

Alice Ndege with two of her children. The plastic sheet on the roof helps keep out rain. The hanging black plastic sheet separates her space from her neighbors'.

Now that I have the loan, I go to Meru to sell plastic bags and buy vegetables there to sell here.

Many women survive by spotting some little niche in the economy, like collecting papers or selling plastic bags. Plastic bags are the blight of the Kenyan landscape. In London, an impoverished section of Nakuru not far from the dump, Anna Wanjiru, the AIDS orphan who was raped by her step-father, earned a bit to support herself and her five younger siblings by going every day to collect discarded plastic bags, which she sold to *Munyore Women's Group*. The women cut the bags into thin strips and crochetted sweaters or sturdier bags from them, using the different colors to create vivid patterns. These sweaters are not as warm or comfortable as those from natural fibres, but they provide extra warmth over a dress or shirt.

Members of Munyore Women's Group with tote bags and sweater they made from strips of discarded plastic bags

Wanjiku Mutua, who was born in Limuru in 1968, later moved with her natal family to some land in Murang'aa that was given to them by the government. But problems at home made her flee to Nairobi to protect her children.

I had two problems at home. My brother was a drunkard and a drug user. He would take a panga and chase me and the children.[16] Also, our land was very dry. We could even stay four years without good rains, so I could not make a living by farming. By this time I already had four children, so I came here.

I sold vegetables in the wholesale market, and sometimes also house to house. But I could not earn enough to keep my children in school. A lady named Njeri told me I could make more by begging.[17] I continued to sell vegetables, but when I didn't have enough money, I would beg until I had money to go back to the wholesale market again. I would only go back to the streets when I thought there was no way my vegetable business would survive.

I have a daughter who is crippled. Now she sells the vegetables because when you are crippled, the police will not bother you, even if you have no license. I buy roots and give them to my daughter, and the whole family lives on what she can earn selling.

---

16. He may have been trying to get them to leave so he would have all of the land. Boys grow up expecting to share their parents' land only with their brothers not their sisters.

17. This was the translator's polite way of referring to prostitution.

Many Kayole women were forced to live in the streets after some piece of bad luck or injustice made them homeless. But Agnes Wamuruana, who was born in Nairobi, had always lived in desperate circumstances.

> My mother did not get married, so we were not at a father's home. I was an only child. My mother did odd jobs here and there, and that's how I survived until I was eight. Then I did small jobs like holding small children. When my mother had work, she would take me to help with children. I would not get paid: I would be fed.

Women who survive the hazards of street life have often been helped by the kindness of other women, as Barbara Kamau was. Georgetta Njoki, the woman who fled her brother-in-law because he beat one of her children fatally, was helped by another women at a turning point in her life.

> When we arrived in Nairobi, I was advised by one lady that the women sleep overnight at the wholesale market, and then in daytime, go around shops and the Mosque begging. I am very grateful to her because she opened my eyes to street life. Without her, I would not know how to make ends meet.
>
> Four times I was arrested and charged in court. I would take my kids with me to prison. They were still small. One time I was imprisoned for four months; another time for one month. They were with me the whole time.
>
> The street women would collect the papers from the shops and the streets and sell them. The children collected papers too. Also, they used to beg, mostly from the Indians. At times they would go to dustbins to scavenge for food because they were hungry.
>
> Unfortunately, from the dust bins, one of my sons took milk that was spoiled. He drank it and died. Three of my children are still with me in the same house. They are big now; they can collect papers and fend for themselves.

For people who live on the street, even minor misjudgements can provoke disaster. Many develop very clever strategies to provide for their children. Margaret Wagatwe has eight children and little food. She sells potatoes, onions, and any other vegetables she can buy. With the help of sponsors, she was able to educate her children, but most did not find employment. Only the oldest daughter had regular work as a tailor. But she died, leaving two more children in Margaret's care. There is no surplus, and often the children go unsatisfied. Margaret has devised a way to make sure that no child goes without food. "If someone is missing, they go to look for the one who is missing before they eat. Since I am not rich, there will be no food left for the missing one to eat, so I taught them never to eat until all are there."

Life is hard. Many rural people don't have enough land to feed their families. Some migrate to the cities in hope of employment. Once there, many find neither employment nor housing, and they may not be able to go home again. Kenya is filled with desperate people, many with little land or income, and some with none.

Portrait J

Hadija Ali

At the African Housing Fund's project for Nairobi street women in Kayole, I interviewed a dozen women who had just been given business loans. Among them, I found Hadija Ali's tale especially moving because of her aunt's struggles to care for her small siblings, and because of Hadija's own marriage and subsequent loss of her husband's property. Hadija talked willingly about some very painful episodes in her past.

I was born in Nairobi. My parents were laborers, picking coffee on the white men's plantations, but I want to go back and give you the background on my mother. She was born upcountry. She had no father, and her mother had no land. Unfortunately, her mother, my grandmother, died leaving four children, two girls and two boys. My mother was the littlest, and the other sister was the oldest. When their mother died, there was no one to care for them. They were taken very far, to a place by the road, and told to stay there. They were told that someone was coming for them, and they would be taken to a new home. A big fire was lighted for them. The older boy wandered away from the fire, and was taken by a hyena. The big sister got so scared she took my mother on her back, and took the little boy by the hand and started running. But God's mercy, she found some people who were celebrating a wedding, so she ran to them. A woman there asked her why she was crying, so she told how they had been left under that tree, but no one had come. The woman took them into her house, bathed them, and fed them porridge. After that, although this woman was not from their area or their tribe, she cared for them and they became like her own children.

Eventually, my aunt found a suitor and got married. My mother and her brother eventually moved to Kiambu, where my mother married. My parents lived on squatter land, and worked on a coffee plantation, but the brother died. My mother had five children. I am the lastborn, but three died, so I am left with only one brother. After my father died, my mother converted to Christianity, so she was buried at the church.

There was an Indian man who used to come and sit by us when we were working in the coffee plantation. He wanted to marry me, so he started giving money to my brother. Eventually, he carried me off without my mother knowing anything about it. It was all arranged with my brother. He was an old man, and I was thirteen, so love was not part of it.

I lived with him fifteen years before he died. He was a Muslim, so I converted, but I was not a devoted Muslim.

During the time we were married, he acquired many things. He had a lorry and properites and so much. But because I did not go to school and can't read and write, these things were taken from me by some people who pretended to be his relatives. He had no real relatives near because he was born in India, and came here alone, but these people were other Indians who knew him. They wrote a paper saying all his things were to be given to them. When he was lying dead, they took an ink pad and pressed his fingers to it to get his fingerprints on this paper, signifying that he agreed that his possessions would go to them. So I was chased from the house where we lived. I had five children who were still small when he died.

There was a social worker who found me and helped me for a long time, until my oldest child became old enough to help me. Then they said that he should get a job and they would no longer help me. So we moved again, but my son became mentally sick. He is still alive, though he is very sick. He drinks a lot, and because of that and the mental sickness, he has aged very fast. He is now completely gray, much grayer than I am. He does not have a particular spot where he lives. When I want to see him, I go to Pumwani and ask if anyone has seen him, and I tell them I want to see him.

After he became sick, I went into trade. I began selling miraa, which I bought from a trader from Meru. That was a good business, I was able to feed the children and to pay rent for a house and bus fare for the children to go to school. But even with the miraa, I had little money.

My brother, who sold me so many years before, said, "Why are you still in problems? You have daughters whom you can sell and get money to keep you."

I said, "No, no, I won't sell them. I'll let them get an education first."

Then another disaster happened. The house I was renting got sold, and the rent was raised so I couldn't pay it. I rented another house which was not suitable for my trade. Then my daughter ran off. By this time she had five children. She had employment in an Indian's house. One Indian man said he would marry her, but he would not care for her children, so she went to Uganda to marry him, and left the children with me.

At that point, I started going to town to beg and earn money any way I could. When I got a bit of money, I would buy charcoal and resell it. There was never enough food, so I could not school my children and grandchildren anymore. We lived like that for twelve years.

One of my daughters was married by a Somali. She was not accepted by his community. He will buy her anything she needs, but he won't give her money, so she cannot help me. The others are not able to help me either, because apart from that daughter, none of them has enough to keep themselves.

But then a man named Paul, who worked with Ingrid,[1] came to the places of begging. He talked to us and told us help was coming. He took us to be photographed. Last year, we were brought here, and immediately given a house.

Now, I will be starting a business. Yesterday, I got a loan of 3,000 Ksh., so now I can start, but I am not sure what to do. I would like to do a trade of second-hand clothes. They are sold one bale for 6,000 Ksh, but I do not have the strength to carry a big load on my back. Perhaps I will sell charcoal.

Someone suggested that I could sell clothes with a partner and split the bale, but I am afraid to do that. Some people are not honest, but I have to be very honest in my business. Last year I accepted Jesus Christ as my personal savior so I can't go back to cheating.

As I told you, I became a Muslim because of my husband, but I was a great drunkard, so I was not really benefitting from being a Muslim. My children are Muslims and maybe they do not like my conversion, but as far as spiritual life is concerned, I am free and must decide for myself. If I still had a husband, probably he would beat me for converting, but since he is dead, I am free.

Now my life has changed to something I can feel good about. Before, when I would go begging, I could come home to my children so drunk I would fall in the ditches. When I got saved, I stopped drinking. That is what being a saved Christian means. You do not drink or smoke or use any drug that will harm you. Converting has really saved my life.

The thing I would like women in the rest of the world to know about Kenya is that most of the people here are very poor, even as I am. My daughter married and started out her life in poverty too. I am old, but still poor, though I have always worked as much as I was able.

Six years later, I tried to find Hadija again. She did not have a business, but was known to beg on Fridays at the Central Mosque. I found her there and we talked again. Her life has become very difficult. Her hearing and sight are beginning to fail. A daughter who is living with her made plans to marry, but decided to stay with Hadija instead, since Hadija is no longer able to wash herself. The daughter who was married to a Somali and her husband have both died.

Hadija comes to town during the day to beg, but goes back at night to the small house she shares with her daughter and four grandchildren. Four of her children are still living, including the drunkard son. None has regular employment, or land to farm. All scramble for casual labor.

---

1. Of the African Housing Fund.

Hadija has become a Muslim again, both because Muslims have been generous to her and because all her children are Muslims. When I asked her about this, she said, "When I pray to Allah, I feel sure I am talking to the true God, but my goal is to be sure I see God when I die, whether Christian or Muslim."

8

Sources of Joy

A life of struggle against hunger or cruelty does not preclude joy. Many of the women whose lives are hardest still find or create joy. Narrating only the external facts of their lives hides the wellsprings of their emotional sustenance. To encourage respondents to describe the brighter side of their lives, we asked two dissimilar questions:

"What are the things that make you happy now?"

"When you have finished in the fields (or whatever applied to the respondent), *and you have some time for yourself, what do you enjoy doing?"*

Pride in their work, creating beauty, appreciation of nature, leisure activities, family or community, reasons for optimism about the future, and above all, religion, were the answers.

Pride of Accomplishment

Like people anywhere, many of the women we interviewed take pride and pleasure in work well done, whether farming, crafts, leading peers or studies. Although it is arduous, many women greatly enjoy the work on their farms. When asked about what they do for their own pleasure, many, many women respond with some farm task.[1]

> I enjoy planting *sukuma wiki* (kale) because it grows quickly and is easy to pluck. But I hate harvesting beans because it takes long to harvest them, to carry them home, and to beat them (so the pods open and the edible bean can be removed).
>
> —Lillian Kibuka, Wundanyi

1. Clearly, some mentioned work activities because they enjoy them. Others may have mentioned them because the question appeared peculiar and this was their assumption about what sort of answer was expected.

I like cattle. As a child, I went with them every day, and up till now I still like caring for them.

—Siyomit, Kajiado

I used to look after cows after I finished school. Then I did *shamba* work with my mother. All the work was good, but I liked going to the *shamba* most.

—Jecenta Atieno, Kakamega

If I have no have-to-do, I like to just prepare things around the house and compound.

—Lucille Bwanga, Kakamega

I like farming and poultry, collecting the eggs and cleaning the poultry house.

—Maria Rotich, Kimaren

As a child, I really liked cooking, fetching water, and cutting firewood. Now it's a familiar routine, so I still like it.

—Anna Mwende, Athi River

For some, creating beautiful and useful objects is an important life enrichment, as well as a source of additional income. Rosemary Njeri creates beautiful batiks for sale in Nairobi with her husband. "I didn't know how to make batiks before my husband showed me. I feel more satisfied in making batiks than working in the shamba."

Often, farm women supplement their incomes through crafts, which provide flexibility and the satisfaction of creating something useful. A craftswoman can pursue her craft intensely when there is little farmwork, and cut back during planting, weeding, and harvesting.

Traditional crafts using available natural materials have provided extra income for many rural women. Monicah Abdullah who was born in Mumias in 1937, was good at making things. Although some of her neighbors were struggling, she supported herself comfortably and put her children through primary school by molding clay pots and weaving.

We talked to women who made pots from clay, wove reeds into mats or baskets, and made ropes from sisal. But, by machine-made objects using synthetic materials are supplanting these traditional crafts, so few women now can support themselves and educate their children entirely through traditional crafts. Flores Mwang'ombe likes to make baskets, but finds it hard to sell the traditional ones. Now, she only makes baskets when she can buy the synthetic materials she can sell easily.

Diane Kimunda of Kipousi Women's Group showing a basket she made using traditional local materials

When I have time, I like to make something, like baskets, but sometimes even these materials you are supposed to buy. I don't have the money, even if there is that little time.

HH: Why don't you use the materials just growing here?

Locally it is possible. But you know things have changed. People call those ones old-fashioned. Some still buy those, but not many. So, much as I'd like to spend my free time making baskets, it's not possible sometimes.

LEISURE

To most grown women, leisure seems an alien concept. Married women have little time. Apart from religious observances, few can devote much time to non-economic activities. Many would not let their hands be idle, except perhaps on the Sabbath.

Only young, unmarried women named a leisure activity that they enjoy now. Mariamu Khalifa is a school secretary in Malindi. Before she married, she said, "I enjoy reading story books. I can spend the whole weekend indoors reading novels. I also like traveling."

Lillian Kibuka is a recent secondary school graduate hoping to find employment near her family's farm in Wundanyi. "I like being home with my family, working together, and going to church. Aside from farm and house work, I most enjoy reading Christian books, singing and visiting friends."

Many families enjoy making music together. Judith Kakai comes from a very musical family in Western Province. At school, she always enjoyed teaching other students to sing. Her family sang together every night. For Wanjiku and Wanjiru, sisters in secondary school, the happiest times at home are when they play music together. "When he's happy, father will come to the kitchen with a guitar. We sing or play a flute and mouth organ. Mother also plays the guitar, so we all enjoy making music together."

Mature women whom we asked about activities undertaken for pleasure often found the question surprising and confusing. Some told us which work they most enjoyed. Others, perhaps unable to think of an answer for present time, described activities they had enjoyed in childhood or adolescence. Olive Majala lives by digging other people's land. "Now, when I finish digging, I just go to sleep. But it was different when I was young. I used to like the local dances around the village. When I was very little, I used to go with other neighbors who were a bit older.

Jerusha Wawuda, a Wundanyi farmer in her fifties who went to school for three years, had nothing to say about current pleasure, but talked readily of the pleasures of her childhood. "When I was a girl, I enjoyed digging and handicrafts, especially basket-making."

FAMILY AND COMMUNITY

Many women mentioned some aspect of their family or community life as a major source of satisfaction. Khadija Mayow, a Somali mother of ten, was one. "This is best time because one of my children is employed, I've finished giving birth, and my husband and I are staying very happily."

Even if they struggle to feed and educate their children, many women regard having a large family as a great blessing and a daily source of happiness. Sayioyioi, an often-hungry cattle herder in rural Kajiado, expresses the feelings of many women. "Even though I go and borrow from one person and another for the children. I'm still happy because out of the seven children that I was given, they are all still alive."

Despite Oruko Omina's demanding work, she gets great satsfaction from time she spends in community service.

> I do a lot of voluntary work. I talk to girls at the church pregnancy prevention, and I counsel AIDS patients for the Kenya Red Cross.
>
> The way I relax is to go to a salon to have my hair done, or get a facial, but of late I haven't done that. I've got a husband who demands everything to be done. So the only time I have for myself is on Sunday when I go to church.

Dekha Ibrahim, the Somali woman whose mother first took her outside on a moonlit night so she would be bright, reflected on pleasures she looks forward to in her future life.

> There are traditional women's parties in honor of Eve, who is the mother of all mothers. It is done every Thursday afternoon as the beginning of the Sabbath. Women collect sugar, coffee, milk. They come to a central point, like the home of a respected lady, and they pray together and they discuss a topical issue like the outbreak of a disease, or it might be praying for someone.
>
> The older women drink coffee together, and the young ones are there to help the older ones to move. It's purely women, and it's something which helps to keep them together. It's a tradition which shouldn't disappear. Some of us young working women are not active in that now, but with age, it is something we want to do.

Nature

The spectacular scenery and abundant wildlife that bring tourists to Kenya from all over the world, also give many Kenyans a deep attachment to their home. Some women strongly prefer rural life even without lifelong ties to friends, family, and land, or concern for children's welfare. Esther Muthoro is a young, unmarried Kikuyu whose mother purchased some land in a Maasai area a few years ago. Esther quickly came to consider this land as her real home, which she loves deeply. She is employed in town, but goes "home" for the weekend whenever she can, and wishes she could afford to live there permanently. "It's a nice place, very quiet, fresh air. In town you can't just go outside and sit, but in the shamba you go outside and nobody sees you. There are animals there, like zebras, giraffes. We love to sit and watch them going by."

Optimism about the Future

Even during the darkest, most discouraging days of the Moi regime, some women found joy in hopes for a better future.

Members of Elangata Wuas Women's Group in Mile 46 told me with pride and enthusiasm about their group's accomplishments, and also told me their individual histories. When asked about happiness, they immediately answered with reasons for optimism. Siyomit, an unmarried woman of about sixty, named several. "So many things have made me happy recently: I am happy to see my children going to school. I am happy that my sons are able to marry. I am happy to have grandchildren. And I am also happy about the help that we give each other in this group."

Beatrice Wanjiru is another member of Siyomit's women's group, but was born in Ukambani, about 180 km away. She came to Kajiado as a child, and was thrilled to see a new part of the world.

> I came to stay with my sister, who was married here. I was young and happy to be in a new place. I was so excited about this place that I decided to stick around. Now, I am happy because there are enough funds this year for the Christian Children's Fund to start a primary school. They helped my daughter until she completed form two. I could not have educated her.

Neperon Naironma is an older member of the group.

> I'm happy that children of the Maasai community are now responding to education. A large number of children are being reported into school and a large number are finishing. Before, children just went to class four and then dropped. But now the continuity is there and it makes me happy for our community. I'm also happy that we are sitting as a women's group. We have thought that it's good to develop our houses. And also I'm happy that we[2] still have unity among ourselves.

Wajir was racked by terrible clashes in 1993-4. Hundreds of people and thousands of animals were killed. In town, everyone feared to go out after sundown. A small band of heroic women decided they would

2. The members of Elangata Wuas.

take responsibility reconciling warring clans and making peace [Portrait N]. When I first visited Wajir in 1996, the terrible clashes were still at the top of everyone's list in evaluating life. A group of miraa traders each talked of their own individual concerns, but when we asked about the community, they were of one voice in their delight about peace. Hibo Hussein, the schoolteacher translator for those interviews, appeared to be talking for all of them in saying,

> Two years ago, there were clashes, and now there's peace. Peace is a necessary and important thing in life because without peace, there's nothing — no kind of development. We don't see any danger ahead that the clashes will be back again. We rejoice that the clans that were fighting are staying together peacefully and so far there's no problem.

Two later visits confirmed that continuing sense of triumphant relief.

Religion

> I did not go to school, but I studied the Qur'an. I love Islam.
>
> —Saumu Hasani, Likoni

Since I come from a culture that discusses religion reluctantly, it had not occurred to me to question women about the influence of religion in their lives. When many women mentioned it without being asked, I realized this was a serious omission. Many of the women I talked with said it had changed the direction of their lives, and given them great happiness.

Islam is clearly an essential force for most of the Muslim women we talked with. Several volunteered their love of Islam, but did not discuss its role in their lives in the same way that some Christian women did. There are probably two reasons for this. There is a strong evangelical Christian movement in Kenya, which has converted many of the women we talked with. A woman whose religious affiliation is explicitly evangelical may have a sense of responsibility to spread the Word in all her contacts. Muslim women may not have felt similarly obligated. The women who spoke of their lives being transformed by religion were Christians of the "born again" variety.

The other possible reason why some Christian women may have been especially inclined to talk about their faith may relate to perceptions of me. Since I am an American, most respondents, whether Christian, Muslim, Hindu, or traditional, probably assumed that I am Christian. This made it easy for Christian women to bring up religion, and may have inhibited Muslim and other non-Christian women.

In speaking of traditional indigenous religious practices, women spoke more of self-protection than of celebration. Many women talked about witchcraft: none mentioned sacrifices, libations, exorcisms or other indigenous religious observances in formal interviews or in personal contacts.

I did not inquire about any of these customs because many people from my culture have condemned indigenous religious practice. Although traditional observances remain important, people are usually reluctant to discuss them with an outsider, especially a stranger. I listened attentively to what I was told, but rarely asked questions about traditional religious observances.

Among people I know well, who could speak more openly with me about this, traditional religious observances remain an important part of their strategies for protecting themselves from life's misfortunes, even for people who unhesitatingly identify themselves as Christian.

Although what follows are comments women made about the role of Christianity in their lives, it does not mean that Christianity is the only religion important to today's women. Many women, like Hadija Ali, [Portrait J] had "been saved" at a desperate time in their lives. The hope and comfort of faith, and the emotional support of other members of their church, provided important sustenance. Simanya Machocho, the Taita farmer who worries about the problem of two instructors, was converted while she was trying to adjust to life as a widow.

> My friends influenced me by persuading me somehow when you are saved you'll forget thinking about your husband. It would help me to forget all the problems, so I got convinced. I feel that it helped me quite a bit because I forgot about everything and went back to bringing up my children.

Loice Mattoi, a farmer and shopkeeper in Werugha, seemed very different when I saw her in 2001 than she had in 1996.

> I got saved in 1998. Jesus changed my life, so I feel free. I have joy and peace in my heart. My salvation came at night. I was in bed, and then a bright light came. I was so disturbed without understanding what was coming, but Jesus appeared and talked to me, telling me to follow him and my life would change. He made me strong to overcome my sorrows.

Priscilla Nyette, the Nairobi maid who had her tubes tied after the birth of her third child, told us that faith had quite literally saved her life when she was depressed and unemployed after leaving her husband.

> I was desperate. I feared I would develop an ulcer or go mad. I didn't know where to go but I didn't want to become a prostitute. I decided to kill myself. So I took the Bible. It was a good friend. I prayed with the children. I'm a Seventh Day Adventist, and good Christian friends started visiting me.

Angelina Mgange had been desperate, became a prostitute in a bar and bore nine children. Her income was never enough. She struggled to feed them, and could not educate them.

> I felt a sort of despair and a point of no return, and therefore I decided to be saved to make a change in life. There was a time that I felt like killing myself when I looked at all my children that were helpless. Someone approached me and told me about Jesus. I believed and changed my mind. I was able to go church and pray. I had been going to a Catholic church earlier but I did not see any change in my life. But when I started praying to Jesus for help with my burdens and my children, I saw some change. He opens ways for me. Now I go out to look for casual jobs.

Ginorah Keya loved going to church as a child. She didn't describe a conversion experience, or a moment of "getting saved." Her faith has always been a vital part of her life. "As a girl, I liked going to church on Sundays very much. What I didn't like was mixing a lot with many people, you know socializing too much. I was shy."

Ginorah told us about her hardships, culminating in the accidental death of her husband, but concluded, "Now, it is only the love of God that is giving me courage in life."

Olive Majala, the Wundanyi widow who lives by digging for other people, described the role of her church this way, "There is a group in the Church. Spiritually and socially it sustains me. When I am disturbed by a problem, I approach the group and we pray together. They advise me, and I get relief."

Many women described specific changes they had made in their lives as the result of increased faith. Hadija Ali and Angelina Mgange stopped drinking. Elmina Okuda and Rosemary Setei gave up brewing after conversion.

Gloria Wangari, a Kenya Airlines employee born in 1969. has faced exceptional difficulties, and met them with exceptional heroism. Just after Gloria finished high school, her mother was sent to prison for murdering Gloria's youngest sister. Gloria became responsible for supporting her surviving sister and brother and trying to meet their mortgage payments from her modest salary. Her brother and sister blamed her for not providing as much as their mother could, and believed it was her fault that the mother had gone to prison. When her siblings had finished school and were working, Gloria bore a daughter fathered by a married man. The man was a good and wise friend, and gave her decent financial assistance. The relationship ended after his wife discovered it. Then Gloria again became desperate.

> I got saved and got known to religion so I had to be very honest. My personal problem was that I was becoming an angry person. There came a time when I was just yelling to my six month old daughter. And I could see the previous circle coming in again. I was seeing my mother in me. When I accepted Jesus Christ as my personal savior, that healing came.

Belief in miracles is an important part of many women's faith. Maggie Mwasi, the Mwatate farmer whose sister-in-law forced her to move, told about an event in her own life that she describes as a miracle. She had delivered several children by Caesarean section, and was expecting to deliver her next child the same way.

> I thank God and am very happy. Despite the doctors telling me I needed an operation to deliver, I delivered in the normal way. After that incident, that miracle, I was so happy that I had to be saved to thank God. I love God very much. Before then the husband was smoking and doing all these things. I preached the news to him and he also got saved. He stopped doing these things and we started living in harmony.

Maggie is an optimist both by nature and as a matter of conviction. Although being forced to move from her natal home was a severe hardship for her family, she found a blessing in it, too.

> If you could compare between now and the last time you saw me, in my head and in my body, I have had many problems, and my health is not what it used to be. But above all, I am so happy, that now, in spite of the problems I have had, now I am at peace. In this new place, no one is pushing me around.

Serah Rahab, the Karai farmer who saved herself from two abductions, has not yet experienced a miracle, but she confidently expects one. She does not see any other source of hope, but has strong faith that God will help her. "I can't know what will happen. I expect a miracle will help me in the future because I believe God will not let me down."

Trudea Kemane, a teacher in a Nairobi elementary school, believes that God has guided her life at many points. During her school years, her family lived in the city, but they also had a farm which needed tending.

> My father told us that whoever will fail his exams will go upcountry to look after cattle. So I felt that my father did not love me, but I worked very hard in fear of leaving my mother (who was in town) and staying home looking after cattle. There was a small Bible I was given by my father, so one day in school, I knelt down and prayed in tears, "God, you see my father does not like me, he wants me to go and look after the cows upcountry. Please help me God, because I do not want to." So I wrote a small note and put in the Bible, I felt some relief from my heart and noticed that actually God had done his miracles.

After graduation, she was posted to a school on an island.

> On the way to that place was a big water which took about two hours to cross. I went on a canoe which capsized and I did not know how to swim. Other people had known how to swim apart from me, so one man that was in front of me got hold of my arm and helped me out, by the grace of God.
>
> I am somebody who loves God and therefore I have not thought of getting married. I have met men but have not seen one of my choice. I just want to leave teaching school to be a preacher. I will have to ask from God. You know even deciding about teaching I asked God and the same way I will do to Ministry. Maybe it is God who has called me and therefore he will just open ways for me. I just want to serve the Lord full time. I really enjoy the mission a lot. In fact, preaching is like teaching the word of the Lord, so it is the same.

For these reslient women, the capacity for creating joy in the face of hardship sustains them. The resourcefulness with which they bear their burdens is nourished by their ability to find sustaining joy and to laugh despite deep sorrow.

Portrait K

Lydia Kalaghe

I met Lydia Kalaghe at a sandy bend on the bank of the small river running through Wundanyi when I interviewed members of Kilili Women's Group, of which she is a member. Kilili was granted the right to dig sand from a plot along the river. When they had enough sand, they would hire a lorry to take it to be sold for building. They also made building blocks by mixing some of the sand they dug with cement. When I visited them at their riverside site, there were men nearby making building blocks from piles of sand. The plot belongs to the women. They had hired their husbands to assist with making blocks. All of the members joined in telling about their group and how it has changed their lives, then Lydia stayed to tell the story of her own life. She's a small, outgoing woman; stooped but energetic.

I am the firstborn of four, two girls and two boys. My mother got us outside of marriage. I was able to start school even though my mother had nothing because school was not expensive then. Unfortunately she died when we were very young, so I could not finish school. I was twelve, in standard six, when she died. She left me a small brother who was only three weeks old. So I had to drop out of school to take care of the young one and there was no financial support to take me back to school.

After my mother died, we lived in the houses of other people. We were often changing houses because no one really wanted the burden of four more children. Finally, we went to my grandmother. She died when I was fifteeen. Apart from the problem of how we ourselves would grow up, we had to care for the small one.

When my grandmother died we remained on her land. It was not really enough but somehow we all survived.

I waited until my brother went to form one when he was a bit full-grown, then I decided to marry. I was desperate to get married because I was hoping for a responsible husband to take care of me. I was desperate for anyone, without looking left or right, so it didn't matter that this man was jobless. I thought maybe it would make an improvement in my life but it didn't work.

Apart from all the problems I had growing up with, I ended up being married to someone with problems, who is unemployed, so my struggle continues.

When I started getting children the problems between us were so bad that I decided to run away from the husband and the children, leaving everything behind. Then I thought that if I leave the children they'll grow up with similar problems I grew up with. So I decided I had better mend the marriage and shelter my children. At that time, I only had boys. I feared that if they grew up without a mother, they would become thieves.

Now I have two girls and seven boys. My husband assists with the children to some extent. He is usually okay now. It's not a straight line. Occasionally he is harsh.

My children are fully grown up. All of them have been able to go to standard eight. They could not go beyond that because we could not pay for secondary school. Two of my first boys are already married.

The lands are not productive so we can't just plant whatever we want. Otherwise we'd be growing everything like vegetables to bring an income. But it is not possible. We work hard on our little land. We plant mostly maize but because of drought and the acidity of the soil, we don't have a good harvest.

Kilili has helped me greatly because I cannot survive on what we can grow. I dig with the group, and then I dig more sand on my own for some extra income. That's all I have.

Portrait L

Ayuta Women's Group

Barwako is an arid village just outside Wajir. The houses are made of bent poles tied together and covered with grass. Inside, an adult has to stoop, and light is limited. Between the houses there is sandy, dry soil with a few scrubby, short trees and an occasional tuft of other vegetation. There are no signs of cultivation. Many of the trades which sustain poor women in other parts of Kenya such as scavenging, contract digging, and selling surplus produce are not possible here.

Nevertheless, a group of remarkable women in Barwako have formed a women's group, found a trade, provided their families an income, and transformed their own lives. I sat with seven of the ten members in their light, airy meeting space, a frame of bent poles covered at the top with clear plastic. The women each wore two brightly colored cloths over their clothes, one over their legs and the other covering the upper parts of their bodies and their heads. In the informality of the interview, they let the cloths slip off their heads, but later, when I took photos, they covered their heads to preserve proper Muslim modesty.

Most members of Ayuta Women's Group are former camel herders who were driven into town by drought. Some would gladly return to pastoral life. Others prefer life in town because it gives them the opportunity to educate their children.

Although all the women present participated in our conversation, Habiba, the leader of the group, did most of the talking about Ayuta's history. Other members were more reticent except when I asked them questions directly. All had previously known the translator, Hibo Hussein, and seemed comfortable with her.

Members of Ayuta Women's Group surrounded by some of their mats

Habiba: We were very many women who have children, and we could not depend on anything. Maybe one day we got something, maybe another day nothing. In 1990, one of our neighbors learned about a women's group somewhere else. We just decided that we have to start a women's group and try to help each other. It was the only way we would survive and make life easy for ourselves. We collected women around the area together. We said, "Now we don't have money, what should we do?" We said we'd start with patience and gradually start to develop. We donated ten Ksh a day each, so the money becomes 3,000 Ksh in one month from ten women. We give it to one woman to solve her domestic problems.

In May 1995, we went to the Social and Cultural Service to register the group so we could open an account. We opened an account with 500 Ksh. At this moment, we have 7,500 Ksh in the account. We started collecting money to start a business. We bought maize, beans, and sugar to resell. And now, this year [1996], Oxfam gave us a loan for 10,000 Ksh.

When we started, some women knew how to make mats, but others did not, so we taught each other and made mats together. We sent off money to Mandera where materials for making mats are cheap. From the first sale we got a profit of 3,500 Ksh. And again we repeated and we got a profit of 2,500 Ksh from the mats. We have paid 6,000 Ksh back to Oxfam, and will pay the remaining 4,000 Ksh when we are able.

Now we are ten in number, but we began as very many. Some were not patient and could not wait for nine months, so they disappeared. Once a week we have a meeting to discuss our problems. The ten who are remaining are sincere to each other and there is no problem.

I asked each of the others how they had benefited from membership in the group.

Muslima: I got the skill of making mats, which I never knew, and I got also the idea of how to start a trade. I never thought of doing trade before. My husband was jobless and both of us were staying at home. Some days there was no lunch, no supper. Since I joined the women's group, I can afford the school fees of my children, I can afford the uniforms of my children. I can afford the daily bread of my children.

Halima: I have benefited in another way too. I have the idea of how to hold a meeting. One important thing that we have learned is sharing problems. Before, we used only to wait for help from the husband. We never knew that a woman could work for herself, and that was due to ignorance. But nowadays, we are no longer in the hands of men, of husbands. We work for ourselves. If our husband gives us something, we can use it in the group. And if he gives us nothing, we are not bothered. We are sending our daughters to school. We know very well about work. People solve their problems in two ways. They use their pens, or they use their hands. We cannot use the pens because we are not educated. We use our hands because so long as we know how to make the mats, we can help ourselves with our hands.

Khadija: I have benefited since the beginning of it. I made money, I got ideas, I made friends. When I got the 3,000 Ksh I bought some animals.

Siyada: The greatest benefit was from Oxfam. Even if we sit the whole day, the whole night, we cannot finish telling.

Saadia: When I came to the village, I was just staying in my house and never knew anything about what was happening. The moment I accepted the women's group, I got friends and I have learned something about what is going on in the town.

Another way their horizons have expanded is that they have started attending adult education classes.

Khadija: Now we are enrolled in school ourselves, the whole group. Immediately after lunch we go to classes. We start at 2:00 and continue until maybe 4:00 pm or 5:00 pm. We want to learn English and Kiswahili. If you come again, we will speak to you directly with no translator.

Muslima: Before, we were afraid, but now we are not.

Habiba: First three decided that they should go to school. When they went, we all decided we should go. We thought at least we should learn mathematics because every month we do some calculations for our group money. Also, when we go to sell, it is a problem if we can't write numbers and calculate. People take credit from us. Sometimes we forget the amount we are offered. Before, we had to wait for our children to come back from school. Now we do all the calculations ourselves. That is why we all went to school.

Maryam: One of the fears we had was that maybe the teacher would write something on the blackboard, and instead of writing correctly, we would write something else. We were afraid, "What if these people laugh at us?"

Member of Ayuta Women's group in front of her grass-covered home. The leather door has been rolled up on a piece of wood.

Halima: If you don't know mathematics and you don't know English, obviously it is hard. But now we are trying hard and in the long run we will be able to learn something. We are doing very well.

HH: What do your husbands think about you going to school?

Maryam: The first time we told them, they said it was good. They help us. We have no troubles with the husbands about this.

Siyada: My husband is educated, a teacher. He always wanted me to be educated, so when I told him about the idea he became impressed and happy.

Halima: But the rest of our husbands never went to school. We tried to persuade them to go to school too. Now they all go. Even the men have realized that one who does not have an education is totally handcuffed. So at night they go to adult schools. Some of the men are doing very well because they have worked for schools. They are very high, doing very well.

Among nomads, girls and boys go with the animals in the daytime, and at night some go to Quranic schools. Wherever the camp is, there is a teacher. Every group takes a teacher with them when they move with the animals. So therefore, since reading and writing are not new to us, we can catch up very quickly.

HH: How long will you continue going to school?

Habiba: Until the last day.

Siyada: We want to continue until we know English very well, until we know Kiswahili very well, until we know every subject.

Habiba: When you come back, we will speak with you in either English or Kiswahili. It's good to have a national language. That is one way to build unity between Muslims and Christians. Understanding and one language can solve the problem of disunity.

As a registered social service group, Ayuta is eligible for government assistance, but also subject to some harassment by chiefs wanting harambee contributions. In 1997, the chief asked them to contribute to a fund for women and vaguely promised them future benefits. They refused to contribute unless they were given a receipt and promised benefits equal to or exceeding their contribution, since the fund aimed to benefit women's groups. The chief became angry and abusive, and threatened to report them to the district commissioner. They invited him to do so.

The district commissioner, who is greatly respected, said it was a very good idea to insist that all contributors be given receipts. He promised them that their benefit would be 150% to 200% of their contribution. They contributed 10,000 Ksh and later received 17,000 Ksh.

When I visited again in 2001, Ayuta's membership had changed. There were fifteen members, but only three had been part of the original group. Some of the original members had returned to pastoral life when refugees were offered animals. They faced hardship because many animals died in floods.

Most members who had stayed in Barwako owned some land and were growing vegetables or other things they could sell, like grasses for mats or construction. Many had a "table shop" selling vegetables, meat, or used clothes. One member had a donkey, which was used to collect firewood for sale. All were attending adult education classes.

9

SEEKING SOLUTIONS THROUGH SOLIDARITY: WOMEN'S GROUPS

When a spider's web unites, it can tie a lion.

—Maasai proverb used by members of Elangata Wuas Women's Group in talking about their accomplishments.

Women's groups are changing relationships within the family. Being a provider rather than just a receiver is boosting her position.

—Dekha Ibrahim, social services worker, Wajir

Throughout Africa, women have traditionally worked together: hoeing each other's fields, helping each other harvest, cooking together for an important event. Women have always organized themselves into various types of groups: age grades, secret societies, work groups. These groups have a defined membership, and some perform rituals that reinforce solidarity.

In recent years, women have responded to increasing poverty by modifying these traditional groups to meet new needs. Now, they form groups whose primary purpose is to give them greater economic security. Development agencies use these modern variants of traditional groups as vehicles for delivering social services or financial assistance.

This chapter tells of the forms these groups take, the strategies used to help members meet their needs, and the dramatic social and emotional benefits that are transforming women's view of their possibilities.

Types of Groups

"Merry-Go-Rounds"

The most common type of group is a "merry-go-round," which operates like a non-interest-bearing bank account. Each member contributes a specified sum. The total is given to a different member each time. Eventually, everyone is given a larger sum than she could accumulate by herself. Merry-go-rounds exist in many forms, and at all economic levels. Some ask a contribution of one shilling a day; others require a thousand a month.

Zuhura Ali, who was born in 1967, is a nurse in a Malindi hospital. Her mother could not afford to educate her, so she was sent far from home to live with an older married sister. For the sister, providing for Zuhura was a heavy additional burden.

> She would give me money and say this is your fare, without knowing if it was enough. So I was not free to ask for anything more. I could get my pocket money only from the money I was given for lunch and fare. I ate very little and kept some of the money. Some other girls in school and I started a merry-go-round in which we kept a shilling each and give it all to one person by the end of the week. There were eleven of us. This was the money I used to buy my bras and my panties.
>
> I still play the merry-go-round even now. In one, ten of us collect 1000 Ksh every month. We introduced another for buying *lesos* [cloths worn as body coverings or as protective cover for other clothing]. We are just two right now, so we buy for each other. We intended to be more, at least four to seven people, so that each person would get four or five pairs of lesos when her turn came.
>
> Our merry-go-round is important because one person cannot raise much money by herself. Money from the group is a lump sum that you can use to settle a reasonable problem. The last time, I got 500 Ksh, and I do a lot with 500 Ksh.

The merry-go-round has endless variations. Sometimes members give weekly, but proceeds are distributed monthly. Sometimes, only part of the accumulated money is distributed and the rest is saved for future investment, or for emergencies. Often, as in the case of Zuhura's *leso* -buying group, the recipient is given something bought with the money, rather than the money itself. Nancy Karamana, who works in an information booth at the airport, explained the benefits of her mother's group:

> Each member receives about 1000 Ksh. None of them is earning. They can contribute maybe fifty Ksh a month, maybe 100 a month, and there are very many women, a group of about twenty or twenty-five.

When it's her turn to receive, they ask her, 'What do you need in the house?' She is not given the money; she just says, 'I don't have cups, I don't have a good bed, I don't have this and that.' Then they go to the market and buy what she needs.

They don't give the women cash. You know, if a member hasn't had money for a long time, she might buy something she doesn't really need. But when she is given what she needs, she is very happy about it. All by myself I would buy a dress, though I have many dresses, but I may not have a cup or a glass. I would rather that they buy for me.

Specific Purpose Merry-Go-Rounds

Many merry-go-rounds, like Zuhura's *leso*-buying group, are formed to give every member some specific item that all want.

In rural areas, water tanks are popular. Fetching water is the most onerous task, taking hours and eventually causing permanent pain, pain that is assumed to be an inevitable part of aging. This task is such a burden that women generally do not expect a new mother to do it. Friends and neighbors carry water for her. Some women's groups are raising money for water tanks for their members. Eunice Karoga, a Lusigetti farmer, has participated in several groups with distinct functions. She told about several of them, but dwelled on the group that should eventually provide water for every member.

I have joined several women's groups: the Morom women's group builds tanks for each member. Gimwe buys cows for the members. Kavarty buys iron roof sheets. Ramogi just started a few months ago to start a zero grazing project.

When we started Morom, we had many problems so we joined together to solve them. For example, if a woman had a child, we would fetch water for her. Since it was so far, we couldn't even get enough water for a woman who had just given birth, so we decided to build tanks to catch rain water. We built four tanks at four members' homes, but now we are waiting for more funds to continue building. We only have money to build during the season when we can dig.

There are twenty women in the group. We drew lots to decide whose tank would be built first, second, and so on.

Maggie Soriko, a farmer born about 1950 in rural Mumias District, belongs to a group that plans a sequence of acquisitions for each member.

We visit one member per month. We give 200 Ksh, two armchairs and a stool for that member. After finishing the round, we are going to buy a set of

> cups for each member. In case of problems, such as school fees, we contribute extra when the problem has befallen.

The neighborhood group that Doris Mathieu and her husband belong to has thirty neighboring families. The group operates as a cross between a merry-go-round and a civic association. Like a merry-go-round, it provides identical tangible objects for every household. Like a civic association, it provides neighborhood improvement by laying pipes to bring water to every homestead. And, like any good self-help group, it has brought benefits of greater co-operation and understanding among neighbors:

> The project started as a women's group. We bring people from outside to help us learn how to use the water well and to keep animals. There was a problem about money, but it's over now. The members called the Chair and solved the problem by looking over the money and forgiving one another.

Income-Generating Groups

The overwhelming majority of Kenyan women are hungry for part of every year. Even women who never have to be hungry may be hard-pressed to provide such comforts as a solid roof. Although merry-go-rounds are both economically useful and socially agreeable, they can't address the most pressing need — additional income. Thus, many groups that begin as merry-go-rounds gradually gain mutual trust and undertake an income generating project. Other groups form specifically to start some sort of micro-enterprise, or make a joint investment.

In rural areas, a poultry-keeping project is often the first joint project undertaken because it can be started with very little capital. *Ingavira Women's Group* in Kakamega District, which began a poultry project in 1991, aspires to start a *jaggery* [small-scale sugar refinery]. As a registered group, they could get a loan, but without business and management skills, they fear they could not succeed and would not be able to repay the loan. So the jaggery will be postponed until they can accumulate capital on their own.

The members of Lydia Kalaghe's [Portrait K] *Kilili Women's Group* have been allocated a strip of riverbank from which they scoop sand to sell for construction.

> We came together because we were desperate so we thought of this project, sand scooping. We approached the local government and were allocated a place for 500 Ksh. During the rainy season, there was enough sand. Now,

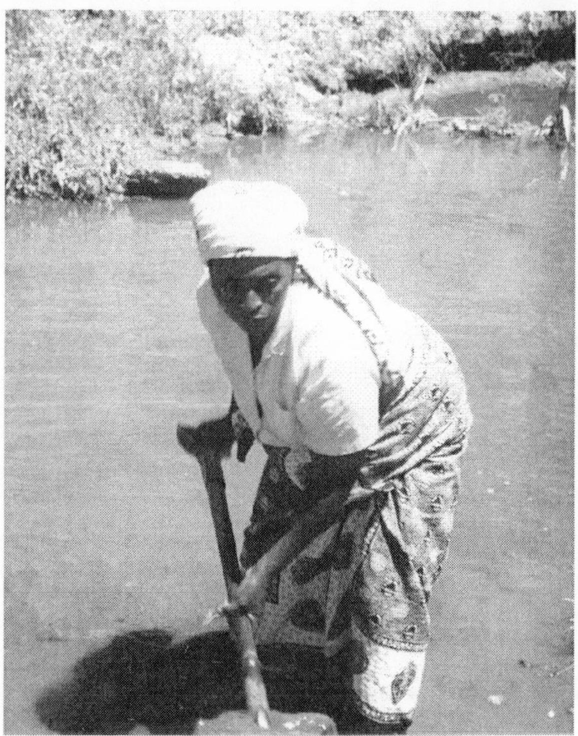

Member of Kilili Women's Group scooping sand

there is a bridge just upstream from our spot, so we don't get as much sand as before.

We had more members at first but two died and some left because they did not want to scoop sand. It is hard. We stand in the water hunched over and scoop as much as we can handle. We carry it to the pile on the bank, and go back to scoop again. Our legs and backs and hands hurt very much after a morning of scooping, and some of us have pains that don't go away. It is not easy work but we don't mind because we need to bring some income.

We scoop together twice in a week after the children go to school, and go home around noon to prepare lunch for our children.

At first we did not have the scoops to get the sand out of the water so we hired people with scoops and paid some small fee. Now we have our own scoops.

Sand is a seasonal thing. When it rains there is a lot of sand in the water but when it is dry, we cannot get sand. Because of that we thought when this sand is out of season and whatever we have scooped out is drying, why can't we be making building blocks?

We are the only ones making blocks, but there are others who sell sand. The whole group can make fifty blocks from the time we report up to midday. We

> still sell the sand also since it's not always that we have cement to make the blocks. So we run these two projects concurrently.
>
> This is good work for a group because many hands make many blocks. To get out enough sand to sell and transport as one person would take too long. Also the government would not give a plot to just one person.
>
> When we sell a lorry of sand or some blocks, we divide the money. A portion goes to the group account and a portion is shared among members. It is maybe just a bit for school fees. In case we didn't have food in the house we would buy food with that. When we are making a lot of blocks, we involve our husbands to better our incomes. Because of the group, we always have something small to keep us going although it does not clear all the problems.
>
> None of us belong to other groups. We are contented with this group. There is a lot of transparency; we can trust each other.[1]

Their group account provides another benefit. Funerals and harambees [community fund raising projects] arise unexpectedly, and neighbors are expected to contribute. For a woman with no reliable margin, these unforeseen needs for cash can be a severe problem. A group contribution covers all the members. For the women of Kilili, this is another important economic benefit.

> Apart from using the group account for expenses, sometimes we are asked for harambee contributions. It is better to contribute as a group because when a harambee or funeral is organized there is something in the group account whereas a member might not have anything to give. That way, everyone is covered.

For groups with almost no capital, the first business they start is often buying and reselling some locally needed commodity. Maize, lesos, building materials, rabbits, charcoal, miraa, and dried fish are some of the goods sold by groups we talked with. Many groups begin with a plot of land given by their church or a member, work it together, and later get a loan from an NGO or the government.

Tegelmoi is a very successful group in Kobujoi: old, well-established, with a history of overcoming setbacks. In 1972, they began planting vegetables together on land provided by a church. Their next step was to rent a *duka* [small shop], which greatly increased their income and provided business experience and employment for some members. Eventually, the owner of the shop terminated the rental agreement. They lost quite a few members, but some continued as a merry-go-round. Later they were given a plot, and the government provided iron

1. Their trust in the treasurer was misplaced and caused disaster. This is explained later in this chapter.

roofing sheets. Tegelmoi built another duka, which has been providing a small income for members.

Charlotte Kogo, an unschooled farmer who has been active in the group since the beginning, explained why the group's success has changed members' lives.

> We Kenyan women are under our husbands and they don't honor us. You see, they take us to be their possessions. A woman toils from morning to evening without a rest. Still, women can start income-generating projects, so that husbands see that the woman can stand by herself. Then they start to respect us. For example, sometimes a family needs school fees, and the group can help.
>
> We all live near each other, but we are very different. Some are a bit rich, some are poor, and some are very poor.

Anna Mwende lives in a settlement in Athi River. Her women's group has an unusual business.

> We dig building stone. We meet at the quarry, work together, and then part. None of us could do this alone because we needed money to hire the plot and some men to do the heavy digging, and buy the implements. The members move stones and clean the stone chips. The rest is done by hired men. We have all agreed to work hard so there are no disputes. All are young and energetic.
>
> We did not know each other before we started this project. We talk freely, so I have gotten good advice. We are happy just to do this one project because it helps us.

Regina Kavindu, another member of her group, said, "I have seen some tribal tensions, but in my women's group, when women start to backbite each other, or gossip about each other, other women separate them and calm them. The cornerstone of our success is unity."

The members of *Namulungu Youth Work Group* are men and women living along the Suo River which divides Nasianda from Mumias. Namulungu started as a merry-go-round. Soon, members decided to work together. One member who had some land lying fallow gave it to the group. Everyone contributed money for vegetable seeds. Now, they are growing vegetables and bananas for sale. Members work jointly on group land; and help each other plant, weed, and harvest on their private lands. Some of the original members dropped out because they could not make the expected contributions. Others were asked to leave because they didn't show up when they were supposed to work or didn't work as hard as expected.

Namulungu built a fishpond. The first time they harvested and sold fish, each member was given a fish "to rejoice for our success." They own some sheep and a pig and will give each member a piglet as they are born. They plan to buy a cow when they have raised enough money from produce sales, and have already planted some napier grass for it. One of the members is paid to care for the sheep and the pig. This has not caused problems or jealousy.

> We work together well and agree on what to do next. All the members work hard. Even the lazy ones work hard because they follow the others. We are not worried about trusting each other because most of us come from this area.
>
> Many people are attracted by our success and want to join us. We will try some on the project and then choose who will be the best ones to join. We want to be fifteen members.
>
> We decide together what to plant. When a member wants some of the produce from the group land, he must buy it.
>
> Our problems are not with the members, but just the common problems of farmers here. We are worried because we don't have a water pump, which we may need to supply water during dry seasons. Also, transportation facilities here are not good, so this gives problems in selling our produce.

When I visited them five years later, they had a water pump and were doing well.

I first encountered *Kese Women's Group* on a visit to Loice Mattoi. I noticed large piles of locally-made construction blocks in front of the house. Naturally, I asked about them. She told me how Kese acquired and then lost land, and must now begin again. Kese operated as a modified merry-go-round, giving each woman 500 Ksh. when her turn came. Most used the money to buy iron roofing sheets, which cost 150 Ksh apiece. Others paid school fees or bought a cow. But the group retained several hundred shillings each month that were banked with an eye toward starting an income-generating project. Soon, they decided they could invest even small sums for greater profit than they got from the interest-bearing account. They began to buy a truckload of firewood, which they bundled for resale. When the firewood had given them a sufficient bank account, they embarked on a more ambitious project.

> We were planning to build rental housing for teachers from outside. There was a plot of land set aside by the government for women's groups. Many groups were hoping to be given, but it was given to us, only we were not given a title deed.

We built a foundation and started making these mud blocks. We made three thousand blocks and bought ten lorries of crushed stone. We were ready to build, but we lost the plot.

After we were given the plot, others started grumbling and complaining, so we think the leaders were incited to take it away. Now, instead, the whole area has been allocated to a secondary school, so we have lost it, and lost all our work. We were not given compensation even for the foundation we built.

We are still ambitious and eager to begin another project. We hope to get another government plot so we can use these blocks.

Khadija Mohammed, who lives in Mtongwe in a large permanent house with electricity, has belonged to two groups that received loans. One group divided its loan among the members so each could start her own business. The other hoped to start a group enterprise, but encountered problems.

The Kenya Women's Finance people came here and wanted to meet different women's groups to give them loans Our group used loans for individual members. I started selling charcoal. From the charcoal, I got enough money to buy a freezer and started selling ice also.

My other group, *Mtongwe Women's Group*, started as five members. We joined the Kenya Finance and were able to get some loans. We also started contributing ourselves until we had 30,000 Ksh. But when we gave the money to be banked, the treasurer took it for herself.[2] This spoiled everything.

We are continuing despite that. We have twenty members contributing 200 Ksh per month, but we are doing nothing else right now. We plan to install a water tap to sell water. We can't start that yet, but we give each other ideas for making money and we help each other if one has a funeral or family crisis. We have lost some members who cannot raise 200 Ksh per month. Some members have lots of money and others do not.

Investments

For groups that have a bit of capital, whether rural or urban, buying a plot of land and constructing rental housing, is a popular form of investment. Nancy Karamana is one of a group of twelve women who staff the airport information booth. They have become friends, and cooperate quite successfully in a self-help group that is accumulating capital to construct a rental building in Nairobi. For this group, deciding what kind of investment to make was not difficult.

2. Like other Bantu languages, Swahili lacks sex differentiating pronouns. Thus "he" and "she," or "his" and "her," are the same. I used feminine pronouns here, but I don't know for sure whether masculine or feminine apply.

> None of us could do this on our own, but we looked at what other women's groups have done and decided we could do it together. We all make the same salary but some have more responsibilities. Sometimes one will skip a month, but pay double the next month. Some who have little are very willing to sacrifice.
>
> Although we don't work at the same time, we get along well. If you come to our meetings, you will be impressed. We enjoy each other, we trust each other. When a woman does not turn up for a meeting, I go to find out why. If there is a problem, she will tell us. If there is sickness, we all go to help her.
>
> We started paying 500 Ksh a month. It will take two years before we can buy, and longer before we can build. This plan will work. In Nairobi you will never lack tenants. The apartments will be booked three months before the building is finished.
>
> The more complicated part comes when you decide to buy land here or there and when you decide what to build on it: twelve apartments of one room or six of two rooms? All those decisions will be made later.

There is always a market for rental housing near rural schools. Teachers generally come from outside, and need housing. Elangata Wuas, like Kese Women's Group, decided to build housing for teachers. They are a group of unschooled Maasai women of various ages living at Mile 46, a remote spot near the Tanzanian border. Elangata Wuas started in 1983, with donor assistance. When we first visited, I only expected to sit with them and interview them. Members were eager to show us their plot and rental housing, and were justly proud of their accomplishments. They refused to be interviewed until we had seen their building. The group had worked hard to accumulate money and buy a plot on which they built a rental building. Before the building was even occupied, it burned down. They suspected arson, but could not prove it. With great effort, they rebuilt a four room concrete block unit with an iron-sheet roof. Morning glories growing up wires on the front of the building give it an inviting, homey appearance. They had a steady rental income and hoped to build more housing and, eventually, a row of rental shops.

The years between my first visit in 1996 and my second visit in 2001 were not kind to them. One year, they had bad tenants and had trouble collecting the rent. Then, drought hit, which meant disaster for all of them. The herds were greatly reduced. Kakeni Mosoni had started with thirty cows and twenty goats. When I saw her again, she had only one goat.

Some members of every family left with the animals in search of water. Those who were left behind had no animals to milk, could not plant, and even had difficulty getting water to drink. They ate only relief food. But, having rental houses meant that they still had a trickle of income that did not depend on animals. Now, members are struggling to replenish their herds and using whatever income they get to build water tanks or buy animals. In 2001, Elangata Wuas was not even running a merry-go-round because members could not contribute.

Like many other urban women, Elizabeth Ndunde, a well-educated Nairobi woman employed by a major NGO, spends her free time in her husband's home village working in the shamba. Since Elizabeth's city home is not far from her rural home, she is able to spend her weekends in the village. She belongs to four women's groups, each quite different from the others. Ndunde's groups illustrate the tendency of modern Kenyan women to form organized groups in their social networks. One is composed of women who have married into Ndunde's husband's family. They cook together for weddings, contribute jointly for funerals, and have a merry-go-round. When they began, they gave gifts to each woman's mother in turn, and are now giving gifts to the mothers-in-law. The group lends money to members at low interest. They considered buying a building plot, but were prevented by internal divisions.

> Although we are all about the same age, from mid-thirties to late forties, we don't all have the same means, and sometimes this makes for problems. Even though we had money for the plot, some people felt that if we bought the plot they wouldn't have the means to develop it. They thought the ones who had the means might end up owning the plot and take it away from them, so they prevented it. We lost that opportunity because of misunderstanding and have regretted it ever since.

Ndunde's second group is more affluent. From the beginning, they sought an income-generating project.

> The second group is made up of women who live in the village, but are not necessarily family. The age range is wider than the other. One is a primary school teacher. Two are so-called housewives who keep a cow and a few chickens. One has a kiosk. But this second group is relatively better off than the first. The members of the second are also more educated than those of the first group, and not so suspicious of each other. When they give me the money to bank, they don't think I'm going to take off with it. When I explained to them the need to be registered with the Ministry of Culture and Social Services, they immediately saw the benefit.
>
> When women's groups started in the village there would be some kind of a feast when we met. But in this second group, we specifically said there wouldn't be a lot of eating — tea and maybe sweet potatoes or bread. We

Nepron (l) of Elangata Wuas, and Irene Katete (r) with bags of relief food

didn't want people to cook, because if you start having elaborate meals, you just eat up the money.

Ndunde's other two groups are based in Nairobi. One was formed at her Nairobi workplace as a joint investment group. They have bought a rental house and some shares of Kenya Airways. Since they are a workplace group, they buy out any member who leaves the workplace. The remaining group, composed of women who had been together at Makerere University, was convened for purely social purposes. "We were in Uganda during Idi Amin's time. We Kenyans felt like sisters. We suffered a lot together. A few years ago, we decided to meet. A whole afternoon was not enough. We wanted to continue meeting."

Soon they decided to invest jointly, despite substantial differences in their incomes and family responsibilities. At the time of the interview, the group was collecting money to open an account, and had not yet decided on their first investment.

Groups with Outside Sponsors

Since self-help groups are transforming the lives of many families, NGOs and churches often sponsor promising groups. Sponsored groups usually serve very poor women, often women for whom running a business of any kind is a new experience.

Some sponsored groups run an income-generating project jointly. Others divide the sponsor's money among the members, so each can start an enterprise of her own. In that case, the group can offer each member business advice and pressure to keep going so she can repay her part of the loan.

Sponsors provide more than money. They may organize seminars that bring women from many different groups together. Seminars train members in business and group process skills, and give them an opportunity to learn from each other. Many groups adopt ideas from other groups. For rural women especially, the opportunity to travel and meet people from outside their home area is a special experience. The opportunity to talk with groups of strangers gives many increased public confidence.

Churches often sponsor women's groups. Ann Nyawanga, Diocesan co-ordinator for women's groups in Kakamega District, advises groups organized by the Catholic churches in her diocese.

> Most of the groups have problems, but the leaders' coming around helps. St. Mary's almost collapsed, but when I talked to them, they survived. Once you talk to them and give examples, it helps. If there is a leader who has done something wrong, we talk to her.
>
> When some member is being stubborn and not doing her share, the Chairlady may even call someone from the church to talk to the member. After four or five times, we leave the member [ask her to leave the group].
>
> Members not participating is a common problem. Also, sometimes members withdraw if they cannot afford the contributions. Sometimes, a fight makes members withdraw. Also, some are very lazy.

Irene Katete works with the Department of Social Services as a liaison to women's groups in Kajiado District. Her role is to help groups develop long-term projects, provide the necessary training in business development and group dynamics, and help them strategize about solutions for their problems.

> Since the 1980s, things have been very tough. Often, a woman has to look after her children alone because her husband may have turned out to be a drunkard who never cares about the family. So women thought it good to come together and help each other.
>
> If any funds come from the government for women, it goes to the women's groups. That is how Social Services started working with the women's groups, registering them, giving them certificates and advising them.
>
> Our main objective is to help participants think long term and not short term. In today's life, a merry-go-round will never last. We help them to develop bigger plans, not just a few shillings going from you to you, but then maybe bead making, then house construction, maybe later to a big firm, or even to a big shop.

For a woman who has not been economically active, joining a merry-go-round or selling vegetables from a cloth on the ground can be a big step, but neither of these will make her economically secure. For that to happen, a woman needs to be supported in taking larger steps that might have seemed inconceivable when she first joined a merry-go-round. If groups start with a merry-go-round, members may be brought to seminars where they will hear about more ambitious projects they can consider. For example, Elangata Wuas started small, moved to one rental housing unit, and planned more houses and a pharmacy.

Sponsors help women develop greater entrepreneurial capacity as they learn business and group process skills. Oxfam was the major organization providing relief in Wajir during the 1990s. When the crisis was past, Oxfam proceeded to transfer responsibility to local hands. Families who had moved to town for safety were given a choice of restocking their herds and returning to pastoral life or staying in town with some assistance. The assistance was delivered via women's groups, and responsibility for continued technical support was transferred to ALDEF, Arid Lands Development Fund. Suli Abdi was a recent university graduate when she began working with ALDEF. Oxfam has given her training and advice as she learns how to help members of women's groups become self-sufficient.

> The woman at Oxfam really inspired me in this work. Before the program was given to ALDEF, they made sure that there is not loophole, that the program is intact, clean, it is serving the poor, it has systems, etc.
>
> One time, some group was not paying their money well. I was just newly employed. I had seen so much resistance from the women. I thought maybe we should just ask the stubborn ones to quit the group. But she explained to me, "You are supposed to be humble and do things in a very diplomatic manner. Let the group decide how to handle the problem, not you to decide for them."

Dekha Ibrahim worked with pastoralists and former pastoralists in Wajir. She sees women's groups as a tool for broader empowerment.

> The women's movement is the vehicle for social change, for economic change, and can lead to political change. That solidarity, women doing things together is a very good vehicle for building up from the grassroots. What is now a social group, an economic group, will later on turn into a political group. It's a good beginning. The next step is to consolidate that by having a voice. I

can see in the future, especially in Wajir, a lot of women in politics — whether at the local level or national level.

Mixed-Gender Groups

Groups like Namulungu or Doris Mathieu's water-pipe-laying group include interested people from the neighborhood regardless of gender. Other groups that are predominantly women's groups may also have one or two men as members.

Kalaha is a relatively new group in Kakamega District. Most of the members have participated in merry-go-rounds and other small-scale projects in the past, but Kalaha is more ambitious. They held a harambee at which they raised ten thousand shillings. They are currently renting some sugar cane land and hope eventually to build a jaggery [small-scale sugar refinery]. In the meantime, they continue to engage in the handicrafts projects that are common to many groups. I attended a meeting at the chairlady's home. Fourteen women and one man sat in a circle on wooden chairs in a large, light-filled double room. Each woman was busily embroidering a tablecloth with her own designs. Even before introducing themselves, the women sang enthusiastically and well, then continued with introductions, responses to my questions, and general conversation. After learning about their work, I asked, "Are you a group of men and women, or a group of women and one man?"

The man responded, "I'm interested in what women are doing, so I support them."

The Chairlady added, "It is not bad to have a man in the group as long as they don't interfere." Everyone laughed heartily.

Josephine Okoth, a farmer in Kabras, has been a member of quite a few different groups. She had a bad experience with a mixed group, and would not join one again. "One group I was in mixed up women with men. They produced some money, but the men made a mess, and the group failed."

Even parish groups have found it best to confine their membership to women, according to Ann Nyawanga.

> In most cases, a man will oppose what women say. When we come to the money questions, they want to be the bosses. If they take the money, it will not reach where it's supposed to go. Sometimes the men seem to underrate women, and sometimes they bring in politics. Those are the major reasons the women don't welcome men.

Mary Kiungu, a Nairobi hawker, disagrees. Fighting between members tore her women's group apart. Now she is in a group with men and women, and says the men help the group function more effectively, "Men are very strong and very good. They want to know more about you before joining. They are serious and know what they are doing."

Beyond Self-Help: Addressing Community Problems

Groups formed solely to help members may eventually take on wider community problems. Or women may use the familiar women's group structure when they create a response to community problems.

Naseru Maa exists to improve the lives of Maasai girls. Their first goal is to enable girls to stay in school. This creates conflict with fathers who want to arrange marriages for their daughters before they have finished primary school. The leader, Sein Milanoi, lives a very traditional life, but has a thoroughly modern outlook.

> We had a big seminar for all the educated Maasai ladies in the district. One hundred and fifty ladies came. The topic was to improve the position of a Maasai girl. Our big problem is the education of girls. We came up with the position that our girls should not be married off when they are nine years or ten years. It is a very bad thing to marry off our girls while they are still in school.
>
> I'm the Chairlady of that group. I tried to hide [from taking this post], but I'm just caught again. I'm so busy. I have no time to sit idle. When I refuse to go for two meetings, the ladies are bitter.
>
> We approach the girls and do guiding and counseling in schools. We visit the girls' mothers in their *manyattas* [compounds]. We counsel the mothers, then the girl and the mother will fight the father. Since we cannot go direct to the husbands and tell them, "Now we'll not be marrying off our girls," we decided to go by a longer way. A few will change.

Other groups do straightforward charitable projects. Karai is a green farming village less than an hour from Nairobi. One Karai women's group has taken on the problems of AIDS orphans. We interviewed three members of different ages. One appeared to be over sixty, one about forty, and the third was a young woman holding an infant. All wore simple cotton dresses and lived, like most other families, in small mud houses. Nothing suggested that they have more than a tiny margin of surplus.

---

3. This was in 1996, before the reintroduction of free primary education.

> We help the orphans in giving them food, clothes, and education.[3] We also help ourselves in a merry-go-round buying different items for our houses. We started in 1986 and have thirty members. In the beginning, there were eighty members. The reason most women left was lack of money, so thirty women have been struggling to keep this group going.
>
> There are more orphaned children than before. People visit the children and give them some small amount of money. Classes have been put up for the children. They had been staying at the school, but now the school will no longer board them, so they will go home if they can, or go to home-stays. This will be more affordable, and we will be able to put up another classroom.

Personal Benefits

Although women's groups are formed primarily to provide economic assistance, they give members non-economic benefits as well: ideas, skills, assistance with shamba work or other heavy labor, emotional support, and advice about family problems.

Women learn a wide range of skills from their groups: skills for a particular trade, such as embroidery or mat-making; business skills like bookkeeping; and group process skills such as conflict resolution or taking minutes.

Quite a few women said that group process skills or business management skills were crucial benefits. For many, group membership opened a new world. Many had limited experience relating to a money economy before joining a group but learned what they needed from the group.

Sophie Amolo is a sponsor of various empowerment projects. The handicrafts shop Amolo started in Kisumu and has helped many women develop the skills to produce salable crafts. A friend describes Sophie as a "one-woman road show." It seems everyone knows her. We arrived in Kisumu without an address for her, but asked around, and found her within an hour. Knocking unexpectedly on her door, we were welcomed enthusiastically, given a hug, a cup of tea, a jacket (as a souvenir, she said), and an opportunity to interview her. She explained why she is doing this work:

> When I first came, I found many young women in the street, searching for jobs. If I asked them if they knew any job, they'd say, "Oh, I don't know this, I don't know that."
>
> I always tell people, "You were not born walking. You have to learn." I ask women, "Can you do this like so and so?" When they say. "Oh, it is very hard."

4. A kind of soapstone easily carvable into bowls and boxes, as well as purely ornamental objects.

> I say, "'Don't have a negative attitude. Try!" At a small distance from Kisumu, women were making things of Kisii stone.[4] When I started, men were bringing the women's Kisii stone products here for sale. They told the women who made them, "Kisumu is such a complicated city. If you go there you won't even find your way back."
>
> I talked to the women and brought two with me. I walked them to the shop, walked them back to the bus stop, and then I left them there. I said, "Now, you go to the shop." So they went. After that, they started to bring their work themselves — and kept the full profit.

This Kisii-stone story is a good example of the diverse skills women develop from participating in a group project. Now that they take their stoneware to Kisumu themselves, these women can no longer be cheated by a misrepresentation of the sales price. They have seen a city and successfully made their way around. They have lost the fear that many rural women have of cities. In addition, having successfully overcome one fear, they have improved confidence in their ability to learn and to do new things.

New Ideas

Women's groups share their practical innovations with members of other groups. Filomena Jeptanui is a warm-hearted, laughing school teacher in her forties. She gave a telling example:

> You know, there are different types of fireplaces, *jikos*. Some have now made better ones, so we have now gone to the houses of women who have them, to learn about them. They even have a warming oven. If you have made ugali [the cooked corn meal that is the staple food in much of Kenya], you put it there and it stays hot. We can make these ourselves. We can also make a pot that will have warm water all the time. So we save time and fuel. We are making these for each other. I have not made one yet, but I have invited the women to come and make one for me — and it costs nothing.

Members of sponsored groups go to seminars given by the sponsor and meet women from other communities. For some, this is a major benefit. Maku, a young professional woman who works in Malindi told us about the changes she had seen in her mother as the result of group participation.

> My mother is the chairlady of *Magaone Women's Group*. They have a successful water project that caters for the needs of everyone in the group. Soon they will start a poultry-keeping project. My mother did not go to school, but she has become so clever from that group. She has changed very much. When she

Kimiri Lenutil of Elangata Wuas sitting near Elangata Wuas' rental house

> goes to the bank for the group she can sign her name. The group has solar jikos [metal pot stoves], which are at our house, so we use them. My mother doesn't buy so much charcoal now. We don't have a fire so much, only for the tea. Also, my sister-in-law is the Treasurer. Since she handles the money for the group, we are up-to-date and can borrow cash.[5]

Members of Elangata Wuas live in a very dry area, so anything that will give them water with less work is an important benefit. At a seminar, they met members of groups who had built rooftop water tanks, and look forward to building some for their members.

Social and Emotional Benefits

Many women suffer terrible isolation. For them, participating in a group brought a much wider range of social contacts. Nkatha Murithe, an educated young woman in Meru had felt cruelly alone.

5. I did not ask whether other members consider this acceptable, or whether she is stealing from the group treasury.

> I was not employed, my husband was not employed, so we lived simply. I joined the Emmanuel Women's Fellowship. The first time I went to the church I was feeling as if I didn't belong. I was not of their standard. I was young and life was not so good to me. But they really welcomed me. I was very much encouraged.

Soon, one of the women employed Murithe's husband.

Personal advice and support has been important Tabitha Nechesa. She does not speak of her own experience, but what she says reflects advice she was given during a crisis in her own life.

> You sometimes can feel, when your husband doesn't help you, that he may have other wives outside whom he helps. And you find your friend advising you to leave him alone, or continue with your business at home — because you cannot follow what he does. That really helps. And you see him changing because you are not following him.

When we interviewed a dozen members of Kitivo Women's Group outside Wundanyi, each woman told her own life story, but questions about the group were almost all answered by Ginorah, a confident and well-spoken woman. I was therefore astounded when Ginorah answered my question about social and emotional benefits by saying that the group had helped her overcome shyness. She used to be too shy to talk, even in a group of friends.

Kese Women's Group in Werugha is a great help to members when they have problems with their husbands. Gracilda Mwakio was helped to stand up to her husband, and has been able to help others in the same way.

> Quite a number of husbands in our group have changed. The group leaders will approach a husband who is mistreating his wife to talk to him. They feel ashamed if people have discussed it, so they change.
>
> Forming women's groups can help women with their family problems. We discuss our problems. You might get some good ideas from a woman who has a similar problem. If I had stayed by myself, I would not have known what to do in my family troubles.

Reasons for Not Belonging

Financial and Time Constraints

Some regions only have groups ambitious to carry out large-scale projects that require substantial contributions. Where these are the only groups, poor women are automatically excluded. In Lusigetti, Joanne Gathone explained why she cannot afford to belong to a women's group.

Loice Mattoi and Gracilda Mwakio in Loice's sitting room

> It's about 700 Ksh, 500 for registration, 100 monthly, and 100 for emergency funds. I started in the group, but left when money was needed. The 500 is used to help a women who has to send a child to hospital, circumcise a son or for a funeral. The group can't help anyone unless she joins, and I can't afford to join.

She was thinking of the groups like Gimwe, the Lusigetti cow-buying group, the only type she knew about.

The late Rose Barmasai [Portrait M] was a well-educated woman with a position of high responsibility. She lived in Plateau, outside Eldoret, and continued to be very much a part of her community, despite her education abroad and employment with a national organization. She started a women's group with her neighbors. Despite her group's success, Barmasai is quite critical of women's groups. In her view, most are structured so they are accessible only to women with surplus time and money.

> Women's groups help those people who already have time, who already have some finance. They would demand some labor and that means for a Kenyan woman, who works up to sixteen hours a day, you have to have another extra two or three hours. It will be asking more than they could give. Those who have been pulled the maximum can never participate.
>
> Those who benefit are the elite — those who already have the power and many times, it is the officials who benefit. It rarely trickles down to the really needy woman. How many times do they get a dividend? How many times could this money take care of school fees of their children?

> The other thing that I see is those who really run these women's groups are the middle-class women; women who have gone to school. The issue of ordinary women will never be addressed.

It can be difficult for very poor women, who are often hungry, to carry out a group project. Agnes Wamuruana had been a member of a group sponsored by the African Housing Fund. AHF's goal had been to start a group, sponsor them for a time, and enable them eventually to continue independently. Her group tried to continue after sponsorship ended, but failed.

> I was in a women's group that made mats and *kiondos* [the world-famous Kenya baskets] all together and AHF would pay us. When they stopped buying our things, it was difficult. We could not listen to what anyone had to say because we were hungry. Our children were crying. Now, we don't see each other. Everyone looks for her own ways.

Bad Experiences with Previous Groups

The problems that cause the most failures are bad leadership and jealousies between members. Qaudensia Oyiro, the woman who used to alternate with her co-wife in living in Kisumu with their husband, has experienced both.

> I used to belong to a women's group, but it failed because of some corruption[6] between members who didn't like each other. In another group, there were a lot of jealousies between the women. We had chosen a chair. Some people liked her, others didn't. This group also failed.
>
> These were small groups, maybe ten, maybe twelve people. Our groups failed before we got big enough to ask for help [money] from the government. The leaders, you know, they take for themselves. If the group is helped from the government, they would take from what they got before passing on the money to the group.
>
> I belong to a group now, not a part of Maendeleo.[7] We women would like to get a little money to start making things to sell. After we get just a little to start, we can beg the government to help us continue. The government must see that already you have done a little something. Then they give help. In one meeting, there were certain girls from the government there. They brought a cow for the group. But then later, they wanted some money from us.

---

6. In Kenya, the word corruption is commonly used in two senses. One is misdeeds by people in a position of trust, such as government officials. The other is mistreatment by people in their private relations. Thus there can be "corruption between husband and wife."

7. Maendeleo ya Wanawake [Development of Women] is a conduit for government assistance to women's groups.

We collected money to get food for the cow. The milk was being sold and money was sent to the bank for school fees for our children. When a woman gave birth, she got a calf. There were fifteen of us. But the government was just hitting us, making business off of us. They give us a cow, then they want our money. We do not trust the government.[8]

But I'm still hopeful. If we can start a group and avoid corruption, we will do well. If we get a piece of land to plant, after eating, we can even pay school fees for the children. Otherwise, life will be very difficult.

Theft of group funds by the leadership is a common problem. Flores Mwang'ombe, who lives in a permanent house outside Wundanyi, also participated in a group spoiled by bad leaders. Instead of being discouraged, she organized two smaller groups so members could monitor the money more closely. One of her groups later helped her quite dramatically in a crisis.

The first group was a very large group because it was the only one — maybe about sixty members. At first we would do the merry-go-round. With that one I was lucky once to get 800 Ksh. That's the time when we were building this house. So I gave that money to the husband, He bought cement for plastering this wall.

But before every member could get something, we changed the idea. We wanted to keep poultry. A misunderstanding formed because the leaders were not transparent. These hens were laying eggs and we had an order to buy. The leaders sold but whatever income they got, they didn't tell the group. The poultry died and that stopped everything. Then they stopped holding meetings. So we have never known how much that project generated.

Instead, we organized small groups in our own village, so now there are only a few members. We don't want to handle a group project because of what happened with that large group project.

I belong to two merry-go-rounds now. The problem is that whenever we meet to contribute, some members don't have money. So they have accumulated arrears. We have resolved: when it comes to your turn to get the money, we deduct the arrears. But still we have problems with some members. When it comes to their turn, they want to get that lump sum. They cry to be given everything, whereas when they were not contributing, others were getting less.

There have been funny complaints. A group of twenty is a little bit big. When we first started we had voted that we were given numbers, one up to twenty to know when each member will be given her turn. For some members, it will mean you will be contributing for a period of twenty months. So some become impatient and starts thinking maybe her name was pushed back.

8. This was in 1996.

But sometimes, private problems are given consideration, and your name can be pushed forward. Maybe you get sick and there is no one to take you to a hospital. In those cases, first it is taken through the officials. When it is passed by the leaders of the group they bring it to all the members and if it is agreed upon, then it can be done. It's not one person's decision.

It really helps if someone is desperately in need of the money. I cite my own example: my husband was sick in Mombasa. For quite some time, I left the children to go and care for him. I did not request, but somehow the members met and thought, "Why can't we give the children this money to help them as both parents are away?" So when I came back, I learned from the children that they had already been given this money to help them eat. I will always be grateful for that.

Maria Kibera, the NGO worker who talked so lyrically about the streams which have now dried up, belonged to one group with people in comfortable circumstances, and another in her village, where people are living on very little.

I belong to the group in my village because I was asked by my aunt whom I admire so much. She is a wise brilliant woman who likes doing things for others. At my father's funeral last year, people did not know how to use the flush toilets so my aunt told them. She did not go to school but she has brought development to my village.

The group has built a *posho* [maize grinding] mill. The group has encouraged women to build a group catchment and latrines. They also make their own ways of generating income. They are all close to the same level, but there are members like me who are outside. If I go there, I just do the same as others and once in a while if I feel I have extra I boost their kitty.

I had been in another group here in Nairobi that broke apart because of being too big to be good friends. I joined them to be able to meet people from Taita. We raised harambee to get money to supply water. We now had money but could not lay down the pipes. Our chairman passed away, and the other chairman was not as strong as the first one. So things started being in disorder: the secretary was missing meetings, the treasurer was not able to bring the last meeting's contributions, and such things. They started gossiping, talking about what they saw in other's houses. Up to now, the money we raised for water pipes is still in a bank and nobody is willing to call for the meetings. These are the problems that fail many groups.

Husbands' Objections

Just as some women are helped in their marital relations by having the support of other women, some women are unable to join a group because their husbands fear outside interference.

Aisha Muhammad lives in the village of Mtongwe, just outside Mombasa, with her husband and seven children. Her neighbors are Muslims, like herself, and Christians. Several of them belong to a women's group. She sometimes talks wistfully with her neighbors about their women's groups, but has never belonged to one herself.

> I don't really need extra income because my husband is employed, and I have a tailoring machine. When we were first married, I was really restricted, but I could shop sometimes. Now I am free to go out. But I have never belonged to a women's group because my husband might not like it.

Jane Gathege is a teacher married to another teacher. Their shamba shows notable enterprise. There are permanent buildings, a zero-grazing project, and poultry. When Jane first moved from Nairobi to Lusigetti, her hubands's village, she felt ostracized by local women. She wanted to join a group as much for social reasons as for economic ones.

> Having come from a different environment, I took some time to adjust and make friends here. My husband was against my joining a group, so I have not. He didn't give any concrete reason for opposing. He said going to work and raising children is enough so if I joined some group, it would be very hard for me to have the time. And of course he has not understood how those groups help women. I'll just wait because maybe someday he won't object.

Roselyne Choge, a schoolteacher, and wife of a school Headmaster, lives in Kobujoi, where the Tegelmoi women's group has had a great influence. Many of her friends are members. Her husband doesn't want her to join. "You know women are very good gossips. Most husbands do not like that sort of thing. If they hear something about a women's group, they say, 'You are just looking to gossip. I'd better stop you from going there.'"

Since Kese Women's Group has been so successful in helping its members with family problems, some husbands have objected.

> Some men have stopped their wives from attending our group because of this. They think we spend all our time in the group talking about men, there is no other good thing we do. If a husband is refusing to let his wife participate, we talk to the husband. You have to tell him what are you doing in the group. But sometimes in the end, the wife is instructed to completely withdraw from the group. That's how two members left. One is a neighbor of mine. We meet here and she is just near here and sees us coming, but her husband says, "Don't step away, don't go to them." The other one was even the secretary of the group.

Some men are unapproachable, too hostile. In a few cases talking to them has proved fruitless. Some still are too rigid to listen to anything even if it's profitable. We gave them examples of the benefits but we have reached a deadlock.

Sometimes the husbands are working in town. They only come home on occasions. So we don't know when he comes and when he leaves. And he's not ready to meet us.

Even if the husband is away, the wife is not free to join us. You know some of these women are really threatened by their husbands. He keeps spies. He tells her whenever he leaves, "I have already assigned some people this duty so I'll be informed." So the woman feels quite insecure. You never know where the information will leak from. It instills fear.

When I visited Kese Women's Group again, I was delighted to learn about a new member. Gracilda told us, "The woman who was kept away by her husband is now a member. When he saw how much the group has helped us, he changed his mind."

Nancy Karamana sees a change in men's attitudes.

Things are changing. Husbands don't mind because of course they couldn't have afforded to buy those glasses for the house. When he comes back from the river he is given a cup of tea with a very nice cup, he would say, "What is this, it's very nice."

So the wife would say, "Well, I told them I don't have this and they bought it for me." and he would say "Oh, very good." So next time the wife asks for the contribution he is ready to give.

The husbands thought maybe there is nothing these women could do and they are just going to waste time. Maybe they are going to discuss us. But the wife might say my husband doesn't have a good shirt so then they would go and buy a good shirt and he would be very happy.

When women have their own money, they are respected by their husbands. He knows that you are capable of caring for yourself even without him, so he respects you.

Rose Barmasai developed a way to help the women in her group overcome their husband's objections.

Men would be very threatened if they didn't feel their power. You cannot change that overnight. But women learn practical skills in their women's groups. They learn new ways to cook. If he gets good food, he comes around.

Some groups used to annoy husbands because they would stay a long time and go home very late. What I did was to make sure that women came at 10 o'clock and at 2 pm we were gone.

Through the chickens they raised and the vegetables they sold, they were able to buy simple things that had always been making quarrels with their husbands.

I went to ask for permission from the very difficult husbands in a joking manner. I would pretend that I had never discussed it with the wife and look for an opportunity to meet him and say, "Oh, by the way, I really wanted to come to your home as we are having a meeting and I would love your wife to come. This is what we are planning to discuss." If they don't want anybody outside to know that they don't like their wives coming, then they will allow their wives to go.

Of course, men are very sensitive about anything that can make his wife more equal. I have to handle situations so that there are not confrontations. After they come, I go to different homes and sit with the men and appreciate them on behalf of those who came for the workshops. The men said that when the women came back from these workshops, they were changed.

Problems and Solutions

We asked everyone who had participated in a self–help group to tell us about problems they had encountered, and what steps they had taken to solve their problems. If women wanted to create a favorable impression of their group, they were sometimes reluctant to discuss problems.

I realized that I should explain my reasons for asking, so I began to say, "Women in other places have no such groups, and might benefit greatly from learning about them. But if they read only about the good things groups can do, and form their own groups, they might get discouraged when they encounter problems. Therefore I want to write also about problems that groups have had, and how they solved those problems, because that would help other women very much." With this explanation, women were usually willing to discuss the struggles their groups had undergone.

The most common problem is irregular payment. Although many groups fail as a result, others have found a variety of solutions. In Nkatha Murithe's church fellowship group, some of the members are well off, and others are not. All contribute, but not equally.

If you have five shillings, you give five; if you have ten shillings, you give ten. If they set a certain amount for every woman to give, maybe some women could not afford. This way everyone can give.

We keep on giving, that money keeps accumulating. When the money is enough, we are asked what we need at home. That way, I have been able to have a lot of things at home.

Once a member of a merry-go-round has had her turn, she has little incentive to keep on contributing, especially in large groups, where the personal ties are looser and the wait is longer. The merry-go-round run by *Kipusi Women's Group* in Mwatate had problems with this. Maggie Mwasi explained their daring solution.

> We started as the ten members, each giving 120 Ksh every month, but that attracted others, and now there are fifty. So every time we meet, we raise 6,000 Ksh to share between two members.
>
> The main rule is that you don't get money. When it's your turn, a certain number of members go with you to a shop to get what you want. The receipt is kept by the officials. If you are not paying your share, our law says that we can come and take what we gave or something else, until you pay the others.
>
> We have done it to three members. We didn't get the original things back, but cash or other things to cover the balance. If you go and find that cups are broken, or the cooking utensils have been spoiled, then the rules say that the elected members can take other things to make up for the outstanding balance. Sometimes, we have gotten goats, which we sell to get the money back.
>
> Some people in the group complained to the chief that their things were being taken, but we told the chief, "Off! These are the rules, and you cannot interfere. These members contributed to the setting of the rules, so you are not going to intervene."
>
> He was also posing a condition that when we raised the money, half of it should be going to him. We told him, "This is our money, and we have to utilize it the way we want."
>
> HH: All these fifty people agreed to these rules?
>
> We all sat with the village elder, and he approved the rules, because the village elder is the immediate hand of the government in the community. He does not agree with that chief, and he is one of the fifty.

Kilili, the sand-scooping group, had the problem of unequal work. When they were scooping, some worked less vigorously than others, and resentments flared.

> What we did to solve that problem was to agree that when we are in that water each one of us has to scoop up her own portion, and each piles her sand separately. So if whatever a member has scooped out does not satisfy other members she is told to go back and scoop more out. If a member does not appear on the workday, she has to come on another day, and get out the same amount as the others.

Other problems range from dishonest leaders to conflicts between members. Joan Kanini, an educated Nairobi woman, has left two groups because of problems. "I left one because the Chairman[9] was squandering the money. In the other group, one of the people came up with a gossip that I did not like. I wrote a letter to the Chairlady about leaving the group and my money was returned."

Joan is now in a group which is much more skilled at solving its problems.

> The members are women who were born in Kilungu, where we were born. The money is very well accounted for. In the meetings we make suggestions about how to use the money. There are many suggestions, including helping the needy instead of ourselves. Everyone feels her suggestions are welcome.
>
> We have bought land and want to build a small factory. It was an easy decision because one member has a brother who is an architect. He gave us good advice.
>
> I don't know what kind of factory they are planning because I do not participate in the meetings. If you don't go, you have to pay a fine, so I pay a little extra.
>
> We never went into anything that would give us problems: we didn't want to borrow, so we raised the monthly contributions.
>
> A few people fell off because they could not keep up with the contributions. One member wanted her time compensated, and when she left, she wanted her contributions refunded with interest. She has not come back.

Despite Kilili's importance to its members, and its success at solving other problems, Kilili has been destroyed as an economic group by theft and consequent inability to repay a YWCA loan. Kilili continues, but now it is primarily a social network and merry-go-round.

> Paulina: We have over twenty thousand in our account at the post office, but Sophie [Mwangemi, the former Treasurer] opened this account with her own name, so we are not able to withdraw. The post office needs a copy of her death certificate. Her husband won't release it.
>
> HH: When last I visited, you had suffered very much from those problems, but were working together again.
>
> Paulina: After that, we continued with sand scooping. We sold six or seven tons of sand, and put it in the account before we knew the problem. But now we have agreed that when we sell, we'll use that money to repay the loan, because that has blocked us from getting a second loan.
>
> HH [to Mary Msinga, the YWCA liaison]: Is this something that the YWCA has considered helping with?

9. This interview was in English, which Kanini speaks fluently, so I am sure that this was a man.

Mary: We are not harassing them. We told them to pay at their own pace. The headquarters in Nairobi will not release money with an unpaid loan. We are still giving them all the other benefits like seminars, but not money.

HH: How many members are still in the group?

Paulina: There are nine. The ones who are active and strong to scoop are five or six. The others are old and cannot do much. Most members left or died. The other three are too old, but we still consider them members.

HH: Last time, you said that when a woman became too old to dig, she could send a family member in her place. Did that work?

Paulina: The parents want to continue but the children are not willing to take over the work.

HH: I almost think you might disband, declare Kilili is over, and begin again with younger, active members. Why do you hold onto Kilili, when there is nothing coming in?

At this point, they all started talking. Mary Msinga summarized their comments.

They love the group. It's not the money in the account, or the loan that brings them together. When they meet, they have a lot to share. In case one has a ceremony, all the members are there. Their problems are dealt with by the group. That's why they remain.

HH: Even when you were economically active, it was your commitment to each other that kept you going.

Paulina: You know with African men, sometimes they are not cooperative, so when I felt like leaving home, the other members encouraged me to stay because of the children, because I have my own house.

Clemence: I am encouraged by the support we get from the merry-go-round. I'm able to make my own budget plan for small things in the house like food and other requirements, without bothering my husband, because husbands do not help. Getting this small money from the group, I am able to solve these problems.

Defence: I am the founding member. Due to my age, I am unable to participate in the sand scooping but I am still very interested in the group. I hope when I die, the members will come to my funeral.

Making Diversity Work

Trust is essential for success, so multi-ethnic groups face special challenges. Zuhura Ali, the nurse in the leso-buying group, explained why one of her groups was determined to solve a problem resulting from being ethnically mixed, and how they managed. Most of the members were from various Swahili-speaking coastal groups.

> We have people from different tribes in our group and sometimes we get problems. One Kikuyu woman had a problem with communication so she did not attend the meetings. She was so harsh because of the communication barrier. She had taken a loan. If she left, she would have left other people with the burden of paying the loan. So we talked to her slowly by slowly, to let her get what we were discussing. She is a good member now.

Filomena Jeptanui's group of twenty-five women has faced and successfully addressed the dilemmas of economic diversity. They scaled back their projects so that the women with the least money can participate, and they have addressed the concerns of employed women who aren't able to spend as much time in the group shamba as others.

> We had big ideas, but we came down, so everyone could keep up. We saw with our small contributions it would take long to do a big project so we decided to do a little project that we could do with our little money. We are planning to plant potatoes. We have another shamba where we have planted beans. We do the small things that we are all able to do. After that, we will see what else we can do.
>
> We want to help each other. For example, we each have a water tank and we want to buy utensils for every member. We hired a small plot and planted tomatoes. We solved the problem of people not doing the work by making this rule: if you can't come you just send somebody. If they chose a day when I can't come, I can send someone, — a member of my family, or I can hire someone to dig for me.

Rose Barmasai's group worked hard to solve the problems that can result when women at different economic levels work together.

> In this group we have those who have good jobs and those who have very little. We decided to buy a uniform, so that we don't come looking completely cheap. We are dressed the same when we come to this group. And at every house we serve the same simple food, so that you don't show that you have more than anybody else. It has been very challenging. One of those who lived in one of the simplest homes we visited was so happy to see people coming to her home, eating whatever she was able to afford, without raising an eyebrow.

Despite the problems that challenge groups, many women in Kenya and throughout Africa are using traditional mutual assistance groups to transform their lives. In a time of deep poverty, self-help groups are giving women a margin of economic security and control. With increased economic control, participants are gaining the skills and confidence to combat injustice in their lives and their communities.

Portrait M

Rose Barmasai

In Nairobi, I met a Dutch Reformed missionary, Sister Marie Lekkerkerker who, on hearing about this book, said, "I know a woman who is working with women in areas affected by the clashes of '92.[1] You should definitely interview her. I don't know her address, but come to Eldoret anytime, and I will introduce you." Months later, I wrote to her proposing a date, but communications being uncertain, I heard nothing from her. Taking her at her word, I went anyway, over roads that could scarcely be managed in a two wheel drive vehicle during heavy rain. Sister Marie gave me an excellent welcome, and asked Rose Barmasai when I could talk with her. Barmasai was a busy woman. She was only able to see me four days later. Sister Marie very kindly put me up until then, providing delightful hospitality. On the appointed day, Barmasai met me at Sister Marie's home and talked to me for nearly three hours about herself and her work, and about many other problems affecting the women she works with. Here she tells about her own life and her work. In other chapters, she gives her views on many of the problems facing women today.

---

1. From 1991 through early 1993, regional clashes displaced 300,000 people. These were mostly people of other ethnic groups who had settled in Kalejin areas. The effect was to prevent these people from voting, and to make their land available to Kalenjins. Although these clashes were disguised as "tribal," high-level government officials were involved in training participants, and police units were instructed not to interfere. Although considerable money has been spent on relief, it has not reached most of the victims, and many have neither been able to return safely nor resettled adequately elsewhere. Extensive documentation of all phases of this is available through Human Rights Watch publications, especially *Divide and Rule: State-Sponsored Ethnic Violence in Kenya.* Similar clashes occured before the 1997 election. Some of these were again in the Rift Valley, others affected areas of the country which had been spared in 1991-3, especially Likoni.

I was born in 1956. My father was working for white settlers as a milkman. Since my mother could not travel with him, she stayed with her parents. My father married two wives. We were brought up in a very tight situation. I rarely saw my Dad. I saw my mother struggle like many other women, struggling to see that we were eating, struggling to see that we had proper shelter. I lived with my mother for six years and then we joined our father in the white settlers' farms. Later he bought a piece of land.

Just before I started going to school, my parents became Christians. It was very difficult to afford the school fees, especially when there were three of us in high school. My school fees were sponsored by a missionary from the Netherlands. Though I had studied well and could have gone to form five,[2] I opted out so my brothers and sisters could go to secondary school.

During my school days, I tripled my work because my mother was sickly, maybe partly because of having many children, or partly because of a lot of work. My mother had ten surviving children and two dead children. As she was sick, I had to do most of the work, cook for the family. I admired my mother's struggles, admired the way she never complained despite the load of work she had, admired her confidence in life. She inspired me to work hard. After finishing high school, immediately they decided I should be married.

I was not circumcised. Since I was being educated by a missionary, I went to many Christian rallies where they spoke against circumcision. When the time came for us to be circumcised, I was very much against it. My mother wanted to support me, but she could not refuse what my father and my aunts and uncles wanted to do. That would have meant a divorce for her. My elder sister, who was three years older, wanted to be circumcised. Men here do not marry uncircumcised girls, but I didn't worry about that. I made a personal confession about my own Christian life. I therefore resisted circumcision, although it was not easy.

The day I was to be circumcised, I came home and prepared because I did not want my mother be given problems. But during the evening I sneaked away to town, where I had a casual job. So that's how I escaped it.

I started lobbying against circumcision in my village. I talked to some of the young Christian girls, saying that we should make a change. Many would stand up and say, "If we can't refuse this, our Christianity doesn't mean anything." They were the first lot of girls in my village who never went through circumcision. But after that the whole village, even those who were not Christians, started refusing. After 1980, circumcision was reduced significantly. But from 1978, I had a group who had never gone to circumcision. The fact that I got married in 1978 and am living happily with my husband made people see that this can happen. The fact that I had a child made people say that you can have a normal married life without circumcision.

When I was in form one, I became close friends with a girl in form four, Sarah. She was a strong Christian. I liked the way she behaved; I liked her

2. Until 1990, Kenya had the British system of O level exams after form four, and two more years, forms five and six, to prepare for A level exams.

character; I admired her family. In 1975, I met my husband when I went for a Christian youth rally. He was Sarah's brother. When Sarah knew that we were dating each other, she encouraged us. What made the marriage possible was that his father had not circumcised his daughter. Even his daughter who was born in 1948 was not circumcised. His father did not want him to marry a circumcised girl. This helped me quite a lot.

I was very sure that I didn't want a lot of children because of what I saw my mother going through. So I had only four children. My husband didn't have any problem with that. The other major issue I wanted to settle before marriage was whether I would be able to help my parents. I would have opted out of marriage if I had not been allowed to educate my brothers and sisters. I started to do clerical work as a civil servant. I had to struggle to educate my brothers and sisters, but five of them have finished school.

In 1985, I lost my mother. She died at a very awkward time, because at that time two of my brothers had just started working. My elder brother who was studying in the USSR was to come home the following year. We had great plans to help this old woman lead a comfortable life, because she had struggled for us. Despite the fact that I was working, I couldn't help her yet because I had my own children and I had to pay school fees with the money I had.

When she died, it was a real disaster for me. After that I started thinking deeply about what is to be a woman. I thought she really died because of lack of food, and maybe too much worry. The work she was doing alone, four or five of us are doing now. She was the supplier of firewood and water; she took care of the family food; she was the nurse of our family; she was the counselor for all of us. Therefore, I wanted to know what was it behind her that really made her stand.

She knew she was dying but she was willing to die as a courageous woman. She tried to comfort me, she tried to give me hope. Many women go through what she went through. When I saw her in the coffin, something in my heart said I needed to do something useful to other women.

Christianity was very central to my life and to her life as well. I tried to look through the Bible and the church and I found that something was lacking. I felt Christianity regards men more than women. I felt that there was lot injustice to women even in Christianity, just like in the traditional societies. I wanted to study theology to find out if the Bible is really very discriminative against women.

I listened to many pastors telling women to love their husbands, but these women loved their husbands more than they loved themselves. I wondered what kind of love is there in the Bible that tells you to love others when you can't love yourself. That was when I really made a decision of wanting to work in the church. But I could not leave the children behind with my husband. I pursued it, discussed it with my husband and the church said that I could take my children with me to college. So in 1986 I was offered married quarters in theology college till 1990.

I was being sponsored by the Netherlands church, so the delegation came to visit our church. We had three hours of interviews. I found some questions very dehumanizing, degrading. They came back again the second day and asked me what I really wanted. Well, it is not ordination, if ordination means marrying and burying people, then I don't really need it. They asked me whether I would be preaching from the pulpit because they can't allow me to preach inside the church. I said I could preach from the ground and people could gather. The judge made an agreement that I would be the first and the last woman to be sponsored by the Netherlands.

Life wasn't easy in the college because I was the first married woman. I was the only woman in a class of thirty. Despite looking after the four children, I still was among the best in class.

When I finished in 1991, they did not know what to do with me. They decided that I should be in the women's program. So I went into the women's programs in the church and changed them completely. Before, the program was just planning how to cook, etc., just making them more and more slaves. I worked on empowerment. I tried to tell them to love themselves as women, to know that they are the image of God.

As famine passes throughout, I tell women, "Look at yourself in the mirror, eat properly, especially protein. Otherwise you can't survive." I held many workshops and tried to bring the boys and the girls to see themselves as equally created in the image of God.

Women started questioning things in the church. They started saying that they are part of the church so they do not need to be kept in a separate space, the women's side. What they demanded was their rightful participation. They started questioning why women are not part of the leadership,

In 1993, I was sent to a training program in Edinburgh, Scotland for women who were working at the grassroots level. When I came back from UK, I was not put in the women's program because somehow the church thought that I was a threat. They posted me to teach. I really resisted because I started questioning why should I teach ministers, if myself I am not able to be a minister. So I went to teach simply because I wanted these young people to change. I taught only for eight months. Then I asked to coordinate activities in the places that were hit by clashes in 1992-93. That is the work I have been doing up to now.

The 1992-93 "tribal" clashes as they might call it, were political clashes, land clashes etc. Land is the main factor, especially the former white settlers' farms. These farms were previously occupied mainly by the Kalenjin community, but when the white settlers came they pushed the Kalenjins far away to land they cannot farm. During the time of colonial rule, those who were pushed out could not live freely. They had to limit the number of animals: any extras belonged to the white man.

The people like Kalenjins who lost land to white settlers didn't get it back after Independence. The first government advised the people from Central Province about land settlement schemes, so they were able to buy the white settlers' farms. Most of them worked for the white settlers so they knew how to occupy their farms. Despite the fact that the Kalenjin community and the Luhya community coexisted, most of the farms were bought by the Luhya community or by Kikuyu from Central Province. During the distribution of land, the pastoral communities were neglected and the agricultural communities benefited.

As pastoral children went to school and became aware of this, they started questioning — why? Kalenjins felt that they had been invaded. People of this community cannot go to any other place to start a business because the community there will be hostile. I saw that happening when I stayed in Central Province for eleven years. Any time someone from another community wanted to start a business there, it was very difficult. They were thought to be stupid and unfit for anything. The Xxx[3] community members in Parliament used very dehumanizing terminology to refer to the Kalenjin.

1992 became terrible because of the "democratization" of this country.[4] The goal of "Democracy" seemed just to be to remove whoever was ruling the country. People believed if they accepted these changes, then things would be worse. It threatened some people because it was one group against another. That is the real interpretation of what the western world calls democracy for this country. A country like the US, which has been independent for the last 200 years, wants Kenya to be the same as US 30 years after getting independence.

I am not disputing corruption, which is there. But corruption has been encouraged by the western world.

We talk about debt that we owe. If a woman gets pregnant today, her fetus will be already incurring some debts before it is born, and it feels that debt even before it's born because the mother won't eat well.

Because our people are so poor, they can easily be manipulated. In 1992, the politicians touched the issues that were there in the society, and the people just reacted. That is how the clashes happened.[5] I am not expecting it to happen again, because people realize that although they fought, they are even worse off than before. The conflict that erupted in 1992-93 developed because of deep-rooted hatred amongst the communities. Therefore, it is necessary that we find a way to solve conflicts, addressing the real issues that cause them. What is it that made them fight? What is it that made them kill people they

---

3. I use xxx to replace an unfriendly mention of another ethnic group unless the specific name is essential to the meaning.

4. She is refering to the reintroduction of a multiparty system, and the clashes that resulted from efforts to displace potential opposition voters.

5. In fact, there is abundant documentation showing that the clashes were organized and paid for by powerful, well-connected people. The Kiliku report, carried out by a Parliamentary Select Committee documents the use of government cars and helicopters to transport fighters to the clash sites. They were paid 500 shillings for participation, 1,000 to 2,000 shillings for killing one person or burning a grass thatched house, and 10,000 shillings for burning a permanent house. The evidence is most easily available in *Divide and Rule* (ibid).

had known for years? Our work is to bring together communities that are in conflict, to address issues of differences.

We are able do that even if the government and the law encourage conflict. We are working at the grassroots level, bringing women together, bringing youth together. We are also working at other levels, coming to the chiefs, the assistants, the district officers. At the last workshop, members of parliament of the ruling party and the opposition parties came together to address these issues. That was the climax.

We are not saying that these conflicts may not start again, but maybe it will be less. The women are a great source of inspiration in peace activities because women usually suffer wherever there is conflict. In 1992 men went to fight, and women were killed or were left with the children. They were the ones who were exposed to the dehumanizing environment. They hid in churches, or one room houses. They were the victims of rape and crop burnings. So they will do anything to fight these evils. We try to educate our own male children about the evils of this fighting and what their mothers went through because of all this.

We try to encourage women who have been raped not to be ashamed. We are using those who have been victims themselves to speak to other victims. We are teaching them to speak to men to discourage them from doing these things, to plead with them to spare the children.

In the right circumstances, women easily come together and easily share their problems. As they share their problems, they try to find solutions. So we are teaching village women to take advantage of opportunities such as ceremonies, firewood gathering. They can tell others to come for just an hour. If it is to talk about their own security, women are willing to come. So that is how we can facilitate their coming together, and include even isolated women.

After this conversation, Rose Barmasai was killed in a road accident. I have heard allegations by people who knew her well that politically connected men targeted her.

10

To Become a Woman and Leave Childish Ways: Female Genital Cutting

The Meaning of Initiation

Anyone who has lifted a Passover cup and said, "Next year may we be in Israel," saluted a flag with heart full of patriotism, or sworn an oath of loyalty to comrades or country understands the desire to belong fully to one's own group. The most treasured belonging is not given easily. It requires sacrifice or struggle. Initiation rituals, whether of males or females, make the initiate not just an adult, but an adult of a particular ethnic group. One becomes an adult Kikuyu or Maasai or Somali through circumcision. In most cases, the power of the ritual is enhanced because it is simultaneously initiation into adulthood and into a smaller, tighter age-set, the psychological equivalent of a sorority or street-gang. Having been bought with blood and intense pain, it is meaningful. This meaning is constantly reinforced by ridicule of those who flinched or cried out during the surgery, and by scorn heaped on those who have not been initiated.

Traditional initiation practices differ from one ethnic group to another. Being initiated in the manner that was proper for one's own group was a crucial part of ethnic identity. In the past, most Kenyan ethnic groups practiced genital cutting for both boys and girls. Luhyas circumcised boys, but did not cut girls. The case of the Luo was different. They did not circumcise: instead they knocked out the front teeth of both men and women. After this had been done, one was eligible to participate in rituals, thus, truly an adult Luo.

The physical pain of initiation is part of the attraction because it gives an opportunity to prove that one can now withstand pain. The brave initiate feels superior to those who have not proven themselves.

Success is not automatic. The initiate always approaches the event knowing he or she must conduct herself honorably or be held in low esteem.

The age at which girls were, and are, cut differs greatly from one group to another. Taita circumcised girls at three weeks to one month old. Gusii circumcise girls between five and eight years old. The Maasai used to circumcise girls in their late teens or even early twenties, but the age has been dropping.

Forms of Surgery

There are three different types of surgery which are loosely and inaccurately referred to as "female circumcision":

Infibulation: This is the most drastic and is the most likely to cause medical problems in menstruation, sexual intercourse, and childbirth. It consists of removing the clitoris, and labia minora (inner lips at the entrance to the vagina), and sewing the labia majora (large outer lips of the vulva) closed except for a small opening. Sometimes the remaining opening is so small that a straw must be inserted to keep it from sealing as the wound heals. The future husband is expected to break his way through the scar tissue during first intercourse.

Excision: This is removal of the clitoris and parts of the labia minora.

Clitoridectomy: Removal of the prepuce (protective skin partially covering the clitoris) and clitoris, leaving the labia minora intact. Sometimes, only the prepuce is removed, leaving the clitoris intact. Only in this case is the term "circumcision" remotely accurate, but it is commonly used for all three forms.

Instruction for Adulthood

In most communities, surgery was only part of the initiation. Usually, a period of instruction about adult behavior accompanied the genital cutting. Newly initiated girls were secluded for a time and given instruction about adult life, usually by an older woman.

Since the Taita performed the surgery on infants, instruction about adult life was given later, during a separate initiation, Mwari. During Mwari, a girl stayed inside and was not allowed to see anyone other than her female instructors, who were generally older relatives.

Simanya Machocho says of her Mwari,

> I was mature, though I do not know how old I was. We were collected together and given an oath of secrecy. Then each of us was shown something that was to be kept secret, even from the others. This was a way of teaching women to keep secrets during their married life. A man would not want to marry a woman who would reveal family secrets. It was believed that something bad would happen to you if you revealed any of these Mwari secrets. You might never be married because what kind of a man would want to marry a woman who is not going to keep secrets?
>
> Everything was explained about sexual matters, and that's why the pretest was how to keep a secret. So whatever they tell you about how to live with a man you are not supposed to share with anybody.
>
> After that, we were not supposed to move around with girls younger than us, in case we might reveal these secrets to them. And they were curious to know what happens because they were going to be the next lot. Everyone is supposed to learn for themselves.
>
> There was a ceremony at the beginning of Mwari when beer was prepared for the men to drink and *kimanga* [a Taita specialty made of beans, bananas, and cassava or sweet potatoes mashed together] for the women. For us, there was ugali and *mnavu* [local vegetables] prepared by our caretakers.
>
> This ceremony went on for three days, after which we went in for the Mwari, which took three months.
>
> On graduating from the Mwari, we were decorated with inscriptions on the face, which you see on me up to now. They were made by a skilled specialist, who was paid a one shilling fee. Mostly it was men who knew how to do this. We had to go and search for a specialist, for there were not many.
>
> After this initiation, we were allowed to go to local dances, where we could meet young men who might propose to us.

Constance Tanui [Portrait F] had a year and a half of isolation and instruction. In contrast, Margaret Mueni, who was circumcised about 1966, had no instruction.

> I was circumcised at ten years old. Some girls were older, some were younger. There were many girls, but we were separated from boys. The girls stayed together overnight in the same house. The next day, each girl went home. We had no "bush school," but we remained close as an age-set. They stayed together and did things together for some time. Now, I am married away, so I don't know if they are still together.

Because she was now to be treated as an adult, initiation marked a change in the relationship between a girl and her father. Various taboos to prevent incest were now supposed to be respected. Jane Kenyajui, who was born in 1958, said, "We were no longer to tell our fathers about anything we wanted."

For Virginia Njeri, born in 1970, the advice was similar. "We were told not to ask our fathers questions, not to face him, not to bend in his presence. We were told that from now on we are the children of our mothers, not of our fathers."

Instruction usually included cautions about pregnancy. Information about sexual practices that would not cause pregnancy was often included. Even Luhya girls, who had no physical initiation, had a similar period of instruction.

Defenders of Tradition

Circumcision confers a distinct sense of superiority. Whenever Florence, a Gusii who lived among Luos, felt a Luo was treating her disrespectfully, she would ask, "Why are you talking to me this way when I am circumcised and you are not?"

This sense of being made superior through circumcision is even stronger among men. Luhyas circumcise boys but not girls, so a Luhya man will often defend his right to "rule" his wife on the grounds that he has been circumcised and she has not. And the fact that Luos do not circumcise boys is often a cause for disdaining them, as Jean Wanjugu found out.

In many areas, the most educated people no longer circumcise their daughters, though traditionalists continue the practice. Where cutting is being abandoned, but is not yet rare, it is highly controversial, and generates great tension. Katherine Karamboi, a teacher at Kajiado A.I.C. [Portrait G], was forced to leave her first teaching post because of her anti-circumcision views.

> Someone in the community came with a sword intending to kill me, so I went to the office and told them I could not stay. The moment you do not embrace their practices, you are an outcast. They think you are not telling their children the right thing, so you should not stay there. It is even hard to talk to these people about such things.

Arguments that an individual girl should be circumcised center on her own welfare. They are: that she will not mature without it, that no man will want to marry her, or that she will be ostracized. But group attachment to custom always involves more than simply considerations of individual welfare. For many, it remains a defining element of group identity.

Arguments with individual girls about why she should be circumcised are put in terms of her own welfare, maturity, and social acceptability, but pressures for maintaining the custom go beyond a belief that it is better for the girl. In Meru, Kikuyu, and Kiambaa, there have been threats and forcible circumcision of women thirteen to sixty-five. At least in Meru, these threats were carried out. Married women are not exempt, belying the excuse that no one will marry an uncircumcised woman.[1]

Grandmothers' Role

In some communities, strong respect for the grandmother causes parents to defer to her on this question. A group of young, educated Somali mothers in Wajir all considered circumcision both unnecessary and harmful, but all expected to circumcise their daughters. They hoped that a form milder than infibulation would satisfy their mothers.

> Habiba: There is no choice about circumcision. All girls here are circumcised.
>
> HH: Is that a custom that should continue, or a custom that should change?
>
> Bahsan: Change! That should change, but it's part of our culture. Now that we're moving from the culture to the religion, it will change. You know in Nairobi or elsewhere you will not hear of the traditional circumcision.
>
> HH: You've all had it in the traditional way. What will you do for your daughters?
>
> Bahsan: Our mothers live with us. They will say it must be done. I can't disagree with my mother regarding my daughter. But for my daughter's daughter, it will change. (Various sounds and words of agreement from the other women.)
>
> HH: You all feel that it wouldn't be right to oppose your mothers?
>
> All: Yes
>
> HH: If your daughter for some reason thought that she did not want it, and was in dispute with your mothers about it (Maybe that's not realistic) what would you do?
>
> Bahsan: It's done when they are very young, maybe seven or eight years old.
>
> HH: Do you think that it's best to do it when they are young?
>
> Dekha: There's the social pressure, even when they are very young. Because it is being done to all her friends in school, she would feel that you are denying her right.

1. Mungiki, a pressure group that claims to represent "true African values" has threatened forcible circumcision of all women in Kikuyu and Kiambaa who don't promptly arrange to be cut. Since they have been responsible for well-publicized political murders, these threats are serious. In 1995 there were forcible circumcisions of married women in Meru.

A few days later, when Dekha was interviewed alone, we returned to the topic of circumcision.

> HH: You said yesterday that your mother will want to have your daughter initiated and you will not challenge her on that.
>
> If you make the small issues become big, then how will you tackle the bigger issues? If you start challenging your mother on something like this, then she will stop reasoning with you on bigger issues.
>
> HH: But you also said that you will not insist that your daughter's daughters be circumcised, so the custom will change. Why should it change?
>
> It's not necessary from the religious point of view, which is the guiding factor and I don't see the benefits of it. I don't see why a child should go through all that pain we give her.
>
> HH: What form is used here?
>
> It's the most drastic kind.

When I talked separately with both Hibo and Dekha in 2003, both had changed their minds. Dekha said three respected sheiks had spoken against it, and she would definitely not allow her daughters to be cut, even if it meant opposing her mother. Hibo emphasized that Islam does not require it, and because it is harmful, it is therefore actually an offense against Islam.

Why Would A Girl Want to Be Circumcised?

Becoming an adult of course means a change in many aspects of life. Girls are eager for the right to go to dances, and to have boyfriends. Peers' ridicule is a problem for girls who are not initiated. Desire to equal her peers is an important motivator for many girls. Sein Milanoi, a Maasai woman born in 1951, left the decision to her daughters.

> My daughters may do what they want. They decided to get circumcised because they're living in Maasailand, where everybody is circumcised. We don't want to be called bad names. Maasais are radicals, they hold to their traditions very much.

Rahab Wambui, a Kikuyu born in 1963, was not circumcised, and suffered the consequences.

> In my class I was the only one who was not, so I was left alone. The other girls felt they were higher than me. They would say, "you, you are not complete. You'll never have a husband if you are not circumcised. You won't stop being childish." Those were the old beliefs.

Still, I didn't want it, because I knew my parents wouldn't agree. They were Christians, even my grandparents were. But now, whether you are circumcised or not, it is the same.

Irene Katete [Portrait B], who is a Maasai, was insulted and ridiculed by most of her friends for not being circumcised.

Teresa Wambui Tericho, a Kikuyu born in 1967, was circumcised when she finished primary school in 1982. Although many Kikuyus consider that it is no longer necessary, she disagrees.

I wanted to be a mature person, so I harassed my parents, asking them, "When will I be circumcised?" They wanted to wait until I was mature enough to understand what circumcision really is.

Since I was eager, I will also circumcise my daughters unless the country changes and says no. According to our culture, we have to circumcise.

The Current Situation

Communities have responded in many different ways to controversy over female genital cutting. Some have almost eliminated the custom. In others there is virtually no change except that some families request a less drastic cut.

Many people find a compromise. Some take their children to a hospital to be circumcised. Susan Malaso discussed changing attitudes.

When I was in school, already some girls were initiated and some were not. This depended in the family they came from. Some girls would want to be initiated because they feel proud to move to a different stage.

I was circumcised during the holidays when I was about sixteen years. It was later than any other girls. It was a surprise to me. It was our tradition so I could not refuse whatever my parents told me. When school was opened, I resumed school. My daughters were initiated because of their grandparents' opinions. I could not object.

I don't think it is important for my granddaughters. I think this will come to an end because many people are educated and don't see the importance of girls being initiated. They know it is harmful because they hear from radios, read from the newspapers that a certain girl was initiated and bled to death. So they are scared.

In most cases, it is those who have not gone to school who still support initiation of girls. Some time back, we used to believe that if a girl was not initiated, she would not have children, and also that men will not like her, and she will be set aside. But now most parents take their girls to hospital. Hospital is safer than home.

Sein Milanoi disagrees that many use hospitals for daughters.

> As we go on lobbying, we are trying to tell the mothers not to circumcise them at home with those instruments that are used for everyone, because of disease. Take them to hospital at least. It's very rare for girls to be taken to hospital, but for boys it's becoming common. People say the hospitals don't know how to operate properly on girls because it's not a common thing in other tribes.

Tabitha Mukhera, a young Gusii woman, would choose the hospital for her daughters only because of concern about disease. "I was circumcised at home. I liked it. If those diseases were not there, I would do it the same way for my daughters."

Mrs. Nangurai told us that those who take their daughters to the hospital for cutting also request a milder form.

> Those who are doing it in hospital just ask for a small snip — just so that others will not laugh at them. They do not want to have people say, "So and so's child is not circumcised."

During the conversation at Bahsan's home, Dekha said,

> Dekha: Some of the TBAs[2] who do circumcision are getting awareness. The best thing is to get a very moderate TBA, who will do a moderate job. Then you have a win-win. You give your mother her rightful place, you also cut this girl (only) on the outside.
>
> HH: (to the other four women) Is that what you would like to do for your daughters? (murmurs indicating agreement from all the other women)

Among the Maasai, circumcision traditions are changing in another way: the age is dropping. Irene Katete told me that the Maasai now usually circumcise girls at about fourteen years old, though when she was in school it was usually done at about eighteen, and during her mother's youth it was done at about twenty. Mrs. Nangurai explained one reason for the change;

> Excess bleeding usually comes in the older girls. There was a time that the government was really concerned and talking about it for so many days. The medical people thought it was their duty to talk to the parents. And then you find when they talked about AIDS, they started doing this circumcision in the early age. It is safer that way, when you are younger, so the age has been dropping.

2. Traditional Birth Attendant. Many TBAs are now trained by NGOs on subjects such as antisepsis and recognizing complications.

Sein gives a different reason for the declining age.

> It has dropped a lot because when they grow up, being in school, these girls might refuse. But when she is young, she has no decision to make. So the parents decide to circumcise when she's young. They don't wait for menstruation, they just look at the body.
>
> A Maasai man does not look at his daughter, it is the lady who will come and say, "Now the girl is grown up." The mothers say when the girl is ready, but the father cannot ask. And when she sees the girl is trying to have some breasts, it is she who will tell the father that the girl is ready to be circumcised.
>
> So we (her lobbying group) are trying to tell them not to report this to the father.

Katherine Karamboi told us what has happened to a number of girls from A.I.C. during school holidays.

> Even some of the girls here who are big enough to say no, when they go home during the school holidays find their parents have arranged for the circumcision to take place immediately, e.g. they go home on a Friday and Saturday is the "big day."
>
> Plans are made without her knowledge. The boma is full of people coming for the ceremony. She is guarded tightly to avoid her running away. So the following morning it is done and she comes back to school and narrates how she could not run away.
>
> The same thing can happen when the girl is given in marriage. This is tricky because, is it is in the interior, the girls are not able to know in time to take the appropriate action. Sometimes we rescue these girls when they have gone through the whole process: circumcision, marriage, and the old man has slept with the girl. Those girls may come here really traumatised.

The Influence of Christianity

Communities that have ceased to circumcise girls often explain the change as a consequence of Christianity. When asked about traditional customs that are changing, Nkatha Murithi, a Meru, thought first of circumcision. She was not circumcised because of her parents' opposition.

> My mother was circumcised, but I was not. My parents are very strong Christians. In this area, most of the people are Christians, so they don't normally practice it. But there are some areas where they are still doing it.
>
> There are women who are encouraging it. Even when you talk to our grandmother, she feels proud of it. In rural areas it is the ones who are already circumcised who are encouraging others to continue.

Where I grew up there were some who were being circumcised, but my mother really encouraged us to stay away from them. She didn't want us to be influenced by staying with them. That was in the villages, not in school.

HH: Are you saying that the girls who were circumcised mostly didn't go to school? Or did some of your classmates also get circumcised?

In school they were trying to eliminate it, so the girls who were circumcised didn't talk about it in school.

Under pressure from church, school, and government, female genital cutting is disappearing in some communities, and becoming less common in others. Some women are refusing to circumcise their daughters, even in the face of intense pressure from relatives. Jean Ndike, a young widow, told of a very early refusal.

My own grandmother, my mother's mother, ran away from her husband many years before we were born, when my mother was a young girl. Ran away with all her eight children because their father wanted them to be circumcised. My grandmother was always complaining that whoever came out with woman's circumcision must be a very evil person. She was circumcised, of course. Even in my time it was usual.

About half of my age-mates were circumcised. We were not supposed to talk about it in school. Where I came from my grandfather on the other side was a very strict Christian. When we were little, sometimes we'd hear there was a circumcision parade passing through, so we would go to look. He would be very angry. We would really hide ourselves.

We would never talk about it in the school. The teachers would probably send away the ones who had been circumcised, and then they would never be able to enter a missionary school, so we did not talk about it.

Joan Kanini, the Kamba born in 1945 who told us about the Kambas early abandonment of traditional drums, said, "The Kamba are very quick to change customs. They accepted Christianity and immediately stopped circumcising girls."

Despite Joan's assertion that Kambas "immediately stopped circumcising girls," the rural Kamba women whom she introduced me to were all circumcised. Kasiki Wayua, who appears to be in her sixties, said:

I was fully grown, about sixteen years old. The only instruction we had was about half an hour before the operation. We were told how to behave when it happened. There were about fifty girls. I don't know if any of them had health problems after the operation.

Kasiki's daughters were also circumcised. Kasiki's neighbor, Regina Kavindu, felt proud when she was circumcised, but did not circumcise her daughters. "The tradition was already dead. Circumcision of girls wasn't good because of bleeding, because the knives are not sterilized, and because it decreases the girl's sex urge."

There is no simple connection between abandonment of circumcision and Christianity. There are Muslim communities where the practice has been abandonned and fervent, devout Christian communities where all girls are still circumcised. Selina is a Gusii and a Roman Catholic. Her entire family is quite devout. All facets of their lives are affected by their piety. Yet all of Selina's daughters and granddaughters who are old enough have been circumcised. Both sexes are circumcised at five to ten years old. Her family routinely takes girls to the hospital for circumcision, but many others in her community do it at home.

Selina's friend Robina, also a Gusii and a Roman Catholic, had her daughters circumcised at home. While Selina and I were talking with Robina and several of her children, I asked one of the unmarried daughters:

> HH: You're a young, educated woman. You know that many other tribes are giving up circumcising their girls, but your community still circumcises every girl. Will you circumcise your daughters?
>
> Yes.
>
> HH: Why? What is the importance of circumcision?
>
> If my husband says it should be done we will do it.
>
> HH: But suppose your husband says, "I don't know. You are a woman. You should decide." What will you decide?
>
> It is not necessary. She should be able to enjoy herself sexually.
>
> HH: Is it harmful?
>
> Yes
>
> HH: Why?
>
> Because you lose blood.
>
> HH: You lose blood, but then eventually you stop bleeding. After you've recovered from the operation, has it done any harm?
>
> Yes, in the days which are coming, many people may get disease. You know the same materials are used for many people, so if one has the disease, many people will be infected.

People of nearly the same age in the same community may have very different opinions and experiences. Anna and Monicah, two young Nandi women who live near each other were both circumcised at age nineteen. They had quite different feelings about it, and did it for different reasons. Anna, who was born in 1967, told me, "I was circumcised at nineteen. I didn't want to. I knew about Christianity, but my parents insisted. I was circumcised alone, but there was a celebration and instruction."

Monicah, who was born in 1963, has a different story:

> I wanted to be circumcised because I had a boyfriend who told me to be circumcised so we could get married.
>
> HH: Did you have the traditional instruction afterward?
>
> Yes, they told me many things. Even now I cannot remember. [This was probably a polite way of forestalling questions about what is supposed to remain secret.]
>
> HH: Did you marry the man who sent you to be circumcised?
>
> No.

Her cousin Pamela interjected, "He refused."

Filomena Jeptanui, born in 1959 in the same region as Monicah and Anna, was not circumcised.

> You know, I had gone to school and didn't see any need for circumcision. It depends too on the person you marry. My husband did not insist.
>
> HH: Did your grandparents or anyone else put pressure on your parents to have you circumcised?
>
> No, there was no pressure. I had only a maternal grandmother, and she had no say in our family. My paternal grandmother had died earlier. Both grandfathers were also dead. Even during the engagement ceremony, my husband to be was asked, "Do you want to take her the way she is, or do you want us to circumcise her?"
>
> You know the parents of the husband may force you, but mine said, "No, we will take her the way she is."
>
> HH: What about your age-mates. Did they ridicule you?
>
> No, and we are still friends. Most of those who didn't go to school were circumcised. The ones I went to school with were almost the first ones to leave circumcision.

Arguments for Change

The reasons most commonly given for opposing circumcision are Christianity, harm to the girl from loss of blood,[3] and the risk of disease. Two women also mentioned decreased sex urge as a negative consequence.

Mrs. Priscilla Nangurai opposes circumcision for educational reasons. She sees circumcision as the beginning of the end of a girl's education.

---

3. From the frequency with which loss of blood was mentioned, I suspect many women don't know that lost blood is eventually replaced if the girl survives.

After she is circumcised, a girl is at risk for a marriage agreement. In addition, since she now considers herself an adult, she may lose interest in school, which is seen as the domain of children.

When the girls reach class five or six, they are circumcised. Circumcision brings them to another stage where they are treated as adults, mature women ready for marriage. After circumcision you are free. Nobody will ask you why you are having sexual relationships, because you are supposed to. That is where our problems begin, with circumcision.

HH: Is it changing? Are all of your girls initiated or are there now families that are refusing?

The majority are circumcising, even the educated. It is about ninety to ninety-five percent. There are very few parents who do not want to do it. Circumcision is the beginning of disaster. After that the girl is a mature woman. She can move around the way she wants. I am not of their father's age grade so I cannot say what they can and cannot do. And also the girls themselves feel that they are now matured women and they expect the teachers to know that they are mature. They become very flirtatious. They expect any man to approach them for sex.

From twelve or thirteen we know that when these girls go for holidays they might be circumcised. So we try to talk to them at that stage.

HH: How many are circumcised in the traditional way and how many in hospitals?

Very few in hospitals. The rest of them would like to go through the traditional way. Sometimes, if you are not circumcised, others would really laugh at you. If you are not a Maasai they will assume you have not been circumcised. They look down upon teachers who are not circumcised, but that is changing. After circumcision women have their hair cut completely. So you come to school with your head clean-shaved. You are kind of embarrassed. Before you would be proud to walk with no hair.

HH: Do the girls who are last to be circumcised get anxious and request it?

I do not think we have reached the stage where the girl can discuss it with her parents. The girls here say, "Oh, I wish I could talk to my Mum. I wish I could talk to my auntie about circumcision." So I have a feeling soon girls will take courage to discuss this with their mother.

HH: So what they want to discuss is not being circumcised?

Especially when they are Christians because of the teachings about not being circumcised if you are a Christian. I remember when my parents became Christians first they said we were not going to circumcise anymore because we are Christians. So if you became a Christian they say you will not be circumcised. Yet the girls are afraid to discuss it at home. But I can see a time is coming.

The lobby group have been having meetings with the mothers. We talk about the importance of education, and now, we are touching on circumcision. Of course when we start talking about circumcision, everybody just looks down.

Now, most women are against forced marriage. But circumcision I do not think yet.

HH: May I ask you one slightly sensitive question? Was your daughter initiated?

No she was not. So I am happy about that. You know I never even discussed it with my husband. Obviously, he knew what I thought. I just kept my fingers crossed that he did not insist, and I said, "Thank God."

Author's Comment

No reader of any nationality will be surprised to learn that I, an American feminist, hope to see female genital cutting eliminated completely and permanently. I applaud the willingness of some western governments to grant asylum to girls and women fleeing to avoid genital mutilation. Nevertheless, I think western efforts to force African governments to outlaw genital cutting are unwise for two reasons: Where it is illegal, people do not have the intermediate option of having their daughters cut in a hospital. Hospital procedures are both less likely to lead to infection and generally milder in extent. I think it is a valuable option in communities where genital cutting is still common.

Secondly: western pressure is counterproductive. As many Africans are becoming aware of its harmful effects, there is a growing indigenous opposition to female genital cutting. Africans should be left to decide this issue without western interference. Only widespread understanding of its harmful effects will end the practice. African opponents of cutting can argue more persuasively when they are understood to be voices for girls, not misperceived as voices of the West.

11

The Other Kenyans

In the years since independence, the number of non-Africans in Kenya has dropped dramatically. On the eve of independence, there were 177,000 Asians and 56,000 Europeans in Kenya. By 1989 the number of non-Africans was dramatically lower. There were about half as many Asians, 53,000 citizens and 36,000 non-citizen Asians; and sixty percent as many Europeans, 3,000 citizens and 31,000 non-citizen Europeans. In the same period, the total population increased from 8.6 million to 21.4 million.

White Kenyans

Today's white Kenyans are Kenyan by choice. They, or their parents, chose to stay after independence. Generally they have been educated abroad and urged by relatives to stay in England, but decided to return to Kenya because they love it.

Corporate and government employment is generally closed to them, except perhaps teaching, but many feel that Kenya is a land of good business opportunity. Often they are in tourist-related businesses.

Love of Kenya

Jean Hartley was born in 1943. She attended Limuru Girls School when it was entirely white, and then went to study in the UK. "I really did not want to live in England. I hated the weather, I hated the people and this was home, so I came back though I didn't know what life had in store for me."

She returned to Kenya in 1967. Because of the push to Africanize, it was not easy for her to find a job. She was not a Kenyan citizen, despite having been born in Kenya, because she had been away at the time of independence. She eventually found a job as a government secretary. In the next few years, she worked in various ministries. Then she went into business with friends and travelled extensively in Africa and Europe. She is an active outdoors person, a scuba diver, a birdwatcher, and deeply interested in wildlife. She became a guide and now has a flourishing company that assists people producing wildlife films.

> The generation of white Kenyans now in their late twenties and early thirties can't really live anywhere else. Although they have uncles and aunts in other parts of the world, they have nothing in common with them, as I found when I went to England.
>
> A lot of people left before independence since they thought the change would be awful. But they hated England so they came back home after a year or so. They went to see Kenyatta and asked, "What can we do?"

Jessica Smith did not like school, and did not go abroad to study, but nevertheless left Kenya for a time.

> I decided to go off and live in any other country. All my friends were locked in some university or school so I went to South Africa for a year and a half.
>
> Maybe I am being an ostrich with its head in the sand. I do feel very positive about living here. We are very blessed in this country because we really have a lovely life, an outdoor life, an active sporty life, wonderful weather.
>
> We enjoy being able to go away on safaris to Turkana. You really get into the wild; you don't see another person.

The White Kenyan Community

Because of restricted opportunities, many who have decided to stay nevertheless encourage their children to look elsewhere. Gillian Veitch is one of the people whose children have left. She doesn't fear living far from them. In colonial times, her family owned a hotel in Nairobi and a large farm outside Nairobi. Her father especially loved the farm, and looked forward to selling the hotel and retiring to the farm. He hoped his sons would take over managing the farm so he could retire there.

After independence, the government bought the surrounding farms from the white settlers and gave small plots to the indigenous Africans who had been working the land. Gillian's father held out for a time, but eventually succumbed to pressure and sold the land.

> The British government agreed to buy back most of the land that had belonged to the British people and give it to local people. My father did not

want to sell, but all the farmers around had all sold; he was a little island. He was quite determined to stay, but things were happening like cutting down the trees after he had spent years in putting them up as a windbreak.

It was mostly fertile farmland that was redistributed. The large arid grazing ranches such as the Delameres or some out on the Mombasa road have been left. I think the people who most wanted redistribution were the Kikuyu. They were not particularly interested in grazing lands. But the highlands are very fertile country, so it was carved up into five acre plots and alloted to the Kikuyu. I have been back to our farm several times to see the people. They are feeding themselves, but on five acres they can't do much commercial agriculture, just subsistence.

When the land had been sold, Gillian's father strongly encouraged his children to find work abroad.

With independence on the horizon, my father sent all of us off and said, "Right, there's no future for you in Kenya so I want you to go and make another life elsewhere." I went to London but I couldn't bear it. It was a cold place with people not talking to each other. But I felt that, having said I was going, I couldn't just come back. So I went to Nigeria in 1961 and stayed to 1963.

When I came back, quite a few of my classmates were still here. But marriage and the work permit system meant that a lot of them dispersed. If an African can do the same kind of job as a white, the white is not going to be welcome. When I got back I could not become a citizen because I was out of the country for more than five years. So I had to do five years on a work permit. I think you need that kind of system. I agree with that entirely!

I don't feel confident about my children's and grandchildren's future here. My son had an overseas education, went to public school in UK and to university. I am not sure about the future of his children. My current husband has two children. They went back to England.

There are lot of farmers and ex-hunters, people in the tourism industry and so on. Their children have just stayed on. People here really have to make a decision whether they are going to stay here or compete in the big elsewhere. The people who love the country decide they are going to stay here as we have stayed. Relatives overseas say to me, "When are you going to return?" But I haven't thought of it.

We've still got lots of people, a few thousand. We've been to school here and known each other from the past.

Jessica Smith was once concerned about declining numbers of whites, but now feels secure about the future.

We're quite a small community. People who stayed after independence have all met each other or know about each other, wherever we live in the country.

A lot of our friends moved away and went to school overseas. So on the social side there was a kind of dwindling away of friends. But now I find lots of people coming back. I find that very encouraging.

HH: Do you worry that when you are old, there may not be much of a next generation?

I think there will be. Ever since independence it has dwindled on, declining, yes, but it will still be there.

Safety

For most white Kenyans, personal safety is a far greater concern than the declining numbers of their community. For example, they are wary about driving at night. Jessica Smith is very cautious.

One is very aware of crime. Driving along in your car and getting stopped, what you do? You check on up on each other, you might phone before you leave somewhere to let someone know you're on the road, and we don't go out at all at night.

Probably if we go out, we stay for night with the person in town rather than drive back after nightfall. It is quite fearful because one wonders how effective the police are. Not that it's their fault, but you ring them up and they don't have a vehicle to come help you, so you have to go and get them yourself, which is a bit difficult if you've had a problem with your car. If there should be an accident where an African is hurt, it can go very hard for a white person. Even if you have witnesses to say it was not your fault, by the time it comes to court, some may have been bribed and or threatened and changed their stories. We are even suspicious of people around us. That is new.

Sandra O'Malley, who was born in Nairobi in 1967, has similar concerns.

We get home before it's dark. Coming late at night is not safe. Then there is car hijacking. Security is not as it used to be. If we are invited for a dinner arrangement, we say we will make it a lunch instead.

One weekend my friend was getting married and I was bridesmaid. We had a hen party, but we made sure to have the men come and pick us up. We made sure we travelled in convoy. What happened? In the middle of the road there was a car stopped, right in the middle, with doors open and a fellow standing next to it, and it turned out to be a pretty suspicious fellow. Fortunately we had a friend coming behind in another car. There were four cars in all.

Marian Slade, who was born in Nairobi in 1939, sees the question a bit differently.

> I've been more unnerved in London than I have been in Kenya. I wouldn't take long drives in lonely places by myself at night, but otherwise I do whatever I really want to within my sphere. I go to see my friends. I don't walk around with a great fear of anything. Of course, it's partly that I know where to go and where not to go.

Social Problems

In 1996, increasing poverty and rampant corruption were these women's biggest concerns for Kenya's future. Jean Hartley felt anguish over the economic problems of her country.

> The gap between the haves and the have-nots is getting wider. The people who have access to money such as politicians and people in high places don't seem to know when to stop stealing. The average man in the street is no better off than he was twenty or thirty years ago. There is desperation and fairly recent social problems like street kids. These kids are next generation's crime in the making.
>
> Many things are much worse now: children involved in prostitution, exploding population. Though AIDS is taking many people, the population growth is still tremendous. That is obviously having its effect on youngsters as well as adults, in unemployment and desperation. Lots of people are turning to theft because they are unable to get a job. But this is a government problem and the government should not let it happen.
>
> If political leaders were at a higher academic level, I think it would be better. If people had been educated probably they would have been exposed to the real world. They would have seen other countries which work. They would be interested in learning from other countries. People who did not have that opportunity may not be able to relate to new ideas.
>
> I would like to see the civil servants, police, and other people, paid a better salary for highly qualified people. When you are not giving high salaries, there will be corruption and people with their hands in the till.
>
> It is still possible to earn a living and run a business without offering bribes. This is where education comes in. Everybody makes noises saying that we must stop corruption. But it does not stop.

Gillian Veitch saw corruption differently, but agreed on the solution.

> We, the Europeans, introduced corruption here. When it was a British colony, everything from tractors to telecommuniations was British. When we

got independence, in came the other Europeans, and in order to try to get a foothold where the Brits had always been, we introduced corruption and then it become endemic. Now it is very difficult to get anything done without paying something. You always need kitu kidogo [a bribe].

It has become almost impossible to reverse it. We will get rid of it only if we have clean sweep in the government. I don't see that happening, unfortunately. Civil servants, police, etc. are not properly paid. When a policeman earns only three thousand shillings a month or so, I really feel terribly sorry for the man in street.

What is happening now is that you've got an incredibly wealthy small section of the community which rushes round in a Mercedes. And then you've got that top level of people with about fifty houses, but they don't seem content with that.

For a long time, Marjorie Macgoye had no telephone because she was asked for a bribe to install one. She refused to pay, and believed that doing so would not solve the problem.

Once you are known to be willing to bribe, people will just keep coming back. They'd be continually coming to fix a problem with the phone. I couldn't afford it.

Things have become so desperate that really, you morally have to find a forum to say it. We know perfectly well these scandals occur in every country. But in a better managed country, if you are found out, you are finished. You have to go somewhere else or you have to change your name.

On the other end, many people are so desperate that they have to grab what they can.

Sandra felt worn down by corruption and bureaucratic unreasonableness.

Corruption is a problem every day, every month. There are so many things you can't do without a permit.

What social security do we get? In the UK, there are stamps for free lunches, uniforms, schoolbooks. People here have to pay for the schoolbooks, uniforms, shoes; it is a shame.

As far as business licences are concerned, it really goes against the grain to pay [a bribe for] that sort of thing and so far I have not touched it. I have done everything by the books and succeeded.

HH: I have the impression that it is easier for a white person, Kenyan or non-Kenyan, to make officials stick to the rules than it is for an equally determined, equally savvy Africans. I think somehow officials fear a white face a bit more and may obey the rules. Is it true?

> I wonder if it is not, although corruption is becoming so blatant now. My husband sent Patrick down to renew the licence for our car. He stood in the queue, got the forms to be filled in, and went back with the filled in forms. But again some other form is required to be filled. This went on for three days. They kept on sending him back for this or for that or for another thing. Just giving him a hard time so he would offer kitu kidogo. Then my husband went with Patrick, put him in queue with him, got to the counter and presented the form as it was, just the same as Patrick had done. The lady started to sign, and then afterwards when Patrick went up, my husband asked, "Why did you not serve this gentleman as you served me?" He was furious, and the whole queue was in unison.

Marian also saw this problem differently.

> Well, there's a lot of "they say..." I personally have never come across it.
>
> HH: You've not been asked for a bribe?
>
> No, or if I was, I didn't see it. I have never bribed anyone a sixpence. I just won't do it. I've run a business and built a house without bribing. I think that people who do are wrong.

When I returned in 2003, white Kenyans were optimistic about the new government's fight against corruption, but personal safety had become an overwhelming concern. A member of their community had recently been murdered in his own compound by thugs, and all felt vulnerable.

Mixing

An important reason why these women can live comfortably as part of a dwindling minority, is that they feel accepted by Africans and, with one exception, feel very secure about continuing acceptance. They also recognize that some of the whites who stayed on have not adjusted easily to their loss of superior status. Jean Hartley thinks the younger generation has mixed easily, but her own has not.

> When I was a kid, the schools we went to were entirely white, but now all the kids are balanced so there is no feeling of being different. My kids have friends and colleagues from all races.
>
> Anybody of my age group who wants to stay has to accept that Kenya has changed and they can't look at it from the colonial way. But some of them can't adjust.

Gillian sees a reservoir of continuing racism among some in the white Kenyan community, but foresses its eventual disappearance.

Here in Kenya, there was a color bar. You were not expected to go into something like The New Stanley Hotel if you were black. However nobody would actually stop you.

My brother and sister lived in South Africa for a while. There, I felt hatred because of the color of my skin, which I never felt in Kenya. And I can't say I blame them. In contrast, when you come to Kenya, people say, "Welcome. We hope you like our country."

I was quite happy to take on the new Kenya. I became a citizen and made friends with people who would not have come into my life before. Now my friends and associates are a mixed bunch. The majority are European descended, but many are Africans.

I don't think there is a color barrier now. I think there is an education barrier. We meet all sorts of people, Indian lawyers, African lawyers, African businessmen of a certain educational and professional level. My husband has a small legal practice. There are four partners, all citizens, mixed races.

I foresee a good future. Now, we are hearing quite a lot of racially mixed marriages. There are quite a few ethnically mixed marriages as well.

Marjorie Macgoye found that her children did not suffer as the result of their mixed racial heritage.

We don't have the idea of the "colored" [as a term for mixed race]. Although I don't mean to say that my children never got teased when they were little. I was rather surprised and very pleased when [my son] George became headboy of his school.

I became a citizen in 1963.[1] I know people who have kept their citizenship elsewhere because there will be education privileges and so on which you are entitled to in other countries. But children belong to the father's community in Kenya. So there can be very serious problems if the marriage breaks up and the mother is not Kenyan. On a non-political field, I would say relations are improving over time. Intermarriages are going on at a very great rate. People who have been to school together, or in theatre together, or played music together, don't have any difficulty about meeting one another. My husband was happy to have every kind of person visiting us at home, not only at my invitation but at his invitation as well.

Marian agrees with the others on this.

I think Kenya is much better since independence. Before, we didn't really know people of the other races. I enjoy it more now. But bear in mind that I was very young before independence, so I didn't really know life. Although we are naturally more acquainted with our own racial group, I think there is a great bridge now between various races. I certainly know more Africans than I used.

1. The year of independence.

Business

Since the government and businesses hesitate to hire them, European-descended Kenyans must mostly conduct their own businesses. Several commented on the opportunities for starting a business in Kenya. Soon after finishing high school, Marian Slade went to work for a travel company started by an English family long before independence. She remained with the same firm and became the manager. Eventually, it was bought by a conglomerate, and she left. She started a sandwich making business that she ran from her home with three assistants.

> I've never found any disadvantages either to being a European or to being a woman. It's just not a problem. I suppose I was the right age at the right time to come into a management position. The business climate is changing. It used to be much trickier, particularly in the travel business. It's easier since currency decontrol. We used to need a variety of licenses. As long as we remembered to renew them it was no problem.
>
> I admire the African Kenyans tremendously because they have had to go from mud hut to microchip in fifty years. We did it in three hundred years. A lot of these girls who are working on computers, their mothers came from a mud hut.

Jessica, who has owned two very different small businesses, finds Kenya very open to entrepreneurs.

> I am not clever, not academic. But I think out here I've had a lot of opportunities. There is so much you can do here if you have an idea: openings for things to be made, or services required, finding a gap in the market.
>
> Lots of Africans are coming up now who are well qualified and who have been to universities and need jobs. Before there was a shortage of Kenya citizens qualified for jobs. But now there are plenty of qualified Africans, so for the first time, the qualified white Kenyans are not being snapped up as they used to be.

A Dissent

Sandra O'Malley, a fourth generation white Kenyan, is very typical in several respects. She was educated in the UK but was not happy there and returned to Kenya eagerly. She and her husband own a business. She agrees that in some respects, Kenya is a land of good business opportunity and a wonderful place to live. But in 1996 she felt far gloomier about future prospects than others I talked with.

My father was a professional hunter so I was born and brought up in the bush. I certainly feel very Kenyan. I went to school in Nairobi in my young years. When my parents divorced, my brother and Mom and I went to the UK in '78. I wasn't happy. It wasn't home.

My husband and I started this company three years ago. We came in with new technology. Nairobi is a small town and if you have anything new to offer, people are excited, so we did very well at first.

Running your own company is easier here than elsewhere because if you find a niche, the competition is not as great. On the other hand, the lack of encouragement and financial support from banks is not easy. To start a company and run it is a lot more difficult than in the UK. You have to have enough of your own capital to keep going.

Finding employment is also different here. Whites can't get jobs like being a supermarket stockist. The ones who don't have qualifications but just want to stay here because they like the climate, the people, or the lifestyle, have to go into their own businesses like crafts shops or exporting. But if you do have qualifications, you start much higher up on the ladder than in the UK.

Many of the people I went to elementary school with have left to study and come back.

This year has been incredibly turbulent. My feelings for the country have changed so dramatically! I don't have the confidence in the country I used to. The roads and infrastructure have virtually fallen down. We had to spend half a million shillings on a generator just to keep the computers running. Often the telephones don't work. The road to Mombasa is terrible. We don't do so much traveling anymore,

All the taxes we pay! I do not mind paying taxes, but the money does not go to where it's supposed to go.

All this will probably change. The question for us is, when? How long can I wait? For six years, for ten years, fifteen years for the changes to come about? We think about leaving, but it's a question of where to go. Generally we do not like the European lifestyle. That is why emigration is towards Australia and America. All my husband's family has left, though they've been here many generations more than my family. His grandmother went to Australia and they are very happy. They like the weather, the people are nice and there's open space, everything works etc. The only thing missing is the wildlife.

We've had a lot more racial tolerance here than in many African or other countries, but the confrontation between Africans and Europeans is getting worse and worse now. In the last few years, I've had little incidents with police, or getting caught up in arguments. The first thing that comes out is, "Oh, go back where you came from." They don't stop to think that maybe you were born here and are as Kenyan as the next person. That really upsets me. I have to say that I feel less and less Kenyan, and it's part of the reason we're thinking about not staying.

ASIANS

Indians[2] and Arabs were actively trading with East Africa long before Europeans arrived. In addition to coastal settlements, they had trade routes in the interior. As the British began inland penetration, they relied on Arab and Indian assistance. When colonizers wanted a railroad, they tried unsuccessfully to conscript African labor to build it. Africans refused the hard and dangerous work of railroad building, running home when they were pressed into service. So, just as Americans brought Irish and Chinese immigrants to build their railroads, the British brought Indian laborers, who could not easily run home. This railroad-based immigration was large enough to attract merchants and artisans who came to supply the emerging Indian community. They came from several regions, spoke different languages, and brought many religious traditions. Although many laborers went home when the railroad was completed, great numbers of tradespeople remained, and the Indian rupee became Kenya's standard currency. Thus, the Indian descended population of Kenya is mixed, just as India is mixed, with respect to religion.[3]

For Some, A Separate World

Asians are thought of as "keeping to themselves." Many Sikhs and Gujerati Hindus do live separated from the general population, but other Asian groups are less isolated. Arunaben Ranmalbhai's life typifies the separateness that still exists in the Asian community. She lives with her businessman husband in a beautiful house in an elegant section of Nairobi.

Arunaben's father immigrated to Kenya as a young man, and worked in his uncle's shop. When he was established, he sent for his family. Arunaben was born in Murang'aa in 1926.

Her childhood was spent in an extended family of forty people. They shared one latrine. Water was fetched from the river, and clothes were washed there. Meals were cooked on a wood stove. There was no electricity, but plenty of good food, and a good school nearby.

Arunaben went to school until she was sixteen, but left when her marriage was arranged. She was allowed to meet and to walk about with her future husband before they married. In fact, they had a long engagement because her father died soon after the engagement was

2. Since the partition of India, the Indian-descended population of Kenya is generally referred to by Africans as "Asians" rather than as "Indians" because people have come to Kenya from throughout the Indian subcontinent. Those Asians whose forebears came from India refer to themselves as "Indians" in the Kenyan context. I have used both terms.

3. Asian interviewees included Hindus, Mulims, a Sikh, a Jain, and a Roman Catholic.

agreed to. The wedding was therefore postponed for a year of mourning. During that time she and her future husband fell in love.

At school, Arunaben had both African and Asian friends, but she did not keep up with her African friends after marriage. As an adult, all of her friends were Indian Hindus of the same caste. Arunaben learned to speak English in school, but now speaks only Gujerati. She has no occasion to speak English, and has forgotten how. She and her contemporaries did not learn Kiswahili or any other African language at school.

Arunaben spends her days at home, but goes out with her husband every evening to visit friends or shop. Prayers occupy about three hours each day. She now spends several hours on exercises to help her combat arthritis. The rest of her time is occupied with housework.

Arunaben wears a sari, but her daughters don't. She never learned to drive, but all three of her daughters drive and have university educations. Arunaben never went out by herself, but she approved of the greater mobility of the younger generation. Arunaben's life is by no means an extreme case of cultural isolation. Several women in their thirties and forties who are active in a Hindu social club consider themselves very fortunate, since some women of their own age are not allowed by their husbands to participate in outside activities.[4]

Rasna Warah, a Sikh born in Nairobi in 1962, finds the separateness of her community stifling.

> As a child, my social world was mostly family: uncles, aunts, grand uncles, cousins. Even our best friends were sort of related to us. But when we went to school, it was a different story. Schools had been desegregated by then, so we had all kinds of other races. My school had mostly Asians and Africans.
>
> I remember once inviting an African friend home and feeling very nervous about it. I didn't know how my family would take it. My grandmother asked her if she wanted a drink. She had a drink and then she just left. I was actually more nervous than my grandmother was.
>
> After I had finished university, I was still living at home with my mother and grandmother. My best friend, Betty, was an African woman. My family liked her, and welcomed the friendship.
>
> I think the barrier to friendships with Africans when I was in school was economic. I lived in a bigger house than my African fellow students. We had a bigger garden and a car. When the economic differences were blurred, it became easier. Betty was clearly of a higher economic class. She was a tennis star, she studied abroad, and she was a woman so she wasn't a threat.

4. We were not able to interview any Asian women who do not have outside contacts.

Although it was difficult for Rasna to socialize with Africans in her family home, now that she lives on her own, it is easy.

Asians in Nairobi are numerous and can live in their own separate world, but this is less true outside of Nairobi. Damu Shah, a Jain who lives in Mombasa, told us that the three races are much more integrated in Coastal Province. Jane De Souza, who was an internationally successful athlete, grew up in Kisumu before 1965, and had a social life which included all races.

> I went to a mixed school run by the nuns. For high school I went to a government school. My closest friends were mostly (African) Kenyans, because of sports. Many Asians here in Nairobi live in a fairly closed community, but it's different with Goans. Religion plays a role too. We Goans are ninety-nine percent Roman Catholic.
>
> Kisumu was a small town, very united, the entire population. For example, when we got married we had to invite everybody, from a butcher to a tailor. There were about a thousand people.

Bhagwati Jani, a Gujerati Hindu born in 1937, is today an important influence in the Hindu community.

> I have lived in Nairobi all my life, but I was born in India because in Indian tradition the first delivery takes place in the mother's place. My maternal grandparents were in India, so my mother had to go to India for delivery.
>
> I had a secluded childhood. We thought segregation was a normal thing. All the Asian children went to one school and the Africans to another. We did not see any Africans those days. Neither did we see any Europeans. Even at teacher's college, I did not know any Africans. All our lecturers were Europeans.

Mina Daya, who was born in India in 1947, but moved to Kenya after marrying a Kenyan Indian, sent her son to an integrated school for six years, but regretted it and concluded that he would be better off in a school for Asians.

> I thought I had done the best for my son and I paid through my nose. During children's break time, I would park my car and observe the child. I saw certain groups were always with the teacher. The African children, very affluent class, the teacher was very kind to them but there was not the flow of love which you see within the same community. Between the English teacher and English children, it was unmistakably there. Also, some of the families were expatriates. Every year some child will leave and my son would say, "Mother my friend has left. I am alone." So I thought my son was going to

be such a lonely person in the world. I said, "Now I want him to be with the community with which he is going to live." So I sent him to an Indian school. Today at least he has good friends.

Prabha Bardhwan, an expatriate Indian living in Kenya for many years, explained that Africans and Asians are kept separate by two very big cultural differences: eating meat, and pre-marital sex. Another way of looking at this comment is that it reveals how separate some Hindus still are, not only from African Kenyans, but also from other castes of Hindus. Not all Hindus are vegetarians, but Brahmans like Bardhwan live in a society that doesn't include other castes or races, though it does include people of similar heritage who may now be citizens of India, the U.K., or even the U.S. But Bhagwati Jani believes the separation between different castes is lessening.

> My father encouraged me when I wanted to marry out of my caste. My mother also accepted that after five long years. Her hesitation had nothing to do with him. The only objection was the caste.
>
> HH: To someone from a different culture, it is hard to understand that. What can you say to help me understand?
>
> There is no logic. There is no reason behind it. The language is the same, the way of dressing is the same, food is the same. Now we have inter-racial marriages, let alone inter-caste marriages. Things have changed dramatically. Traditionally, you had to live with your mother-in-law, as I did. There was no way out. But now you can live separately.

Neera Kapoor, a dancer who was born in Kenya in 1953 but has lived all over the world, laments the one-sidedness of her family's friendships with Africans. They enjoy social contact with many African friends and colleagues, and frequently invite them home. But she said that they are never invited to visit their African friends in return.

Family and Community

There are important similarities between Indian culture and indigenous Kenyan culture. In both, marriages are traditionally arranged by the parents. Indians live patrilocally in joint families, just as African Kenyans do. The primary responsibility for carrying out the work of the household generally falls to the wives of the sons. For several of the Indian women we talked with, though they were educated and may have had independent aspirations, meeting the needs of their husbands' families had to come ahead of other goals.

Anita Patel was born in Nairobi and has lived in Kenya all her life except during the time she was at university in India. But Kenya achieved independence during the time she was away. She is therefore not a Kenyan citizen, which has not been a problem for her. Her marriage was arranged shortly after her return from India. Her husband and her children all have Kenyan citizenship.

> I stayed in a joint family where things were done together. My mother-in-law was not healthy. My husband's sisters were working, one was a secretary and another one was an accountant, and therefore I was just to stay at home.
>
> It is good to bring children up in a joint family, because this can enable one to afford something he would not have afforded alone.
>
> I still live in a joint family although I am a bit separate because I am grown. When you are young, you need to be guided and therefore it is good to be in a joint family, but now we are big people who can decide what to do on our own. When we were together, there were restrictions in that whenever we wanted to go for an outing, we could not go.
>
> I think it is easier now, because old people have changed a bit and the younger generation has also changed. Most of the work at home is done by househelp, so a young bride will find some chances for working. I think this is a good change because the education that is given to children should be put to the right use.

Under the best circumstances, joint families are able to support every member in her independent activities. Jane de Souza was able to continue competing in international sporting events because her mother-in-law took over household responsibilities for her.

Mina Daya's life was decisively channeled by her love for and sense of duty toward her father-in-law. Mina was born and educated in India. She married a Kenyan Indian student of the same Brahmin sub-caste as her own. She moved to Kenya in 1971, but was not happy.

> When I came to Kenya, I disliked it because, compared to India, it was much more orthodox and slow moving Here, the women cannot do this or that. This has kept me at a certain distance from my generation, but the younger generation, I feel very comfortable with.
>
> There was kind of cultural and professional shock when I came. I had an Indian passport so the Government wouldn't give me a [dentistry] job in hospital. I was sitting at home, I do not know the language. As a new bride, I was expected to meet a lot of people on a social basis, relatives and so on. So during that time I was really unhappy.

With her father-in-law's support, she went to England and practiced dentistry there while her husband remained in Kenya.

> After the 1972 coup in Uganda, my father-in-law was intensely worried that his son would be left in a country where there might be turmoil. So they thought it was a good idea if I went to England, and got a registration there so if time demanded we could go and settle down in England. For me, it was a good kind of escape. Later I went to US and got my green card. All this I did in order not to settle in Kenya. But my husband is the youngest and only son and my father-in-law was really pining for him.
>
> All these years I had avoided having a family. I thought, "I won't start a family until I am settled." My father in law supported our idea. But in '79, he said, "Now what? You are not going anywhere. Now I want to see grandchildren."
>
> He died in '85. By then my husband was pretty well settled and he had never wanted to leave this country. It was only me.

Beju Sumaria, Arunaben's daughter, gave up her desire to emigrate to India because her parents were opposed. She married but did not get on well with her in-laws.

> I went for studies in India. In India, the culture was so rich. After coming back, I wanted to go back to India. But my father told me that, since my elder sister got married and my younger sister went to England for further studies, I should stay and do what I wanted to do here in Kenya.
>
> My parents used to give me all that I needed. They were getting upset about me not marrying, so I said, "Just for this little thing, why should I upset them?" I had nobody in mind to get married to. I decided that the man my father will bring, I will look at him and if he is nice then I will get married. It wasn't the right decision.

Beju's father found a man from a prosperous Mombasa family consisting of a father, step-mother, the husband-to-be, and a younger half-brother. Beju was married, left her job, and gave birth to a daughter. She felt very lonely in Mombasa, away from her family, friends, and previous occupations, but did not seek employment. "For my daughter's sake, I have never started a job. She is all alone and I have to be with her."

Beju lived in Mombasa for fifteen years, and worried constantly about her poor relationship with her in-laws. Eventually, she returned to her natal home to care for her mother. After a period of separation, her husband was able to move his factory to Nairobi, and has joined her at her parents' home.

The bonds of joint families, a source of strength and of restriction, are beginning to break down. Many of the sons and daughters of this affluent group are being educated abroad. Some choose to return to Kenya, some return for other reasons, and some do not. Those who return may have employment outside the family business, and a wider social horizon than their parents.

In Anita Patel's family, as in many others, we see the separation of the races decreasing with the next generation. Her children are both studying in the U.K., where they have friends of many nationalities.

> My generation hasn't had much exposure to anything outside the Asian community. But my children were in mixed schools where there were many people from different communities.
>
> When my children return to Kenya, they will not remain isolated in the Asian community because they are used to other communities.

The 1980's coffee boom brought many Asian families a tremendous increase in wealth. Several people said that this changed family and community life in undesirable ways. The economic advantage of joint families becomes less important. Bhagwati Jani explains how that wealth brought many individual opportunities, and fragmentation.

> Family life is breaking down. The children are moving away from the parents and vice versa because every one can buy comforts and things that they think are important like houses, cars, land, and holidays, and can have people to work for them. So it has become a less caring society.

Rasna shares Bhagwati's sense of loss of family and community closeness.

> Life here has changed a lot in the last twenty years. There is less sense of community. Class divisions have grown very wide even within our small Sikh community and within the Asian community in general. I think it has become extremely materialistic and very shallow. They are super-rich. Most of the middle class emigrated to western countries in the 60s and 70s.
>
> Before people were held together by a very strong sense of community and purpose for being here. But now everyone is trying to outdo everyone.
>
> I miss the extended family and a sense that we were all in this together. I could never give my child the sense of community I had as a child: the grand parents, uncles and aunts always popping in, enriching your life.
>
> It has plusses and minuses. I wish people could have that sense of community but not impose those restrictions on the members of the community.

> I don't know if Kenya will remain a multi-racial country. This is Africa, and the way some leaders talk, you never know what will happen to our community. A lot of the younger generation will go to study and never come back.

Mina Daya sees the effects of sudden wealth differently than Rasna and Bhagwati do.

> The Indian community has changed so much, and money has played a big part. Traveling improved, most of the children started going abroad for studies and I think that also brought a lot of western influence. They have renewed confidence in themselves. When you see the outer world you sometimes can make out what is good from bad.
>
> We definitely have progressed, but we have become too much of a showing off community. We are hard working and have very good virtues, but not being able to keep a low profile has harmed us.

Prosperity and Posterity

All parents hope to give their children a good life, and if their life has been difficult, they hope to "give their children a better life" than they had. But the Asians who expressed this hope seemed to use that phrase in a purely material sense. Many felt it was important to provide "the best" in every material sense, and expressed no concern that showering children with objects could lead them to develop materialistic values. Or perhaps citing the desire to provide for one's children seems the most respectable reason for seeking wealth far beyond meeting one's needs.

Beju Sumaria's expressed reason for limiting her family was this desire to give her daughter "the best," and her concern with the condition of the world.

> By my own decision, I have only one child. I decided to stop because of my concern about the world. We felt it needless to get children who we can not give 100% care to.
>
> Our daughter decided that she wanted to study in England. Her father thought she should have everything the best. She was in the best school here, so he said, "We will look for the best school there and if you can get into that school, then you can go."

For the same reasons, Beju is willing to forego becoming a grandmother.

> To me grandchildren is not important. If she has children, then she has to give them the ultimate. The children should then have the best food, the best

clothes, whatever the parents can afford, the best way of living from their income and also have the best friends. You should introduce children to all the best things in life.

Whatever they need, they should be able to get. You see I could take my daughter to music classes, and dancing classes, tennis classes. We should make them people who are happy in the world, not distressed.

African-Asian Relations

Relations between African Kenyans and Asian Kenyans are often tense. Asians are frequently in business, often very successfully. Their perceived wealth, and their separateness, can cause resentment. Africans employed by Asians frequently complain of being underpaid. There is a widespread belief that Asian employers do not comply with minimum wage laws, and that they prefer to give responsible and well-paid positions to other Asians. The tensions are similar to relations between African-Americans and European-Americans in the United States, except that in Kenya, the disadvantaged group is the overwhelming majority. Of course, this hostility toward Asian Kenyans reinforces the tendency to remain separate.

Damu Shah, who was born in 1939, concedes that in the past, Asian households were not good to their help, but she believes that the younger generation are much better employers than their parents were.

Mina Daya thinks the complaints about Asians as undesirable employers are largely unjustified.

> Our Asian mentality is to get the maximum out of a man. That is the mentality of any business community. So that is where they [the employees] are right [in complaining]. But the [African] workers just want to waste time. You have to shout at them. Business unions are always breathing down your neck. You cannot underpay. But we people are result-oriented. If you don't shout, they don't want to work, will come and say, "I have a headache." If you allow one person to do that, you will see another ten people come with the same complaint.
>
> So over the years we have studied the mentality of the workers and developed the system. You cannot fire and hire here like other places. In other countries you have a solid union background. Unions are prepared to understand your argument and correct the workers also. That is not here, so people develop their own system. I don't think they should complain about that.
>
> In any Asian household the working hours for househelp are longer. All of them get paid according to set wages. If the servants stay on the premises, they get three good meals a day. Because of our charitable beliefs, we always take care of the children. I think they have a lot to gain from an Asian household.

We believe that you can do charity for either food or education, and education we always put higher. One or the other of the [househelper's] family will always get education money. Medicine is always looked after. I don't say 100%, no I cannot say that, there is always a small section of people [who don't]. The only thing that really they can point a finger at is long working hours.

Beju Sumaria attributes the economic differences between the Asian and African communities to lack of unity among Africans.

Our children go to school together, but we have different perspectives on life. The culture and the traditions of Africans are very different from Indians.

The Indians in Kenya have a priority to work very hard. When they came here, they were at the same levels as Africans, but due to the unity in their community and their hard work, they are in a better situation. Indians were very much concerned about their families, tried very much to educate their children and worked very hard.

Rasna Warah is married to an African Kenyan who lived in England for several years while she was in Kenya. They were married secretly in England. At first she hesitated to tell her family because they had not accepted a cousin's marriage outside the Sikh community. Her mother accepted the marriage slowly.

Maybe my mother thought that once I married him, I might become destitute because he is an African. She thought her friends would abandon her instantly, but they didn't, so she became more tolerant.

When I was very young, my aunt married an Ismaili Muslim. My grandfather refused to go to the wedding. Another cousin ran off with a Swahili in the early eighties. Not only was he a Muslim, but he was black. That was the talk of the town for a year or so. They didn't say that she had married somebody who might make her unhappy, it was more, "what will my friend say when I go to the temple tomorrow?" The gossip is the real thing they want to prevent. You should never allow people to gossip about you, especially about your daughter. It's OK if your son goes away and has twenty girlfriends, but your daughter, never.

My husband understands the situation. He was the one that said we should not advertise too much while we were dating. He knew that we could not marry here. He also knew that I was worrying about whether I would be accepted back. In England, I was imagining that everybody here hates me. But none of that happened. And now mother has even met him.

But I am still scared of living with him here because I don't want the added stress of walking down the street and wondering if my relatives have seen us; what they are thinking. I suppose I am still trying not to embarrass my mother.

I have seen so many mixed white and African children. They seem to be very normal. They are not tortured by other children. Before it was a problem. Among the Asian-Africans there is a wide range of skin colors. Of course, my child will have black hair and dark eyes, not blond with green or blue eyes, so the mixture will not be noticeable.

Mina's growing frustration at dealing with social problems she could not solve finally drove her to isolate herself. For most of her career, she worked in a Nairobi slum, but moved her practice to Westlands, a wealthy section of Nairobi, where her patients were Asian and European, less commonly African.

I moved my practice here because of the insecurity. The area where I worked for fourteen years started going down so much. I stopped practicing in the afternoons. I would come only in the mornings. The police station was just across the national highway, but no police would come if there was trouble.

Another thing that really depressed me in that area was the parking boys. I used to see child prostitution, the drug trafficking, and those beggars drunk and lying on the roads. When you see this kind of society, you do not want to live among those people or you, yourself, are going to deteriorate. You cannot change them single-handedly.

I was forty-seven. I thought, I will be able to work for another ten or fifteen years maximum. So I wanted to come to a place where I could practice progressive dentistry. I very often go to refresher courses and seminars. But I could not use what I was learning because people could not afford that kind of thing. I thought let me now practice what I have learnt all these years.

If you go to that area now, it is so bad. Three years have gone and so many shops have closed and bars have come up. I have not made a bad decision.

Two Views of Charity

When we used to make chapatis, we would give the first one to the dog. This signified that we should share what we have with the needy people around us.

—Beju Sumaria

Charity is a religious obligation for both Hindus and Muslims, and something Asians are proud of. They consider it an important virtue of their community. There are thousands of Asian charitable endeavors benefiting Africans. Many Asian Kenyan's primary contact with their African compatriots is through works of charity. In Mina Daya's view,

Asian charitable contributions should make them a valued part of Kenyan society.

> Why do the Africans hate us so much? We do so much for them. We even have religious days for doing charity. We go to the slums. The Asian community conducts so many medical camps, collects money to buy medicine. Asian doctors go to the rural areas. But having done so much, there is still a lack of trust.
>
> Speaking for myself, if you have helped someone for twenty-five years, you have done so much for them, they know you are willing to do more in time of need, if understanding and trust is not there, how far can you go?
>
> All races have certain allergies for others. But please don't misunderstand me: it is not the failing of only Asian society. We should have picked up the serious or genuine people from the other community and tried to train them. We could have trained a very small section of a particular [i. e. African Kenyan] society which could have helped a larger part of society. But we fed them instead, always gave them the material things. Many people did not have clothing, so we gave them clothes. But they took the clothes and sold them. We did not make them self-sufficient.

Bhagwati Jani understands why all this charity fails to create mutual respect or to build unity.

> I think there is a great difference between giving that amounts to charity and daily contact with people in need, responding on a daily basis in an informal way. All of us have moved over to impersonal charity. If I give money to some charity that eases my conscience. But then I may not bother as to where my money is going.
>
> It is more of a problem than when I was a child. I remember my father used to work outside Nairobi and sometimes he could not manage to send home money. But there were the neighbors to take care of us. My brother was sick and the neighbors sat with my mother all night. But nothing like that will happen now. If I have money, I give money to the charity. There is no personal involvement.

Unity requires visible good will and fairness on both sides. Paying fair wages, treating all employees with respect, and filling responsible positions without regard to race has more effect on goodwill than charity.

The Future

Mina Daya is pessimistic about Kenya's future because of the failings of individuals.

There is so much of hatred. Tribalism is the main problem. There is so much hatred among the different communities. They have so many common enemies, but still they cannot unite.

When something changes inwardly, you can bring about a constructive change. But here nothing changes, so a person will float wherever the benefit is, wherever the selfish motive is. Religion has not taken a deep feeling here.

You read in the newspapers that today Kenya is the third most corrupt country in the world,[5] but Kenya is the size of one of the suburbs in India.

The Indian community also needs to change a lot. We are facing the problem of not being welcome in other countries. But we cannot help being the successful because we are a hard-working community.[6] We are financially on the better off side. So we have a few extra things and then the showing off comes.

Jayshri Shah fears for her community's future, not because of hostility, but because of growing competition.

Most people have education and jobs are scarce, so there will be more competition. We will be better if we acquire better qualifications from college which can enable us to get good jobs. We are not even one percent of the population. It is very hard to get jobs and therefore, connections[7] will help greatly. This is done everywhere, even in the U.K.

Bhagwati Jani isn't as confident about growing integration as some others.

Barriers of caste, creed and religion are breaking down. On the other hand inter-racial integration has diminished. Whereas the caste boxes were made of wood, the racial boxes are made of iron and are very difficult to break.

An African sees an Asian and he says "Ah! he is a rich person." He is not.

An Asian sees an African and says, "He is stupid." He is not.

The Africans may say, "Because I am a Kikuyu, I am good at business." That is rubbish.

To be able to look at people as human beings with good points and bad points is something that comes through education. Please do not judge people because God has got that function still in his hands.

At Home in Kenya

Like white Kenyans, Asian Kenyans have often been educated abroad, usually in India or the UK. Some disliked the UK and were

---

5. This was 1996.

6. In fact, not all Asians are prosperous.

7. An African Kenyan who read this assured me she was referring to bribery.

relieved to return to Kenya. But their experiences with India were often positive, and some would be happy to live in India. Others have strong loyalty to Kenya. Generalizations about the Kenyan Asian community are riskier than generalizations about the Kenyan European community. The Asian community is larger and is divided, as India is divided, by religion, region, caste, and language.

Some Asians feel insecure in Kenya because of the hostility they perceive. Some fear expulsion, as was done in Uganda. Others feel confident that will not happen in Kenya because they are economically significant, and expelling them could cause economic chaos. Anita Patel does not fear expulsion in the immediate future, but she can imagine it happening eventually.

> If the country is not stable, this will be a problem for Indians. I do not mean that things will start being like in Uganda where people were being expelled. The situation in Uganda was very bad, so Kenyans are taking care that it will not happen in Kenya. But some MPs are talking about Asians, and people are scared. As time goes on, the change of the leaders may cause that.

Many other Asians are much more confident of their future in Kenya. Jane De Souza's husband, Felipe, and Bhagwati Jani have very similar reasons for feeling confident that Asians will never be expelled from Kenya.

> Felipe DeSouza: I think [the expulsion from] Uganda has been a blessing for Kenya. The turmoil was the result of the Asians being sent out, and our leaders can see that.
>
> Bhagwati Jani: I don't worry about expulsion any more. The rich people here in Kenya are all three races and they are interested in keeping it. This is capitalism.

A white person such as I will be told people's thoughts about racial questions through a very selective filter. People will speak to me about hostility toward Asians, but not about hostility toward Europeans. So I am not the right person to judge, but it seems that the position of Asians is quite different from that of Europeans. There seems to be far more hostility toward Asians than toward Europeans, despite the history of colonial oppression. There is a persistent mutual mistrust, which is a real barrier to comfortable coexistence. But there are efforts on all sides to break down these barriers. Zifanikiwe![8]

8. May they succeed!

12

1995-2002: *Dreading the Future*

> The future will be worse. I can't think of anything to do about it. We are really trying today, and if things are this bad today, how will they be in ten years?
>
> —Jerusha Wawuda, Wundanyi farmer, 1996

From 1995 through 2002, nearly every woman we talked to expressed great fears that the future would be bleak. Poverty had become much worse in recent years, so people expected it to continue to worsen dramatically. The greatest fears were that school fees would continue to rise steeply, so that fewer and fewer children would attend school, and that unemployment for young people would increase, with a consequent rise in crime. The major non-economic fear was the spread of AIDS.

As a person from a distant culture, clearly more financially secure than most women I talked with, I felt unable to respond with any words of hope or mitigation. What can one say to a woman who struggles to feed her family, when she has good reasons to fear that her children will suffer even greater hardship? To deny it is insulting and false. For me to point to some bright improbability would offer no reassurance, only show how distant I was from their reality. There was nothing to say. I could only sit in solemn and humble silence.

The members of Kitivo Women's Group expressed fears that seemed to be nearly universal.

> Elizabeth Anton: It is getting continually worse now, so it is going to be even worse.

Constance Nyambura: When we were growing up things were better, things were cheaper. There was digging, there was harvesting. But now because we have continued digging in the same place the time has changed. Poor harvest, poor rains, poor economically. It is shrinking to infinity.

HH: In twenty years how will people eat?

Constance Nyambura: We are thinking of business. But without food what are you going to eat, and how are you going to get money to start a business? No matter how we look at it, we don't seem to make ends meet. When I think of the fate of my children it is even more sad. As difficult as it is now, during their time it will be worse. We are praying for our children.

Diane Kimunda: Though some of our children are educated and some of them are working, I don't think that they can support us since they have their own needs. We cannot build our hope for our future on our children.

HH: Since your children are working, are they going to be able to take care of themselves?

Diane Kimunda: I don't think it is possible.

HH: Do the rest of you agree with her?

(Emphatic and universal sounds of assent.)

Women who belonged to a thriving women's group were generally much more optimistic about the future than others because the possible future accomplishments of the group gave them reason for optimism. Members of Elangata Wuas had high hopes.

Kakeni Mosoni: Maybe in ten years we will have completed everything. Maybe the shop will be going on and other and activities will come along.

Soytonado: Also in ten years time we may be able to have a chemist shop that will generate money to help any group member who is having a big problem. Now the group gives money to use for small, small things. In ten years the group may provide for major needs.

Many people believed that changed public policies could go a long way toward improving decaying public facilities and providing access to land and employment They believed that the appalling level of public corruption was the major reason for these problems. In 1996, Jean Ndike, the daughter of a member of Kenya's first government, reflected on the then-current government.

People are not as they used to be. My father was a senior minister and he did not own a car. He worked for the country. His whole heart was with the country up to the time he died. And he would never, how do I put it, try to benefit.

In those days no government minister was supposed to drive a government car. The government used to buy tractors for ministries with lot of work, the agricultural ministry used to buy Land Rovers. Now, they buy the most expensive cars. Everybody is doing this.

These problems are recent. OK, maybe there were some few before, maybe ten, fifteen, twenty people in the whole government who would take advantage. Not like now.

This is public money! It breaks the peoples' hearts when you see the way the money is used. Yet the taxes in Kenya are so high. Those days the aid we got from other countries was properly utilized. I wish the people we have today were like the first ones.

Many others supported Jean's assertion that "everbody" in public life was corrupt, from the highest level of the government to people with a much smaller responsibility. Maggie Mwasi cited an example of local corruption seriously harming the children of her village.

When I was little, we paid school fees but everything was included. Now in order for your son or daughter to go to school you pay the school fees but then there are books, etc. You even have to provide where your children will sit in school. We must pay for a desk. The school keeps that desk, but new families are still charged for a desk. In the future, all of this will be worse than it is now.

Many women believed the low standards of honesty and dedication by public employees could be reversed. Oruko Omina had a dire warning for corrupt leaders.

The percentage of people in this country who are benefiting from corruption is very, very small. It might be one percent. The majority are suffering. The money is in the hands of very few people who have not worked for that money. They own Pajeros and big farms. You find someone with a big farm lying fallow, and other people going hungry. Corruption is responsible for the big difference between the wealthy and the poor, and it doesn't look as if it was getting any better.

There are a lot of Africans going to school. They learn and then they don't get jobs. You find three quarters of even advanced graduates on the streets. And when they get to that level, what do you expect? You are in for trouble.

If things go on the way they are going, there will be no country at all. The poor are now getting poorer. That small percent, one hundredth of one percent continues to get richer, and this disparity will just blow up one day.

Jean Hartley was discouraged about Kenya righting itself any time soon.

Nairobi itself is falling apart. Holes in the roads get bigger, garbage gets higher.

Things are falling apart, corruption is dreadful. I don't want to get into politics but I think it is difficult to foretell what is going to happen to the country without getting into politics. I think with the government of the moment, things will not get better. They will slide further downhill.

There is a chance. There is a whole new generation of middle class Kenyans. They cannot be bothered with politics. They want change but they can't see any positive ends politics serves, so they won't vote. Unless we can get those young Kenyans in their thirties and forties interested I can't see how things are going to get changed.

The basic structure is sound. I don't think the international community would let it completely fall apart. I cannot see a situation where the rest of the world paces the border to Kenya and says, "Let them get on with it" like they did in Burundi.[1] There is too much international business here. Other governments have far too much interest in Kenya.

Eileen Waruguru saw no hope for the future without thorough political change.

Life will be very hard unless there is a change of government. The way we are suffering today, it is completely bad. That is why the opposition parties were formed.[2] People could see that things were not running smoothly and they wanted to fight the government.

If all goes well, and there are some changes, maybe we have some hope. I want to think that whatever the opposition does, at least they want to improve things because they know things are not as good as they used to be.

At the time she said this in 1996, she had her own beauty salon from which she was supporting herself and assisting her three children. She has since had to close the salon because fewer and fewer people could afford her services.

Society

Many people commented on the ways that spiraling impoverishment would affect human relations. They have a variety of perspectives. A woman who appeared to be about forty years old made an especially dark prediction in the Mumias church conversation.

1. She was refering to massacres following the assassination of the President in October of 1993. Amnesty International estimates that over 50,000 people were killed in genocidal violence between October 1993 and December 1995. When I first spoke with Jean in August 1996, there had been a recent coup in Burundi. In Rwanda, the UN belatedly sent a peacekeeping force with too little power to stop the slaughter, but in Burundi, not even that was done.

2. Opposition parties were legalized in 1991 as the result of intense pressure. A strong domestic effort to repeal the one party rule was supported by donor nations, and aid was suspended.

All these evil things used not to be there, but now, there are very many problems. Our children are not able to get what they need, so we do not know what is going to happen. Maybe it will just be a matter of murder, take something, and go.

Grace Nyawira [Portrait H] seemed to be bursting with thoughts about the future, as she bursts with ideas about everything. Growing poverty, the mistreatment of women, and poor governance all played a role in her thinking.

Life will be very tough in the future. If now we cannot take care of our children, what about our grandchildren? Without land, education, and so on...

It seems that some years to come, marrying and getting married will come to an end because most people would prefer to live single, as married life is just hell to many.

If there were a woman president it could be very good as women are wiser than men and we could be in a better situation than today.

Sofia Muthoni blamed the emerging belief that women should be equal to their husbands for deterioration in marriage, yet she favored education for girls and equal employment. She expected this would reduce poverty because women usually use their money for their families more than men do. "I think that life will be much harder than now. There is no way life will get better in future unless girls are educated and can hold the same posts as men to make life better for their families."

Doris Mathieu, who works through her church to create social welfare programs, was concerned about poverty and the erosion of social life.

If some people have things others don't have, there will be jealousy. Marriages and burials bring people together, but since they are no longer celebrated, women's groups and church groups need to help.

The population will go down. You won't find anyone of my age who has more than two children. She can't even manage to educate two.

Members of the Ilbissil women's group feared for their children for social reasons even more than for economic ones.

We are praying God that we live to help that next generation because it will be a generation that is mixed up, confused. They are a generation without a culture so they are doomed in life. There will not be anything like marriage, it will just be like you have a girl and you sleep with her, forget about her, life continues. Poverty will increase: Thuggery, theft, and so many terrible things that we foresee happening in the next generation, simply because people won't have a culture to guide them.

Sophie Mwangemi shared the concern expressed by members of the Ilbissil women's group. She would like parents to develop explicitly shared standards to give the next generation more consistent guidance. "I think it is going to be worse. But in my own opinion things could be improved if people could carry out a house-to-house campaign and agree as parents on how to educate and bring up their children."
Elizabeth Ndunde feared excessive urbanization.

In fifteen years, there will be even more people crowding around towns. The current school system doesn't equip people to live in rural areas. We're still being told that to work means to live in town. This migration will continue unless factories are put up in rural areas to absorb them. It used to be that men came to town to work and left the wife and children at home, but this is becoming more and more difficult because women also want to come to town and do something economically useful.

The form four girls we talked to at Shamoni Secondary School had known each other for years, yet there were still deep philosophical differences to discuss. The result was a lively and passionate group discussion.

Bilha Chiluyi: I think they should invite each community to share together, such as games, and people sharing their culture. But even if they do that, we understand very well that where people have little money they will be poor. We think our government, our Kenya today it has no maximum resources to give to everyone. With what the government has, it will just build some schools, and only those who are able will attend school, and those who are unable will just stay at home.

Carolyne Ashiko: Let me tell you something. If everyone were rich at the same level, there's no one who would hear one's advice. So we need to have those who are rich and those who are poor because the poor ones, they can at least listen to the rich.

Bettye Khayati: If there are rich and poor then we have discrimination, and when there is discrimination, there is fear.

Carolyne Molenje: If one is rich, he will only think about himself. He will not have an eye to look for the little people.

Knight Opaka: During our colonization, we see that our African people, due to the power that some had, they would overtake others. Do we think that the poor one will appreciate what the rich one is doing?

Carolyne Ashiko: He will not appreciate, but you see, in fact he will now be working to produce those foodstuffs. But if everyone will be rich, no one will listen to the President. There would be more corruption[3] in the country.

Bettye: But those poor ones who work as laborers, or whatever, if they are unable to feed themselves, then there is no peace.

Carolyne Ashiko: If you are poor, you find someone to work for and he will feed you. Then there will be peace.

Bilha: There will be no peace. For example, if you are a rich man, though you will be giving me a salary, I will be looking at you with a bad eye.

Carolyne Ashiko: But so long as you are surviving...

Knight Opaka: I will be surviving, but there will be no peace.

Personal Expectations

Many women drew a distinction between their expectations for the country and their own personal expectations. Susan Malaso, who comes from a financially secure family, was quite optimistic about her own children's future, although she shared the general pessimism about the future of the country.

Life has really changed, especially on the side of education. Education has become very expensive, not like our time. Now there is daily inflation. Jobs are scarce. Children are just loitering about, looking for jobs they don't get. In future, I don't know where our children will be.

The population will increase. Poverty. When many children will be born it means that parents will not have money to feed those children.

HH: How do you expect your daughters' lives to be different than yours has been?

Maybe they will like to build big mansions. Bigger than the one we have at present. Maybe they will like to have big cars, and walk in big towns, instead of coming back home and walking there. So those are the things that will make their life different from ours.

HH: Do you expect that all of your children will spend their adult lives in town rather than here?

Not all of them because children are different. Some like looking after their father's animals. In fact I have one who says he will not be employed. He will just stay at home at look after the animals. We are very happy about it because now my husband is far from home but our son is at home taking care of the animals.

3. I assume she meant corruption in the general sense of decay, especially decay of order and civility, rather than specifically misuse of office for material gain.

A reasonable husband becoming abusive is a familiar story. Ruth Atieno, an educated Kabras farmer born in 1975, feared that her "not so harsh" husband could turn into a tyrant. She thinks his treatment of her will be the most important factor in her future happiness, since as a wife without means of her own, she is not free to leave.

> I can't judge the future because it will depend on the husband. He might change. I hope he won't become harsh in the future, that he will be a good man.
>
> For Kenya, I'm not thinking anything good of the future. I don't see peace, since the government is corrupt.

Members of Ayuta Women's Group provided an inspiring exception to widespread despair. Their enthusiasm for their new educational attainments generated optimism about an easier future for themselves and their children. Their confidence in themselves was infectious.

> Khadija: Life will be very comfortable for us in ten years to come. We are in school, so next time you come back to Kenya, we will speak to you in English.
>
> Halima: We think in twenty years to come, the living standard of our children will be very comfortable. The standard of education will be very high. We will all be educated, our children will all be educated, and we will have plenty put aside.
>
> Siyada: In twenty years time my children will all be educated and I hope they will have a good living standard. and a bright future.

But Siyada later expressed some ambivalence. Although her children's education gave her reason to hope they would do well, when she considered the economy, her optimism was tempered. "Life was very cheap before and nowadays it is expensive. Who knows what will happen to my children? The way I'm thinking if there is a drought, there is a drought everywhere. Because of that, I think life for my children in future may be very hard."

What Can Be Done?

We often asked, "Is there anything that can be done in the present to make the future better?" Many answered by endorsing family planning. Other answers concerned ways that people could maximize their personal resources, hopes that better adherence to religious precepts would solve social problems, or hopes for better management from government. Joan Kanini answered immediately, "To make the future better, work hard. Especially in the public sector."

Filomena Jeptanui had a conservationist's perspective. She talked about steps families could take, beyond family planning or sexual abstinence, to ensure that limited plots with declining fertility would yield the maximum possible return.

> Life will be very difficult. People will have to plan. They can plant trees. People are doing that, learning the importance of trees.[4] People should build houses in one area so there is land for planting. Also, people are starting to use higher yield cows. It is better to have one cow that will give a lot of milk than ten which give less, and there is no land for grazing.

A group of miraa traders in Wajir was optimistic about the future. Since their community had quelled an epidemic of violence through committed and effective community work, they believed peace would endure. Their pessimism about the economy was outweighed by optimism about peace.

> We don't see any danger ahead that the clashes will be back again. We are hoping and praying hard that peace will continue with no more clashes. At the moment, the communities that were fighting are staying together peacefully and so far there's no problem between them.
>
> "An idle mind is devil's workshop." Our fear is that the more the youth will be idle, the more they will think of how to get something and stealing and banditry will be high. But if the youth are occupied, then there will be no more problems.
>
> We are hoping that life in Kenya in twenty years to come will be full of joy. Our total peace, education will be perfect, and we are hoping that life will be comfortable. Our prayer is for peace. If we get that peace, then everything else will be okay.

Saadia Abubakar spoke for many who believed education could be the key to future success.

> My life is changing from worse to better. Life in future will be good for me, and for other people who're able to adjust to modern life by educating their children and planning their families. Children should be educated so they will be able to get jobs. I would like my son to get enough education so that he will be better off and will help me.

---

4 The Green Belt Movement and other projects are encouraging tree planting, providing seedlings and education about the value of trees. But each time I return to Kenya, large new areas have been deforested.

For others, it will be very hard because money is valueless. Ten shillings was enough, but now it can not even buy a single thing like sugar.

Religion

Religion, a source of comfort and support in the present, and hope for an afterlife where the injustices and tragedies of the world are left behind, is also a source of hope for a better earthly future for many people.

Serah Rahab, the Lusigetti farmer who confidently awaited a miracle in her personal life, applied her deeply held Christian beliefs to thinking about Kenya's future as well. This made her optimistic. "Life will be better each year because Christianity will spread."

Bahsan's friends had divergent points of view about the future of their religion.

Hibo: In twenty years, there will be a woman president and life will be better for women.

Sarah: Tribal clashes will be worse because each tribe wants leadership.

Kaha: It will be difficult as far as religion is concerned because there are so many religions coming up and some will leave Islam to join them, and some will be influenced by other religions.

HH: Do the rest of you agree with that?

Bahsan: No, I don't. Now religion is better observed than before. Our knowledge of religion is much better than our parents and grandparents. But many people who know nothing about Islam may come here and influence people.

Dekha: Originally the Quran was translated in Somali, and now it is in English, Swahili, and many other languages, so people know much more about it, so religion will get much stronger. But what is going to decline is Somali culture because that is in the heads of the elders. That will decline, and that I fear.

Rose Wanjohi, a maid in a Nairobi hotel born in 1951, saw all the problems that indicated a grim future, but overcame her own despair by placing confidence in the Holy Spirit, the church, and the actions of individual Christians.

The future will be very difficult. People won't be able to raise as many children. The land is getting smaller and the jobs are very scarce. Salaries are very small. What we earn, it's not even enough to eat. In the past, we didn't have street people because the community cared. But now there are too many. People don't help others.

Rose Wanjohi with the food she sells at lunchtime to other members of the hotel staff

I think there will be a Christian revolution. We are trying to get people to know that God gives and God takes, and whoever has more must help. When the poor hear the word, they don't have to go to the street begging. Once they go to other Christians, once they've received Jesus Christ, God will help. If they just stay in the street and smoke, people won't help, they just run away because they are not like human beings. The Bible says, blessings will follow us. Now, if I didn't have a fear of God and a strong will, I would be worse, I could go drinking.

The church will help. The Holy Spirit will help. We are praying very much for our government. It will help the Ministers; it will help the government. Through the Holy Spirit, Kenya will become the best.

A Possible Reason for Hope

I see the future as being pretty bright. I have a lot of faith in the youngsters of the middle class. A lot of them are bright, have travelled, and know the world. They're idealistic and caring, and will make good leaders.

—Marian Slade, Nairobi businesswoman

Although most respondents felt pessimistic, particularly with regard to public affairs, two aware and articulate women, from very different circumstances saw similar reasons for long-term hope. Dekha Ibrahim was talking about her own region, but some of the things she said applied to other parts of the country as well.

I think Wajir will be a better place in twenty years. Right now we are struggling and in a transitional period. Our children are going to school and the positive political attitude right now will help it develop into a better town.

> I am sure that even at the political level, the kind of leadership in twenty years will be so different. And with better leaders, you can create wonders even in such a desert.
>
> Right now, a lot of people are talking about how to improve the schools, how to improve the hospitals, how to improve political life. We have the opportunity and we have a lot of willing people around.
>
> I'm optimistic because of the interest of the young people in politics. At one point people thought that politics was for the elderly and that the younger people should have nothing to do with it. But the young, who are sort of clean-minded, are thinking of joining politics. The political awareness is very high. It will depend on the situation in Somalia and in the rest of Kenya. I am sure that the kind of leadership that we are going to produce in the next twenty years will be a lot better than what it is today.

Aoko Odembo expressed hope for the country as a whole.

> I think what Kenya is going through is what every country in the world goes through. I don't think Kenya can get more corrupt than we already are. The loot has already been looted. The generation that is coming after me will change the face of this country.

Perhaps. The election of a new government in the last week of 2002 initially inspired tremendous, nearly universal, euphoria. By September and October 2003, when our last interviews were conducted, the enthusiasm was dissipating. Although there was still a great deal of optimism, many Kenyans were disappointed by the failures of the new government. They had settled into something between the deep despair that characterized the last years of the Moi regime and the buoyant hopes of a few months before.

Portrait N

Making Peace in Wajir

National boundaries are irrelevant to camels, and a nuisance to humans who travel with them. The northeast of Kenya is ethnically and culturally Somali. The long civil war in Somalia has thundered throughout the region. Until 1990, the entire region was a government "security operations zone," which permitted unrestrained police and the paramilitary General Services Unit to control movement, exclude outsiders, and censor the press.

Wajir, forty kilometers from the Somali border, is the center of this large camel-herding region. The population of 270,000 remains close to nomadic life. Some spend part of their time in town and part herding. Others were born pastoralists, but now live permanently in town. All have close relatives who are pastoralists.

Wajir's streets are lined with the plain, unwelcoming walls of houses. Hidden inside are courtyards with trees, water, and shaded verandas where most family activities take place. Women hesitate to go out without a male companion and will usually insist that their sons accompany them when they do errands. Women invariably cover their heads, although their faces are visible. Their brightly colored and patterned shawls provide the color in a dusty landscape.

Vegetation is sparse. Camels and goats roamed the streets when I first visited. Five years later, because of drought, they had been replaced by hundreds of relief trucks. From 1992 to 1994, severe drought killed thousands of animals, and nomads flooded in seeking relief. Their food and health needs overwhelmed the town.

In 1993 and 1994, the violence that tore Somalia apart inflamed the entire region. Clashes between different clans killed hundreds of people. Families whose animals had perished desperately needed relief, but killings impeded the distribution of relief supplies. Three traveling health care workers were murdered, so no more were sent out. The only services were in town. But even the town was wracked by violence. Townspeople stayed locked in their houses after six in the evening.

The raiding and killing were done by men, but after the killings began, some women actively incited their men. Adey Addeha, a charcoal seller, described their role.

> Women say poetry, poems, and riddles to demoralize men and make them feel that they are no longer men. Or women say they will go and fight instead, because the men are always defeated. Such things uttered by women make the men fight. When the men leave for war, the women are happy. They sing songs telling the men that they will be brave and win.

A small group of women, some of whom had lost their herds and numerous relatives, were determined to stop the violence. Dekha Ibrahim explained how they managed.

> In 1993, we were at a wedding party. All the clans attended and we felt safe, but when we left, that safety was gone. We decided women could restore peace because they cut across all lines. There is a Somali saying, "a woman has no tribe." She is born of one, married to another, and a child born of her is married to another one.
>
> We asked women from all three major clans and the corner tribes[1] to approach elders of their clans. We organized a meeting for women of all clans at which the elderly women took charge. After much talking, one elderly woman said to a younger woman of another clan, "I was a friend to your mother and father, Asli. How is it today that we are enemies? What has gone wrong?"
>
> Asli stood up and hugged her, and all of us started remembering how we had loved many people from other clans in our lives.
>
> We discussed two women who fought at the market two weeks earlier. It became a clan dispute because the police never came to the scene, and the elders did not intervene in time. Women went to the station to report on the issue, but the police never even listened. If the first lady who fought had been charged with a criminal act, it would have ended there.

1. The "corner tribes" are the other small clans. For purposes of this meeting, everyone who was not in one of the major clans, even Arabs and other non-Somali residents, were included with the corner tribes.

The women agreed to have a Joint Committee from all clans to listen and diffuse tension in the market. In case of any violent act, they will report to the chief, to the elders, and to the police, so that action can be taken immediately.

School holidays were coming, so we went to the secondary schools to dissuade the youth from violence during the holidays. Young people told us, "We have no problem. We don't fight in school. All we want is education and time to study. The problem is the elders. Convince them to stop, then we'll have no problem." When they went home, they refused to raid, and convinced their parents not to do the dirty work.

We realized that our work was dangerous, life-threatening. What if the government will not agree to what we are doing? What if one of us betrays us? If we are locked up, what do we do? We don't know who is actually spreading this violence: it could be the government, it could be any of the community members.

We sent delegations to meet the clan elders. Elders of the corner tribes said, "Thank you. You young people have done good work. We are ashamed because this should have been our role, but it is not too late for us to take our role. Give us backup support; we will meet each clan."

At the first meeting, by telling each other the truth and challenging each other, the elders took it forward. People of the Ogaden clan said, "Why did you call us? It's Ajuran and Degodia fighting, it has got nothing to do with us."

One elder told them, "Maybe the people who are fighting now aren't wearing your hats, but you are hiding them, so don't throw yourselves out of it."

The elders asked us all sorts of hostile questions. "Who sent you? Were you sent by the government? The UN? Who is financing this?"

The turning point was when one elder called Mahat Golja stood up, started a prayer and said "Aren't you ashamed? I am eighty years old. I have seen eight clan wars, but I have never seen two things that are happening now: I have never seen men killing women and children and raiding milking animals. I have never seen children leading adults, children talking for peace and adults just refusing peace. Look at our gray hairs, and still we are asking them questions. Aren't we ashamed?" After that, everybody was for peace.

A standing committee of elders from each clan was formed. Raided animals were returned, and the BBC interviewed one of the elders. Women went to the new district commissioner (DC) hoping for community-government co-operation. Dekha explained the history of problems between the community and the authorities.

Before 1990, nobody would have accepted anyone but the security forces talking about peace. Thirty years of harsh rule did not work, so the government became receptive to community efforts.

The army knew how to act harshly, but they didn't know how to act softly. So, after the end of the "security operations zone" they were doing nothing. When there was a problem at the market, since they were no longer allowed to beat up the women, they stayed out.

The old DC used to refer disputes to the elders in cases which should have gone to the police. The elders had no vehicles, and could not handle the job of the police. The old DC was removed because of public pressure. The new DC listened to people, and consulted the elders. We told him, "We, the children of this area, would like to intervene."

There was one incident where thirty-five people were killed and a vehicle was burned. The DC came personally and took the suspects. This time, there was no revenge because people felt it was being taken care of by the courts. He told the elders, "If there is an incident in your area, and you don't tell me who did it, you will go [to prison]."

The country was going through hard times. It was the beginning of the multiparty system.[2] People didn't know whether multiparty meant no government or no law. The police just decided to stay out of conflicts.

When the military was going out somewhere we said, "Please tell your young men not to grab the women, or kill them, because that is going to undermine the whole peace process." Of late, there have been no incidents of violence by the army. This has brought the community and the government closer to one another.

Systems that were not working earlier started working. Now, if there is an incident, the police go. When the DC goes for fact-finding, he takes the elders and the youth. The morale of the people started rising. For two months, there was not a single incident.

Having established a sort of cease-fire, the committee's next concern was to develop mechanisms for resolving conflicts before they became violent. They wanted to create a body that would be widely trusted. Dekha explained how they succeeded.

If we made it a government institution, the community would not feel comfortable. If we made it completely community based, then the government would not be comfortable with it. So we thought of a forum which would bring the community and the government together. It consists of politicians, religious leaders, businessmen, women, and elders.

The committee is spreading out into the villages to involve a wider group. Our activities are in three phases. One is rapid response. A group of elders and the security committee go to the scene of any incident, whether it is a breaking of a shop, or a raid, or a fight. If it requires a dialogue, there will be dialogue; if it is a criminal act, then the police take action.

2. As a result of internal and international pressure, Kenya readopted a multiparty system before the 1992 elections.

Second is the creation of dialogue between different communities.

Finally, we sought to improve the welfare of the youth who are used during violence, so that they could not be easily manipulated. We got government and community funds to revive two polytechnic schools that had been closed because of structural adjustment.[3]

Making and keeping peace has become a true community project. People in every part of Wajir and every clan are involved. Destitute nomads who had recently fled to town for food and safety felt as much responsibility for peace as did these long-established community workers. In 1996, members of Ayuta Women's Group [Portrait L], explained how they saw their roles as peacemakers.

Habiba: At the moment, we have united all the tribes. The people in the clashes were our husbands, our sons, and our brothers. We were desperate to stop the killing, so we talked to them about destruction. We women are the vulnerable group, because if a husband is killed, the mother is left to take care of the children. If we stop clashes, it is our benefit. We help each other without asking each other's clans.

Saadia: Sometimes, the men don't want to end their clashes, so women have to lead them. But now even the men are fed up and want peace.

Peace has endured in Wajir despite hard times. From October 1997 to March 1998, there were terrible floods in northern Kenya. This is an area of such low rainfall that there are few river channels. So the water stayed in stagnant pools, and Anopheles mosquitoes bred. Hundreds of people died from malaria. At the same time, in other parts of Kenya, gangs of heavily armed thugs were displacing suspected political opponents in preparation for the national elections. I wondered whether such terrible circumstances had undermined Wajir's peace. In 1998, Dekha explained how they avoided clashes during the elctoral campaign.

Before the [1997] elections, we had a luncheon for all the candidates. Campaign speeches often incite violence. We asked candidates to contribute to peace in their campaigning: to use words of reconciliation, not words of fighting. There were cross-clan political alliances, and no incidents. One MP, Mohammed Abdi, realized that the dances traditionally used to rouse supporters could be an incitement, so he vowed not to use them. We had elders at every polling place to watch for incidents, but there were none.

3. International Monetary Fund Structural Adjustment Programs, which require the government to cut spending on social programs to reduce expenses.

> At the Peace Festival in November 1997, we gave awards to people who had contributed to peace. We had a soccer match for the youth, and conflict resolution workshops for the elders. Almost all the elders participated.

In November 1997, nurses all over Kenya went on strike over working conditions. They had no drugs, and could only watch patients die. But in Wajir, because of the floods, there were many donations of drugs. Dekha continued.

> One problem now [1998] is that health care funding has been terribly cut since foreign aid is drying up. One of the nurses went to the other nurses individually and asked them to help. They did not return to the hospital, but worked privately, for no pay, administering drugs and caring for sick people. That really helped the community.
>
> We have had only one recent incident. There was a raid of 500 cattle. But the elders made sure that all the raided animals were returned to their owners.

Why have peace-building efforts succeeded? These women have made every possible effort to conform to community norms so as not to alienate any segment of the community. They defer to elders by asking them to lead meetings. They look for opportunities to shower established leaders with public praise. Conflict often occurs in a time of great hardship. These courageous women have tried to increase everyone's stake in peace, and to build conflict resolution mechanisms that the community could trust. Through community insistence, the irresponsible DC was replaced by someone willing to work with and respect the community. By involving youths, women, and the elders of each clan, they have created a broad-based and enduring peace-keeping effort.

On subsequent visits to Wajir, I found pride throughout the community. The Peace and Development Commission (PDC) has remained very active. The co-ordinator, Nuria Abdullahi, a solid, capable woman, has been working throughout Wajir District to create village councils skilled in conflict resolution. She has especially been targetting herders On my last visit, in 2003, we were only able to talk for a few minutes. She told me that the PDC has become an important resource for communities all over Kenya that need to develop peace-keeping mechanisms. As we parted, she joked, "Peace has become our export product."

Dekha now works in Mombasa, broadening the peace-keeping efforts. Among her projects is finding support for conflict-resolution training programs. To be as up-to-date as possible, I called Dekha just before going to press. There was more exciting news from Wajir. In

December, two clans co-operated to defuse a situation that could have started a war. Two men of different clans, an Ajuran from Wajir and a Garre from Ethiopia, had been trading with each other. The Ethiopian was found murdered, and the Kenyan was suspected. To pre-empt revenge, relatives of the suspect took responsibility. They guarded the body, informed the dead man's relatives, and committed themselves paying the victim's clan proper Islamic restitution: a hundred camels. They found their guilty fellow-clansman and confined him. As a result of their effective initiative, the aggrieved clan felt that they had been treated respectfully and fairly by the murderer's clan, and had no wish to wage war. The killers' relatives are working to raise money for restitution, and have so far paid twenty camels.

Not long afterwards, there was another serious incident with four men killed. The incident of the murdered trader convinced them that it is more honorable to seek a solution than to seek revenge and inspired them to look for a peaceful resolution.

Epilogue

The New Kenya: Rebirth or Repackaging?

> Since this government was elected the people have a lot of confidence, but there has been a silent war to derail their plans. There have been accidents, and some of them are dying. This is not KANU; this is Satan. It shows that this government is doing the right thing to be so much attacked by Satan. Satan is not happy with the government's plans.
>
> —Dorah Zighe, farmer (Wundanyi)

The government that came to power in the last days of 2002 had a profound effect on people's lives within the first year. I went back in late 2003 to ask the women whom I had previously interviewed how they saw the new government and how it had changed their expectations. Many people, especially in rural areas, cited evidence of tremendous progress and were enthusiastic. City people gave the government mixed reviews.

From the time Kenya became independent in 1963 until the last week of 2002, the country was governed by one political party, the Kenya African National Union or KANU, which became increasingly corrupt and increasingly unpopular. At first, Kenya had opposition parties, but in 1982, President Moi created a one-party state. In 1990, multipartyism was restored as a result of both domestic and international pressure.

Kenya's many ethnic groups do not easily trust each other. Most voters have limited contact with and, therefore, limited confidence in other ethnic groups.[1] Political parties generally represent one ethnic

1. Former President Moi belongs to a small sub-group, the Tugen, which is part of a larger group called Kalenjin. I did not interview any Tugen women, but in 1996 one Kalenjin woman said of Moi, "Other people don't like the President, but we like him because he comes from here." In 2003, she was as enthusiastic about NARC as most non-Kalenjin rural women.

group. Voters tend to support political figures of their own ethnic group because those are the ones they trust, those are the ones whose speeches they can understand, and those are the ones who will reward them if in power. It makes sense, but it also makes creating national unity difficult. So, unseating the KANU government required assembling a coalition of different parties representing different ethnic groups, the National Alliance Rainbow Coalition or NARC. Creating the coalition required making promises to many people. Not all of those promises have been kept, which is one source of dissension within NARC.

NARC united behind a single presidential candidate, Mwai Kibaki. Kibaki, a Kikuyu born in 1931, was a founding member of KANU. He was Moi's first vice president. Over a long political career, he held many different ministerial posts. When multiparty democracy was restored in 1991, he founded the Democratic Party, and was the leading opposition candidate in the 1992 presidential election.

Kibaki's government was greeted with widespread euphoria when it came to power in the last week of 2002. In late 2003, some people remained euphoric, but many others were disillusioned.

Conventional wisdom tells us that when hopes for a new government are very high, they are based on an overestimate of what can be done in a very short time, so disappointment is inevitable. Speaking as one outsider, I think conventional wisdom is wrong in this case. I talked with large numbers of unschooled women who lived far from the centers of power and communication. Yet all of them seemed to understand perfectly that real change takes time, setbacks are inevitable, and progress must be slow.

Where there was disillusion, it was not the result of unreasonable expectations, but of seeing promises broken and reasonable expectations partially betrayed. In fact, the greatest disillusionment was among people who read newspapers, had access to television, and could talk with people in diverse occupations and income brackets.

How do Kenyans assess the new government in which they placed such hope? My last comprehensive interviews were done in September and October 2003. Despite occasional references to later developments, what follows is only a collection of views at one short period.

What's Working?

HH: How has the new government changed life in your community?

[A long, pleased sound ending in ululations.] We are very happy about it. The local leaders, through the influence of the new government, have now started working well.

It was very hard for us to sit and meet with councilors and MPs. But these days, we meet quite often, deliberate on our problems, come up with possible solutions. We are seeing them implement what they promised during campaign time.

We are no longer intimidated. We feel like dancing, and jumping high! It's our prayer that the same government continues to function so that we may see stability in the country

—Loice Mattoi, farmer, Werugha

The introduction of free primary education was greeted with nearly universal jubilation. As we have seen, the beginning was rough, but everyone hoped schools would operate more smoothly before long. One other area received nearly universal praise: health care. Medical care was better and less expensive. Charity Ngilu, the Minister for Health, is highly dedicated and competent. Gracilda Mwakio, the Werugha farmer who saved herself from beatings by reminding her husband that her mother died from being beaten, gave an example of her experience.

Now, when we go for checkup, or a test for malaria or HIV/AIDS, it is free. The beds and blankets are clean now, and the buildings have been repainted.

I was coughing. When I went to the hospital, the doctors carried out a lot of examinations, including blood tests, which was not like before. I also took one of my children who had a dog bite there. Before, they'd say they didn't have any kind of injections, but this time, they gave him injections, and he is okay.

People don't queue for a long time. With the previous government, you'd go there, queue the whole day, with no one to attend you. Now you can be there for five minutes, and someone will come and ask how they can help.

I had to pay 100 Ksh for the blood test, but the rest was free, for my son, too.

Dekha Ibrahim commended NARC for improving services to nomads. "Setting up educational and health care facilities for nomads has been a long-time challenge. The new government has helped by providing mobile health care facilities and teachers through standard three. After that, children can go to boarding schools."

Performance of Civil Servants

Signs were posted in government offices telling people they had a right to be served and should not be asked for money. This had an effect. Filomena Too's good experience with the District Education Office [Chapter 6] has been repeated throughout the country in offices of many different ministries.

Hibo Hussein was greatly involved in Wajir affairs, and therefore heard many people's experiences with government.

> There is no corruption. In any office, you are served like a Kenyan. Before you had to take something in your pockets. I know so many friends who have been served this year and when they tried to give something, the office said, "No." Even the police are different. They used to beat people, to harass people, but now they are very friendly. It's the same people, but a different attitude.

Teresia Wachuka was the widow of an adopted son. Immediately after he died, his relatives chased her and her three children from the land where they had lived. She became embroiled in a court battle. Her experience in court was a contrast to how the courts operated when Catherine Obungu and Esther Wangui tried to get divorces.

> Earlier this year, I was called to attend a court hearing. I saw the people at the court really doing a good job. For example, we arrived late at the court to find that we had already been called, but the officials still went ahead to look for our files. In the previous government, they could not have bothered, especially if we arrived late.

Not everyone was served this well, but throughout the government, even in the most reluctant offices, citizens were served better than before. Rasna Warah had to use a little persuasion.

> I went to report a stolen car and was told by the policeman, "I'm too busy."
>
> I said, "I thought things were supposed to have changed?"
>
> He rightly took that as a threat and said, "Well, maybe I do have a spare minute." Now, if you threaten a police officer, you will be served.

Local Government

Kenya has a highly centralized governmental structure, although devolving power to lower levels is under discussion as a new constitution is being drafted. Local councils are elected, but chiefs as well as district and provincial officers are appointed by the national government, and are accountable to them.

A number of people said the administration of local affairs had greatly improved. In many places, the same people were still in place, but often they were performing better. In Nairobi and Kisumu, rubbish was being collected. Peter Andajo is a supermarket manager in Kisumu.[2]

> It's the same people, but the city council is a bit better. The water supply is more regular and better quality, but the bills are higher. Garbage is collected in the city center, so the city is cleaner.
>
> I deal with all government permits for the store, so I go into many offices. Some ask for kitu kidogo [a bribe], others don't.

In the past, Nairobi's electricity and water rates were greatly inflated by corruption. Under the NARC government, the rates came down. Rose Wanjohi, the hotel maid who kept despair at bay through Christianity, was much more confident about the future. She talked enthusiastically about changes she had seen under the NARC government. Electric rates were one concrete improvement in her life.

> Before, in one month, my electricity bill used to be 350 Ksh. But now, I am paying 150 Ksh. The water bill used to be 1000 Ksh for three months, now it is 300 Ksh or 350 Ksh. People who used to eat our money were thrown out. That is why people are talking very clean of the government.
>
> We used to have piles of refuse by the roadside. In Umoja, we used to pay people privately to collect our refuse, and clean our drain. Now the city council is doing it twice a week, but they do not have enough vehicles because the former government didn't repair them.
>
> HH: Before, did you ever complain to the city council?
>
> Who would listen? Now people listen. Although they do not have the resources, they are doing what they can. The councilors are new. In the offices we still have the old staff, but now they serve you without asking for something.

One aspect of improved local governance is that hawking regulations are being enforced. In Nairobi, license requirements for hawkers can no longer be evaded, but in smaller cities, hawkers don't need licenses, and are now given a spot at the market without paying a bribe. Stricter implementation in Nairobi has hurt Grace Nyawira [Portrait H].

---

2. Although I returned to talk with the same women, often a son or husband was present during the interview, and the men were sometimes more vocal than the women. So, in this chapter, I quote men as well as women. Peter Andajo is Roselyne Okumu's husband.

The new government has really affected me, because I depend on selling in the town center where I have sold for years and have customers who know me, but now I cannot sell there.

HH: There used to be a system of buying daily tickets. Is that system gone?

That is impossible now. Now you can't hawk there without a license.

Kibaki's Minister for Local Government, Karisa Maitha, was said to be active and effective. Many Nairobi residents commented on a decrease in street crime immediately after the change of government. Petty crime was reduced in many parts of the country. The NARC government instituted a training program for unemployed youth, the street children of big cities and "loiterers" of rural villages. The youths receive intensive basic skills training, and are given preference in a variety of suitable government employment.

In Wundanyi, where the road to Mbale crosses the river, there is a small market. Even though it is right beside their digging spot, members of Kilili Women's Group used to fear walking there, even in the middle of the day. When I saw the ladies of Kilili in 2003, we sat in the heart of the market area, with no young people around. Paulina Nyambo told me that they felt safer, and the others emphatically agreed.

Before NARC, we always saw groups of youths hanging around here. There were so many youths loitering, but now they're finding employment, and the army is coming for recruitment. It has already reduced crime here because there aren't so many idlers. They have been taken to the local Youth Polytechnic and are learning skills. The government engaged the village elders to identify idle youths to send to those institutions. So many learning institutions that had collapsed have been revived. There is more peace and security.

Rose Wanjohi and her son Patrick were very happy about the benefits the National Youth Service had already brought to Nairobi, and the role it could play in the future.

Rose: The government has done a lot to take back the streets. The Nairobi streets are very clear now. You can walk without fearing the street children. Some have been taken by the churches, others are being trained in the National Youth Service, and the little ones have been absorbed into the schools.

Patrick: The National Youth Service collects the boys, puts them into a camp to teach them discipline and introduce them to a trade. They could be mechanics, carpenters, etc. When they come out, they can be absorbed into the economy. The ones who want to pursue a career in the armed forces are given a priority. Because of their training, private security firms[3] will want them.

> They have discipline and are enlightened on security issues. We can employ them as security guards, drivers and mechanics.

Maggie Mwasi of Mwatate is a community powerhouse. Politicians seek the support of her large and influential women's group at election time. Her political opinions were based on considerable contact with the current councilor and his predecessors. She was thrilled with the new councilors elected in her community, and with the national government, but not happy at all with the appointed chief in her area, a KANU holdover. Maggie wanted to organize a harambee, a local event to raise money to take her son to Mombasa for medical care that could not be given locally. This sort of fundraising, for either private or public purposes, is a long-time Kenyan tradition, though it has come under fire because it was much abused by political figures during the previous regime.

> You are not supposed to collect money from people without getting a permit from the DC [district commissioner, the highest district official] with documents explaining why you need to collect money. The DC refuses me because the protocol is that I have to go through the chief. The chief has been here for a long time, knows the ins and outs, but he doesn't help.
>
> The chief has been the same for many years. He is a difficult and selfish person, never willing to help. It isn't easy to get rid of him. The councilor we can remove by vote, but not the chief. I'd prefer it if we elected chiefs, so if he starts letting us down, we could go talk to him.
>
> The recent past councilor, whom we voted in twice, we have now voted out. He visited the women's groups to know all our problems, walked around with us saying he'd help with water and other needs, but he never came back. In the last elections, he started going around again saying, "I need your votes." All the women's groups met at the chief's place, and said we weren't going to vote in councilor so-and-so, because he never fulfilled any of his promises. The new councilor is not able to assist much with funds, but we're happy. He gives guidance and direction, or refers us to people who can help.
>
> I'm very satisfied with the NARC government. But the chief has been the same since KANU, so it's been hard to realize the total change that NARC promised. It's my wish that the government get rid of all these people who worked under Moi and start afresh.

Some holdovers are performing more conscientiously than before. Others are not. Benjamin Rotich of Kimaren complained that their chief, a holdover, still follows corrupt practices that were nearly universal before, "If you have a case to discuss with the chief or sub-chief,

---

3. Patrick Wanjohi is in charge of operations for a private security firm.

you must take 1000 Ksh." In other respects, he has seen important improvements.

> Under the former government, they would come and take your property like chickens, dogs, cats, cows that they could sell to get money, just any property in the compound, even if it was not yours. We would feed them sometimes 500 Ksh. Then they would go for about three to four months without asking. But now it is finished. There's no such act in the new government.

In the past, even when local officials wanted to help, they were often frustrated in their attempts to get higher levels to address citizen's concerns. Gracilda Mwakio of Werugha suffered for years from her chief's inability to get money to which she was entitled. The problem was solved when NARC took over.

> From the councilor to the local MP, people have been meeting and consulting on how to build projects for the community.
>
> When my husband passed away, we had shares with Kenya Brewery. I tried for many years to get the money, and I didn't know where to go. Whenever the chief wrote letters for me, the offices always found excuses not to help, like criticizing the chief's English, saying, "Oh, it isn't clear, go back." I gave up, in spite of having all the necessary documents.
>
> But this year, when I approached the chief, he wrote a letter on my behalf, and forwarded it to the right authorities in Nairobi. Now I have been brought forms and the next thing to do is wait for the money. I was even told the amount, 147,000 Ksh, which I never knew.
>
> Even with my husband's NSSF [Social Security] dues, they would not pay before. This time when the chief wrote, I went, and got paid.
>
> Recently, I got a letter which said that there was some interest from the NSSF fund, and I was paid here, without going to Mombasa or Nairobi. I wouldn't even have known about interest.
>
> When they gave me a check, I told them there was nowhere for me to cash it, so they assisted me in getting cash without keeping part of it for themselves.

Citizens Talking to the Government

Many people, not all, felt better able to communicate their concerns to local officials than under the KANU government. In Nyansiongo, Robina Mukhera saw this as one of the important improvements. "Last government, if you wanted something, you would always be told, 'Wait a bit.' But now they want to listen."

Local officials in other places were not always as receptive. Zildah Kirwoi was dissatisfied with the inability of ordinary citizens to talk at a public *baraza* [meeting] in Wundanyi.

> In Kenyatta's time, anyone could ask a question at a *baraza.* In Moi's time, when the chief called a baraza he said what he wanted to say, then called only on certain people who would say what he wants. That is the same in this government. If a person like me goes to our chief we will be mistreated. If we go privately to talk about some problem, we will be criticized at a public meeting. We will not be welcome. We might queue for the whole day and never see him, or he might even drive off with his security force while we are waiting.

In the past, citizens often feared to voice criticism of the government openly. That changed, and Zildah rejoiced.

> In Moi's time, I would not even talk sitting here in a private home about any complaints, but now we can even talk about these things while we are walking on the public road. A chief could hear that, and we would not be maltreated.

Gladys Oluchumba of Mumias gave one reason why it had become easier for women like herself to talk publicly about her concerns. Gladys was referring to a different sort of baraza, one called specifically to discuss a problem within her family, not an open public meeting. But for her, talking even in that slightly less public forum was an emboldening new experience.

> The new government is always talking about the importance of empowering women, encouraging us to start self-help groups. Now, we feel very free to talk in public, to say what is on our minds. Anyone can talk at a baraza. One reason that women feel more free to speak is that now they are electing women elders.
>
> Before my husband died, he was quarreling so much. He removed the door of my house and tried to make me go away. I complained to the sub-chief, who went to talk with him. He quarreled with the sub-chief and was arrested. Then he quarreled with the police, but after the police and the sub-chief talked to him, he came home and replaced the door. The sub-chief called his relatives for a baraza. They came and I told them everything. They counseled him and he started behaving better.

AN ACTIVE CITIZENRY

In addition to fine promises, some fulfilled, there was a new sense that citizens control their own destiny, and that of the country. NARC emphasized citizen involvement, and the message was heard. Rasna Warah explained the change.

> Kenyans were dying from the corruption of KANU. NARC gave the country optimism. Suddenly, people are very proud to be Kenyan.
>
> People's attitude toward government has been permanently changed. Since they were able to get rid of KANU, they can also get rid of NARC. They aren't scared to vote out an unpopular government. It's a big mental shift.

With possibility comes responsibility. Patrick Wanjohi accepted the obligations of citizenship.

> I would have no explanation in future for my children if they have to go through the struggles I am going through. We now have democratic space to air our grievances and would not fear or hesitate to name the thieves among us, be they our tribesmen or even brothers. Kenya is no longer a one-man show.

Oruko Omina was greatly influenced by Kibaki's early call for citizen participation. A close friend of hers found evidence of corruption in the AIDS Control Council. As public health workers, they were outraged that this important work was being undermined. Omina and her friend worked for months to generate public concern, which ultimately resulted in the head of the council being removed.

> I would like to believe that there is always a way, and the way will come from the people. The people must create their own forum for pressure: lobby groups, activists. We have the power, we even managed to remove the previous regime.
>
> A colleague in the National AIDS Control Council realized the director was corrupt. We still had the euphoria that the new government has zero tolerance for corruption, so we thought we should expose her. We got all the evidence and started distributing it to everybody, every member of Parliament, all opposition leaders.
>
> We had the NARC Minister for Health on our side. She put pressure on her colleagues. She even went up to the President and said we cannot have a corrupt person in that office. I got my friend in the media to write stories about this. They wrote everyday, and people were saying, "Come on Kibaki, take care of this."
>
> It took us eight months. And it takes everything out of you, but if it gets done, you get satisfaction.
>
> I have lost people very dear to me to AIDS, and I thought that if this thing could be properly run, these people would have lived their full lives. So it touched me personally.

> And too, the call of duty to my nation. NARC had told us, they want us to work together. Kibaki had said he could not do it alone, he wanted us all to work as a team. You do not have to be in any big position, whenever you are, do something that will help.

Citizens came to believe they could create change, so there was an active, engaged, responsible citizenry. Dekha Ibrahim put personal responsibility for creating a better nation at the heart of her work. "People of my generation are moving away from seeing ourselves as victims. We have control over destiny. In the new Kenya, we are going beyond blame; creating instead of blaming."

In contrast, Mary Msinga of Mombasa thought that blaming people publicly was an important new source of accountability.

> The KANU government banned all the local media, which only left KBC [Kenya Broadcasting Company, the government radio and TV station]. But today, they have revived others, like Citizen Radio.
>
> If our chief does damage you can tell about it. You can tell them anything about that chief, and they will shout, over the radio, using the real name, "You, chief, you upset this place, why are you doing this? Chief, you promised this, you promised this, and you aren't following through." Every day you can hear them. And they won't have citizens being intimidated.

Appointments

> I greatly respect Kibaki's appointments. All merit their posts. I don't think it matters at all that he doesn't have a perfect balance among the different tribes. Morale among civil servants is very good now. People are coming to the office at eight and working all day. Those KANU civil servants who were appointed without qualifications are running scared.
>
> —Ajema Kikuyu, NGO Director, Kakamega

Kibaki's appointments got mixed reviews. The complaints were that some ethnic groups were underrepresented, that ministers were too old, that corrupt people who were thrown out were hastily replaced with equally corrupt people, and that many corrupt officials of the former government were still in place.

NARC managed to be elected only by uniting a number of different parties representing different parts of the country and different ethnic groups. Inevitably, under those circumstances, the government was criticized for its appointments — most groups believing that they had been given less than their rightful share of appointments. On the issue of ethnic diversity, there was clearly no way the government could please most people.

Many senior ministers were over seventy. This distressed some people. Others agreed with Dorah Zighe, "We face big problems, and young people may not have the experience and exposure to know how to deal with them. As everything becomes stable, young men can take over."

Because KANU had held power since independence, all experience was in their hands. Inevitably, many functionaries at all levels were kept in the same posts. Some seemed to be as crooked as ever. Others who formerly accepted bribes or refused to provide services were behaving responsibly. Some of the competent people who had sunk to the prevailing level in the previous government were performing better. The new atmosphere not only threatened them if they failed to perform, but also supported and encouraged them if they wish to accomplish something constructive. According to Patrick Wanjohi, many were doing more than just trying to hold onto their jobs.

> The Kibaki Government has created an open atmosphere for people to be accountable to the public. Before, if I saw something going wrong and talked about it, chances were that I would be arrested and put in [prison] or killed. But now, if I see something going wrong, I know where to report it, and action will be taken. That is giving Kenyans hope.
>
> We cannot say that corruption is wiped out completely but a lot of the bad people are being forced into the stream of the good people. Saitoti is an example of that. I think he regrets what he did in the previous government[4] and is trying to make up for it.

Oruko Omina insisted that it was not only holdovers who brought corruption to the current government.

> Some crooks were replaced right away, but with what kind of people? If you are going to replace one corrupt person with another, you have not solved anything. They did not take time to think through who won't do what the previous person did. You hear people say, "They have replaced the old one with this one? He is so corrupt!"
>
> People are angry that they always appoint the same people. Kenya has so many other good people who are not used.

4. George Saitoti is now the Minister for Education, after holding many posts in the previous government. He was deeply implicated in the Goldenberg scandal, the most spectacular incident of corruption in Kenya's history.

On the other hand, there was widespread agreement that President Kibaki appointed capable people, which was a significant accomplishment in a coalition that had to include many factions.

Tackling Corruption

People from other cultures may have difficulty imagining the pervasiveness of corruption of the Moi regime. Corruption was routine, on both a grand scale and a petty scale. Margaret Obonyo has already told us of being asked to buy petrol if she wanted police assistance.

Like nearly everyone in Kenya, I encountered it frequently when I was living in Western Province, even though I seldom left my village. Once, I went to the public map office in Nairobi to buy maps of various parts of the country. I was asked for a bribe for performing this routine service.

The anti-corruption drive has taken many forms. In the first heady days of the Kibaki government, outraged citizens interfered when *matatu* drivers gave policemen bribes to overlook safety violations. In one case, passengers took the policeman's accumulated bribe money and gave it to charity. That only lasted a few months. Soon, though drivers handed their bribes over a little more discretely, it was still the expected response to being stopped, and the protests ceased.

Oruko Omina and her friend found the system for reporting corrupt behavior overwhelmed with complaints when they tried to get action on their AIDS Control Council evidence.

> We called the Permanent Secretary of the Anti-Corruption Authority every day. At one stage he told us he has more than 3000 cases to deal with. We said, "We do not care. This is our case, and we do not see you doing anything."
>
> Those 3000 complaints were real. People in Bamburi Cement, etc., any parastatal[5] you can think of, took the trouble to write everything. They wrote about tribalism; how people were brought in without qualifications, jumped over people qualified for promotion, and had a salary just tailored for himself or herself; and how they siphoned money for this and that.

Judicial corruption robs citizens of any means of redress for wrongs, and is perhaps the corruption that harms them most. The NARC government responded to complaints about corrupt judges by appointing a commission. The Ringera Commission report revealed egregious misbehavior.

5. Bamburi Cement is one of many government owned businesses (parastatals). Under the previous government, the parastatals were a major source of patronage, so it is not surprising that many complaints about corruption came from them.

A notorious senior principal magistrate brazenly held a bribery auction. He told one complainant that he had already been given a 50,000 Ksh bribe by the accused and that if she wanted the accused to be convicted, then she should pay an even bigger bribe.

Then there was the magistrate who split the robbery proceeds with the defendant...

[Another] was caught in his chambers shoving bundles of currency notes into his pockets, and when challenged threatened to jail the man...

Another judge...gave judgments without hearing the evidence.[6]

Five of nine Appeals Court justices, half of the thirty-six High Court judges, and eighty-two magistrates were named. Most resigned. Others will be prosecuted. There was some dissatisfaction with the report because even though many were named, others widely considered corrupt were not named

Judges depend on the executive for their tenure. During public discussion of the Ringera Commission report many people thought that here, as elsewhere throughout the government, the problem could only be solved with constitutional reform. Peter Andajo expressed a widely-held opinion, "Without judicial independence, it will be the same before long."

Despite nearly universal agreement that corruption is a major problem, some people worry about the elaborate systems created to prevent corruption. We have already heard Filomena Too's and Katherine Karamboi's concern about the burdensome accounting needed for school funds. Permit granting, too, is cumbersome. This in itself can become an invitation to corruption. Dr. Edward Kamau, who lives in the US but continues to spend part of his time in Kenya and maintains business interests there, is trying to get a permit to mine gypsum in Kajiado. He was given a formidable packet of forms for necessary approvals, and referred to someone who could help him through the process. This person advised him to use specific companies to conduct the necessary environmental and cultural impact assessments. This resembled the abuses of the former government.

Rasna Warah complained that the government was behaving inconsistently in its pursuit of corruption among highly placed officials.

The person in charge of corruption came from Transparency International, and is now in the cabinet. That's great. But NARC has so many people who were already known to be corrupt. They shouldn't have been given such

6. *Daily Nation,* October 8, 2003, p. 2.

> prominent positions. I am disappointed with the Saitoti appointment. Instead, they should have some key prosecutions of prominent people.

Karisa Maitha, Kibaki's first Minister for Local Government, was widely praised as an effective and energetic minister, but he has been accused of corruption in several ways.[7] Following my conversation with Rasna, and reading charges against Maitha daily in the newspapers, I thought perhaps suspending him until the charges had been investigated would bolster confidence in the government's determination to root out corruption near the top. Rose and Patrick Wanjohi disagreed.

> Patrick: If Maitha is suspended, a lot of people will feel insecure. A lot of people of Maitha's caliber are being attacked by jealous people.
>
> Rose: The Government said unless there is concrete evidence about these allegations, Maitha is not going to be sacked. Nobody has come up with any more evidence. You can call it a witch hunt. You do not expect Kibaki to react to hearsay and witch hunting etc. If everything is true, then he will take action.
>
> Patrick: You know, there are people from the opposition trying to undermine these ministers. He was offered bribes to try to trap him. The problems have all got to do with politics. KANU politicians do not want things to go smoothly for NARC, because this will make them look worse.
>
> One may say that this is coming from a Kikuyu.[8] That's true, but the current Government has all my sympathies, not because of the tribal issue but because of what it has promised.

Later events have seemed to confirm the fears of the gloomiest forecasters. The Ministry of Finance soon became embroiled in a very public scheme to spend huge sums on systems of questionable value. Although Oruko Omina and her friend succeeded in forcing the removal of a corrupt official after eight months of high-powered pressure, NARC has not been quick to act on evidence of corruption at the highest levels.

Economic Development

On taking office, NARC set a goal of creating 500,000 jobs annually. This was not a proposal to add half a million people to government payrolls each year. The plan was to create infrastructure and mechanisms

7. Rather than being sacked, he was appointed Minister of Tourism and Wildlife in June 2004 and died in September 2004.

8. The Kikuyus are the largest ethnic group. The first President, Jomo Kenyatta, was a Kikuyu, as is Mwai Kibaki. Most Kenyans acknowledge that Kikuyus have been more favored by Kenyatta and Kibaki than by Moi, a Kalenjin.

that could attract industrial and agricultural investment. It did not happen as they hoped.

Partly this was the result of some very bad luck. Tourism is an important sector of the economy. At the end of the Moi era, it accounted for 12% of the economy. In May, 2003, the US State Department issued a travel advisory, and tourism dropped dramatically. The travel advisory also made attracting foreign investment difficult.

The bombing of the Paradise Hotel in Mombasa six months before provided an excuse for the travel advisory, but many were not convinced it was the reason. What were the reasons? Americans easily assumed the warning was based only on danger. Kenyans saw other reasons. Many believed that the U.S. wanted to build an air base on Manda Island, off the Kenya coast, and the travel advisory was a pressure tactic. Whatever the reason, this new source of economic woe was a tragedy coming just as Kenya had a chance to rebuild itself.

When I asked what else the government should be doing, almost everyone answered with some scheme for economic development. In rural areas, there was great desire for factories to process the local agricultural products. Benjamin Rotich lives in Kimaren, surrounded by bright green fields of tea and roads that are often impassable during the rainy season.

> We want roads improved. During the rainy seasons, many times the lorries cannot come. We may have to wait three days to a week. We are paid by the kilo, but our tea dries out and loses weight if it waits after being picked. Sometimes we even have to throw out the leaves when there is no lorry. If we could have a tea factory here, it would really help the farmers.

Even for city people, rural development is a very high priority. Both city and country people understand that rural development is essential to greater national security and prosperity. Although Rose and Patrick Wanjohi live in Nairobi, the confidence they felt in NARC when we talked in 2003 rested on plans for agricultural development.

> Rose: Now, Kenya is moving. It was eaten to the bone. They are trying to revive the economy because it was zero. Industry collapsed.
>
> Patrick: One of the strategies for creating jobs is to revamp the agricultural sector. The Livestock Ministry has come up with a plan to revive the Kenya Meat Commission.
>
> Rose: A KCC [Kenya Co-operative Creameries] factory is coming up.
>
> Patrick: What was there previously got spoiled by corruption. For example, coffee used to employ a very large population of Kenyans. When coffee prices

came down, the little profit was being taken by the Coffee Board of Kenya. The farmer ended up with absolutely nothing. Farmers were taking loans to be able to buy fertilizers, chemicals etc., but the returns were so bad.

Now, the Minister for Co-operative Development and the Minister for Agriculture are working to revamp the Coffee Board, make sure that the coffee prices are competitive, and that a lot of the money that comes in goes to the farmers. They are starting a new system where they do not export coffee beans. The coffee beans will be processed here and sold abroad as a finished product.

By July, 2004, Patrick Wanjohi's earlier enthusiasm for NARC had soured. Since he has access to email for his work, I have heard from Patrick since completion of the interviews. In a short time, he has been converted from an enthusiastic supporter of NARC to a disappointed critic. On the subject of agricultural development, he said:

> There is so much talk, but without incentives to farmers, nobody wants to go down that road. Large tracts are lying idle due to absent landlords while so many landless people could be introduced to large-scale farming through co-operatives. We are tied down by shortsighted interests.

Expenditures

To people from many other countries, government revenues being spent on legitimate government functions, might appear unremarkable. To Kenyans, it was cause for celebration. Many people noted ways that the government was spending money to address real needs. Robina Mukhera of Nyansiongo was very pleased that, after years of pleading, finally a police station was being built near her home. She told us, "Thugs are being reduced."

As anywhere, citizens were distressed that too much was spent on some things. Rasna Warah spoke for many in saying, "I can't forgive NARC for giving themselves huge raises. They earn more than top executives." After this, members of parliament voted themselves car allowances of 3.3 million Ksh each. Yet, other civil servants wait long for raises, and are not paid well.

After the death of Vice President Michael Wamalwa in September, 2003, all government functions were closed down for two weeks of official mourning. Mina Daya, saw the obsequies as one example of a pattern of unwise expenditures.

> They are not being wise about money. They said government money should be spent in the rightful way. Yet here they are spending so much on a V.P's death. He should be given state honors, but two million Ksh spent on just bread alone for one day, to feed the people who had gone to attend! That two million could have set up a home to educate street children.

More recently, the government proposed to help the family of the late vice president pay for two houses. This disgusted many who see legitimate government programs underfunded.

CONCERNS

President Kibaki has long favored a hands-off management style. He believes in appointing good people and allowing them to do their work unhindered. It can be an effective style if overseen by someone alert, capable, and interested. But it requires oversight. From the beginning, the NARC government had a particular burden. Since it is a broad coalition, ministers were appointed for competence and affiliation, rather than because they were part of a tested team. Each seemed to be competent in his (or her, in the best case) area, but they were not a team. They feuded publicly: each day's headlines screamed the squabbles among them. There was a loud citizen outcry to stop feuding and get on with business, but Kibaki kept his hands off, and did not — as far as anyone could tell — discipline anyone for feuding.

Long before the election of the NARC government, citizens began agitating for constitutional reform. The Moi government resisted, dragged its feet, but eventually took two steps. They appointed a commission led by constitutional scholar Yash Pal Ghai to draft a new constitution and created a broad citizen review group, popularly called "*Bomas*" after their meeting place at *Bomas of Kenya*. The Ghai Commission was only partway through its work at the time the NARC government came to power.

NARC initially promised a new constitution within 100 days. After 600 days, the process was still not complete. "Bomas" resulted in a good deal of wrangling and delay. Those delays were not the fault of the new government, but there were other delays that NARC caused. Before the election, NARC supported calls for an executive prime minister. After becoming president, Kibaki said that was a tactic to reduce Moi's power, not a position of principle, and he no longer favored the change. This backtracking disgusted many people, but many also agreed with Kibaki's argument that an unclear division of power between the president and a prime minister would be unwise. The question of whether to leave executive power in the hands of an elected president or to have an executive prime minister was the most contentious issue the Constitutional Commission had to resolve. Oruko Omina thought that Kibaki and his associates had quickly become addicted to power, and reneged on promises for that reason. She and I were sitting together eating fish when this conversation occurred.

> Suppose before the plate came, we said we would divide the fish, but then, when I start eating, the fish tastes sweet, so I may decide I don't want to share it. Now that they are in power, power tastes sweet. That's why they have changed their minds about the prime minister's post, and about sharing appointments.

President Kibaki's health also causes concern. Shortly before the election, he suffered a mild stroke. People who had known him for a long time say he seemed very different. This probably reduced his capacity for vigilance, and forced him to trust his ministers further than should be done in a coalition of fighting cocks. His promise to remove corrupt civil servants is the bearing wall of the anti-corruption campaign. But it is not clear whether he still has the capacity or attention to fulfill that promise. There have been serious new corruption scandals involving some ministers, but none have been removed.

In sum, how do Kenyans see the future? At the end of 2003, many rural people were as delighted as Loice Mattoi. They understood fully that change would take time, and did not resent that some promises were not fulfilled immediately.

On the other hand, city people who read newspapers and have a wider circle of acquaintance were becoming discouraged: the reason was not that some promised changes had not happened within one year. Their discouragement arose from seeing misdeeds, false steps, lack of co-ordination, and wrangling within NARC. Oruko Omina's summation expressed this ambivalence. "The excitement is dying off because people don't see something tangible. I talk with people who are discouraged and I say, 'No, no, no, it's coming.' There are times when I believe that, and times when I don't, depending on what I've just seen."

By August of 2004, many who supported the NARC government enthusiastically in late 2003 were dismayed. Patrick Wanjohi commented:

> It is now evident that the liberators are adopting the old cloaks we intended to cast away and forget in order to forge a new beginning.

> The government has not settled down to help Kenyans due to internal squabbles within the ruling coalition. It is very disappointing to realize how self-centered our politicians are while we (ordinary Kenyans) wallow in abject poverty.
>
> New cases of corruption have emerged. I could go on and on. It is simply pathetic.

The NARC government still has time to purge itself of corruption and carry out the promises that created so much hope. A great reservoir of goodwill remains that can be used to rebuild Kenya. Leaders can choose to repeat the mistakes of their forebears, or to respect the Kenyan people and run the country for the benefit of citizens of every ethnic group, women as well as men.

My country, the United States, inevitably has a role to play too. Our actions in supporting Moi, our influence in the World Bank and IMF, our eventual realization that Moi was not governing responsibly and consequent aid cut-off, and our support of multipary democracy all helped bring Kenya to where it was at the time of the 2002 election. Since then, resumption of aid, the travel advisory, and pressure for an anti-terrorism bill that will assist our purposes, have greatly affected the scope of what the new government can accomplish. No country exists in a vacuum, and the US makes a large footprint.

Author's Comment

Kenyan culture provides many heroes to emulate. Some are in this book. Some are found in every neighborhood. If Kenyans are able to follow their own wisest traditions as they create new norms of justice, they will leave their grandchildren an extraordinary country.

GLOSSARY

8-4-4	The system of education in place since 1985 with eight years of primary school, four of secondary, and four of university.
Asians	People with who came to Kenya from throughout the Indian subcontinent are now usually called Asians rather than Indians because they may have come from Pakistan or Bangladesh.
baraza	Public meeting.
bhang	Marijuana.
boma	Compound of adjacent homes for a family or larger group.
bui-bui	Voluminous black robe worn over clothing for modesty.
chang'aa	Local whiskey.
Green Belt Movement	Environmental movement started by Prof. Wangari Maathai. Afforestation has been one of their long-time goals.
harambee	A community project. Used for schools supported by the local community, rather than the national government, or for individual or local fund-raising efforts. Literally "let's pull together."
jaggery	Sugar refinery or sugar refining equipment.
jua kali	Small-scale enterprise which can be conducted outdoors. Literally "fierce sun."

kabisa	Completely.
KCPE	Kenya Certificate of Primary Education, or the exams at the end of primary school.
KCSE	Kenya Certificate of Secondary Education, or the exams at the end of secondary school.
kiondo	Traditional woven basket popular with tourists as a handbag.
kitu kidogo	A bribe. Literally "something small."
Ksh	Kenya shilling.
Maendeleo ya Wanawake	Government supported organization dealing with women's affairs. Literally "Development of Women."
matatu	Small van which is the dominant form of local public transportation.
miraa	Khat, [Catha Edulis], a common stimulant whose leaves are chewed.
mitumbo	Imported second-hand clothes.
Mungiki	Organized pressure group claiming to represent "authentic African values." Implicated in many forms of thuggery.
mzee/wazee	Elder/elders. Terms of respect.
mzungu/wazungu	White person/white people.
okhukwesa	Luo word for marriage by abduction.
panga	Machete.
shamba	Farm or field.
sukuma wiki	Kale, a widely used vegetable.
TBA	Traditional Birth Attendant. Often used by health related NGO's for delivery of basic health services.
ugali	Paste made from maize meal. The staple food in many parts of Kenya.
unga	Maize meal.
zero grazing project	System of keeping cattle penned and feeding them grain. This allows for easy collection of manure and sometimes urine.

Index of Personal Names